Beyond Resilience

Is success pattern-based? Is the journey of successfully building new banks or services (either from scratch or in the context of a going concern) predictable enough to be repeatable? And if there are patterns, are they within our gift to replicate?

Beyond Resilience: Patterns of Success in Fintech and Digital Transformation asks these questions and seeks answers among the people who have first-hand experience of building new things and who live to tell the tale.

This book is not a hagiographic founder story that elevates the founder's own narrative to a montage of challenge and resilience, grit, perseverance and a soaring successful crowning at the end: a narrative that, figuratively speaking, can play out while 'Eye of the Tiger' is blaring in the background. Nor is the book a series of vendor testimonials that cover in a few thousand words each their own triumphant digital projects. These stories are not untrue but can be too generic to be illuminating, too vague to be helpful and too hollow to be the whole truth.

Filled with interviews from leading fintech entrepreneurs, this book strives to tell the whole truth about building new things. It shares the stories of leaders who admit that as they built their businesses, they learned a lot, changed a lot, and made mistakes and had to course-correct. The book attests that leading new fintech ventures or digital transformations, whether they are started with a blank sheet of paper or within an established entity, is hard and unpredictable. It requires control. It requires consistency and integrity. It requires standing strong either alone or with a team. It requires going beyond resilience.

Leda Glyptis is a seasoned fintech executive and former banker, with a career spanning two decades. She has worked in transformation and technology functions across a variety of financial services verticals and companies including BNY Mellon, QNB, 11:FS and 10x. She is the author of *Bankers Like Us: Dispatches from an Industry in Transition* and of the highly acclaimed *#LedaWrites* column on Fintech Futures. She is a frequent keynote speaker and contributor to industry publications and works as an external advisor to boards and executive teams for banks and technology companies of various sizes in several geographies.

Leda is Visiting Professor of Practice for the University of Loughborough, London, focusing on fintech and the digital economy. Leda holds a BA and MA from King's College, Cambridge, and an MSc and PhD from the London School of Economics and Political Science.

Beyond Resilience
Patterns of Success in Fintech and Digital Transformation

Leda Glyptis

CRC Press
Taylor & Francis Group

AN AUERBACH BOOK

Cover: Web Large Image (Public)

First edition published 2025
2385 NW Executive Center Drive, Suite 320, Boca Raton FL 33431

and by CRC Press
4 Park Square, Milton Park, Abingdon, Oxon, OX14 4RN

CRC Press is an imprint of Taylor & Francis Group, LLC

ISBN: 9781032493541 (hbk)
ISBN: 9781032498096 (pbk)
ISBN: 9781003395577 (ebk)

DOI: 10.1201/9781003395577

Typeset in Garamond
by Newgen Publishing UK

For my tribe, always.

Contents

Preface

When I started this work, one of the things I said to all of my sources was 'this is not a gotcha': I am not interested in catching anyone out, in getting a scoop or following industry gossip of which there is plenty. My interviewees got to approve their quotes and review how I was presenting their distilled experience. This was important to me and I am sure it was important to my publisher for obvious reasons both practical and ethical.

But in giving that comfort and protection to the people who shared their stories with me, did I leave myself open to being given so many platitudes? I was asked the question a couple of times (that's what you get when you hang out with a lot of journalists): how do you know your sources didn't lie to you? How do you know that what people described is real?

I mean.

Obviously I don't.

And I also got the other question, equally obvious and fair and it goes like this: you only shared the part of the story the folks shared with you. You know and I know and the industry knows there is a bigger picture.

Yes. True.

But given what I asked them to share with me was experience and perception, their view of the world and the journey... I don't think lying was ever an issue. At the end of the day, the only arbiter of your lived experience is yourself. There is no objectivity to it. And the fact that they didn't tell their full story is a given. This isn't their biography. It's just a set of observations from them and a set of conclusions from me.

The better question would have been 'how do you know that what they describe is what it felt like to work with them, how they see their efforts and companies is what it felt like for everyone else too'. And the answer to that is... I don't. And that is also ok. I bet that, for every person who agrees with the view the folks on these pages share, there will be another who doesn't recall things the same way. And that is to be expected and that is actually fine.

It is how it goes. If someone says they are proud of the culture they built and you used to work for them and find yourself thinking 'I hated working there' you are both right. They are proud of where they got to *and* you were not happy there. Both these things can be true at once. And often are.

If you read someone saying talent is everything or making product pivots fast is key and you think 'you didn't do it when I worked for you'... maybe that is distilled wisdom. Maybe they learned something through that experience, the experience of getting it wrong... maybe the incident you are thinking of is an aberration and maybe they have a different view of what is 'fast' than you do. And, yes, maybe they know that is the right thing to do but struggle to actually do it. It doesn't change the value of the insight. It colours it and contextualises it but it doesn't change it. If you read this and thought 'I agree with that point but I don't like that person: I know them and neither like nor trust them' I would argue that is also ok. The value of their observation is not diminished by whether you value their work.

My point is... people have shared their truths here and that is what it needs to be seen as. Journeys of immense complexity and personal toil as shared by the people who went on them. Whether you like them or not. Whether the way they remember it is how you remember it or not. Whether it worked or not. And a lot of it didn't.

Ultimately, every single person I spoke to said they learned a lot, they changed a lot, they made mistakes and had to course-correct and so I have no doubt that people who crossed their paths during different phases of that journey will have slightly or radically different experiences of what they are like as people. And that is normal and good and valid. But it doesn't change the three simple facts I have learned in this process:

This work is hard. Whether you do it with a blank sheet of paper or within an established entity. It is hard and unpredictable so you need to control what you can at all times. Control is more important than creativity, funnily enough. Who'd have thought.

Secondly, you need to do a lot of hard things at once with consistency and integrity. There is no way around this. And you can't do things in sequence. It's everything, everywhere all at once or bust.

So it is important to work out whether this is a ride you will personally enjoy, whether this rollercoaster is for you. And there is no shame if it isn't. But if it is something that feels right for you: remember standing strong is essential, standing alone is a choice. A choice you don't have to make. And this is the third simple fact I learned...

Find your people and share the journey. With its ups and downs, curveballs and moments of abject despair and bittersweet triumph. They will not experience everything the way you do, they will not recall everything the way you do and that may be part of the value they bring right there.

But mostly it is the camaraderie.

It is a long and bumpy road. Don't travel it alone.

Acknowledgements

Writing this book was infinitely harder than writing the first one which, frankly, I did not expect. Part of it was the fact that I had created a certain set of expectations for myself. So a big thank you goes to my editor, John Wyzalek at Taylor & Francis Group, for keeping me focused during what turned out to be a hard process.

But, really, the biggest challenge was the fact that a large number of people I like, trust and admire trusted me with their stories: stories that you will read in these pages. Synthesised and retold.

I am in the debt of every single one of you who took time to speak to me, on or off the record, about your journey and experiences. I cannot thank you enough for your energy, your vulnerability and honesty and for sharing your truth with me and my readers so generously. This book wouldn't exist without you and I am an infinitely wiser person having gone through this process.

A huge thank you to Tanya Andreasyan and Kevin Johnson for reading through the manuscript and offering many helpful suggestions and pointers.

Any errors, misrepresentations or omissions are mine and mine alone. As is the joy and privilege of having gone through this process with you all.

Chapter 1

Unlocking Greatness: Seeking Everyday Patterns in Extraordinary Journeys

A Space on Your Bookshelf

Are you one of those people who organise their books thematically?

I am.

Fiction separated from non-fiction.

Books by the same author grouped together, books on similar or adjacent themes, clustered tightly. It has its own rules, this esoteric librarianship, as I like the thematic units to logically lead onto each other and sometimes you wish you could have multi-dimensional shelves (that would be comfortably accommodated in Terry Pratchett L space[1]) so you can have everything an author ever wrote sitting together horizontally but also everything written on similar topics vertically aligned to each book with collaborative, co-authored works stretching into a different dimension altogether.

Not possible, I know.

First-world problems also, I know, and more than a little obsessive, perhaps, but there you have it. We all have our foibles and this is mine. And the reason this is

---

1 Getting the first Terry Pratchett reference in early, you will be pleased to see, if you are a regular reader. For the uninitiated, the L space is the notion that large quantities of books warp space and time around them. The principle of L space is an extension of the 'Knowledge is Power' and, shock horror, isn't real. But I can't help wishing it was.

DOI: 10.1201/9781003395577-1

pertinent is because I found myself looking at my book collection and asking myself where *I* would place this volume when it's out in the world.

If I look at my business book collection, they bunch together around some well-trodden themes ('digital is here', 'innovation takes discipline' and 'why do transformations fail', largely). Books about what we are doing wrong today and what we should do better tomorrow are stacked neatly next to each other. But what about the things we are doing well *enough* today to build a bridge to tomorrow? What about the topic in the middle?

Well. When it comes to that elusive topic, what happens between realising things are broken and before you have made your fresh start... my otherwise extensive book collection has a gaping gap, the books practically running away from each other in two distinct blocks: on one side, we have the books (including my own first book *Bankers Like Us*[2]) that describe the realities of the business world today, where we go wrong and what can be done about it. Those books range from the deeply academic and technical to the more observation-based, they span industries and decades and can be grouped under the rubric of 'where things are broken'.

At the other end of the shelf are the fresh-start books. Books on innovation and creativity, books on change, digital aspirations and tools to get going. Some include case studies from other industries, some extensive references to unicorns made during the fintech boom and their unfinished stories. But even the books describing businesses that are still building, are mostly about 'getting going'.

> There are a lot of books about where we are getting things wrong in our industry.
> A lot of books about what the future needs to look like and how to get going.
> But what about the things we are doing well... today?

Get going where?

To the future of course.

Be it starting something new or refreshing and renewing what you have, there are *a lot* of books about what that needs to look like and how you can get started. A lot of books about those first steps and early stages of change.

Excellent books.

Many, excellent books. With, usually, more cheerful covers than the first lot.

And in the middle?

In the middle there is not much.

There is the odd founder story: a hagiography, often self-penned, that elevates their own narrative to a montage of challenge and resilience, grit, perseverance and

---

a soaring successful crowning at the end. Narratives that can all play out while *Eye of the Tiger* is blaring in the background. Figuratively speaking.

There is also the odd collected volume, usually published by a software vendor (I can see four of them accusingly stacked together on my shelf) where their clients are invited to share a couple of thousand words each on the triumph of their digital projects.

> There are a lot of founder stories: a soaring montage of resilience and perseverance playing out while *Eye of the Tiger* is blaring in the background. Figuratively speaking.

Not untrue, those stories.

But too generic to be illuminating. Too vague to be helpful. And too hollow to be the whole truth.

It is easy to dismiss this empty space between the two blocks and say that perhaps there aren't enough success stories to tell. But that is not true. There are plenty.

We have been doing this long enough: changing the old, building brand new things: businesses, products and digital capabilities. And although doing things for the first time *mostly* fails, it doesn't always. That is, in fact, how human progress works. So of course there *are* success stories. But *where* are they?

Why is that part of my bookshelf not busier?

Surely the success stories are both uplifting and helpful. In that you can probably, hopefully, learn from them on how to succeed yourself.

Or can you?

Is success pattern-based? Is the journey of successfully building new things (either from scratch or in the context of a going concern) predictable enough to be repeatable? And if there are patterns, are they within our gift to replicate?

Asking those questions and seeking answers among the people who had first-hand experience of building new things and living to tell the tale, is where the idea for this book started.

What Is Success Anyway?

Funnily enough, the word 'success' was picked up by every person I approached to interview for this book. And it wasn't a case of 'awww you are writing a book about whether there is a pattern to success and you want my glittering story to be a part of it'.

Nope.

Not that.

It was more… 'whoa… *success?* That's a big word and a slippery concept. What do you mean by it?'. Which, if anything, showed I approached folks who were humble about what was behind them and realistic about what lay ahead. There is, predictably, an ancient Greek phrase for everything and the one that applies here is 'never call someone happy till the end[3]'. Success falls in the same category as happiness, I guess, and the very idea of 'calling it' while their careers were far from over made people uncomfortable. The idea of success is off-putting in its glittery perfection. But perfection is not what we are looking for.

As part of this work, I spoke to founders (you will meet them as we go) who had lucrative exits and don't feel like they succeeded yet. They felt that their exit wasn't even a good metric of success. I spoke to people building or transforming businesses whose targets were met, the goals they set themselves at the start of the journey exceeded and they are not comfortable with the idea that they are 'success stories'.

> When speaking of success, don't think of something permanent, glittering and lasting.
>
> Think of something that made it through the challenges it faced… without dying.
>
> At least for a time.

Because they are humble. And hungry. And because they are not done yet.

But also because 'success' feels like the end of a journey, it is a shiny word and, when you apply it to yourself, not devoid of arrogance.

I also spoke to people whose businesses folded, and they hesitated before the word failure for all the same reasons. Not everything failed. Or things worked very well for a time or under certain conditions. What can you learn from that to do better next time? Isn't that as useful a piece of knowledge as success itself? What qualifies as a successful venture anyway?

Especially when, in discussing definitions of success with the wonderful people who gave me so much of their time while researching this book, we found that the things people set out to do when they began their journeys changed, morphed, grew and transformed with everything they learned, built and did every step of the way. For everyone, the goals they set themselves, the 'success' they set out to pursue at the start of their journeys kept shifting with everything they learned and everything they achieved or failed to achieve. So success, whatever it is, is not static.

That is to be expected. But it is hardly helpful if we are trying to pin the concept down.

So when can you call a venture a success? Is it a time thing? A size

> Success is neither glittering nor permanent.
>
> But there is a robustness about a venture that succeeds. For however long that cycle lasts.

---

3 The phrase is believed to have been said by law-maker Solon to the famously rich King Croesus: μηδένα προ του τέλους μακάριζε…

thing? A time and size thing? Do you need to get to x size and stay there for y amount of time?

What are the criteria? When do you call it, so to speak?

How long does a venture need to be running before it is out of danger (careful how you answer that because Enron and Lehman Brothers and Blockbusters are cautionary tales for us all).

Is that even the right metric?

Although there is an undeniable, retroactively identifiable *robustness* to the things that 'succeed', it is dangerous to consider the term as conveying something permanent and lasting. A business can be a success and still not be forever.

So when talking about success, I actually set my eyes much lower than the heady apex of perfection in human endeavour. I shall explain what I mean in a moment. But first: a digression.

I am a political scientist by training. You probably already knew that.

In political science you consider a country's transition to democracy as successful, complete and stable if there have been two handovers of power following a free election after which the loser leaves office without picking up a gun or taking a swing at the winner on the way out.

Two rounds of the game played with everyone following the rules. That's all it takes to meet the criteria of the definition. That doesn't mean it won't break in the future. It means it is deemed stable now.

My students hated this definition, by the way. It felt lacking in ambition and optimism. But it is a definition so widely accepted in political science that arguing against it is the equivalent of deciding to start your physics career by debating gravity. You can. But it won't get you far. And it is a good definition *exactly* because it is something an accountant and a philosopher could agree on.

End of digression.

That is how I define success.

New things fail in droves. I will share some facts, figures and depressing statistics with you later on in this chapter, but it is sadly a given. New stuff, be it a new venture, a new initiative, or a transformation process towards a new state, mostly, largely, *usually* fail.

Success, for the purposes of this book, therefore, is the art of *not* dying.

Not dying doesn't guarantee continued success or survival.

Nothing in life does.

But it sets you apart from the majority anyway.

Doing something new and navigating the 95% death rate, making it to the far side of that and carrying on. That, much like the definition of a stable democracy, doesn't guarantee continued success or survival. Nothing in life does.

But it sets you apart from the majority anyway.

So, if we define success in this pragmatic albeit impermanent way, and we return to the question of 'why are there not any more books about it on my bookshelf' the answer may be: because that sounds messy and murky. And sort of circular.

People like stories with a clear ending.

Money Men[4] is an excellent book full stop. Even if the bad guys aren't caught in the end (sorry, spoiler alert), the story is known and the narrative arc is fully played out. The classic books for our industry such as *The Lean Startup*, *Sprint*, *The Four Disciplines of Execution* etc. etc. etc. are excellent books because they are not contingent on anything outside of them being true for their truth to hold. Go do the things in them and your journey will be a little smoother.

The space I found myself wondering about was neither fully played out nor clear and objectively true and shiny. Even if I found the patterns of success (and I did) would they be clear and ready to be used again and again?

As ever, I found myself drawn to the messy part of life, the messy middle of the creative process. The part of the story that is usually montage fodder because the work is hard, non-linear and it comes with many 'maybes' and a lot of 'it depends'.

That's my kind of territory.

So: into the messy middle we go.

To speak to people who tried to do new things, in a world where new things fail in droves, and lived to tell the tale. I was lucky enough to get a glimpse of their thoughts on the experiences.

The question I needed to answer was: is there a pattern, discernible and repeatable, that you or I or any other ordinary person can learn from to apply in ways big and small when we set off on our own ambitious journeys of creation and change?

This Is an Open Book Exam: Here Is What I Found

Obviously, I want you to read on.

But as this is not a whodunit, I trust that knowing the answer is as important as knowing the intricacies of how to apply it so the spoiler isn't an issue. So here it goes:

I looked at a wide array of 'new' ventures in financial ser-

> There is a pattern to success.
> But there is no magic formula.
> The pattern is: you have to do a lot of things, consistently, at the same time, for a long time.

vices. The research sample included new businesses, new products inside existing organisations, new businesses inside existing business concerns etc. I did not look

---

4 *Money Men: A Hot Startup, a Billion Dollar Fraud, a Fight for the Truth*, by Dan McCrum (2022).

exclusively at one particular type of venture or effort although I looked exclusively at financial services examples and I did look for 'new' ventures with a strong technology component. What I was interested in was the process of going against the grain. Starting something from nothing is, by definition, an uphill struggle. But so is changing something established and mature.

So our examples come from across the spectrum of 'new new' work.

Although all examples in this book are from the financial services space, the insights are actually industry-agnostic.

I stuck with finance because that is the space I live and work in, the space I understand in great and occasionally excruciating detail. But the insights are in no way tied to the subject matter of the businesses, as you will see for yourself in the pages ahead. The lessons learned and the dos and don'ts of entrepreneurs and leaders shared could apply to you regardless of whether you work in health-tech, fashion, e-commerce, engineering or music. The businesses examined are all financial services providers of some sort or another. The insights gleaned have nothing to do with what the business does, however, and everything to do with how it is set up.

> The examples in these pages are all from financial services.
> The insight is universally applicable and industry-agnostic.

And what I found is: yes.

There are quite a few patterns across the success stories. But there is no magic formula. The overall pattern can be summarised as 'you have to do a lot of challenging things, consistently, simultaneously and for a long time'.

We will dedicate the rest of the book to what those things are, the pitfalls to watch out for and the temptations to over-index one over the other of those things. The mistakes that are easily made and lessons learned the hard way. There will be cheat-sheets so you may benefit from the learnings of others, if you are that way inclined. And I hope you are. There is a lot of valuable stuff here that people who have been there and done that generously shared. But, for the avoidance of doubt, the refrain of it all is: the pattern boils down to a lot of complicated, *hard* work over a prolonged period of time.

> Up close opportunity always looks like hard work.

Within that envelope there are many tips. But no silver bullet. Up close, opportunity has a habit of looking a lot like hard work, as my old boss used to say.

The second prevailing pattern is that this work is hard in its own unique ways. And that very fact in itself attracts a particular type of person. In exactly the same way some professions attract a particular type of personality. First responders and surgeons, firefighters and art restorers all have some shared personality traits in common, be it patience and a steady hand or something more esoteric. In exactly the same way, this work seems to also attract a certain type of person.

The first word that comes to mind is extraordinary, and you will forgive me if I am a little smitten with the people I have amassed on these pages. I trust that by the time we are done here, you will be too.

Some of the personal stories shared felt like movies in the making and although I did not set out to find extraordinary personal stories, there is no denying that I found them. Some of these personal stories felt like gifts I had not yet earned and the retelling felt like a gift passed on.

> Doing new things is hard. It takes a special kind of grit and determination. It demands a lot of you. And it takes a toll on you. A personal toll.

But it isn't even about the mind-blowing origin stories. Because although they are common among the people drawn to this work, they are not actually necessary. Many of the folks I spoke to here had them and you will read about them in this section because, frankly, I can't *not* share them. They are mind-blowing and instructive even if they bear no resemblance to your own life.

But it is important to stress that the Origin Story itself is not the pattern. Many had them. And just as many folks who succeeded at this work did not have such a story.

A dramatic or traumatic origin story is not necessary. And, also, as we all know well from our own lives… humble beginnings or a tough start in life doesn't guarantee humility, wisdom or extraordinary ability. Hollywood be damned.

What makes the people attracted to this work extraordinary is perhaps my own perception. Or the fact that they allow themselves to be drawn to and moulded by a journey that has more than its fair share of reversals. So it goes without saying that it takes grit to do this work. Where each of our characters got the grit from varied. What didn't vary was that they had both grit and resilience.

And it feels imperative to state that every person I spoke to exhibited grit of a kind that you don't find in your normal garden-variety endeavour, so to speak. There is no denying that doing new things is harder than doing things that are already being done… so it takes more grit, determination and optimism. It takes more work. It takes more of *you being able to get back up after every fall.*

And it takes more *out* of you.

That's another pattern. This is a lot. This work comes at a price.

Maybe that is why that part of my shelf is not so crowded. Because this is a story of hard, complicated work that takes a huge personal toll.

It is worth it. To the people who do it. And to all of us who benefit from their endeavours. But it is not easy and, even when you learn from others and spare yourself some costly mistakes thanks to their tips, the hard work remains.

That's the book. This book.

No silver bullets, though a lot of brilliant ideas you can apply immediately if you so choose. No magic beans. And yet, there is magic in the rarity of this elusive notion of success, however defined. And there is magic in its pursuit.

Looking for Buried Treasure: The Rarity of New Things Succeeding

At the risk of sounding a little conceited, *Bankers Like Us*, yes yes: my first book, made a compelling case about what failures have in common. The entire volume is dedicated to the myriad of highly predictable and infinitely repeatable ways in which, when we try to drive change in the financial services industry, decision-making often ambushes itself and trips up its own best intentions. How organisational inertia and individual habits eat intent for breakfast. How good people end up making bad choices that compound each other and add up to terrible effects.

It's a thrilling read, if I may say so myself. You should read it (hint, nudge).

But success stories? What do they have in common? If anything.

Other than being extremely rare.

And this rarity of success is common in all new ventures, affecting both startups and change work inside established entities. The reasons for that and the statistical thresholds used by the various studies vary a little. The theme tune does not. Opinions may differ as to what exact percentage of startups succeed. But all studies agree the number is low.

Some find that 20% will fail in the first year, 50% within five years and 65% within ten years[5]. Venture-backed startups in the fintech space tend to see between 70 and 75%[6] failure rates according to some analysts, while others put the overall failure rate at 90%[7].

A total of 95% if you are in crypto[8].

> Most startups fail.
>
> Most transformation efforts fail.
>
> There is pattern to the failures: the high failure rate and the reasons behind it are well documented.

5 https://www.investopedia.com/articles/personal-finance/040915/how-many-startups-fail-and-why.asp

6 https://www.ncbi.nlm.nih.gov/pmc/articles/PMC10197061/#:~:text=Therefore%2C%20the%20FinTech%20market%20is,%2C%202019)%20after%20the%20founding

7 https://explodingtopics.com/blog/startup-failure-stats

8 https://www.upsilonit.com/blog/startup-success-and-failure-rate#:~:text=On%20average%2C%2063%25%20of%20tech,fail%20in%2075%25%20of%20cases

The sources vary. The reports vary. Both are plentiful. The qualifiers against which data is parsed also vary. What doesn't vary is the failure rate: it's high.

No matter how you cut the data, the failure rate is consistently high. There is no hiding from it: most startups fail. And the reasons for that failure rate vary, but not hugely.

Failure comes because money runs out. Because of poor product market fit. Or being in the wrong market, which often happens because of inadequate research and/or lack of expertise in the requisite area among the leadership team.

Amazing isn't it?

That the reasons for failure are so basic.

Surely the answer can't be: don't be an arrogant fool who tries to solve a problem you don't understand or *try* to understand (no research, remember) oh and keep an eye on your cash flow.

Done.

This book could end up being super short after all. Only it's not that simple, is it?

Because removing the reasons for failure doesn't guarantee success. There is, as ever, a more complicated story in play here. But before we turn to that, it is important to stress that it's not just the startups that are plagued with failure. Change work inside a big organisation seems to have similar failure rates.

The number that's bandied about with a lot of confidence when it comes to the failure rate of transformation and change programmes inside big corporates is 70%. This number covers all change work in the digital space, of material size across financial services. That of course includes technology, organisation changes, talent and product shifts in various configurations and permutations. It comes in a variety of shapes and sizes, as you would expect, and no matter how you cut it efforts of this kind tend to fail at a rate of 70%.

That's not great, is it?

Where does this number come from, I hear you ask. Hilariously, it comes from the people tasked with designing and implementing those transformations. So they should know. McKinsey states the number as fact[9], so it must be true. Deloitte does too[10]. In fact, everyone does[11]: a quick Google search will yield reports from every major consulting firm, most of the boutique ones plus articles across *all* industry publications that place failure rate for digital transformation initiatives inside financial services organisations between 70 and 75%.

Occasionally, you find a report that sets success rates even lower.

In the book *The Engagement Banking Revolution*, sponsored by Backbase, the authors claim that the success rate for digital transformation inside this industry is

---

9   https://www.mckinsey.com/capabilities/transformation/our-insights/common-pitfalls-in-tran
    sformations-a-conversation-with-jon-garcia
10 Deloitte Human Capital Consulting, *Digital Transformation: Are People Still Our Greatest Asset.*
11 https://www.globaldigitalassurance.com/why-70-of-digital-transformations-fail/

16% because that's how many banks bother to even define metrics of success before embarking on a costly, multi-year digital transformation programme.

Funny cos it's true.

These numbers are not pertinent to the narrative that follows in this book, by the way, other than to say success is rare for change work.

> Removing the reasons for failure doesn't guarantee success.

And if 70% of digital transformation work fails, inside banks, the reasons fall into two categories.

Bucket 1: just like startups, banks fail because of arrogant leadership who think they know best without either having or seeking subject matter expertise… without commissioning research… or believing the research, once they see it.

Damn those experts.

Bucket 2: unlike startups, doing a new thing inside an organisation that already does something established and comfortable, often fails because of leadership that lacked conviction and gave up. It's patience or courage that runs out, rather than money. The effort not failing as much as fizzling out, being distracted, bloated or running out of steam before it gets to the end.

> Arrogant leadership that doesn't validate assumptions or doesn't believe research when they see it, is a common reason for failure in both startups and big financial services organisations.

Seasoned innovation survivor Kevin Johnson reflects, referencing the Innovator's Dilemma[12] 'it is about headspace, and how an organisation is set up to do what it does today. If you're a multi-billion dollar enterprise, the new thing you are building has to make millions to even be noticed, so if not nurtured through its early years, it will fail'. And that doesn't mean what you are thinking. In an organisation generating hundreds of millions in revenue, if your venture 'is making 10s of thousands, that doesn't cut it' reflects Kevin. So it's not running out of money that will kill you. Perversely, you may make money and still lose the battle for headspace.

In big banks, running out of money is rarely a factor (though never say never) and waning product market fit is a slower death. So slow that, although it can and does happen, it is often not understood for what it is. The currency for survival inside a big bank is not cash but attention. And that attention can be lost as banks and big corporate entities of all kinds get in their own way more than any small organisation can.

They will compromise long-term outcomes for short-term wins, they will allow personal biases to carry the day and they will work in a silo or try to become digitally

---

12 *The Innovator's Dilemma: When New Technologies Cause Great Firms to Fail,* Clayton Christensen, first published in 1997.

enabled without losing any of the technology that they are meant to be replacing. The reports and articles on these topics[13] are so aligned as to be repetitive[14] and they all point to the same poor leadership decisions which we all know about. And we know all about them because I already wrote a book to explain why we keep ending up making the same bad decisions time and again when the fact that they are bad is so well documented.

Kevin Johnson, Head of Innovation Competence Centre, Euroclear
Previously Innovation Lead at ING and head of Swift Innotribe

I wrote that book. It's *Bankers Like Us*. It isn't *this* book.

Go back to 'GO' (yes a Monopoly reference) and read Book 1. We won't be talking about people getting in their own way in this book other than to acknowledge that the vast majority of them do.

In this book, our focus is the other side of that story.

The 5–10% of startups that succeed and the 30% of digital transformation efforts that succeed are minority plays by anyone's standards, but very much there. These numbers are low but they are not rounding errors. They exist in adequate numbers and they are very much able to teach us something that we can then consciously apply when we go about our own ventures.

Apart from the obvious pointers along the lines of… you know… don't spend more money than you have or you will run out; and ensure your business is solving a problem someone *actually* has; and *you* understand; and if you set out to transform your business because your technology is old, crumbling and causing failures maybe don't keep that technology as a key part of the future you are building?

> Successful startups that go on to thrive… and successful transformation efforts that take root… may be rare but they do exist.

Apart from that really obvious stuff, is there a pattern?

Because killing the 1950s mainframe is a prerequisite to moving forwards. But it is not a guarantee of success so the question is: is anything?

I already told you the answer and I know you are ready for the details now, but first I want to talk you through my process. It is a habit that was drilled into me while in academia and I can't quite shake it off. If that is of interest, read on. If not, skip ahead to the next section, I genuinely don't mind and you won't miss anything critical for the rest of the book other than how I went about choosing the interview subjects.

---

13 https://www.cio.com/article/228268/12-reasons-why-digital-transformations-fail.html
14 https://www.forbes.com/sites/forbestechcouncil/2023/02/21/seven-reasons-why-digital-adoption-projects-fail/?sh=7b6e85f45b9a

What I Did Next

When the mission is to look for patterns on the road to success and having defined 'success' as the art of not dying despite an often-inhospitable environment for what you are trying to achieve, you then need to look at an adequate number of cases that fit the bill in order to see if the patterns you are hoping are there, really do exist beyond your own wishful thinking.

If I am looking at experiences of doing something brand new either inside an existing business or outside it, the sample size is potentially huge: looking at startups, scale-ups, corporate-backed ventures and big companies that successfully reinvent at least part of themselves across any FS vertical or geography means that I am looking at patterns across a vast population. Even with the failure rates discussed above shrinking the survivors considerably, it is still a lot.

> Success, when building something new, has certain discernible and repeatable traits.
>
> And it is important to understand what those are because we live in an era of unprecedented constancy in the speed of change.
>
> So we will keep needing to create new ventures and transform the old.
>
> That imperative will, in fact, only become more pressing.

If the intention is to create a sample of any statistical significance, I would need to speak to thousands of people across hundreds of companies across every possible geography. Without meaning to trivialise the significance of a wide enough sample, my approach at the start was a little less rigorous.

I started with a sample of 50 companies across 14 countries split fairly evenly between big companies and new ventures at various phases. My intention was to 'see how it goes'. I would adjust and add to my sample as I went depending on what I found. Oftentimes in academic research, you find that your hypotheses need rework. Only one way to find out: start testing.

Which is exactly what I did.

And it worked.

The pattern emerged very fast and it was crystal clear.

So, although I did add to my sample some additional experts who didn't belong to either category but had worked with both of them long enough to have insightful observations of their own, I did not extend the sample much beyond that original pool of 50. If this was academic work, the peer reviewers would be spitting feathers right now so I have a little section on my sample selection below just for them. And for me. Because I love that geeky stuff.

For everyone else, the whole point is that I believed (and now know to be true, having done the research) that the work of creating something new in a digital economy is hard and fraught with failure but when it does succeed it actually has certain discernible and repeatable traits in common.

And it is important to understand what those are because we will keep needing to create new ventures and transform the old. That imperative will, in fact, only become more pressing as the digital era is only at its dawn and technical capabilities will continue forcing us to reinvent everything from communication to commerce, government to ethics and everything in between.

> The combination of innovation, cross-vertical cross-pollination and tighter cycles of adoption means that technological complexity will keep creating new possibilities that new businesses will forever seek to explore and new pressures that existing businesses will forever need to adapt to.

We live in an era of unprecedented technological change. The combination of innovation and cross-vertical cross-pollination, tighter cycles of adoption of new technologies and products in society and the relentlessness of Moore's Law[15] means that technological complexity will keep creating new possibilities that new businesses will forever seek to explore and new pressures that existing businesses will forever need to adapt to.

So it helps to understand what steps you can take to make your success a little more likely next time you go into this type of work: the creation of something new. It doesn't matter what your new thing does. It matters a lot to you and your team and customers, of course. But it doesn't make a huge amount of difference to the exercise of setting it up. No matter what your business does, or intends to do, the process of setting it up for success has commonalities.

Keep Skipping Ahead: More Research Methodology Explanations

This is not a fully-fledged research methodology. It's more a methodology section 'lite' for my fellow geeks and pedants. And for me. Because once a social scientist, always a social scientist. So indulge

> The prevailing narrative of the heroic-founder CEO standing alone against the world is immensely unhelpful.

me while I get this out of my system or I will feel like I need to return my PhD back to Senate House and I don't think there's a process for that.

---

15 Moore's Law is not a law. Sorry to disappoint. It is an empirical observation and it goes like this: the number of transistors in a computer chip doubles every two years or so. As the number of transistors increases, so does processing power. The law also states that, as the number of transistors increases, the cost per transistor falls.

    So essentially we will always have exponentially more *and* cheaper computing power. Ad infinitum.

This book started with the hypothesis that, as there is a pattern to why ventures fail, so there is a pattern to why they succeed. I conducted 55 in-depth interviews with people who are or have been in or close to successful ventures defined as new initiatives that managed to survive and see the light of day. Some of those successes had longevity. Others did not. Some came on the heels of failed ventures. Others did not.

The people I spoke to were originally chosen for what they have done: the businesses and initiatives they have been a key part of. I spoke to a variety of folks in a variety of roles. That was intentional. Because diversity of opinion and perspective is a good thing, obviously. But also because if I had just looked at founders or just CEOs or just people with a particular job title or characteristic, I would be telling you a self-fulfilling story and you deserve better.

I would also be feeding into the immensely unhelpful narrative of the heroic founder/CEO standing alone against the world. And that is not how the world works. That is not how businesses work.

A heroic CEO is not actually necessary for success. Having one won't hurt your chances of success, to be clear. But even if you have one, they are not *enough* for success. A heroic CEO is simply not a factor. So, although I spoke to CEOs, I also spoke to their teams, to create a richer tapestry of viewpoints. Besides, you need *teams* of people who are drawn to this work in order to do this hard, messy, transformative work. So I spoke to people fulfilling different functions across different teams.

> A heroic CEO is neither necessary for success nor a hindrance. It is actually not a factor.
> You need teams drawn to this work, much of which is unheroic and quiet.

All interviewees in this book, irrespective of whether they were a founder or not, irrespective of whether they were in a startup of a bank, were asked the same set of five open-ended questions[16] as a baseline, but then the interviews were allowed to flow to the places that were most important for the subject without being guided or led. The repeatable questions were designed to allow me to build a framework since qualitative research is more loosey-goosey than surveys and statistics, so you need a repeatable framework of non-leading questions for consistency.

Basics.

---

16 The questions were:
   1. Tell me about your career journey;
   2. How did you define success at the beginning of your journey with [the particular venture we are speaking about], what were you trying to achieve and how were you planning to know when you had achieved it;
   3. What were the hardest things on this journey;
   4. Have you moved the goalposts on yourself and the business: have your definitions of what success is changed;
   5. Have you changed on this journey.

In every interview, you ask the same questions as a baseline.

If you are lucky, you get more than you ask for and then you can then seek clarification, you can delve into the stories and follow the thread of detail.

If you are lucky.

And boy did I get lucky.

I got conversations of such immense richness that each could have been a book in its own right. For this, I cannot thank the people who participated in my research enough. No research discipline and questionnaire design could guarantee to get me to the wealth of insight that I have the privilege to share with you on these pages. I got there with a combination of luck, experience and the grace of the people who chose to share their stories.

For the research design part (that I know you *really* are bored with now), it is important to know two more things:

1. The sample size

If there was considerable divergence in what I learned, I would need to create 'control' factors and go out and do many more interviews to decipher the reasons behind the divergence. Thankfully for me (and for your frayed patience) the alignment in views was spectacular to an unexpected degree.

2. How I picked my subjects

And the only answer I can truthfully give you here is: subjectively.

Which, yes, defeats the point of a rigorous research methods section but bear with me here.

All the folks I interviewed had two things in common.

The first is experience. Although the ages of the folks I interviewed cover a 30-plus year span, they are all some ways into their career journey and have experienced challenges and reversals. That was intentional, as it guarantees both for the richness of their experience and because I consciously wanted to avoid the first-time founder hustle narrative. There are some first-time founders in this story. But they are experienced in business having cut their teeth in other structures, startups or corporates.

Secondly, all the folks I interviewed have my profound respect. Some of the folks I interviewed I have known for years and love very much.

> The market is awash with arrogant founders liberal with their use of hyperbole.
>
> It's all 'taking over the world' and 'getting shit done' and 'hypergrowth'.
>
> They are the founders who, if they fail, they learn little. If they succeed, they learn even less.

And even then, I discovered things about them I would never have known were it not for this book. Others, I met for the first time for the purposes of this work, but I actually knew of them and their work before I started writing and I reached out to ask them to give me some of their time for this project exactly because I have admired their trajectory.

Lastly, I have specifically and intentionally avoided the rockstar founder space.

The financial services industry and the economy at large are awash with arrogant founders, liberal with linguistic hyperbole. It's all 'taking over the world' and 'getting shit done' and 'hypergrowth'. They are the founders who, if they fail, they learn little. If they succeed, they learn even less.

Arguably, this phenomenon is a passing trend, a moment in time and were you to catch these figures ten years from now, it would be a different story. So I endeavoured to do just that. I focused on people later on in their lives' journey. Largely because I never had any time for that hyper-bouncy, glossy narrative and I have no interest in their stories. If you do have an interest in their stories, you are in luck, as they command quite the following so there are plenty of things written about those characters at various stages of their rise... and decline... And the patterns therein (spoiler alert: it's mostly hybris).

And yet we don't learn. But that's another story. Maybe that's the next book.

For the purposes of this one it suffices to say that none of those folks were approached, interviewed or harmed in the making of this volume.

A Small Digression on the People I Specifically *Didn't* Speak To

Doing empirical research only to confirm your own biases really defeats the point of trying to be methodical about it all so, having made the decision to *not* write about this particular type of founder, I had to check myself. So. Here are my reasons:

1. They have been written about at considerable length, both from personal experiences and reflections in books such as Sophie Theen's 'the Soul of Startups' reflecting on her time recruiting for Revolut and from the vantage point of industry observers. There are multiple (and I mean *multiple*) articles on the tell-tale signs and ever-presence of toxic founders[17].

    It is telling that Founder Syndrome[18] has its own Wikipedia entry. There is a lot to be said here, but it has been said by others and it is continuously being

---

17 For instance https://www.keystonelaw.com/keynotes/navigating-four-toxic-startup-founder-personality-types-god-wiz-ocd-and-fng

   https://www.saasacademy.com/blog/toxicculture

   https://medium.com/panacea/how-to-avoid-startup-suicide-toxic-founder-relationships-a8a0d746a82b

18 Defined as the difficulty faced by organisations, and in particular young companies such as startups, where one or more founders maintain disproportionate power and influence following the effective initial establishment of the organisation, leading to a wide range of problems.

said already. I don't feel it requires a literature review or indeed more words added, even though I agree it is a phenomenon that merits attention. A set of behaviour that merits analysis and reflection. And maybe less adulation.

2. This book is *not* a gotcha. I have no intention of airing dirty laundry or interviewing people whose work I neither admire nor respect in the hope that they will be tricked into saying something that will allow me to compromise them in their own words. I am not an investigative journalist and this is not that kind of book. *This* book is meant to look back only so that we can look forward: I intend for it to be a helpful resource for people going about hard, complicated work.

3. I don't actually think the bravado-filled 'always falling upwards' brigade has much to teach us that doesn't fit on a bumper sticker. I appreciate that it is a sweeping and highly emotive statement I just made there... but there you have it.

Even though I suspect their stories are fascinating and their thought processes will probably be riveting, those founders (and many corporate officers who emulate the tone and swagger) lack the humility required for self-reflection and therefore I don't see how they may give useful answers to my questions around failure, challenge, doubt and the things we can learn to make it easier for the next cohort of folks coming into the fray.

The lone founder or CEO standing against the odds is not a trope I am interested in. So I didn't speak to anyone who fits that mould. You have been warned.

> I don't believe that the bravado-filled 'always falling upwards' brigade have more to teach us than can fit on a bumper sticker.

I ran that decision by my friend Liz early on in the process. For a bit of sanity-checking of my own biases. Liz Lumley not only is a seasoned journalist but also has held a variety of industry roles[19] working closely with transformation leaders and founders. What she had to say reinforced my conviction to select very carefully whose wisdom I cared to distil for you.

'I heard once at an event '*the best entrepreneurs are naive and arrogant*'. That seems to be a widely shared belief. But we are in financial services. What industry has ever needed naive and reckless *less*? And yet we somehow have bought into the idea that an entrepreneur is someone who jumps off a cliff and builds a plane on the way down. Hang on.

What were you planning to do once you climbed the hill? What was the plan and why were you not equipped for it?'

---

19 Since being interviewed for this book, Liz has moved from the Banker to Chainlink Labs.

Of course life throws curve balls. Of course business is full of surprises and of course even the best prepared entrepreneurs will miscalculate. That is not what Liz is talking about and what I was trying to avoid.

There is a romanticised founder-centricity in our industry. And it cuts both ways. It paints a founder pitted against the world, staying true to their vision through whatever the haters say, which effectively romanticises ignoring feedback which, ironically, is consistently identified as a cause for the extremely high failure rate we have already discussed.

Liz Lumley, Deputy Editor, the Banker
Previously Director of Product Strategy for VC Innovations, MD for Thought Leadership for Rainmaking and award winning journalist

Plus it diminishes the actions and value of the drivers of change inside big organisations just because to get anything done inside an established entity you need to placate and negotiate.

Because they cannot always go in a straight line or on the fast lane.

So the idea of the heroic, singular founder is unhelpful whether you are a startup or a corporate and yet our entire industry has encouraged this image. 'It's all part of the t-shirts, and the slogans and the language' continues Liz. 'It's all a little cultish if you stop and think about it. There is a messianic mission narrative. The image of the disruptor and rebel.

The language we provide when speaking about entrepreneurship in fintech is at odds with the industry we are trying to enter. Frankly some of the books in this space have done more harm than good. *Hustle culture* is the vocabulary we provide. And it is unhelpful.'

It creates tensions inside your organisation and across the market. It is simplistic. It is not informative. And it is actually symptomatic of a greater ill whereby people enter the business arena with their eyes firmly on the finish line rather than because of any real interest in the journey.

'In fintech, a lot of people started a business because they wanted an exit, not for the problem they are solving' observed Liz. 'People talk about their exit strategy before they even have product market fit. In this spirit, serial entrepreneurship is a badge of honour.'

Weirdly, may I add.

Because we both idolise being so focused you don't take no for an answer... and idolise doing it again irrespective of success or failure. 'How about you focus on the business you actually want to have instead?' continues Liz. 'Achieving viability as a business is hard. Essentially a real entrepreneur is someone who has built a business that is stable enough to pay taxes and hire people.'

So I avoided people who saw their stories as me vs the world... and opted for people who tried (and largely succeeded) to build scalable businesses, not get rich.

Even if, in some cases, riches ensued. And I was rewarded with insight and reflection and more than a little actionable wisdom. Which was the whole point. So each chapter will end with your *Call to Action*, things you can start thinking about. Things you can do. They won't always be easy. But you didn't expect them to be, did you?

The people I spoke to were humble in their truth. Not one of them said 'I am now a millionaire because I am a natural, self-taught genius' which is rarely true and never helpful. They were all keen to speak about the things they got wrong. Which is *always* helpful.

You will notice that some of the stories here are not attributed. Not many, but a few. In a couple of cases that is to protect corporate sensibilities. In two further cases it is because of open, ongoing litigation. So although their insights imbue this book, a few of the folks interviewed are not named to spare them additional complications.

It goes without saying that I remain grateful for their time and insight.

So yes.

I interview people I admire from up close or afar and I looked for something between their answers which is why you won't see any interview transcripts here even though you will see a lot of quotes. I looked for a pattern in their experiences and their reflections and I found it in spades. But I also found nuance and insight that I wouldn't have known how to look for in a research design format. This insight was their gift to you, via me. So I am coming out of this smarter and grateful.

The challenge of how to synthesise these amazing stories is not small and any failures in doing them justice are mine alone. Please bear with me and enjoy.

So: on with the show.

> The idea of staying true to a vision is romanticised to such an extent that it romanticizes ignoring feedback.
>
> Which is, ironically, consistently identified as a cause for failure in all change work.

Do You Want the Good News, or the Bad?

Are you a 'bad news first to get it out of the way' kind of person? I know I am.

So the bad news is that the patterns emerging from these stories as to what we can and should be doing to ensure success are not easy to implement. The good news is that, as already mentioned above, the pattern is very much there and it can guide some choices you make throughout your journey to shore up the ship, so to speak. I trust that this bad news does not surprise you. You didn't expect there was a magic trick, did you?

So here is what comes next.

This book is essentially a laundry list of key things you need to think about when you engage in work that goes against the grain. The list is itemised and thematically organised. The things to do and think about and be mindful of reflect the insight shared by the people I interviewed and based on the experiences of people who have done this before and they will be shared with you in a format that is clear and pre-scriptive ('go do this thing, immediately').

You will see a lot of quotes and a lot of names in support of the insight.

Some of the names will be familiar, if you are from the finan-cial services industry. Some may

> Achieving business viability is harder than serial entrepreneurship.
> **Liz Lumley**

not be. Have no fear, I will introduce and re-introduce the people and their story every time they speak so you don't have to hold that information in your head as you go. There is enough to do without needing to remember a huge cast of characters.

The idea is that the stories in these pages should go some way towards helping you plan ahead. Or at least scan for dragons and monsters when you are mid-journey.

I will tell you about all the plans that were made and didn't quite work out. I will talk about the factors that ended up being more important than any amount of planning. I will tell you about some of the basic stuff that you already know is important and yet often still treat as auxiliary. How discipline eats innovation for breakfast and culture beats strategy right out of the gate. And I already know

that some of the stuff I have to say, you will be tempted to scoff at and say that *this is not the most important thing*.

And it's up to me to find a way to show you that you may be wrong. Just like those guys who choose to not trust the research or what the experts tell them. Those very guys who make up the failure rate numbers for startups and corporates alike.

> You may be tempted to look at some of the findings in this book and think 'this is not the most important thing'.
>
> Just like the decision-makers who make up for the high failure rates: not believing the research over their personal preference.
>
> Try not to do that.

I guess it is not news (or at least shouldn't be) that doing something brand new, be it on your own or inside a com-pany, is hard. It takes optimism: because if you believe in the possibility of a positive outcome you are more likely to put a lot of work in. It needs work, because doesn't everything? But it also needs a willingness to take advice from people or a hint from the market around you. And a resolve to *not* take advice or a hint when they are distracting. And the wisdom or good luck to know the difference.

The advice in this book will be clear as day but not always easy to follow. I've made that point already. But it is important enough to repeat. Which I have done now.

We are almost ready to roll with the actual main body of the research (already).

There is just one last thing.

You Probably Think This Song Is (Not) about You[20]

The first iteration of this chapter went straight for the jugular.

After the introductory stage directions above, I went in straight to meeting the cast of characters whose wisdom is distilled in this book. Not what they had to say about the specifics yet, but a glimpse into who they are. It felt appropriate to start there. It felt respectful.

But re-reading the chapter created a very strong sense of... *what about me?*

As I mentioned earlier, the people I spoke to have achieved momentous things. And some of the folks I spoke to have incredible origin stories. Not all do. They all have incredible resilience and wisdom (the combination is important as one without the other doesn't get you far in this business). For some, the origin stories emerged as a powerful way of showing how their particular thoughtful resolve was forged.

But in my first attempt at telling these stories, it almost looked like there is no room in this business for people who had a blissfully uncomplicated start in life.

> Although I have avoided the me-versus-the-world founder, there are a large number of folks on these pages with cinematic backstories.
>
> They are not critical for success. But they often are where people's mettle was forged.

What about those guys?

I have made it very clear that the heroic founder standing tall against the world isn't what I am looking for and yet looking at some of the stories I am about to share, there is no denying that there are heroic figures here. They may not cast themselves that way, but that doesn't change what they are. People who went through serious hardship often with a smile on their face. People who tested their mettle in life, not just business, and prevailed. Amazing stories of amazing people. So what about those of us who don't have such stories?

What about Me?

Someone who doesn't necessarily have a cinematic backstory? No more than garden variety hardship? Someone who had an easy childhood and now wants to build a tech business... or transform a bank or card issuer or insurer? Surely there is room for me here, right?

Yes.

There absolutely is. The backstory is not essential. But a particular type of personality is. And that part is unavoidable. The backstories are just a dramatic and stark way of highlighting what that particular personality type looks like. So when it comes to the 'what about me' question, the answer is you can absolutely succeed at

---

20 Paraphrasing Carly Simon's 1972 song 'You're so Vain'.

this work without a dramatic backstory. Provided your personality (forged in whatever way) fits the needs of this journey and the journey tickles your fancy.

I spoke with Gareth Richardson, COO of Thought Machine about this. Little digression here: Thought Machine have been a competitor for me during different parts of my life, so this is the first time I can actually openly admit I really like what they do and really *really* like their logo. There, I've said it.

Gareth Richardson, COO Thought Machine
Previously MD for the Atlantic Region, GFT Group and Rule Financial's Global Head of Delivery

So I asked Gareth exactly that: is there room for real people in the entrepreneurial journey? His view... was it depends by what you mean when you say 'real'.

'I am from a lower middle class background with average grades and dyslexia.' Doesn't get more real than that. But. 'But I am driven and purposeful in what I do. There is no one way to do this work, but I think there are a few common traits people need. As a general rule, to be an entrepreneur or a change agent, I really think you need to fundamentally be an optimistic person.

I generally will jump into things in a way that stretches me, always optimistic about the outcome. But that has to be tempered by strategic thinking.

> There is absolutely room for 'real' people in the entrepreneurial journey.
> Depending on what you mean by 'real'.
> *Gareth Richardson*

People, it seems to me, are often emotionally driven. More than they should be. They try to dress up decisions in other ways but they often don't take a brutal view at what they are dealing with. They are not objectively/brutally strategic, first principles based or just conscious about why or what they do.

Take core[21]: it is an obvious problem to solve. The largest banks in the world need you to solve it. The business case has been written for 10–20 years. The technology is there. If you can achieve that, you will change an industry, be supported/cheered on to do it and will get an outsized result for you and your team. But it will be hard and lots of people have failed before *because* it is hard. So go for it but

---

21 Core banking is an area I am so steeped in, I almost missed the fact that some of you have fuller lives and hobbies and may not know what Gareth is talking about, so for those who may not know exactly what we mean here, it is merely a part of the banking stack. Gartner defines 'core' as a back-end system that processes daily transactions and posts updates to accounts and financial records for all deposit, lending and credit-processing capabilities.

There is nuance to this but fundamentally if it sounds fairly simple it is because it should be. Essential. But simple.

be thoughtful. Pick big enough problems and solve them – don't spend your time adding a widget to a home screen (just because you can) and expect that this will be game changing. Be conscious about what you do and why.'

So is there space for real people? Yes.

Ordinary though? That is another matter altogether.

Real people willing to do the hard work are not *just* welcome here. They are absolutely essential and more likely to thrive than those who believe greatness is the key and, even worse, believe they have it.

Jesus Don't Want You for a Sunbeam[22]

As I said at the very beginning, a heroic figure is not necessary for success.

In fact, a self-selected heroic figure is often a problem as statistics of labour churn in companies with toxic leadership show. But, for the avoidance of doubt, the issue is the self-anointing, not the hero themselves.

Observe.

A few years back, a founder asked me to join his board.

We started the process of conversations and light-touch due diligence on both sides. The business was young but seemed sound. The team was mature and seasoned. The CEO was chocolate-labrador levels of keen but experienced and yet something didn't sit right. If you had asked me at the time I would have made a vague gesture and muttered something unintelligible. It's not quite right but I don't know how. The founder had no such qualms. He wanted me. He made me an offer and allowed me time to think about it. But as I had not leaped at it with the enthusiasm he required, in a move designed to sway me, a personal manifesto hit my inbox on a sleepy Sunday morning. A vision statement that was, I suspect, meant to clinch the deal. And in it, the phrase I will never forget that did seal the deal only in the opposite direction: *I believe I am on a mission from God.*

Worthy cause by the way. The business was trying to have a genuine impact on local communities in their regions of operation. But the direct line to God is where our roads parted forevermore.

I admire people who are fuelled by belief and conviction. In fact, conviction and optimism help on this journey and a belief in God is always a strength for those who have it. But you don't need to be anointed to do this work. And you definitely shouldn't believe you are, even if others may suspect it of you.

Everyday greatness is possible. But the 'everyday' part is key to ensure it doesn't slide into a farcical parody of itself.

On January 26, 2024, Scott Galloway wrote: 'Few virtues are more celebrated in America than perseverance and grit. Commencement speakers offer a similar battle cry: "Never give up!" Jesus, what bullshit. Entrepreneurs aren't voted into the hall

---

22 Song by Nirvana, released 1994.

of fame unless they have a story about mortgaging their house to make payroll or cleaning the first apartments rented on their platform. Sir James Dyson made 5,126 prototypes of his bagless vacuum cleaner, only to be rejected by every manufacturer in the U.K. Jack Ma was rejected by Harvard ten times. Grit is great. Perseverance is a virtue. But, narratively, it's overrated. Greatness is a function not just of grit, but of talent, luck, where and when you are born... and knowing when to quit.'

And that is the point. Some of the folks have those inspiring backstories. Some don't. Have some dramatic music in-built into the journeys. Others don't. They all have everyday greatness though. And that is what this story is all about. *Every* story in this book.

And it is greatness, make no mistake.

A lot of the folks here are humble (unlike your man above) *and* great. There is no denying there is nothing average about them.

> This book is for everyone.
> The insights and tips in this book are for everyone.
> But the journey of building something new from scratch is not.
> And that is ok.

So can the average person still learn something from this book? I say: absolutely.

Even if you are not doing 'exciting new' stuff but running a small business or working in a big department of a big company doing Business As Usual work, there is something to be learned here if you have your eye on a leadership role.

There is a lot here that you can take and apply no matter what you do. Especially if you are doing new stuff, but not exclusively.

No matter what you are doing, this book is for you.

But it is fair to say, harsh as it may sound, that the entrepreneurial or intrapreneurial journey, the change journey, the building new stuff from nothing journey... *that* may not be for you. It is pertinent to say that the 'building new stuff' journey isn't for everyone. And, additionally, not all stages of the journey are for everyone.

Not everyone will have what it takes to go on this journey. And what it takes is not a history of hardship or vision or greatness. Not

> The experiences of people who have driven change are useful for everyone. No matter what work you do.
> The work however may not be for everyone.
> And not everyone will want it.

at all. But it does take grit, determination and a tolerance for pain that many people don't have and frankly don't wish to have. It's not that you can't as much as you may not want to. A lot of people may *not wish* to take on this level of stress. May not want to take these gambles.

So if you read these pages and go 'jeez that's not for me' then that is also a win. Because life is short and the journeys described in this book are not smooth sailing. To decide they are not for you, is actually a meaningful outcome.

Equally, to use your own experience and some of these stories to calibrate what stage company, perhaps, what shape (new venture inside a big corporate, transformation work or brand new venture) is right for you is also a win.

Ultimately, in reading these pages you are invited to reflect on whether these experiences are right for you. Not so much whether you are like the people described here but whether the experiences described are for you. Not least because the people described here are as different as they come. And their experiences show that you don't need to be on a pedestal, you definitely don't need a mission from God, you don't need a history of hardship and challenge to do what they did. But you do need grit, optimism and an immense capacity for hard work and bounce-back-ability. So sometimes the traits that go with being attracted to this work go hand in hand with resilience gained through early hardship or with an inflated ego.

The latter tends to burst and shatter and outlive its usefulness much more easily than the former.

So as I go into some of those incredible stories of grit and resili-

> There is something extraordinary in the grit and resilience of the people who are attracted to this work and who do this work well.
>
> Even if this is not you, you can learn so much from it to apply to whatever context is right for you.

ence (and yes I realise this is the longest caveat emptor ever) please sit back and enjoy the gift of people sharing their backstories with us. Don't think 'what about me?'. All of their lessons are still useful for you even if you didn't experience great hardship. Many of the people in this book didn't either. All of their insights are still applicable. All their stories resonate even if they are not same-same.

Still, it takes a lot to do this work. It's not for everyone. And no matter how much I want to stress that this book *is* indeed for everyone, I would be lying to you if you told you this work is.

It is not.

That much is clear.

There is no escaping that this work is hard. It attracts some egos, for sure. But there are also some extraordinary people quietly getting on with some very hard stuff and not dying. Succeeding and creating and having an impact.

And it's time to meet them. The longest drumroll exercise ever, is finally over.

Every Day Is a School Day. Even Sunday

Building things that haven't been done before means you operate without a blueprint. Inevitably, you will get things wrong and will need to revisit. You will need to re-do, re-think or pivot. It goes with the territory.

And while you are going about this tough, unpredictable work, you will be offered advice by people or by the universe in the shape of experience and instructive examples. And you will need to determine whether to follow said advice or not. And when.

Every day is a school day, the saying goes. And although we don't always realise it, the formative, useful experience life gives you that will help you do the job better don't always come labelled as such. The learnings are not always dramatic. Often they are, don't get me wrong. Some folks have those 'stop press' stories: life moments that you know are momentous even as they are happening. But most of us don't have those. Most of us

Monika Liikamaa and Denise Johansson, co-CEOs of Enfuce
Enfuce offer card issuance and payment services globally.

acquire learnings and experiences as we go through life doing other stuff. Most of us can't always pinpoint the exact moment when the lesson came. Sometimes the lessons come through your life, outside the office. And sometimes they are work-related, in things that you did, witnessed or suffered in the work arena before you came to do whatever it is you are doing now. Realistically and in most cases, the useful learnings come at you from both directions: life and work. In and outside the 'office'. It is up to you to notice, decipher and absorb them.

Speaking to the co-CEOs of Enfuce, they observed that those things may not be entirely unrelated. Your life before and outside work shapes you in a particular way. Your experiences in your early years in the workforce shape you in certain ways. They all make you more alert or receptive to certain things. And all the lessons come together in their own time. Everything plays its part. But it is not linear.

Denise reflected that 'neither Monika or I have the easiest backgrounds. We have similar childhood stories. Not the prettiest. Not terrible. But nothing came easy in life. We had to work for everything. We saw that in each other when we met. We were already far into our careers and we had that in common'. And yet.

Knowing what you need to do and having the confidence to do it are not the same thing and don't always arrive at the same time.

Although the experiences they already had were useful: in identifying each other as a good partner and co-founder, in planning and setting up their business (as we will see in the next chapters) and getting ready for what they wanted to build and how they wanted to go about it, those experiences didn't protect them from everything. They didn't protect them, for instance, from taking the wrong advice in the early days. Not least because, ultimately, there will always be parts of the work that are new to you, no matter how experienced you are.

'In our early days' recalls Denise 'the mistake we made was listening to someone who looked like they knew better than us but actually didn't'. An easy mistake to make. But a costly one. 'In the early part of our journey, we used a big consultancy firm for our A round and we let them lead us. We barely got to pitch our own company [to prospective investors]. The consultants were pitching their own story. They said we should go for a 20 Million investment and we went with it and before long we had it on the table... but something didn't feel right.'

You may argue that having gone that far with the consultants and with money on the table, the only option is to take it. You've come this far, right? Plus it's hard to turn cash down when you are fund-raising, a topic we will turn to at length later in the book. Plus, if experience didn't protect you from going this far down the road, what good is it at the 11th hour?

> The world is full of 'average'. And that's ok. Ok for them. If you have ambition, you can't do 'average'.
> **Monika Liikamaa**

Plenty good, as it turns out.

'We went back and regrouped' recalls Denise. 'The money was on the table. But we didn't want to lose control of our company and actually telling us to give up control at that early stage was terrible advice. We didn't take the money. We kept control of our business. And we stopped taking advice that wasn't right for us.'

Monika concurs: 'During the first three years we listened to much of the noise. Now my tolerance for bullshit is zero. I get annoyed before it even hits. I have no patience for stupidity. I have realised that the world is full of average and that's ok.

Ok for them.

If you have ambition, you can't do average.'

This is a very helpful benchmark for working out which advice to keep and which advice to reject. Because of course the advice you will receive will invariably suggest you do things differently. More of, less of or just different to what you are doing now. Sometimes the advice will be right for you. And sometimes it won't. And you won't know which is which till after the fact.

> Building new things means operating without a blueprint.
> Knowing what to prioritise and what to park.
> When to double down and when to pivot...
> Most of it takes vision, determination and experience.
> For some, the experience comes from previous ventures. For others, from their life.

So how do you choose?

How do you filter?

Focus and determination are absolutely key to any personal and professional journey. You will never be a pro athlete if you give up at your first injury. You will never learn to play a musical instrument if you are not ok with some pretty shrill noise before the sweet music comes. But at some point, maybe the shrill noise is how you know the clarinet is not for you.

When is *you doubling down* perseverance and when it is obstinance?

This is a topic we will be coming back to a lot in the chapters to come, especially when we discuss product market fit considerations and that startup classic: the pivot. But knowing when to call it and when to double down is not a science. It's not even an art. It's a gut feel. And you won't always get it right. You may take the wrong advice for quite a while until you realise it's not for you, like Monika and Denise did. You may reject good advice and regret it (as we will see in later examples in the book).

> Maintaining your sense of perspective is key to doing things for the first time and learning in the process.
>
> If you are only driven by your own vision, you may miss a lot of cues along the way.

The key is to engage with the advice, keep focus on what you are trying to do but try to avoid pig-headedness if you can.

The thing you need most of all is a sense of perspective. How else do you even begin to tell the forest from the trees? And where does that sense of perspective come from?

This is not just a philosophical question. It is a practical one and one you should ask yourself as you are building a team: where do you get your sense of perspective from? And where do the people you surround yourself with get theirs? Hint: if the answer is always and only 'their own sense of purpose' then I can introduce you to your man who is on his divine mission. You will get on like a house on fire.

But for the rest?

Sometimes it comes from past professional experience. And sometimes from life.

Now, getting a glimpse of someone's personal life, of their private story, is a gift and not something you can ask for in an interview. 'Tell me about your childhood' is absolutely not an acceptable interview question. But asking folks about moments in their life or career that they are aware were formative may tell you a lot about what forged their metal and set them on a path.

This is not a Hollywood montage set to uplifting orchestral music. It is more visceral than that and that is why it is important. Because one of the hardest things to do in change work is keep going. It is inescapable that most of us learn the skill way before we come into our very first (real or virtual) office. The key, of course, is in the learning. As I already mentioned, challenge doesn't make saints of us all. It doesn't always teach people the same things. Sometimes it doesn't teach people anything. A formative experience is only that if it actually taught us a lesson that is useful for whatever came next.

First Person Singular

Dharmesh Mistry is a familiar name in the financial technology space. He has been up to his eyeballs in banking transformation, having led major projects in some of the biggest banks in the UK. He had also been the Chief Digital Officer of one of the biggest core banking providers globally, plus he is one of the few people who was not only a serial founder but also the captain of multiple successful exits. And a thoroughly nice guy to boot.

So *of course* I wanted to hear his view on what patterns he was seeing, what was repeatable and what was not. What I didn't anticipate – stupidly, in hindsight – was fighting back tears during the interview.

I hope he didn't notice. I have my reputation as a hard-ass to protect.

'There are pivotal moments in everyone's life' said Dharm. 'Mine

Dharmesh Mistry

CEO of vision 2020 consulting

Serial founder (including Ask Homey and edge IPK)

NED, advisor and co-cost of *Dave and Dharm Demystify*

Seasoned CTO, CDO and a former banker (like us... I couldn't resist)

was a conversation I overheard as a child.' I have an image in my mind of a young Dharm tiptoeing to the edge of the landing, holding onto the banister, eavesdropping. 'My parents were talking about selling our house and moving into the shop in order to save it... or selling the shop to save our home.' Before that moment, Dharm may have had a loose sense of financial difficulties in the household. After that moment, the immensity of the pressure his parents were under was undeniable. Inescapable. And although, at the time, he was too young to do much about what he overheard, the moment didn't leave him. The feeling didn't leave him.

> Entrepreneurship involves taking risks. But it doesn't need to involve risking everything.
>
> Having your own boundaries when you start is key.

'My focus on securing my home over anything else for the rest of my life started then. Whatever professional or financial decision came next, the primary consideration was *never* facing that dilemma again.'

The story is both highly relatable and counter-intuitive.

We think of founders and entrepreneurs often as people who take immense risks, who put it all on black and spin the wheel, who put their vision above all else, an image that I have historically found both inaccurate and deeply unhelpful.

The entrepreneur who throws caution to the wind to build a dream is a very Silicon Valley image but the reality is, those lads (and lasses... but mostly lads) who throw caution to the wind like the myth demands, they tend to have a safety net. Maybe they had a dad or spouse that could pick up the tab on all living expenses while they pursued their dream without a salary. Or savings from a successful first career. Or they had a plan B. Or bags of middle-class confidence.

The point I am trying to make is that the commonly established language of *needing* to take these huge risks often makes the image of the entrepreneurial hustle feel entirely inaccessible to many coming from a more financially insecure background.

Why don't you start your own thing is a question many successful corporate employees are asked. I was asked that a lot over the years. Often with slight mockery barely concealed in the sentence. If you are such a firebrand, why don't you go off the reservation and do your own thing?

If you are ambitious and good at what you do, someone, somewhere will ask you why you don't pursue the idealistic founder path, often seen as some sort of evolutionary apex. The unspoken answer is often 'because I have bills to pay and nobody to pay them but me'. But also, perhaps, because I didn't have the fire in the belly someone like Dharm had. And that is as important.

So listening to Dharm was like a bombshell: here is an entrepreneur who worries about the same things as you. Whose daddy isn't his safety net. Quite the reverse.

> None of us have a choice but to play the hand we are dealt. How we play it is up to us.
>
> Do you wrap yourself into a small parcel and accept defeat before you even start just because the first roll of the dice isn't all sixes?

Here is an entrepreneur whose early life was not just moulded by a conversation he overheard but by responsibilities he assumed as a result very early on.

'I didn't go to university' says Dharm. 'I got a job to help out because dad was bankrupt by the time I finished school and I had to help with bills.'

Before you think 'poor Dharm' though… Stop.

'I also felt that, having written a cross assembler for a 6502 chip in my A-Level project, I was good enough to skip Computer Science at Uni.'

Boom.

That's where I wanted to cry, by the way, in case you were wondering. It wasn't the part where his childhood was burdened with responsibility. It was the part where the burden didn't crush him. None of us have a choice but to play the hand we are dealt. How we play it, however, is up to us. What we do with the circumstances we find ourselves in is what fundamentally becomes the measure of a person.

Dharm did not wrap himself into a small parcel and accept defeat before he even started just because the first roll of the dice wasn't all sixes.

I was all fired up. People who don't let their circumstances define them: that's what we need for change of any kind. For creativity and progress in industry, society, technology.

Which Part of Your Circumstances Define You Is Up to You

If I tell you someone was raised by a single mother of four, isn't your first instinct to say 'oh poor thing'?

It is, admit it. It's ok. It's understandable. But you would be wrong.

As Dharm points out, we all have pivotal moments in our lives. Not of our making, not of our choosing. But what we learn from them, what we take away and which direction we go into during the pivot of said moment is, in a million ways, up to us.

Valentina Kristensen is a case in point.

She was raised by a single mother of four.

That was not a situation of her making. What she chose to take away from it though was. There were challenges, there were difficulties and yet the defining image she took away from this journey was empowering: 'I came into the workforce knowing that a woman can be the boss: I had only ever seen that'.

Again, the moment when you feel like someone turns on a light. When you are having a conversation with someone that makes you go 'hang on'. I had known Valentina for years by the time we sat down to speak about her journey with OakNorth and the Bank's success (more on that later, have no fear). I had known her for years and yet I didn't know her personal story. We often don't know each other's personal stories. They are a gift that can and will be bestowed if the moment is right. But they are always there, our stories. As are their reverberations.

Valentina's mother was an entrepreneur whose business started from the simple imperative to make enough money so that she could keep custody of her children and look after them. Valentina's mum, just like Dharm, didn't become an entrepreneur to 'take over the world'. She became an entrepreneur to look after her family

Valentina Kristensen, Corporate Affairs Director at OakNorth

OakNorth Bank is a bank for entrepreneurs, founded by entrepreneurs focusing on lending to scaling businesses (typically with between £1m–100m in turnover) based on a forward-looking view of cashflow and granular data, not just past performance. The bank acquired its full license in 2015 and in the first seven years of operation (the bank launched in September 2015), has lent over £8.5bn to entrepreneurs across the UK.

> Being an entrepreneur entails doing things for the first time... all the time. Being comfortable with that is key.

and ended up building a hugely successful business by the bye. And in running that hugely successful business, as a woman standing alone, she created a very powerful truth for her kids: not an abstract sense of 'it can be done', not a vague sense of 'if you see it, you can become it' but a lived reality of *it* being done. With all the challenges and triumphs of it all.

Watching her mother taught Valentina not just that a woman absolutely can do all the things that come with running a business (fire, hire, do the payroll) but also that she can do all those things *without having done them before.*

There is always a first time.

Everyone needs to start at some point and taking a chance is how you do it.

> A lot of the people successfully navigating this challenging space came into it unburdened of romanticised notions of what entrepreneurship is actually like: the lived experience of seeing it done is more powerful than any motivational quote.

That was Valentina's lived experience. Her normal. Her starting point. And the formative experience she both learned from and held onto: each action as significant as the other.

Being raised by an entrepreneur also taught her that working hard is normal. It's not about work–life balance 'work isn't a thing apart from the rest of your life'. It is a thing that you have the opportunity to do and then get paid for. Work–rest balance is a useful idea but work–life balance is a false separation, especially in a startup or for an entrepreneur: then work is all-encompassing. This is not a 9–5 situation. It does take over your life. You work hard, but you can go places.

Valentina came into this world of hard work with no romantic notions of what it would be like. So she never had the reality check many face before they get on with the work. She never needed it.

We often talk about the power of representation in inspiring and guiding future generations. We all buy into the language of 'if you can see it you can become it' but the reality is a lot more complicated and a lot more exciting than static images on marketing collateral and television adverts. Seeing a female pilot in the latest Virgin Atlantic advert is great but it doesn't really

> Doing new things for the first time requires a lot of hard work. It is not a 9–5 life. And it is not glamorous work for most of the time.
>
> It helps, if you have no romantic notions of what entrepreneurial life is like, when you enter it.

tell me much about how to get there or what my trade-offs will be along the way. The lived experience of watching someone do things for the first time in close proximity, now that is a life lesson for the ages.

Although I am not advocating that you should ask team members interviewing for a role or founders pitching for funding to tell you their life stories (seriously: don't do that. It would be creepy and intrusive), I am very much saying that those life stories temper their steel. The people who go into and weather the storms – material and emotional – of founding, growing and exiting a business and then go again, the people who navigate this jungle with humility and a level head (yes yes this is a dig towards one and all tech founder who is vaguely wondering why his business folded and yet is going again with the same energy, a supposedly radically different idea and yet the same pitch deck, only now in purple).

Doing business comes with a lot of daily choices. Building a business comes with even more of them. You need to be doing a lot of complicated things at the same time. It is hard and it gets frantic. The reality is execution will falter if the people on the boat aren't made of sterner stuff, like this lot. They were not handed anything. They did not set out to prove a point or take over the world (seriously, next time a founder speaks of 'world domination' in their pre-revenue, series B deck, I will reach for a cattle prod). They just went about their journey not contemplating for a moment that they would just watch life play out. That willingness to get in the game without rose tinted glasses is key to what comes next.

Optimism without a naive conviction of guaranteed success is a powerful commonality across people engaged in this kind of work. As was teachability.

By the time these folks become leaders and change-makers, they have already cut their teeth in learning from everything that comes at them, in the office and at home. In the spaces in between and the world at large.

Learning Life's Lessons Isn't for the Faint of Heart

When discussing how hard it was to make a major pivot to her business, Kaidi Ruusalepp chuckled and said 'hard is a very relative term. I was born in the Soviet Union'.

I knew that. Of course I knew that. I know Kaidi is Estonian… I know roughly her age and I know enough history. Not to mention… I can count.

So I should have been able to work out for myself that, yes, Kaidi was born in the Soviet Union.

But I hadn't thought about it. So here's a way you can reflect on people's journeys without asking for a testimonial: think. What do you know about them that may help you piece together what they have lived through, where some of their fire comes from.

Memo to self, as well as to you, my friends.

I am an unashamed fangirl of Kaidi's quiet magic, by the way.

I have been for years. Now I have a quote I can point at to summarise the fizzy feeling of watching her unlock possibilities. When I asked her about how her lived context affected her outlook, she said 'we fought ourselves free and built a new story for Estonia, we created a tech-savvy transparent country'.

It's a fact.

Estonia is the poster child of what a digital governance mindset can achieve. And yet, she continues: 'we are still treated like we are soviets... even inside the EU and NATO: treated as a new kid on the block (after 18+ years of membership)' and what does Estonia do? Carry on. Fight on. Refuse to be defined by what others see. Continue learning and changing and shifting and proving people wrong. That is the lesson. It doesn't matter what others see in you. It matters what you see in you and where you are going. The road there won't be linear. 'So keep an eye on where you are going or you will get lost.'

That's what Kaidi chose to do.

As a female founder. As someone advocating for the use of blockchain technology in the early days of adoption. As someone going against the grain.

'This country has no fear to make change' says Kaidi 'We can all learn from that.'

There is something mind-blowingly wise in the ability to contextualise yourself even when you are not forced to.

Kaidi Ruusalepp, founder and CEO of Funderbeam

Funderbeam helps private investor networks and founders to handle their syndicated investments, post investment flow and secondaries.

Funderbeam was awarded as the Best European Fintech startup in 2017. Kaidi is also the member of the Digital Council of the President of Estonia.

Kaidi is a former CEO of Nasdaq Tallinn Stock Exchange and of the Central Securities Depository. Co-Founder of Estonian Service Industry Association. Ex Member of Startup Europe Advisory Board at European Commission. The first IT lawyer in Estonia, she co-author of the Estonian Digital Signatures Act of 2000.

I was interviewing Kaidi as a successful founder with an imminent exit (more on that later). As someone who has both stood her ground when it was hard to do so and changed when it was sensible to do so. A terribly difficult balancing act we will be returning to time and again in this book. The circumstances of this conversation fundamentally lent themselves to unleashing ego. To saying 'I' a lot. To patting yourself on the back a wee bit.

But I got none of that.

Not from Kaidi, not from anyone in the 50 plus interviews conducted as I was researching this book. Not an iota of ego.

> Do you have the wisdom and presence of mind to learn from your context, even when you are not forced to?

For sure, there was bias at work as I have already admitted: I hand-picked these people, I steered clear from the Other Kind. But the extent to which the reflections the founders and corporate leaders gave me were ego-free was surprising at first and then hugely illuminating.

Because one of the things that emerged strongly through the interviews even though it was never said in so many words was people who threw themselves at seriously hard work, narrow verticals in a specialist industry and yet never lost sight of the bigger picture, the wider context and, ultimately, what matters.

Really matters. When the chips are down.

'My first startup was in Tbilisi, Georgia, where I was born and raised, when we were still part of the Soviet Union', says Zor Gorelov, a founder I have admired from afar for so long and when we finally spoke, I felt I had been robbed of years when I could have known him.

> You don't need dramatic beginnings to be able to tell the forest from the trees.
>
> But you do need the ability to keep an eye on the bigger picture and what truly matters to you, in order to navigate this journey.

He is smart, helpful, warm. I was robbed, I tell you, of all the years he could have been my friend, before our paths crossed. But back to his story.

'We built medical information systems for hospitals. Unforgettable Perestroika days. We were building systems because Georgian hospitals wanted to have computers and there was literally *nowhere* to buy them from at the time.

Zor Gorelov, Founder CEO Kasisto
Kasisto offers conversational AI solutions for banking and finance
    Previously CEO of SpeechCycle Corp and BuzzCompany.com

So we built from scratch and were paid in cash. My grandmother was my banker. I would come home with a shoe box full of cash she would keep safe for me.

We would fly to Moscow, buy computers, find the right people, usually foreign students who were travelling out of the country and could help us get American or Italian made parts for PCs. We would come home and use those parts to build the computers, then loaded them with custom-built software and sold them to the hospitals.'

Entrepreneurship at its rawest and purest form: there is a genuine market need. And it is a gap because fulfilling the need is evidently very hard and complicated. Think of that every time you hear of another copycat solution and niche 'nice to have' product.

But I digress.

Zor had built a successful thriving business. He was making money. And he could have carried on. It was a good gig. Only he wanted more. For himself and his family. Not just money but a different life. So success in this business became a means to an end. Only, because of the black-market exchange rates, a *pound* of Rubles got you a dollar. So this thriving business made enough pounds of Rubles for three one-way tickets out of the Soviet Union.

'I was newly married at the time' recalls Zor. 'My son was two. We decided that we needed to get out of the Soviet Union and all that cash allowed us to buy three tickets. That was it. But we left.

We were 25 years old, 1989, we lived in Europe for a few months with no money.' Quite a change, from having shoeboxes full of cash. Not many would walk away from success of this kind. But Zor did. And many years and four successful businesses later, he has no doubt in his mind 'I still consider this as my most successful "exit".'

> You need enough optimism to try things never done before… and enough realism to know when to change.
> Above all, you need to keep an eye firmly on where you are going as the road is never straight and you need to be able to tell the curves and the diversions apart.

Let that sink in.

It's a mic drop moment and should be the end of the chapter if not the end of the book. But it's not. It is the beginning. That is the point. It was neither the end of Zor's story nor the end of the journey of working out what makes for success.

'We eventually landed in the US, started what was then my second company in the mid 90s. This was my first enterprise startup' continues Zor.

That makes kasisto (the business he founded and still ran at the time of this interview) number four with three successful exits preceding it, even if the first cannot be measured in dollars and valuation narratives. And for the avoidance of doubt: there is nothing wrong with the dollars, we all like the dollars, but if the dollars were the most important thing, the suitcases of cash would have been reason enough to stay exactly where he was. And if you are thinking 'ok yes but my situation is different, I am not in the USSR' you are missing the point.

There is something powerful in people putting all their creative energies into building business solutions, doing hard work and not getting caught up on short-sighted metrics of success.

Yes, I mean money.

It is not only inspiring to see. But also it is key to the success itself. If being successful is the end game, you get caught up in the way you measure it. If you have a bigger picture mindset, you make bigger picture choices. If your life, ambition, sense of self-worth, you name it, is bigger than the venture you are working on, you will make more level-headed choices. That's the way it goes.

If you are sitting here thinking 'thanks for nothing, my parents are still together, I was not born in a challenging political landscape and I was financially supported until I was independent' then more bully you. And I am not saying that ironically. But even if you didn't have cinematic origins, you do have some origins. Your formative experiences may be less dramatic, less story-worthy but they will still be exactly that: formative. What forged your metal? What strengthened your mettle? What made you who you are? You don't need dramatic beginnings to have a clear, unromantic and realistic view of the work you are getting into and an ability to keep an eye on a picture much bigger than any single choice in front of you. No matter how large it looms. What you need is realism balancing out the equally essential optimism. And the ability to tell them apart at all times.

Because this work is hard and it takes determination and commitment to leave things a little better than you found them. And that is another commonality, another pattern that emerged across all the interviews: passion.

They Travel Not for Trafficking Alone[23]

I am not naive and I can be a cynic with the best of them. But one more thing the people who do this work successfully have in common is that they are not. Cynical.

Although I know that we operate in a capitalist context and profit is king, in the course of this work I found myself speaking to bankers and finance professionals for whom monetary rewards are second order considerations. They are not in this for the Wall Street glitz. They are not in it for the money. They see their role and its impact on the world differently.

Coastal Financial Corporation's Curt Queyrouze (who we will get to know better later on in this book) speaks of 'a constant awareness that our primary job is to protect consumers'. Being profitable comes second.

> It is hard to believe but, in order to be successful in this business, making money has to be a second order consideration: it should be there… a successful business is a profitable business. But it cannot be the principal driver.

Yes in a capitalist society. 'Of course we need to allocate resources and make margin but that doesn't change what we are here for. And that is to protect.'

Half a world away from Washington State, USA, Royden Volans and Rolf Eichweber who we will meet more extensively later on in this book, who were, at

---

23 The golden journey to Samarkand, James Elroy Flecker
I know you know. I know I have told you before. Just in case you had forgotten…
We travel not for trafficking alone:
By hotter winds our fiery hearts are fanned:
For lust of knowing what should not be known
We take the golden road to Samarkand.

the time we held this interview, building a bank in South Africa for Old Mutual[24], an insurance giant. Their view of their mission is so aligned to Curt's I would have thought they were comparing notes behind my back if I didn't know that they don't actually know each other.

The way Rolf and Roy see it, their mission is to build a bank that is cheap enough to run so that it can combine profitability with the ability to lend cheaply to those who need it the most, when they need it. Their mission is financial wellness. The bank is how they make a positive impact on society. Their job, in other words, is to protect.

'Protect and grow' clarified Euroclear's Kevin Johnson. 'And I'm not talking business growth here, but growing society. Helping

> When I started, I didn't realise I was building a business. I was driven by the conviction that *this* needed to exist.
> **Teun van den Dries**

people not be defined by their circumstances. It's almost the *teach a person to fish* parable here. That is our job.'

And this sense of mission is equally strong among the entrepreneurs.

I know you don't enter business without commercial drivers and I know that many founders and entrepreneurs, including some of the ones I have spoken with as part of this research, have done well. And yet it was not feigned when monetary considerations were dismissed as secondary or incidental.

By bloody everyone.

I am not that motivated by money myself but I struggle to wrap my head around why you would work 14 hours a day in financial services of all things and genuinely deeply consider money a secondary consideration. And, before you ask: yup. I was tempted to dismiss it as posturing.

Teun van Den Dries
Founder and CEO Karman +
    Previously, Founder and CEO
of Geophy (formerly Officerank)
and then Executive Vice President
& Head of Geophy, Walker and
Dunlop post acquisition

It was tempting to say 'well of course you would say that… but do you mean it? I think not'. And yet these are people who *literally* put their money where their mouth is and none more than my friend Teun van den Dries. Let me start by disclosing that I admire and love this man. Let me continue by disclosing that, over the years, his ability to stay focused and on course despite what was going wrong around him has fascinated me, inspired me and scared me in equal measure.

Observe.

---

24 Old Mutual Limited is a pan-African investment, savings, insurance, and banking group.

I met Teun when he was CEO of a company called Officerank, that eventually became Geophy which in turn, after many trials and tribulations, exited to Walker and Dunlop and we all lived happily ever after. How is that for a montage?

Only that is not at all how life felt in the long version of the story and, in the interests of full disclosure: I chaired the Geophy Board during this process so have first-hand experience of the stress, toil and effort it all took. And I was a friend to Teun before, so I know how much personal sacrifice his journey has entailed. So let me just say that at the start of this story, the happy ending did not seem so certain. Quite the opposite.

> Founders more often than not reach a moment when early success requires immense personal sacrifice from them and their families if they are to do double down and build on it.
>
> Often people building something new… are not motivated by the desire to build a business but by a conviction that the thing they are building *needs to exist.*

I remember having a drink with Teun, circa 2015 in London's Royal Exchange building. He had just signed Goldman Sachs as a client. Which is a huge get.

But we were not celebrating exactly.

Because he was just about to sell his car plus use the money in his kids' college fund to keep the company going. Incidentally, when I interviewed the humblingly brilliant Daniela Binatti, co-founder and CTO of Pismo (much more on her later) she told me a chillingly similar story: she and her co-founder husband sold their car to keep the business going, their only consideration outside their mission? Making sure their girls stayed in the same school and were not disrupted. Everything else was fair game when bootstrapping.

Dani and Teun were building very different businesses, one a data analytics business for real-estate based in the Netherlands and the other a core banking and payments platform in Brazil. And yet the pressures they found themselves under were very similar and actually very common. That is what founder life looks like in the early days.

Teun's dilemma, in so many ways remains the most iconic founder moment I have personally encountered. That deep tension between the success milestones and the price they exact. That recurrent personal sacrifice.

'Do I remember this correctly?' I asked Teun seven years later as I was beginning research for this book. We were sitting less than a mile away from where that car-selling conversation had taken place but the world was a very different place by then. Geophy had had a fantastic exit and Teun was already looking to the next thing.

'Yes. We were running around, we were out of money completely.'

So what kept you going, you lunatic, I asked. Why didn't you just… stop?

'I knew I was right' he said with a smile. 'Everyone else didn't seem to realise it yet. The world can be a little slow sometimes.'

Hold onto this thought. We will need it later. For now, I doubled down: what makes a young father of three take such risks? Because at the time the car selling conversation took place, Teun was in his 20s and his three kids just starting school.

'The first few years of Officerank', says Teun, 'I didn't realise I was building a startup. Sure there was a huge probability of failure but I didn't see it as a risk: if this doesn't work, I will just do something else. But as I started working on this problem (asymmetrical access to information) the conviction that *this needed to exist* became stronger. But it was still a project. I had no clear idea when I started that I wanted to be a business. That happened with time.

Officerank pivoted to Geophy as an exercise in pragmatism. We were totally out of cash. Personal bankruptcy was on "final final notice". We had no investors or real revenue yet. When I started, I didn't know the rules of the game. I didn't know that raising a seed round is a thing that is available to you.' So he found out the hard way at great personal cost, both material and emotional. You don't put yourself in line for bankruptcy in the pursuit of a mission lightly.

Have no fear, dear readers, we will come back to Teun's story. You will find out how Geophy was saved. But for now, let's stick to our topic... money as a motivation. Or not.

Knowing what he now knows. Having been through what he has been through, over many years of hard work, stress and personal sacrifice, Teun comes out of Geophy with a lucrative exit. Never you mind how much. Enough. More than you or I have put together and then some.

Dramatic music, emotional finale.... And what does he do with all that money? Yachts? Loads of drinks with little pink umbrellas in them on a serene beach?

Nope.

He pumps all of that money – yes... *all* of it – into Karman +: a venture seeking to mine near-earth asteroids with the aim of providing carbon neutral energy resources for Earth.

Seriously.

What drives these decisions?

'This feels like the highest impact thing that can affect climate change. It is a neglected problem that needs de-risking and nobody is picking it up. This is an opportunity for me to have the impact I want.'

Not money then.

'My first business was about impact too: access to information is asymmetrical. How do you democratise that? Officerank tried to solve that problem. Success would have been *becoming the standard everyone was using.*'

What happened instead? Teun chuckles.

'Once you are in the game, you have to play it. We discovered that the clients of the service fundamentally benefit from the asymmetry. This problem being solved, doesn't help the customer base. You are a business: you need to be realistic about whether the people you are solving a problem for... need it solved.'

Geophy's roadmap needed to head towards money. And the only way to do that is by solving a problem people want solved. And they did. We did. And it worked.

And Teun had a founder's dream come true: an exit. Validation *plus* cash.

And yet it is pretty evident he is not satisfied. He doesn't consider that success per se. 'For me the question is how can I have the impact I want to have in the world. Now I have the money, Karman + is about impact.'

Making a Dent in the World

That word, *impact*, came up again and again in interviews and you will see it creep in across these pages even in chapters that are not technically about that. Impact.

It is easy to roll your eyes and go yeah sure whatever, assuming it's what people say about their intent wanting to paint themselves in a particular light. And yet you have to sit up and take note when the actions support the words. The choices people make, the roads they *don't* take.

Zor walking away from a profitable business in Georgia for a different life for himself and his family or, Teun eschewing a life of leisure and pink drinks with little umbrellas in them for the pursuit of impact, once the money lands.

That pursuit of impact is a double driver. Impact itself is the greatest motivator. But the journey there seems to be a reward in itself.

'There is something massively liberating in the invention phase' Teun continues. 'I have a thousand ideas per week. Two survive my own due diligence and get another thought. One or two of those ideas per year may be something that makes you go *we have something here*. A lot of what you pursue or not is about bandwidth. So you develop a process of working out if an idea is valuable. Ultimately, the reason I am doing Karman + and not something easier is that it is not easier.'

> I have a thousand ideas per week. Two survive my own due diligence and get another thought. One or two ideas per year may be something that makes you go *we have something here*.
>
> The reason I am doing Karman + and not something easier is that it is not easier.
>
> **Teun van den Dries**

Building an economy in space... working out how to beam non-intermittent solar energy down to earth. 3D printing structures in space. Why?

'Because electricity should be carbon free and cost free' says Teun. So you are crossing into a brand new domain?

Not really, he reflects.

'Every problem is a people problem. Can I get really good people to do work they find exciting? The skillset can apply to any situation, I just chose this because it is the most immature and can have the biggest impact.' If you perceive your role as having a positive impact on people's lives, then the way you measure your success shifts. No matter how much (or little) money you make doing what you set out to do, if *impact* is the mission, then money is an imperfect metric.

Uday Akkaraju, who we will get to know a lot better in a subsequent chapter, founder and CEO of Bond.AI says this about his business: 'We have product market fit. But we haven't yet tapped enough of the market. We have a long way to go and we know what we need to do. It will be a constant theme until we are done.' And when are we done? What is success for an impact business? 'When you think about the fact that more than half of the world struggles financially, we are not done until that's no longer the case' continues Uday.

'Does that sound naive or philosophical? Perhaps. But that's the job we set out to do.'

Money is a second order consideration.

That sentence, almost verbatim, came up again and again. And if you expect Uday to say it (he is running an impact business after all), it is perhaps less obvious that Antony Jenkins, ex Barclays CEO, Board member for entities

Antony Jenkins CBE
Founder, CEO and Chairman of 10x Banking, a cloud native core banking platform
    Formerly CEO of Barclays Bank PLC

including Fannie Mae and the UK's Prudential Regulation Authority, founder and CEO of 10x Banking, said the exact same thing.

When I asked him what success looked like when he set 10x up, he had this to say: 'At first it was proving the hypothesis. Then it was having a positive impact broadly defined. It may sound arrogant to say it... but I see the work we do here as my legacy to the industry. Of course I want to win all the deals but actually if we catalyse and achieve a different way of thinking then we have won. There are classic routes for a business like 10x (IPO, industry sale) at any point along the journey, choices emerge. Money is a second order consequence of the business you build.'

If you think that holistic way of thinking about the industry is unusual, think again.

OakNorth, the company Valentina works for, who we met earlier in this chapter, set out to build an intergenerational business that would be there for entrepreneurs long term. 'The

Seeking impact means you seek to solve a real problem... that has complexity and needs time and scale in order to work.
    Seeking impact is not fast work.

founders are not motivated by an exit. It isn't about that', said Valentina. 'We are building an inter-generational business, a business that will outlast us. If we deliver value for our customers, we will get the valuation and yes this is a business that makes money but that's not all there is to it.'

Winter is coming, though. What about the upcoming recession, I asked her.

She was optimistic.

Yes there were challenges ahead but maybe they would just separate the fintech wheat from the chaff, so to speak. Investors would start focusing more, measuring the right things. Decision-makers would become more intentional.

'The businesses that come out of this will be more robust, more credible' continued Valentina. 'OakNorth has 1% market share currently, so we still have plenty of runway for growth and a lot more to do before we can say we're a challenger bank that's genuinely *challenged*. We are not going after a specific number, but if we can become the de facto choice for scaleup businesses who would otherwise find it challenging or a painful process to secure a loan, that's success. We are solving a complex problem that will take time to solve at scale. That is why it *has* to be an inter-generational business.'

At the time we did this interview, Valentina Kristensen was heavily pregnant. 'The problem we are solving needs time and scale and commitment' she said. 'I am 34 today and OakNorth will hopefully still be a business when my son who is currently in my belly is 34. That's what we are aiming for.'

Contrary to what we often say in the industry: many startups care more about being long-term impactful businesses than being paper unicorns. Not all. But enough to matter.

PensionBee (who we will be speaking about at length very soon) constantly think about what they need to be as a company in 20 years: What do their customers need over the next 20/30/40 years for a happy retirement? Their IPO was a step in the journey. The journey itself is bigger than that.

This sounds nice, you may say, but it is an impossibly difficult horizon to wrap your head around when your young business is two or three years old and struggling to become established. It takes deep commitment to the cause to not get distracted by the day-to-day pressures of getting started, of making it to the end of the month.

And you would be right to fret: it is hard work. It is easy to lose sight of the bigger picture when the pressure is on.

Nektarios Liolios, co-founder of Radish, dear friend and teller of truths, would tell you that this is sort of the whole point. This will sound familiar by now, but no less

Nektarios Liolios, NED, Advisor and co-founder and CCO Radish Co Founder The Future Farm Formerly co-Founder Rainmaking Innovation, Co-Founder and CEO Startup Bootcamp Fintech, founder of Innotribe at Swift

potent for it. 'I started Radish because I wanted to work on real problems... that are financial services problems... but that the banks won't touch. At 52, I felt that whatever I did *next* needed to be about impact, not dollars. Tech allows us hyper personalisation and legacy organisations can't accommodate that. So how can I use what we know is possible to help communities others can't or won't help? The LGBT bank

I worked on before Radish[25] had the same underlying principle. It doesn't matter what the specific needs of the underserved look like. If you think beyond what is currently available, what can you do about providing products specific to the needs of a community *and* be profitable? That is where Radish came in. We tried to find a way to help real lives. It didn't have to be lending. It could have been insurance or any other risk-rated product. And the challenges we have faced setting up have had nothing to do with the product and everything to do with people.'

> If your aim is to have a material impact, you go straight for the problems that are hard to solve. Because most others won't. Exactly because they are hard.

The choice of focusing on risk-rated products is deliberate. Risk-rated products are hard. The space is deemed risky. Many traditional providers don't touch certain communities. Going into the thick of the hard problems is a conscious choice. Focusing on the needs of a community that needs you and you choose to make them your mission is a choice. Building a business that aims to be here decades into the future to continue providing a service is a choice. Obviously you need things to work, you need things to go your way. And that doesn't always happen. In the time since doing this interview, for instance, Radish reached the end of its journey. But that doesn't change the fact that you need to be seeking longevity rather than a quick buck. You need to be coming into the space looking at the impact you need to have, not the shape of the corporate vehicle or the optics of the journey.

These time horizons and metrics are about the communities you serve, about your ability to continue serving them. Not about return on equity. Not about exits. The chapters to come will show beyond the shadow of a doubt that an impactful

> If you want to solve a real problem that is not currently being solved by someone else you will very quickly find out that doing so… is hard.

business can also be a thriving one, but I am not quite done with the personal motivations of the people doing this work.

Those fires in their bellies matter. Because the stories aren't always straightforward ones and success rarely comes easy. And sometimes success doesn't come at all, despite the people involved pouring love, energy, hard work and commitment into their

---

25 Nektarios was part of the early team that brought us the idea behind Daylight Bank. Daylight had to close its doors not long after launch https://techcrunch.com/2023/05/22/daylight-the-lgbtq-neobank-calls-it-quits/ among pressures on product market fit and more than a little controversy as to some of the ideas of the CEO https://nymag.com/intelligencer/article/daylight-financial-banking-lawsuit.html but it was an remains a reference point of community-focused banking solutions.

work. And that is when keeping an eye on where you were going matters the most. To remember why you tried, even when you didn't quite manage to get there.

The Course of True Love Never Did Run Smooth

When I first met Juan Guerra it was 2014 and he was wearing an elephant onesie.

At the time he was CEO of StudentFunder, a firm seeking to enable social mobility through peer-to-peer lending[26] aimed at helping people finance post-graduate and professional education. The elephant suit was, if nothing else, a conversation piece. It broke the ice. It was cute.

But it was also a reference to the Hindu god Ganesh, Remover of Obstacles.

The right god for a builder of new things to worship.

By the time we had the conversation for this book, ten years later, the elephant suit was packed away and life was very different for

---
Juan Guerra, CEO Revolut Mexico
Previously Head of RappiPay Mexico, Chief Innovation Officer at Citibanamex, Director at Waterfront Ventures and Founder of StudentFunder
---

Juan, now CEO of Revolut in Mexico. 'When you met me at StudentFunder, I didn't care for fintech' Juan reminisces. 'I just wanted to help people study. I got lucky. 2012 was a good time to be in London doing fintech. Four years later, the government stepped into the very space I had been working in and, although that was bad for us as a business, it solved the social problem we were aiming to tackle.'

It meant the people Student Funder were trying to help got help. Albeit from elsewhere. It also meant Student Funder went out of business.

'For me, personally, it all turned out to be a really valuable experience in the end. I just didn't know it then. [At the time] I felt like a loser.'

> When pursuing a mission at great personal material and emotional cost and the business fails... often through no fault of your own... you lose much more than a job.

The business had failed.

Which is bad enough. But it wasn't just a business. The personal commitment to these ideals is real. During the StudentFunder days Juan didn't take a salary for two

---

26 Peer to peer lending is what it says on the tin: it is a way of obtaining a loan directly from another individual, cutting out the bank or financial institution. The lender still gets interest and the tech used allows for transparency that protects this (at least in theory) from becoming a digital version of an old school Money Lender.

years and, for part of that time, he had student borrowers occasionally sharing his room as they had nowhere else to live.

Putting your money where your mouth is, taken to a whole new level. And, in this context, when that business fails, it is more than your day job that is gone. It is your job, your mission and a whole host of personal sacrifices that go down the drain. As well as your sense of personal purpose. The emotional toll of this is huge. And the risk of that happening is ever present. Remember? 95% of startups, 70% of corporate change fail. And that failure often comes *after* a lot of hard work.

'I never cared to get rich. At the time I didn't need to think about looking after two baby girls like I do now. I was driven by what I would consider to be selfless motivations… with a fair dose of ego too, to be honest. It felt good to know I was helping people better themselves.

I was lucky that following my passion gave me useful skills. Think about it. I could have been passionate about soup kitchens… and the work is as important but the skills wouldn't have led me to the boom of fintech.'

Juan sees part of this work as 'paying back his debt for the birth lottery' because although he could have been luckier in life, and who couldn't, he considers himself luckier than 98% of the people in his country and beyond.

> I want to change this industry. This industry sucks. In its most extreme form it keeps poor people poor. I can change it. Not many people can. But I can. Exactly because of the knowledge and experience I have gained over the years.
> **Juan Guerra**

What do you do with that luck?

'Can you look back and say you helped some people… through your work, through your policy influence… through your choices? StudentFunder had a unique challenge that made it particularly brutal. You wouldn't know if the premise worked before the first 7-year cycle closed of students being funded… graduating… and paying back in full. The model would not be truly tested before that time and real traction and scale would come after that. It was a long window and the work became emotionally harrowing.

Imagine interviewing people for a loan not knowing if you can fund it. Not knowing if you can make payroll. Living in this binary situation for years. It takes its toll. But it keeps you focused.'

Of course it does. It's a daily dose of Russian roulette, I comment.

'I have mellowed since then' he smiles.

That, of course, is a relative term. The day this conversation took place (December 12) was a bank holiday in Mexico. And here he was. At his desk. Working. Is it possible that this is what holding back and keeping a balance looks like, I asked with a raised eyebrow.

'I am in the middle of applying for a bank licence (for Revolut Mexico, now granted[27]) so you need to do what you need to do when the company needs you to do it. This is my second time applying for a banking licence. Doing it with a small committed team of 16 people. We have to build it, prove it and if it gets traction, away we go. I am an entrepreneur building from scratch again... but with the solidity of Revolut's platform behind me. The motivation now, however, is that I want to change this industry. This industry sucks. In its most extreme form, it keeps poor people poor. And it's just a hassle and a pain for millions. I can change this. Not many people can. But I can. Exactly because of the knowledge and experience I have gained over the years. And that is what I am trying to do.

In five years' time success for us will be if we have made ourselves one of the top three banks in the region and, through that, change the narrative of access to money.

But for now... the hardest thing is waiting. We have to wait: internally for head-space and resources, and externally for the banking application that moves according to its own timeline and is no walk in the park. But these are relatively high quality problems to face.'

'I don't need to be a martyr. But I know the path is not linear. Sometimes it can feel random. So let's make it a random walk towards prosperity.'

The elephant onesie is packed away, his StudentFunder days behind him and many days spent in corporate offices went by between then and now. And yet the work Juan is trying to do hasn't changed much. All that has changed is where he is doing it. His days are very different perhaps. But what gets him out of bed in the morning is not.

Rolf Eichweber, Build CEO, OM Bank, South Africa

Formerly CEO of Tyme SA (now TymeBank) with extensive banking, tech and wider FS executive experience

'We are trying to make people's lives better, to democratise access to money. The impact is not as deep at first glance, perhaps, but the reach is wider. We can make a small difference to millions of people. And as we raise the standard for the industry, the impact will amplify both in terms of depth and breadth.' Thus spoke Rolf Eichweber, at the time leading the build of OM Bank in South Africa. We were speaking on a breezy terrace in Johannesburg, a few months before he was granted a conditional banking license for Old Mutual's own challenger.

---

27 https://www.fintechnexus.com/uk-neobank-revolut-gets-mexico-banking-license-eyes-remi ttances/#:~:text=Revolut%2C%20the%20British%2Dborn%20unicorn,a%20bank%20 in%20the%20country

I must confess that, having studied Nationalism as part of my postgraduate degree, I have had any and all notions of national pride beaten out of me (figuratively speaking, although I had some professors whose withering stares have left permanent scars). So this idea of dedicating your life to do good for *your* people, going back to your country of origin to bring the knowledge you have gathered back to them... or staying in your country of origin despite things being easier or shinier elsewhere... that's an idea that surprised and surprises me. And yet it drives passion and commitment more often than you think. Because Juan is not the only one who keeps entering the fray again and again for the good of his people.

I asked Rolf Eichweber what on earth needs to have a possessed man for him to decide to build a bank from scratch more than once. Because this is not Rolf's first rodeo.

'I don't want to stop' he exclaims with humbling self-awareness. 'I want to do the next thing and the next thing. There is a hunger in me.

My dad was a mechanic. He used to come pick me up from school in a battered car, in his work clothes and I was so embarrassed, as a young kid, that my dad had grease on his clothes. It took me years to appreciate how proud I should be instead. But this knowledge of having further to go than the others around me to get to the same place has created a hunger in me that has been driving me since.'

That hunger, usually triggered by a traumatic event, is common to the types of people who won't sit still, reflects Rolf. Over the course of our chat he shared the personal stories of a few folks we both know. Folks at the top of their game who came up in abject poverty and hardship. It doesn't matter who they are. What matters is how often it is people like that who make things happen.

> The CEOs I admire have two things in common: an ego cut down to size often by a traumatic event in their past... and a hunger for more.
> *Rolf Eichweber*

'Every time I meet a founder or CEO I really admire', reflects Rolf, 'they share the same common traumatic experience and shock of loss from somewhere in their past. These things give you cause to confront your ego. Maybe it hasn't happened to enough CEOs but that shock of loss causes you to lose something fundamental around your ego. You become a much better leader after such a shock.'

That combination of an ego that has been cut down to size and a hunger for more, makes people like Rolf see the world around him differently. He didn't say that. I am saying that. What Rolf said was this: 'In a country like South Africa, rife with division and difference, you have to decide whether you will stay and do good or not. I chose to stay. And I did not want to do charity.'

Funnily enough, 'I did not want to help through charity' were the exact words that Juan used. I wanted to do good but not as charity. The idea that we can do good and do well at the same time resonates with me deeply. I like it. I believe it. So

I am there with little flags and bells on when I hear of all these entrepreneurs and intrapreneurs who want to help people. Through business not handouts.

And I love the simple compulsion to do better.

'I also believe' continues Rolf 'that inside Financial Services, we haven't gotten it right yet and it is possible to get it right. It is possible *if* we get the tech right. What we lack is intent. In South Africa there is a group of customers whose fear of money keeps them captive. Banks don't do this on purpose. Their cost structures, legacy etc. mean that a traditional bank services those who *get* money really well. But the other half are alone.'

Only they are not. Because people like Rolf and Juan are here with them.

Your Call to Action

Irrespective if you are hiring, building a team inside a corporation or getting a startup crew together, if you are an investor assessing a potential investment or a candidate working out if you want to join a team, these are a few things that make for good leaders and colleagues when the going gets tough.

- Look for people who do not let their circumstances define them and who find fire and inspiration and lessons in those circumstances, not excuses;
- Look for people with the humility to appreciate what really matters in life and the understanding of how their work may impact or hinder those things that matter;
- Find people who do what they say and don't just say what they think you want to hear;
- Look for those who go looking for hard problems to solve.

Chapter 2

Sometimes You Choose Your Moment, Sometimes the Moment Chooses You

Once Upon a Time

… there was a prince… or a king… or a wizard. Right? Isn't that how it normally begins? There is a specific and opportune moment in time… and there is a key actor. And then we have a story built in the interplay of the moment and the hero.

The hero, the key actor is the main figure, of course, and a catalysing factor for the story. Not everyone can (or wants to) undertake a quest: be it slaying the dragon or transforming the fund accounting technology estate of your organisation. Be it freeing the princess in the tower or building a new business from scratch.

Not everyone wants to be that heroic figure.

But for those who do, it is useful to remember that, important and catalytic though they are, the actor always operates in context. There needs to be a dragon to be slayed, an organisation needing to be transformed, a technology ready to be used towards whatever effect your business is set upon. The moment in time creates the opportunity, after all. As much as the hero does, if not more.

So in this chapter we will talk about time: moments in time, first times, second chances, right times, wrong times and the art of timing.

Specifically, when going about change work, you need to think about timing in three ways:

DOI: 10.1201/9781003395577-2

1. **Timing in terms of *you*,** your experiences and experience.
   In other words, when you find yourself in the moment, in the context described above: how ready are you?
   What I found in this work is that first times are rarely the only times. And they are almost never the best times. Hindsight being 20/20 is why most successful founders, intrapreneurs and transformation leaders are not on their first rodeo.
   Learning and doing better is key to doing well. Fancy that;

2. **Timing in terms of the market.**
   There are few situations in life where being early is an impediment.
   Tech adoption and business fall in that category and being too early in the adoption cycle of a new technology, or early with a business idea that needs the market to form before it can succeed, in those situations, the early bird doesn't get the worm.
   In fact, being early may hurt you, unless (and this is important) you are doing it intentionally and are prepared for what comes next. Which means, you are only too early if you cannot afford to wait, if you are not equipped with what it takes to wait long enough. But if you expect to have to wait, are prepared to wait and are equipped for the wait then you are not early. You are just first. Waiting, in this context, largely means having reserves of nuts like a good little squirrel and money to last you whatever the adoption cycle and market readiness ends up looking like.
   Being early is the same as being wrong, said Jamie Smith on a call a few weeks before I sat down to write this chapter and he has a point. It is exactly the same unless you did it on purpose. Then it's strategy. More on that below;

3. **Timing in terms of where you were standing when the meteor hit,** so to speak.
   Exogenous factors will always be in play, in life and business.
   Sometimes they will feel like curveballs that slow you down. Other times they will be a boon. Which is which may not be immediately obvious when it happens. Stay alert to what is happening around you. When life is decidedly *not* giving you lemons, maybe you should think twice about the plan of making lemonade. Equally, when history conspires to help you, take the help.

There is a lot there and although it's all about timing, it covers a broad and diverse set of considerations that are only loosely linked to each other, other than being a question of time.

The one key aspect of timing that I *won't* address in this chapter is the timeliness of difficult decisions when running a business, as that will be addressed in later chapters in the context of product readiness (or the need for a pivot), decisions to fire, hire, accept money or take help. For now, all I will say on the timeliness of decision-making is that, for any business, the right decision delivered too late can kill it, just as easily as the wrong decision or no decision at all. If you realise you need to manage your cost base, for instance, but drag your feet for six months or a year before doing what you know you need to do, then the job you now have to do is harder as the cost deficit you need to manage is bigger. If you identify a toxic team member whose conduct is hurting morale and productivity and don't address the issue for months or years, their effect on your wider team gets wider and deeper... and the wider team's faith in you as a

> Exogenous factors will always be in play. Sometimes they will feel like curveballs and slow you down. Other times they will be a boon. Stay alert to what is happening around you and when history conspires to help you... take the help.

leader erodes. If your product market fit is elusive and you ignore the data in the hope that conviction will carry you through then you are in the company of many, none of them successful.

We won't talk about that kind of timing here because we will talk extensively about the need to make changes inside a business and how to know it is time in the next sections under each of the verticals (product, funding, team etc.). And we will talk about the need for a leader to keep themselves in check at all times to ensure they don't lose sight of their own blind spots and make unforced errors like described above in the final section. For now, it's all a question of time.

Not Their First Rodeo

Asking people and particularly founders how much *they* have changed (and learned) on their journey to-date rapidly became my favourite part of the interview.

'When I left Morgan Stanley in 2000' recalls Simon Merchant, CEO of Flagstone who, at the time of writing was in the process of closing one of the biggest funding rounds in the UK that year[1], 'I was cocky, arrogant and totally unaware

Simon Merchant, CEO Flagstone
Multi-exit founder and former banker (also in recovery, like me, but a lot more successful)

of what I didn't know. My own evolution has been gradual but accelerated at Flagstone and with age, as you get growing self-awareness. And you learn to balance

---

1 https://www.flagstoneim.com/press/flagstone-receives-108-million-investment-from-estancia-capital-partners/?utm_source=null&utm_medium=null&utm_campaign=null&utm_term=null&utm_content=null

that real hunger to learn, a desire to work with great people you can learn from which is ultimately the whole point.

I was top-ranked at Morgan Stanley for my ability to go from A to B but, looking back, you know it's a core skill set of course, but it is not enough. What you actually need for leadership is not just to get from A to B but to take people along with you from A to B and that is a different skillset. You need to change in order to be a scale-up CEO.'

This stands to reason.

You need to learn how to do a lot of new things to get your new venture to fly, many of which we will go through in the chapters ahead. Those new things will change and evolve as your business grows and evolves and, as a leader, you need to keep learning.

Realising you have to learn how to do new things and keep learning new things, though, is in some ways half the battle. The rest of the battle are the learnings themselves. You are on the road of building or changing and you realise that what got you here won't get you where you are going. You need to learn new things. You admit it. You are not too proud. But *where* do you do that learning? Where do you learn about those new things? Who do you learn from? Where and when does the learning happen? That is the other half of the battle. The most critical half, in many ways. As the answer is, unsurprisingly, that you do this learning in the work itself.

You can of course read books such as this one and listen to folks who have been there and done that, but most of the learning will be done through doing new things for the first time. This is the inevitable extension of the obvious statement that *you cannot learn what you need to know by doing what you used to do…* you have to do the new things. And of course you can learn through observation and study and through seeking (and taking) advice but mostly you learn by doing.

Which in turn begs the question of how do you benefit from the knowledge you can only get from doing the doing?

The answer is as obvious as it is uncomfortable and that is: by going again. That doesn't mean that I expect you to fail the first time. Just that I expect you to do better the second time round. But, also, that I expect you to want to go again. And again.

'My first venture sold' continues Simon. 'The investors made a lot of money. I made money so that I wouldn't need to work again for cash. That gives you a sense of accomplishment and that in itself is addictive. So I invested half the

> The skill sets required to lead a new venture can only be learned in the doing itself.
>
> So the only way to really benefit from what you learned… is to go again.

money I made into charity projects in Africa and early stage companies in tech and media and created a portfolio lifestyle for myself, doing three or four different things in a day. I did that for two years in which time my own self-awareness kicked in: I am an entrepreneur at heart. I am not a good non-exec. That is not my skill set. As an entrepreneur I need to feel I have a real impact. Rolled sleeves. Boots in. So I combined my skill sets and my values and I decided to start again. And I am very aware of my privilege: from an education and career point of view. And with privilege comes responsibility: so I want to make a difference. I felt unfulfilled tinkering around the edges and, after I had recharged my batteries, I was ready to go. I felt I had something great in me. So I did it again.

Flagstone is my third business. I talk to a lot of other people who don't understand why I do what I do. Why I keep going back into the fray.'

I am with those people, truth be told. But Simon is not alone. Both in terms of the puzzled looks… and in terms of the 'going again' part.

The Last Knowledge

The Greek version of the phrase 'hindsight is 2020' is the appropriately dramatic 'oh my last knowledge: if only I had you first', which, incidentally, was my original title for this book. 'The Last Knowledge', not the whole thing. But still, I got some very weird looks when I road-tested it and at least three folks told me they expected it to be a book about war and death, so I went back to the drawing board, came up with a different title and we were all spared the awkwardness.

But the idea of learning from the journey of people who've been there and done that: who have that last knowledge, so to speak, the knowledge that you can only get by going through something having

> Entrepreneurs rarely stop at the first venture: irrespective of whether it was a success or failure.
>
> They go again because they enjoy the process… and because each time they feel they have learned how to do better.

been through the experience, is a key driver in my research. Ultimately, I was looking for that 'last knowledge' that people acquired through doing the work that they wished they knew at the start. My thinking was we can all learn from their ventures before we go on ours. What I found was that people acquired that knowledge and put it immediately into practice by going again. And again. As Simon above.

Remember in the last chapter when I asked Rolf Eichweber why he was putting himself through founding a bank for the second time, joking that surely, once is more than enough pain to last any normal person a lifetime?

We talked at length about that. Because I was fascinated to hear that enjoying the process was undeniably part of it. Echoing Simon Merchant, Dharm Mistry and many of the others I spoke to, Rolf enjoys the work. That is in itself a good reason to go back and do it again. Believing he could do it better, however, was the main driver: 'The reason I am doing this again is a personal belief that *I* can do it better. Better than last time.'

Is it a pursuit of perfection, I wondered? Do you just keep going? 'It is not open-ended' chuckled Rolf 'it is also a question of how much longer I can take it, how much pain I can take' concedes Rolf. 'Like an endurance sport.'

And like any pro athlete, the fiercest competitor and harshest critic is always yourself. No matter how many medals you win, the real measure is always a PB, a personal best: did you beat yourself today? Was today the best you can be?

And in many cases, founders go again because the first time didn't work and they have a point to make, a point to prove, or impact they feel they are yet to make.

'If I look at my time at Tyme' reflects Rolf 'I failed[2].

I know that we were successful by any external measure. But what I feel *I* truly got was the confidence and understanding to go and do this again and do it better.' And that is the magical thing about experience: it gives you clarity on a whole host of choices. Things you would repeat. And things you would do differently. Which is exactly what Rolf did. Having the experience under his belt, Rolf did things differently. For instance, he chose the set-up of and the foundational partner for his second venture very differently: 'Working with an insurance company this time was deliberate. Insurers understand the need to pivot. They know they need to digitise. Banks disintermediated them already, as insurers come into a customer's financial life later in the cycle. Plus, inside an insurance firm you are not a threat to anyone's P&L. In fact you are an ally to everyone in a fight against a whole host of shared challenges. An insurer gets working with regulators, they are a financial services firm already and they have a superpower they don't see: they are aligned with the idea of long-term value creation for customers. They get it.

> It helps if you have done something before: it helps you arrive at certain decisions much faster and with greater conviction.
>
> It also helps if what you are doing has been done before inside your market: it deals with a lot of early questions much faster.

If you can bring in a far more effective unit cost and good UX and align that with a long term view, you are poised to have a fantastic platform to 'beat the banks' at their own game. And you are aligning the business strategy with the intent behind the money.'

---

2 Tyme, if you are not familiar with it is a success by anyone's standards: both from a valuation perspective and from a profitability perspective.

https://www.finextra.com/newsarticle/43539/south-african-neobank-tymebank-hits-profitability

https://www.bloomberg.com/news/articles/2024-01-16/tymebank-south-africa-sees-unicorn-status-in-next-fundraising

Having done it before helps make short work of a lot of these decisions: decisions that are neither obvious nor easy to execute but at least you can make the calls and start the work with greater speed and clarity. It helps if you've done it before.

There is also one more thing. It helps when *it* has been done before.

Not just that your own team have done what you are trying to do before, but that the thing you are doing has been done before inside the market you are operating in. It helps that some of the basic questions of 'what is this' and 'is this ever going to work' and 'oh what?' have been answered before and you can get on with the programme of building. That was also a consideration for Rolf and it was twofold: first of all, 'Discovery Bank[3] had done this already and it's easier to be the number two adopter in an open road.

Plus Old Mutual, the parent entity, had owned NED Bank before, so the exercise wasn't alien to them. And in fact, despite a couple of false starts in this space, they were prepared to go again: having learned. Proving that failure is ok if we learn from it.'

The lesson here, by the way, is not necessarily 'don't expect to get it right first time': there are many founders in this book and in this world that were very successful the first time. Most of them still went again though.

The lesson is you probably will do it better the second time, which isn't surprising. But also that, in the doing, you may learn things that you may find propel you to go again so you can apply them. And this last thought should be sobering.

> Despite a couple of false starts in this space, being prepared to go again, having learned is key.
> Proving that failure is ok if we learn from it.
> ***Rolf Eichweber***

That doesn't mean you should avoid any and all firsts: this book wouldn't exist if people actually took that route. But it does mean that lived experience (yours and your team's) can help manage some of the variables in your journey. Maybe you are building a bank for the second time and doing it differently, maybe you are doing it for the first time but with people who have started ventures before, maybe you have never built a business before but have extensive knowledge of the problem statement you are working towards solving. Whatever you choose to do, having some relevant experience helps. But it won't be enough. So whatever you end up doing: keep learning.

And don't wait for the finish line to digest and apply that learning.

---

3 https://www.discovery.co.za/bank/join-discovery-bank/, a South African digital bank also backed by an Insurer, like Old Mutual.

Start Learning Early. Don't Stop

Learning by doing is not a startup prerogative, in case you were wondering. Big organisations also get to do things for the first time and learn and go again. They tend to do the learning in a public forum (innovation centres and showcases) and the ingestion of said learning in a more private and restrained setting (boardrooms and closed-door sessions). They are careful and circumspect, those big players, because they have a lot to lose by getting things wrong and, frankly, so do you.

You don't want your bank experimenting wildly and paying the price of the 'move fast and break things' approach to life, because so will you, if your hard-earned savings are held in the bowels of a giant that topples or your loan gets called up or your pension is devalued over-night because they moved fast and broke things.

So learning and experimenting and doing things for the first time

Simon Boonen, Product Manager Payments and Collections at ING Wholesale Banking
Previously, Fintech Consultant at ING
ING is the largest retail bank in the Netherlands, one of the largest banks in the world and a pioneer of digital services

may not look like the natural domain of big established entities but that doesn't mean they don't play there. If they didn't, they would probably all have gone the way of Blockbuster.

Learning new things is very much done inside big, established concerns. It just looks different.

ING Bank is a giant by any metric. It is also one of the first banks to really delve into the digital domain. Doing new things for the first time ahead of the curve.

ING direct launched in the late 1990s. 'That was a different time and age, of course' says Simon Boonen, formerly a fintech consultant within ING and now working in the corporate banking division 'but we were among the first to launch an internet-only bank'.

They started early and never stopped. What followed has been 'decades of work and adaptation'.

Of course what we understood as *digital* then is a million light years from what we mean when we talk about digital capabilities now. It's a bit like my parents' ancient amplifier from the 1990s, still gathering dust on their bookshelves even though it hasn't been used in years. It has 'digital' and 'hi tech' written on it and although now that looks funny, back when it was produced it was *true*. And we needed to get that right to be able to move to where we are today.

In many ways, being on the digital journey since the 1990s means that you know, beyond the shadow of a doubt, that this isn't a marathon and it isn't a sprint, it is a new way of being. It is a forever thing. It is a journey of constant technological reinvention that is less sudden and scary if you've been on it longer. It is definitely less scary if the big steps banking institutions need to take today, with pressing regulation and cloud-first resilience top of mind, are not first steps.

Because deciding to launch a digital-only bank on a static webpage in the 1990s and designing resilient, scalable cloud solutions are very different things. But also they are not. First of all, what seems retrospectively simple now (just a static webpage) was not simple at all at the time. Plus, working out how to do things for the first time with no blueprints and metrics of past performance feels exactly the same no matter how complicated the task you are taking on feels after the fact. The only thing that helps, is how many times you've done it before.

> When we look back, the world of the early days of the internet looks relatively simple.
> It wasn't.
> But comparatively it now appears so.
> **Simon Boonen**

ING took the leap when the internet became *a thing* (for comparison and for the benefit of my younger readers: I interned in an office with dial-up modems for *most of the workers* as late as the early 2000s. The rest of the workers didn't have networked computers at all. When doing my PhD, also in the early 2000s, the university offered graduate students computer rooms because none of us could afford continuous internet at home. So yeah.)

When the second wave of digital transformation started. 20 years ago, when continuous system-to-system-to-person connectivity and real-time information started becoming notions consumers, regulators and service providers could understand and support and rapidly *expect*, the organisational muscles needed in order to react were already in place and in use for ING.

'2007–2012: those were rough times for the world' says Simon 'but they also brought profound change. Movements came together: the rise of the mobile-first world, social platforms, the emergence of cloud storage and data analytics. These were separate trends that strengthened one another' and in their interplay they radically changed the world as we knew it. 'When we look back, the world of the internet looks relatively simple' reflects Simon. 'It wasn't. But comparatively it now appears so.'

And that is vitally important. Nothing feels simple when you are faced with it for the first time but for those who cut their teeth earlier and don't wait for things to go away, the complexity of dealing with an avalanche of change becomes more manageable. Not least because you work out how to work things out. And that is a skill that is harder to learn the later you leave it because it takes time and the later you leave it, the more you have to do, the more you have to learn, the more you have to understand and juggle and the less time you have to learn at a pace that suits you.

That is when the temptation to 'wait things out' kicks in, by the way. When the alternative seems so overwhelmingly difficult, organisations and people are tempted to just give it a wee bit of time in order to see if trends would really catch on. To see if complicated and costly decisions would *really* need to be made. That temptation is strong and we have seen it play out a lot across financial services.

Sometimes, the hesitation bears fruit, as every firm that didn't pour millions into metaverse studies now gets to feel smugly superior to those who did. Sometimes a little hesitation is prudent, as those who decided to avoid experimenting themselves but rather become fast followers and rapidly copy the innovations of others when they are seen to work know all too well. There is a group of decision makers that turn the traditional meaning of RnD (research and development) into *rip off and duplicate*, as a good friend told me once.

> Making decisions without a blueprint is hard. Which is why many big organisations hesitate, opt for 'wait and see', hope for certainty.
>
> And sometimes things fall by the wayside and decision-makers are lulled into believing that inaction is a strategy.
>
> It isn't: you just got lucky this once.

Funny cos it's true. And although there is no glory in it, there is a lot of sense. But wouldn't it be better if you had decided not to 'wait and see' on the metaverse? If you had decided that it is not for you and used all your energy and resources on what *is* for you?

Because hesitation is not the same as deciding not to do something. Hesitation still keeps resources engaged. So, although it is possibly less costly than the wrong decision, it will never be as beneficial as the right decision and it will be a cumulative resource drain as all the things you are deferring deciding upon need to be kept under observation. Humans, reports, Proofs of Concept (POCs), more reports. It takes time. It takes money. It takes effort. Money and time and effort you could have spent learning something you actually intended to use. As the song goes[4].

So for everyone who waited on their cloud adoption… and waited on their API-first architecture uplift and invested a bit more in their on-prem solutions to avoid having to make big decisions around migration for a little bit longer, for those guys waiting means that the things that seemed scary then are now bigger, more complicated, creakier and have grown fangs. And things with fangs are much harder to face or control.

---

4 *You take up my time. Like some cheap magazine. When I coulda been learning something. Oh well, you know what I mean,* Pulp, Like a Friend, 1998. Oh yes: back from the era of ethernet cables. The classics, kids. The classics.

Control What You Can, Always

When talking about organisations doing things for the first time, especially in established financial services entities, you inevitably find yourself talking about innovation. And although I am nervous around the language of 'innovation', I accept that digital transformation initiatives have often been wrapped in that paradigm. Even though the reality is nobody needs *invention* to come from our FS providers.

Just adoption of already scaled technologies that supports their continued relevance to the economy they serve. That is not innovation. But it is something more than Business As Usual. The way I see it, you need a bit of creativity, a lot of responsiveness and a reality check that *digitisation is not a choice.* But I accept innovation is the language we have often used to

> Nobody needs invention from our established FS providers.
>
> We need the adoption of already scaled technologies in line with the economy.
>
> That is not innovation per se. But it is not quite Business As Usual either.

describe all this and, as long as we all know what it means, I am ok with that. And I am ok with that because it needs to be a sustained effort so I care less what we call it and more how we go about ensuring we stay the course.

So I ask: how did ING do it?

'On the journey we learned that innovation is something you can control for' explains Simon. 'You can create focus through governance in order to foster learning and also through governance handle failure so that you can keep the culture alive.

The organisational set-up that achieves this needs to be, and for us has been, high on the agenda for the management board. We have made it a senior management responsibility as well as a domain for employees across the board. Because that is the question: how do you equip the teams outside the innovation department to take on challenges in their day to day and help them enjoy work more, help their clients more? How do you help make it everyone's job? None of this is easy but it is the job.'

> In the process of constantly learning new things, the process of not getting discouraged, not losing the learning itself or your momentum is more important than the 'innovation' part.
>
> Governance is how you keep your organisation on the path of innovation, if that is what you choose to call it.

Indeed. None of it is easy, none of it is linear and most of it won't work the first time. So the experience of going through the process and working out the variables you can and should control, through governance, process, oversight and metrics is how you get to do better next time. It sounds counter-intuitive, to have governance and process and committees for innovation.

But as I said above, innovation is what we agree to call it. It is not about invention. It is about adoption. So actually the 'innovation' part is optional. The governance and control part is not. Because as we already said this is a forever state we need to be in: the ability to assess and deploy new technology with the corresponding operational changes needs to be a thing we get consistently good at. And that involves no invention, little innovation, a lot of creativity and grit and all process, governance and metrics.

And before you ask: of course, banks have often put the wrong kind of metrics around things they thought they understood and wasted time, effort and a lot of their employees' will to live. Of course that has happened a lot. And it will keep happening.

But it's not the only story.

When trying to navigate constant change using your learnings to identify what you can control and controlling that for the preservation of resources, time and energy is a superpower. It goes against the feeling that innovation should be free-flowing and unbridled and that is one of the many reasons why I feel the language of innovation may be unhelpful. It's not about that. It's about creatively finding your footing again and again every time the world shifts around you. As it will keep doing.

So to do that without panic: control what you can. And to know what you can control, it helps having done it before. If you are thinking 'great advice, Leda, needing to fail first' then you are not paying attention. Failure is not the point. In fact, a lot of the early attempts discussed here were unqualified successes by anyone's standards – other than perhaps the individuals themselves who knew what they wanted to achieve and didn't feel quite 'done'. The early attempts may have been smaller or less complicated, like ING's early digital forays. Or they may have been a conscious attempt at learning.

All This Time, I Could Have Been Learning Something[5]

Ken Johnstone, CPO at Mettle, NatWest's digital challenger for SMEs, looks at his parent bank's trajectory and the experiments and investments made early as exactly that: an intentional learning journey. NatWest launched digital challenger Bó (*avec* accent) roughly at the same time as Mettle was coming into being. And then killed it. Not immediately. Not wantonly. But eventually, deliberately and decisively.

> **Ken Johnstone, Chief Product Officer, NatWest Boxed and Mettle**
> Mettle is a digital SME bank by NatWest

---

5 Same Pulp song. Because we are still on the same theme. And also an opportunity for me to say that I saw it performed live the year it was released. 1998. Because sometimes being older comes with amazing perks.

We will talk about pivots later in this book but this wasn't a pivot as such, Bó didn't *become* Mettle. Mettle already existed albeit it was still early days. The two initiatives, programmes of work or ventures (whichever way you choose to see them) were launched in parallel. They were not identical or interchangeable but they were not a million miles apart either.

'Bó and Mettle were almost like AB testing' says Ken.

'Bó set out to build a business. It was focused on building technology, focused on growth and less focused on solving a customer problem. Mettle was the opposite. We didn't worry about growth at the beginning. We didn't worry about proprietary tech yet. The focus was on figuring out *who* needed us most and exactly *what* they needed.

We decided to focus on the small business end of the market, understand their challenges through a JTBD[6] approach. Out of those Jobs, which ones can we, as a bank, really help with? Let's start there. It's easy to work out an amazing solution for a problem that doesn't exist and become so emotionally involved in it that you don't see that. But the question of *what problem you are solving* is the most important one: what problem are you solving and why is your way of solving it significantly better than anything else out there?'.

> In the process of learning, not everyone will take away the same conclusions. Not everyone will agree with the decisions. It may get messy.
> But that is what learning looks like: it is not always safely contained in labs.

Hold onto that thought, we will be coming back to it a lot when we discuss product market fit and the problem you are solving in your business (whatever its size) later. Becoming emotionally invested in the thing you would *like* to be solving and being deaf to the needs of the market is an easy trap to fall into. An easy mistake to make. A common one. And a lethal one.

So hold onto that idea, for it is important.

And if a bank the size of NatWest doesn't come in all guns blazing and assuming they know all there is to know about building a digital business. And rightly so. Maybe so can you.

But you need to be prepared to be scrutinised and criticised.

In an industry where innovation and creative digital application is usually done for public consumption and column inches, it is perhaps not surprising that any

---

6 JTBD: Jobs To Be Done is a framework for understanding with precision and clarity what a user or customer is trying to achieve.

JTBD approaches tend to hide behind most successful and impactful user journeys.

There is plenty of literature (books, videos and articles depending on your preference and attention span) or you can speak to Ryan Garner. Both because he is a Nice Guy and because there is a reason why everyone calls him the JobFather. He knows things.

decision in this space draws attention and it is important to state that the bank's intentionality in its learning journey wasn't necessarily seen as such by the industry press. When the news hit that Bó is no more and the press was quick to castigate[7].

The language used at the time to describe the decision to close down the challenger was intense. Failure. Abandonment. Defeat.

Makes for good headlines, I guess. The story was a lot more mundane and BAU, although admittedly perhaps not if Bó was your baby. And I do remember chatting to friends, at the time, who had left other roles to join Bó. They weren't happy. And they weren't happy because they weren't done. They wanted to keep building the thing. They believed in their mission. They didn't feel the story was mundane.

> It is easy to work out an amazing solution for a problem that doesn't exist and become so emotionally involved in it, you don't see that.
> What problem are you solving and why is your way of solving it significantly better than anything else out there?
> **Ken Johnstone**

And that is the point. The process of learning and, even more so, the necessary decision-making around what you will invest in as an organisation, what you will *not* do and where you will control the variables you can control won't please everyone. And it may not necessarily look or feel great as it is happening. Some of the observers will be swift with their commentary. Some of the people inside the process will take away different lessons from others. Some will not like the choices made.

The lessons that decision-makers actually take away from experiences will not be universally learned the same way.

The process of learning may look like ING's early digital credentials. But it also may look like this AB testing NatWest engaged in, complete with hard choices around what to keep and what to stop spending time and money on. Choices that are not guaranteed to be the right ones. Choices that cannot always be popular. And either way, choices that are visible to a market quick to criticise. Which is why it is often easier, all told, to do nothing, arguably 'for now', and let time pass and other people get beaten up by the press.

---

7   https://www.verdict.co.uk/bo-digital-bank-rbs-natwest/#:~:text=After%20just%20six%20months%2C%20the,its%20digital%20banking%20brand%20Bo

https://uk.finance.yahoo.com/news/royal-bank-of-scotland-bo-shut-down-monzo-mettle-071439805.html?guccounter=1&guce_referrer=aHR0cHM6Ly93d3cuZ29vZ2xlLmNvbS88&guce_referrer_sig=AQAAAH6xOdvy18t6V6tmdYMStG-9NO0v6nyP6H3Z_lXaoLwXBSP1TODrR1nX-7Zhm7BXuBeeT4hnfJswQZZFqkfj3wku9qjceseu00fd9JaMWkPUL0Tuc_kKcKhUBj7NtWb9XMlmHAmKGOJ4cDeqMdP1ei_hXYlESBqu5pnFWtmWmVSK

https://www.choose.co.uk/news/2020/natwest-close-bo-digital-bank/

But the reality is the world waits for nobody and if you need to learn in order to stay relevant... *this* is what learning looks like. It's not always safely contained in lab conditions. It is not always popular. And you need to do it anyway because the alternative is a waste of time and energy and relevance.

So. The bank tried two models. One worked better. They were merged[8]. The most effective parts of each were kept. We will be getting back to Mettle later in the book and delving further into those

> Although nobody wants to fail...and nobody wishes failure upon anyone else... the reality is, failure is usually a better teacher than success.

choices and trade-offs. For now I want to stay with the simple, irrefutable fact that most of the successful, sustainable stories be they startups or successful programmes inside corporates are *always* the product of sustained learning. Sometimes intentional. Sometimes through the simple act of engaging, trying, building and learning from success or failure. And although nobody wants to fail and nobody wishes failure upon anyone else (mostly) the reality is, failure is usually a better teacher than success.

Kasisto's Zor Gorelov, who I know you remember from the last chapter, went on to found three further successful businesses after leaving Georgia. 'My first [post Georgia] business was in the dotcom days' he remembers. 'I was a young CEO and we exited after five years. I *literally* learned nothing. People wrote checks back then. as long as "the internet" was part of your business.'

It worked. It was good. But it was too easy to teach any repeatable lessons. That wasn't set to last.

'Post the dotcom bust, we had nuclear winter in tech investment in NYC. I remember getting a term sheet for my second startup that I considered offensive. And then 9/11 came. So we started funding ourselves. Let me tell you, the term sheet I had rejected a few short months ago, started looking good then! But it was during this time when I learned so much as CEO. It was during that period when things were hard, when we navigated our way through the 2008 financial crisis and managed to get back on track and grow the business to a successful exit that I learned the most. After that exit, Kasisto has been born out of applying what I learned. About being a CEO. About building a company that puts employees first.'

Knowing Which Way Is 'Up'

I genuinely believe that everyone sets out to be good and do good.

---

8 https://www.paymentsdive.com/ex/mpt/news/rbs-shuts-down-digital-bank-bo-merges-accounts-into-mettle/?

I fundamentally believe that is everyone's intention, even if it is not the outcome. And of course we can argue about definitions of goodness and subjectivity and all that but, fundamentally, the reason people fall short is that things get in the way. Sometimes it's just harder than you thought and you are weaker than you hoped.

And sometimes, even though it is hard and you are strong and ready for the hard work you just don't know which way is up. Sometimes you don't know right or wrong until it plays itself out. You may make decisions absolutely believing they are the right ones and then life teaches you otherwise.

> People set out to do and be good.
> But sometimes you realise it's harder than you thought... and you are weaker than you believed.

So once you've learned the hard way, as Zor says, then you know better and can do better. But even after you've graduated from the School of Hard Knocks, so to speak, doing *better* doesn't just happen. It has to be intentional.

Pismo, now a Visa company in a deal that really rearranged the core banking chessboard, was co-founded by four people. Daniela Binatti, CTO who you already met earlier in this book, Ricardo Josua (CEO), Juliana Binatti and Marcelo Parise who is also Daniela's husband, bringing the level of personal commitment to the venture to the humanly possible maximum.

The four co-founders had worked together since 1999. Which is in itself hugely important. As Dani puts it 'in order to do something crazy like this, you need to be with a group you trust.'

This group started their journey with Conductor: a payment processor platform (a company later sold to a PE fund).

They didn't leave Conductor to launch Pismo but, as luck would have it, they all left roughly at the same time albeit for different reasons. Serendipity at work. Because they regrouped. And were willing to go again. Together. Because the lessons learned aren't always about change, sometimes they are about the things you shouldn't mess with, like a great working partnership, which are as important as the things you decide to change.

> The learnings of your life to-date don't come by osmosis.
> You need to stop. Lift your head up from the day to day.
> Reflect
> Then do things differently.
> Intentionally.

And change they did.

'When you look back' reflects Daniela 'you realise you spent 16 years, head down... so overwhelmed with daily problems... and then you lift your head... and realise you have the opportunity to build something from scratch. You know how to do it... you know the capabilities of cloud computing. You also realise the things you would do differently if you went again.'

So they went again. But this time differently.

'We spent a year white-boarding. What were the problems we had the first time round? What are the things we want to focus on or do differently this time? Relationships with clients, transparency with the team: how much do you share and how? How vulnerable do you choose to be? How different do we want things to be from the first time? We definitely *actively* chose a different way of talking to our own teams, a different way of facing challenges and a different way of showing up with clients.'

It has to be intentional.

Learning what fuels big change doesn't just happen by osmosis. You have to be intentional about what you are going to do differently. And you also have to be intentional about what the journey ahead will be, or at least what your intention is for the journey. Because this is not a journey of building and discovery alone. It is a journey that you need to take people on: customers and team members. Because if you are about to do something new, something different, it is new to them too and different to what they are used to and, as Simon Merchant already highlighted, the hardest thing is not getting from A to B but taking an entire team with you on this journey.

So your intent, your vision and your values have to be made real for your teams and clients so that they know what kind of journey you are taking them on, especially when the destination is neither reached (yet) nor 100% clear. You need to give them a reason to go on this journey with you.

'Our approach' continues Daniela 'is to show clients immersive detail on how we do things. They are invited internally to share with their teams. We know education is a big part of this. In 2016, when we started this journey, cloud computing was still a hard concept for banks to get used to. We were regularly asked for the address of our data centre! We had to educate and go step by step.

And in those early days, the language our customers used was

> When dealing with a lot of change and a lot of things being done for the first time you need to relentlessly identify every key variable in your control. And you should control it.

all about the dangers of leaving the comfort zone. But as the world started shifting towards cloud, the conversation for banks shifted: you had two options really. Outsource or build: buying a solution tied you to the product backlog of whichever company you chose to work with and you would still have nothing different to provide your client than all the other customers of said company.

You can't provide something differentiated to your clients if you are on the same core as everyone else. But the alternative of building yourself is a lot.

We have a solution that bridged that gap. But it took time for the clients to get to the place where they saw the gap they needed a solution for.

So at first we evangelised a lot.'

Are you taking notes?

First reflect on what you learned. Then decide what you will do differently. Be intentional and specific. Then accept you will have to take people on a journey until your different way is understood and accepted.

That goes towards both cultural and behavioural choices inside a firm and a product that represents a new way of doing things in the market: a new way of thinking about your core, in Pismo's case.

'We had to share the idea that there is a solution in the middle of that road that allows you to be in control of your operation and that allows you to motivate your team by using and accepting new technology. That allows you to be in control of your roadmap.'

That was Pismo's market positioning and it may not be yours. But the realisation that you have to manage your way to product market fit is a universal fact. Plus, in a world of constant change, controlling what you can is a key to sanity. Feeling like you are in control could, of course, be an illusion.

That is why it helps to have done it all before. It is an almighty reality check. So if you manage to really reflect and be truthful with yourself and your team about the variables you *can* control and intentional about controlling them, you are onto something.

Not Making the Same Mistakes Twice

Remember, a few pages ago, when Denise and Monika, co-CEOs of Enfuce, found themselves faced with a potential 20 million investment on the table and the nagging sensation that taking it would be the wrong thing to do for them because it would relinquish control of the company really early on in the journey? How hard was that decision to make, I asked.

'Deciding not to take that money was never a negotiation between us' recalls Monika Liikamaa. 'We were open with each other and fully aligned. Leaving the 20 million: it was a gut feel but we felt it was best for the company and best for us as individuals.' So they walked away from the money.

> We spent time thinking 'what if'. We negotiated all trade-offs before we had anything to negotiate. And codified our agreement.
> *Monika Liikamaa*

Dear reader, if you have ever fund-raised you know viscerally how hard that is to do. You probably got a little nauseated reading this. If you have never fund-raised, then let me tell you: saying no to the money that will help you build your vision may be the right thing to do (and as we will see in a later chapter: it often is) but it is an extremely hard thing to do.

So. How did they do it?

'We have each other' says Monika. 'We support each other, we are each other's sounding boards. We, in fact, have codified a lot of that in our shareholder agreement. How we expect to work together but also *what happens if*.' What happens if they disagree? On product or management or personnel? What happens if tensions emerge? How do they resolve them? 'We thought, early on' continues Monika 'what happens if one of us dies. If one of us has a family problem, gets divorced, has an accident. We negotiated the trade-offs before we had anything to negotiate.'

They took the time, just like Pismo, to think through the company they wanted to build and the relationship they wanted to have as co-founders and took the time to think through permutations and scenarios that would put pressure on the vision, the company and the relationship. And where does that wisdom come from? You guessed it.

'I had a really bad experience in my first rodeo' recalls Monika. 'I trusted my co-founder and was screwed. I got the learnings but I didn't get the money.' Those learnings went into a different kind of conversation at the beginning. And it wasn't just a conversation.

> We talked about everything when we had nothing to divide and agreed parameters when we could be objective.
> **Denise Johansson**

'We have a solid shareholder agreement because of Monika's bad experience' reflects Denise. 'We talked about everything when we had nothing to divide. It is easier to think about legacy, options and what is right then. It allowed us to think objectively about how we would protect the business in each situation.'

'We did it before money became a parameter' stresses Monika. 'When we had this discussion, we went to the law firm and said there are these parameters, we have no money but when we do, this is how we will do it. Usually, such agreements are there to protect VCs. Ours was an agreement… around our agreement.'

The intentionality is key. Be it a white-boarding session or a codified agreement, taking the time to intentionally reflect on what you have learned to-date is key. Allowing the learnings of your life to-date and your team's life to-date, to bear on what you do next doesn't happen by osmosis.

You need to take the time to do it actively.

And part of that active engagement with the learnings is the choice of who you need to bring on a journey with you.

Once you have done that, you start on the journey afresh. And although past experience helps a lot, there will be new things ahead of you. Things you have not seen before, things you could not prepare for. And you will need to apply all you know and make hard decisions when the data commands it. Because no amount of experience is enough to protect you from every eventuality so whatever you do, you need to be able to be brutally honest with yourself, about where you are. Be it in a market not ready for you, against the wall of cash-burn and product development… halfway up a steep hill or between a rock and a hard place.

If That Is Where You Are Going, I Wouldn't Start from Here

It is one of those singularly unhelpful things, isn't it, when asking for directions and the person you ask sucks their teeth and goes ah… if that is where you are going, I wouldn't start from here mate.

Thanks… *mate*.

But 'here' is where I am so I don't have much of a choice, have I?

I use this imagery and language a lot when speaking to big organisations, be it incumbent FS firms or scaled companies who made some early choices in capital deployment, hiring or product development that they now regret. Hindsight and whatnot.

Of course, all these folks have no choice but to apply what they now know, starting from where they are.

You can *only* start from where you are.

But starting from where you are doesn't mean accepting you will carry everything forevermore like the proverbial snail. Sometimes the learnings of what brought you here lead you to a product pivot or a big change in your company or direction. And sometimes, they lead you to draw a line under your current endeavour and start again, choosing to do something different your second time round. Whether 'going again' looks like a continuation or a departure, it is the same process of learning and doing things better. And you should remember that stopping and starting something entirely different is actually an option and sometimes the right choice.

I talked to Uday Akkaraju about how, in the process of writing my first book, I worked out what I wanted to write next. I could tell you that what I realised is that *this* (the one you are now holding) is the book I *actually* wanted to write. But that would be unfair to both my first book and whatever I do next. It isn't about finding your true calling as much as graduating to your next set of questions and feeling a burning desire to go about answering them.

Uday Akkaraju, CEO at Bond AI
Bond AI a human-centered AI platform for banks, powered by its proprietary empathy engine

---

Uday knew exactly what I was trying to convey. 'Bond AI is not my first business' he said. 'And it is a very different venture to my previous business. A bit like you and your book.'

That doesn't mean Uday was not committed to his first business. He was. It also doesn't mean that, having done it once, he took the learnings and went for effort 2.0 in the same vertical, applying all the hard-earned lessons. Some people may well do that, of course. Or you may go do something entirely different rather, applying all the hard-earned lessons learned the first time round, because one of the things you learn is that the product specifics were secondary to the hardest thing.

'Because I had been through this journey before' he reflects, 'I knew that the hardest thing would be to find the right people. It's not a technical matter.'

That was the learning. And similar to the learning Daniela and her team brought to Pismo, that started with a year's worth of white-boarding to consolidate the intent to do things differently, the biggest learning of the second time for Uday is to take the time.

> The single biggest learning of second-time founders is to take the time and invest in the things that are important to your business.
> Your values. And your sanity.

Take the year to really be intentional about what you will do next. Take the time to find the right people for your team.

'We have a really involved selection processes' reflects Uday. They invest a lot of time. Time that, when the pressure is on, invariably feels like it should be spent elsewhere. *Not* spending the time elsewhere is the discipline of the lessons learned the hard way. 'In the final round of interviews', notes Uday, 'I like to have dinner with [the candidate] and their spouse or partner. I want to see them relaxed and in their own environment. I want to see the interactions. I want to see buy-in into the vision, not the job. And of course this is hard to get right and it gets harder as the company grows and you can't do it this way any more. We may have to find another way to do this soon. But whichever way you do it, finding the right people takes time. You sort of need the stars to align. Because you want a team of people that are different. Not in terms of diversity tick boxes but you need them to have different life experiences and perspectives.'

> You need to be disciplined about time.
> If you allow yourself to feel like you are racing against time internally, you won't succeed.
> You are not racing against time but towards your own goal. And it takes time.
> Taking time is actually key in everything. Including the time you, as a CEO, as a leader, spend alone. Having that discipline to ensure you have time with yourself. Otherwise the subconscious stress can get the better of you.
> **Uday Akkaraju**

We have a whole section on the importance of getting the team and the team dynamics right, by the way.

So see this less as a spoiler alert and more as a sneak preview.

Because, as I was writing the section on the importance of the right team, I could hear the cynics snorting in my mind, I could hear all the people who don't take the time exclaiming that these are business book abstractions that don't apply in real life because *busy people don't have that kind of time.*

So although we are going to be talking about teams... a lot... because they matter *singularly*, it feels important to double down on exactly the things people take time over, or rather the things people's experience taught them they should take time over. Because this is a chapter about time after all.

'You need to be disciplined about taking the time' continues Uday.

'If you allow yourself to feel like you are racing against time internally, you won't succeed. You need people to understand how what they do contributes and the measure should not be racing against time but racing towards your own goal. Not just for hiring. For everything. Time is actually key in everything. Including the time you, as a CEO, as a leader, spend alone. Having that discipline to ensure you have time with yourself. Otherwise the subconscious stress can get the better of you.'

Put that in your pipe and smoke it, busy bankers.

I wrote extensively about the Cult of Busy in *Bankers Like Us* and the damage it does to a leader's ability to think clearly and perform at their best. So, yeah, Uday's learning was music to my ears, I won't lie.

But the point here is not that Uday chose to spend the time on something I also value. The point is that he took the time on something *he* values. He took the time and continues to take the time to focus on the thing that matters. Just like Monika and Denise took the time to write out their testament.

> You should always take the time, never the shortcut.
> **Monika Liikamaa**

Because the scenario planning and the alignment matters. But also because it shows a discipline that will imbue other things. 'You should always take the time when you could take a shortcut. Take the time. Not the shortcut.' reflects Monika. 'In the early days we took the time to write out our testament. We wrote down what our partnership would look like if we had to make a whole host of decisions. We thought about scenarios of pressure and make commitments so that when the pressure was upon us, we couldn't take the shortcut. We couldn't understand, for instance, how our competitors were growing 100x. Then we saw they cut corners in compliance and AML (anti money laundering). We are playing a long game and don't cut corners.'

Taking the time to think abstract thoughts or taking the long route when a shortcut appears available seems counter-intuitive when you are under pressure. When Pismo took that year to white board what kind of company they want to be, it was arguably a year they couldn't spare. Because every day you are not making money is a day you are burning money and we all know what happens to startups who run out of cash: they die.

So taking the time is hard, just as hard as saying no to cash is and for the same reasons. But it is vital. For all the same reasons also.

In 2024, Pismo concluded a landmark deal with Visa. Although Pismo will continue running independently and remain rail-agnostic[9], this transaction means that they have unparalleled access globally. If the mission of Pismo was to create a global, transformative legacy, this is the key to the kingdom.

And do they? Of course they do.

'I want to be part of the transformation of the industry' reflects Daniela Binatti. 'Think about it. Can we build companies that build systems transforming systems and standards built 40/50 years ago?'

Yes they can. And they did. But that first year spent on the whiteboard was not about 'how do we get a giant the size and shape of Visa to buy us'. It was not 'how do we build a business that becomes an acquisition target'. It wasn't even 'how do we transform the industry'. It was rather: we have been together for a long time, doing good work. How can we do better?

This section has been about having the discipline to take the time to do the things you know are important even when they don't seem urgent. Because they are important and you know that. I guess it is also about what teachability looks like.

All I Missed, Led Me Here to This[10]

Life is not linear. And sometimes the reversals and 'lessons learned', frankly, you could do without. But sometimes all the obstacles become a key part of the journey.

Soups Ranjan, CEO and co-founder of Sardine, reflecting on his own journey admits that you have to really want this. No matter how hard it is or how hard it gets. 'You can't be laid back about this.' It takes a lot of work. And courage. And sometimes it takes even more than that. 'I am an immigrant to the US' reflects Soups who had always wanted to build a business of his own. 'The reality for me was that I would have had a visa issue unless I had a majority-owner co-founder' which he didn't want to do.

'When I got my permanent residency and that was no longer an issue, my kids were too young, I didn't have the courage to not have a stable income. But I eventually made the choice. And it was one of many hard choices along the way.'

Serial founder, former banker and all-round digital OG Dharm Mistry who we already met in the first chapter, looks back at his career in a similar way. As a series of moments that came with their own options, constraints and opportunities. His own circumstances and 'banked learnings' drove his decisions. When he took a leap and when he didn't. Those circumstances and knowledge also meant that he knew it was time to move on because 'this here goose is cooked'.

---

9 For those of you for whom the issuer world is a mystery, this just means they are allowed to work with Mastercard or, indeed, any other Visa competitor to deliver services to customers.

10 10 points if you recognised the line from Darius Rucker's 'This': Thank God for all I missed, cos it led me here to this.

He didn't say that. I said that. He doesn't talk like a 1930s rancher. But my old boss used to say that a lot (because he was raised by a 1930s rancher, funnily enough) and it stuck.

Dharm thinks he's been lucky. I think he's been teachable and alert to opportunity. Observe.

Dharm, as you probably recall, could not go to university because of his family's financial situation. So, after school he applied for a whole host of jobs and before long got two offers worth considering. One was working for a big bank (in their data centre for the then staggering amount of nine thousand pounds) and the other was as a trainee with Lloyds at half the money.

And that's the one he took. The half-the-money job.

> Most entrepreneurs had to make a series of hard, realistic, contextual choices leading up to starting something new.
>
> And a whole host of hard, realistic contextual choices after that.
>
> Throwing caution to the wind to follow a singular passion only happens in movies.

Counter-intuitive, perhaps, given the whole career over school thing was happening because he needed the money. But he saw a way to bridge the gulf: he took the role that offered training.

'I was absolutely convinced that writing code makes you money. I had a maths teacher at school who drove in once in a brand new car. Not even the headmaster had a brand new car! So I asked him how he got to afford the car… and he told me he had built a game. Coding, was how. So I started testing for him… took computer science O level.' The rest, as they say, is history. His mind was made. Technology would be his future. The fact that he couldn't follow a linear path to it was incidental. He was going anyway.

'The Lloyds trainee programme was a great compromise for me. Less money but still a possibility to pay the bills while learning and doing something I loved. So it began. I remember I would get to the office at 7 in the morning, work through to 7–8 in the evening but only clock in 9–5 to avoid looking bad for doing extra hours!

And I was lucky. Some fortuitous re-engineering project came my way and I got to see the systems and processes of the bank up close. So I built a prototype of what a branch person could see if we created a single view of the customer.'

That is not luck, dear readers. But you knew that already.

What comes next isn't luck either.

'One day, I walked into the office of the then Head of Retail, around 6.30 in the evening after the EA had gone home, and asked for 15' of his time to show him what I had built in my own time. The concept was 'single customer view'. Back in 1990, no one was talking about data in this way. I didn't realise how revolutionary this would later become in the industry.

He loved it. He said *this is the kind of thing I need to show my team so they can start thinking bigger.*'

If you are thinking: he was good and he was smart and he was bold, but he is right, he did get lucky… stop. Because none of this is luck despite what Dharm says because he is not an arrogant man. At the end of the day, he was not the only trainee working on the re-engineering project. He was not the only person who had access to the systems and data. But he was the only person who reflected, spent his own time to build a prototype and then had the courage to show it to the boss. That is not luck. That is hard work, determination, initiative, creativity. But even more significantly, his reward for all this, didn't come as you may hope.

> I love the impact technology can have if you do the right thing.
>   And if you do the right thing, you will have an impact *and* you will make money.
>   **Dharm Mistry**

'I presented my prototype to the entire team' continues Dharm 'and word got back to my boss. I was so happy! I was expecting a top review. Instead, I got a three out of five for setting expectations above what we can deliver. She didn't even ask to see my work, the prototype that caused this.

So I left.'

There is a world where the lesson someone in Dharm' position learnt here was to keep his head down. In fact, a lot of people in big organisations or organisations led with an iron fist learn exactly that lesson.

I worked in a company a few years back where the CTO had a terrible habit of giving people very public and very personal dressings-down when they admitted to an oversight or error. It was ugly. It was frequent. Tears were not uncommon.

So people learned to hide things. It was the inevitable lesson learned. And a terrible one for the organisation. Because, of course, the only worse thing than a mistake is a mistake that goes uncorrected because people are scared enough to hide it and let it fester and augment.

The reason I insist none of this is luck and all of it is teachability, determination and perseverance is that what Dharm learned from this experience was what *he* is capable of. He didn't learn to keep his head down because he wasn't interested in learning how to best navigate the environment he was in. He learned what he could *do* and went in search of a better environment for his ambition and preferences.

Sometimes where you learn the lesson is not where you apply it.

But where most people at this point put their head down, in frustration, and do as they are told, Dharm moved on. 'I love the impact technology can have if you do the right thing. And if you do the right thing, you will have an impact and you will make money. So I moved on.

The next bank I joined wanted to do some stuff with the newfangled idea of the internet. *Do you know much about it,* they asked me. No, I said, but give me a weekend to find out.' Cocky, much? Actually, not at all.

The fine line between arrogance and confidence is very much there. Let me find out. I am teachable, let me learn. This phrase should be emblazoned on the walls of every company. That ability to learn, however, usually comes with an ability to value the process of learning.

> The same experience won't teach everyone the same thing: someone may learn how to navigate the environment they are in. Others may learn what they are capable of and go in search of a more suitable environment.

So, when Dharm well and truly caught the startup bug and took the plunge away from banking, he was offered a CTO role right out of the gate. I mean. Wouldn't you want the guy who can work out the internet over a weekend as your CTO? I know I would. I know the people who offered him the job did. But he refused.

'You lunatic' was my reaction when he told me the story, years later. In response, I got a signature Dharm chuckle and his reasons for it: 'I said: let me deliver first'. He felt he had some learning to do, to operate at the CTO level. He also knew he could do the learning. The two are a superpower, when combined. That's how he saw it. 'If I succeed then let me step up, rather than stepping down in case things don't work out.' Not a lunatic, it turns out. So I will be quiet.

'We built the world's first online insurance application. It was successful and led to substantial sales. Then we had a successful implementation, with a bank launching online banking and the very first mobile banking solution in the UK. I had delivery success under my belt so I went back to the founders and said *ok now I can do the job of CTO*. And they gave it to me without the pay rise you would have expected. The idea of promises and expectations not met can travel across big and small organisations.' Can't it just.

Cliffhanger time. We will come back to Dharm, this particular business and what happened next. We will, I promise you. For now, I am staying with the subtle theme of 'having done some of it before' as a clear pattern of what the people who live to tell the tale have in common. That's what I promised you, right, the ingredients of success? Well it turns out that up close it all looks like hard work done over a long period of time in a nonlinear fashion.

Knowing What I Know Now

Before the emergence of Monzo, Revolut, N26, as well as before Mox[11], Deniz Güven who became the founding CEO of Mox, had actually built something similar to them all, way before all of them. In Turkey back in 2013.

---

11 In case you have been living under a rock or fintech is new to you, launched in Hong Kong in September 2020, Mox is a virtual bank backed by Standard Chartered, in partnership with HKT, PCCW and Trip.com.

Mox delivers a suite of retail banking services and lifestyle benefits.

Yes, yes. Mox was his second attempt at such an endeavour.

See what I mean?

While working for Garanti Bank/BBVA, recalls Deniz, there was a significant focus on customer experience and acquisition. In 2010, nobody was thinking about 'digital' in terms of the radical transformation of society and the economy that later followed. The focus across the board was heavily on experience and what happened on the glass.

And yet in a move that proved visionary, in 2010 Garanti Bank established a separate balance sheet for the bank's digital arm. The intent was to ensure that executives viewed the digital business as a distinct entity. The effect was to allow the digital entity to develop with its own business model and economic model.

That was a turning point from viewing the capability simply as an alternative channel to building a digital business for the bank. This approach proved to be a major success, allowing Deniz and his team to present their achievements in a different light to management and have conversations on a different baseline.

This model also became the baseline for what Deniz then did with Mox. If it ain't broke, don't fix it territory. Because sometimes the learnings of your first rodeo are through success, you know. Not all life's formative experiences need to hurt in order to be valuable.

> **Deniz Güven, Investor & NED**
> Previously CEO of Mox, a virtual bank backed by Standard Chartered, in partnership with HKT, PCCW and Trip.com.

It is important to stress that the decision to create a new bank outside the main institution (which is an established shape now) was not the obvious choice then. We are so familiar with the construct now that it is almost impossible to imagine it as groundbreaking but there was a time when it was a new and untested idea. And even once you got everyone to agree on the idea, the execution was also untested. Every governance, process and operating model decision was new and untested.

By the time Deniz came round to building Mox, when it came to facing into the governance questions that inevitably emerge when you are building a regulated entity inside a larger regulated entity, his experience with Garanti was invaluable for Mox. Not because he copied the playbook. But because he could anticipate the first few sets of questions and challenges. He had data points and lived experience that meant that, although what he was doing was new, some variables could be controlled.

And that's another little titbit to remember (don't worry about writing it down, it will be in the liner notes at the end of the chapter) the value of this not being people's first rodeo is *not* that they've seen it all before. It is that they have learned how to answer the first set of questions that inevitably come your way when you are doing something different. They are better equipped for handling those, so their chances of even getting to the next set of questions is considerably higher. In Deniz's case, for instance, he knew that getting the governance right was not an afterthought. It was table stakes and only if it was agreed and locked down early on, would they get to answering the real critical success or failure question for the bank which was product market fit and economic traction. But I am getting ahead of myself.

Back in Turkey, the team established Garanti Bank's digital arm, known as "iGaranti", with its own technology infrastructure, products and team. Surprisingly for something so new for its market, the new venture gained traction quickly, acquiring 500,000 customers within six months. Other organisations began to take notice and emulate their model. Success! By some metrics at least. Only it's never that simple.

The business was growing but its economic model was not calibrated for profitability. When they started, they were exploring the art of the possible, not trying to build a viable business. With hindsight, Deniz reflects, they should have focused on profit-generating products. Instead, the team prioritised innovative features such as QR payments as they considered the challenge to be primarily an innovation game, so they neglected the credit aspect.

> The value of past experience is not that people have seen it all before. Far from it.
>
> It is that they have learned how to answer the first set of questions that inevitably come your way when you are doing something different.
>
> They are better equipped for handling those, so their chances of even getting to the next set of questions is considerably higher.

This goes back to Ken Johnstone's earlier point about *what problem are you solving?* And who needs you to solve it for them. Because ultimately that's who will be paying for it.

Our industry has learned the hard way the need to address a real market need and problem and not just do cool, shiny stuff to prove our innovation chops. But the way we have learned this lesson, as Deniz points out here, is by not prioritising profitability and paying the price.

The iGaranti team were not alone in over-indexing innovation proof points over digitally-enabled commercial proof points, by the way. But Deniz learned two invaluable lessons from the experience that he brought to bear when he built Mox. Governance. And commercial clarity.

Having the learning and knowing how to do it doesn't translate into wanting to have another go at it though.

When he moved from Turkey to Singapore and from Garanti to Standard Chartered, where the concept of Mox was born, initially, Deniz had no intention of building another digital bank. In fact, when originally offered the role, he was reluctant to take on the project. He wanted to expand his own horizon. He didn't want to be the man who keeps focusing on a single endeavour. He didn't want to do the same thing again, even if he knew how to do it better.

But it was undeniable that he did know how to do this exactly because... All together now... it was not his first rodeo. So he said yes.

He firmly believed and firmly pursued a strategy that set up the new bank outside the main bank, organisationally, and with a commercial model that established Mox as a JV (a joint venture). We will be coming back to the importance of structure and governance as it merits its own chapter. For now, it's all about those second rodeos.

The choice to set up Mox as a JV seems so obvious and inevitable now: now that Mox is live and successful. But at the beginning of the journey there was resistance to the idea. Of course there was. There always is.

> The thing about having done it before is that your horizon of predictability and your span of control when building something new is greater.
> The more you can control, the fewer surprises you face.
> The fewer the curveballs, the greater your chance of success.

Remember Dharm's boss who gave him a low rating for 'raising expectations'? How many stories like that happen in offices every day. I had a bank CTO tell me (admittedly many years ago) that the Cloud would never catch on. I wonder what he's up to now. Resistance is always a factor. Resistance from people with power is a fact of life. Which battles you pick, which battles become the proverbial hill you die on will have a lot to do with your personality. And a lot to do with the things you know to be true.

So Deniz stood his ground.

If he was going to do it again, he was going to do it right. That's my sentiment. Not his words. But it is an important stance. The pattern of someone coming out of the fray and choosing to go back into it in order to maximise their impact, leverage their learnings to do better is one of the strongest things to take away from this. This work is not for the fainthearted. If you were hoping that this book would give a 'how to drive successful transformation in the economy in five easy steps' you have come to the wrong place. Go read the 5 AM Club and have a smoothie. Both are known to work. But they solve for a different kind of question. The question we are trying to face into here is how to make doing complicated, hard things a little easier.

And, frankly, saying 'learn from your mistakes, then go again' is the opposite of 'easy', truth be told. But if you are looking for patterns in this work then there is denying that *this* is a pattern. People going back into the fray. And doing better. And I am fascinated by these people who just go again because now they know more and will do better.

Doing Hard Things, Better

'What on earth motivated you to found a startup, after a hugely successful corporate career? I would be sipping pina coladas on the beach and I don't even like pina coladas.' That's me speaking. It's a question I asked Antony Jenkins, the former CEO of Barclays Group. At the time we had this conversation, he was my boss and 10x, the company he chose to found several years previously, was a scale-up, no longer a scrappy startup. I didn't ask the question lightly. We were in the trenches of building a business together. Our days were long and the pressures constant. Building a business isn't a lifestyle choice. And Antony, after a very successful corporate career, wasn't doing it for the money. And he wasn't doing it for the fun of it because it's rewarding alright but 'fun' isn't the word I would use.

So, seriously: Why do this to yourself?

'I am not someone who can lie on a beach and drink pina coladas for any length of time' he responded with a smile. 'It is who I am.' Which is a big part of 'why' the folks who grace these pages go again. But it's not the whole story. Having done hard things, they know how to do hard things better. So they are compelled to solve the next problem.

'I founded 10x after a gruelling time at Barclays, doing very hard things as part of the job, both in terms of necessary but difficult decisions (such as shutting down businesses) and in terms of

> When I started this work, the easy part was the intellectual part.
> Imagining what *10x better* looks like was not the hard part.
> *Antony Jenkins*

deeply complex work (such as rolling out programmes to shift the organisation's culture). So when I started this work, the easy part was the intellectual part. Imagining what *10x better* looks like was not the hard part. Execution is always the hard part.

I have always been fascinated by the interaction of technology and financial services and always believed *we* can do better. I have always believed we can re-architect the way we work to achieve better outcomes. This sense of mission is key.'

That sense of mission, that hunger for impact that we already spent a considerable time on in the previous chapter, is what makes people go again and again. In fact, the people seeking to have a profound impact through their work are exactly the sort of people who will go again until they are done. Remember Old Mutual's Rolf Eichweber from the last chapter?

When I casually mentioned to him that his work to-date with OM Bank was a success 'so far', he stopped me dead in my tracks. The project is a success so far, without a doubt, he conceded. But it is too early to know if the mission has succeeded and that's the only success he cares about.

'If we look at Nubank' he reflects 'they are making a difference to people's lives *and* are profitable. They have met their mission. So success for [OM Bank] will look like our unit economics standing up and proving we are best in class; our NPS saying that our integrity shows through; and people globally wanting to join our team. Someone in Sweden saying *I want to work for this team.*'

Oh and one more thing. 'The team will be 50% female. Countries that treat women better are economically better off by multiples.' So success will be elusive until the determined impact is achieved. And if a venture doesn't achieve it, our folks here go again. So make no mistake: there are a lot of challenges along the way of transforming an industry but 'the hardest thing is the journey itself. That's the hardest thing' reflects Nektarios Liolios, co-founder of Radish.

The Journey, Is the Hardest Thing

Nektarios' own 'transforming an industry' journey started with Swift innotribe. 'We were striving to energise internal transformation and build community inside a traditional, conservative organisation whose very motto was *failure is not an option*. So finding ways to ideate new solutions and then build them was hard.

How do you begin to understand horizon 3 innovation and know what to do with it inside the industry, if getting things wrong and going again is not an option?'

That was the exam question. And it was hard but, as we know by now, it is doable. People, once inspired, find ways. And that is partly the point. 'And look' Nektarios continues 'tensions

> When we started this journey, we were trying to get people ideating and experimenting at a time that, inside our organisations, failure was not an option.
> *Nektarios Liolios*

emerge. You need to find a way to handle the tensions. As a business, you will have those alongside the specific challenges of each phase of the work.' That is the deal. Each phase of the work will be hard. You go in *knowing* that and prepared to do better. But what 'doing better' looks like keeps changing.

Antony Jenkins agrees: 'As we get established as a business, new challenges emerge. Ultimately, you have to be in the game to win it. And 'winning' is in constant flow. What constitutes winning keeps moving. You should be raising the bar for yourself as you go.'

But you also need to know where to start, the problem you are solving needs to be real and then, once you have that focus, you can raise the bar by increasing your focus, relevance, speed to market. You name it.

Getting that focus, however, is hard. And often where past experience is most useful. 'In our case' continues Antony, 'in the B2B world, I had the advantage of having been the client I am selling to.'

Do I need to keep saying 'not their first rodeo?' probably not, right? But I like saying it so here it goes again: Not. Their. First. Rodeo.

'I understand the space and I know that you can create demand more easily in a B2C world. No focus group ever created the Sony Walkman or the iPod. No focus group came up with Spotify. Nobody said *it would be nice if.* The ideas came first and then changed the behaviours. We didn't know we needed things but gosh once we had them! B2B doesn't work like that and you need to be alive to it. You also need to understand the fundamental technology you are relying on and the relationships of dependency. Sure… zoom and Microsoft Teams have enabled us to work remotely, for instance, but actually what really enabled remote work was high speed broadband. When thinking about tech change, you need to think about tech stacks on top of each other. There is no Spotify without mobile phones. Or if each song took five minutes to load and forever to stream.'

> Zoom and Microsoft Teams have enabled us to work remotely, but actually what really enabled remote work was high speed broadband.
>   When thinking about tech change, you need to think about tech stacks on top of each other. You need to understand the fundamental technology you are relying on and the relationships of dependency.
>   *Antony Jenkins*

And that raises a valuable point in itself, as well as a segue for my next section. Because no matter how much you learn and apply forwards, those dependencies will still have a potentially bigger impact on your business than your intent.

It is clear by now that the people we are looking at here are the folks who look at the world and wonder '*if I poke it, will it go boing*' and sometimes it does and sometimes it doesn't. And although there are many factors to why it may or may not go boing (and we will get to every single one of them in the chapters to come, scout's honour) sometimes the thing doesn't go boing because you were too soon. It will go boing soon. Just not yet.

And since this is a chapter on the effects of time… and the first factor is this not being the first time, let's turn to the second factor: this not being the right time.

But first…

Your Call to Action

- When doing new things for the first time, control every variable that can be controlled. Don't fool yourself that you can control everything or that you can control nothing. Both are dangerous tactics.
- Creativity and governance are not mutually exclusive. You are building a business, be disciplined and learn from every single experience.
- If whatever you are doing now is your first rodeo, find some people to join your team for whom it isn't their first time. You can thank me later.

- Take the time to do the things that matter. You will always feel time is in short supply because it is. Spend time on the important, not just the urgent.
- The intellectual part, imagining what your business could be like, is the easier part. Not easy. But easier. Execution is hard. It needs discipline, control and teachability.

I Just Wasn't Made for These Times (Yes the Beach Boys)

Is there such a thing as being too early for success?

Curt Queyrouze, President of Coastal Financial Corporation in the US, thinking back to his own career, has this to say about timing: 'In 2006/7 I left banking and was COO for a startup for a couple of years. 75 employees trying to build a real-time auction platform for receivables. We had a CTO in California in the days before zoom and a vision for a plat-

> In 2006 I was COO for a startup trying to build a real-time auction platform for receivables.
>
> We had a CTO in California in the days before zoom and a vision for a platform business before its time.
>
> A great product. Too early to become a business.
>
> **Curt Queyrouze**

form business, before its time. They couldn't get the product launched and they hired me to understand how banks approach invoice factoring and bring them on the journey.

And here this company was, 75 employees with an average age of 27. Amazing energy but not sustainable, not quite speaking the same language as their customers yet and, in the end, the economics couldn't work out. The auction platform itself was solid and sold to NYSE but the scale needed for profitability as a stand-alone business couldn't be achieved by a startup then.'

Give this a moment.

The idea was strong so even though it was before its time, it didn't die. But the business around it did. The idea succeeded, the product worked. But the business failed. Realising the distinction is important. Because a good idea alone, does not a business make.

> No matter how good your technology, for your product to succeed you need a market ready and willing to consume it and a go-to-market commensurate to the task.

No matter how good your technology, for your product to succeed you need a market ready and willing to consume it and a go-to-market commensurate to the task.

Lizzie Chapman, a pioneer of digital credit in India before BNPL had entered our lexicon, reflects back to her time with Zest money: the product worked and had market traction. Check. The market was large and investors were willing to fund the business. Check.

But it was early 2016.

Zest was first of its kind. So building the product and raising capital – both extremely time and energy consuming activities – were not the only things the team needed to do. They also needed to evangelise, just as Pismo already described. They needed to get the market ready. Which, of course they did. But which is also extremely time consuming.

Still, what choice do you have?

So evangelise they did. Successfully. So successfully, in fact, that by 2017 others entered the fray. There was competition.

Lizzie Chapman serves on the boards of Cloud Nine, Mahila Money and IndiaQuotient Currently building a new SaaS venture in stealth mode

Previously CEO and co-founder of digital credit pioneer Zest Money, executive director of DBS's DigiBank, India country head for Wonga, Goldman Sacks and the Wellcome Trust

There was also validation that this space was ripe for disruption. The problem was the new entrants were fresher. 'They had a better story. They could focus time and energy on their product, as the market was more aware.' The energy that the Zest team had to pour into evangelising to create the market had borne fruit, just not for themselves to reap alone. Now, the team had to pour energy into keeping up with a competition that benefited from their early work. The pressure of creating a market for a new product was replaced by the pressure to keep the product feeling *new* for investor beauty parades (a topic we will return to). 'So we had to keep coming back with crazy ideas to keep things fresh. This is hard and leads you to irrational decisions. But unless you have gas in the tank, you have no options: you have to keep the investors interested.'

So what interests them drives where you spend your time. That stands to reason. And it goes against the insights of the previous section about being disciplined and deliberate about how you spend your time.

> If you need to evangelise to get the market ready for your product… remember you may be spending a lot of time and energy getting the market ready for your competition also.

Do you see the connection?

I thought so. We will be talking about the influence of investors and boards in a later chapter, have no fear. And although nothing is ever a stand-alone factor, being early is invariably and axiomatically harder work than being later in the very same space. It costs more time, effort and headspace. Which means it costs more money. It also means you are the first to work out what achieving the thing you set out to do looks like in practical terms: what would it take for the idea behind the venture to succeed.

'We were essentially trying to kill the bank' reflects Lizzie. 'Coming in wanting to lend to underserved people. We underestimated how hard and expensive that would be and we overestimated our ability to raise money.' And probably took the wrong kind of money.

> If you are new to what you are doing and what you are doing is new to the market, it is very easy to underestimate what it will take to succeed and over-estimate your ability to do it.

Although we all have regrets and hindsight is always 20/20, can anyone say hand on heart that they would have done things differently, the first time round? Without the benefit of hindsight?

'Someone comes along willing to fund your growth when you *know* your product can do what you are saying it can do? Knowing what I know now, how much money and time it takes to disrupt an industry, the question wouldn't be about whether I take the money or not but playing a different game' reflects Lizzie. 'If I had known then that it would take 500 million and not 100 to achieve what we set out to achieve, I would have played a different game.'

She knows now.

But the first time, there is no way of knowing. That comes with every first rodeo. And Lizzie's learning journey was compounded by being a market-creator.

'Being early also means you are the first one to size what you are trying to achieve in practical terms. Sometimes you discover that there may be more practical ways to get to the impact you seek. Is that the same as being 'too early' or just one of the disadvantages of being early? If your idea got market traction, your technology worked but you suffered from being too early for adoption (like Curt's example) or pursuing a forbiddingly expensive route (like Lizzie's example) is it failure? And does it matter?

I mean. Of course it matters to the people in the fray, but in the grand scheme of things, is that construct even helpful?

Is Being Early the Same as Being Wrong?

'This is innovation after all. The chances of failure are high' reflects ING's Simon Boonen. 'But we started with the mindset that we either succeed or we learn. There is no failure.' Which is just as well, if you can stay true to it. Because the reality of trying new things for the first time, especially inside a big organisation, is that, often, they neither succeed nor do they fail. They just stop. Because they lose momentum or support or because the idea has no market of an appropriate size for an ING to get out of bed.

Not exactly as Simon would put it, I guess. But he does agree that 'timing is a huge factor. And a major reason why a number of initiatives inside ING stopped. Looking at lapsed initiatives you see some ideas that were ahead of their time: the problem/product fit was there but the product/market fit was not so the MVP couldn't become a scaled solution with rigour because of external timing.' No matter how good the idea, no matter how true your intent. If the market isn't there, nobody is buying.

Arthur Leung, CPO of Shawbrook bank, agrees: 'A lot of the time a company's success has more to do with timing than talent. A product or idea may be great but in the wrong decade. Call it luck. Call it timing. The point is that in

> **Arthur Leung, Shawbrook CPO**
> Previously Director of Product
> at 11:FS Foundry and Curve
> Investor and advisor to startups

a parallel universe, you launch the exact same idea five years later and it's a different story.'

Fair. As is the point Arthur goes on to make: 'Luck is a polarising idea in our industry: founders and entrepreneurs tend to think they are in control and of course that narrative goes against notions of luck.' I am not lucky. I am good. Apart from when we fail, in which case *we didn't get lucky this time*. 'This prevailing narrative goes against accountability and ownership sometimes' reflects Arthur. 'But since you rarely succeed the first time… Do you continue to randomly roll the dice until you succeed? Or do you learn with each iteration.'

That's where ING's 'we don't fail, we succeed or we learn' comes into play.

'For instance we had an IoT "banking of things" pilot a few years back' recalls Simon Boonen. 'A really good idea, but too early to get traction in the market. There were too many players and dependencies on the wider value chain plus the state of emergence of IoT ecosystems wasn't there yet. We were too early. The idea was good.

The timing was not. Unlocking micro payments hadn't quite happened yet. So of course looking back you know now that timing was key, as in so many things.'

Wise and sober words. It wasn't

> A big bank with a thriving business, how do you make a material difference to that? Ultimately that is the ball game. And of course people have short memories and expectations of speed and everything always feels slower than you expected.
> *Simon Boonen*

our time, so we go again. Only it's not always that simple. Going again requires time, money, energy and support.

Inside a big organisation, 'going again' means renewing that permission to succeed or learn, that permission to (don't say the word) fail. And despite decades of practice, it's still hard to keep going and we should never lose sight of that. It's easy to talk about innovation and failing fast and going again but the reality is a lot messier than that and there are always detractors inside big organisations ready to point at each false start, each faltering step and call it a failure and a reason to stop doing it.

'The hardest thing' highlights Simon 'is that despite decades of doing this and actually doing this well, this work is still a 'nice to have' inside the bank. Such a big bank with a thriving business, how do you make a material difference to that with any innovative initiative? Ultimately that is the ball game. And of course people have short memories and expectations of speed… and everything always feels slower than you expected.'

So actually getting the timing wrong, getting a good idea too soon, may kill you, unfair as that may seem. Knowing that is a super power. Being able to recognise that, ideally before it happens, is a super-power. But even if you only recognise it post facto, it's still valuable. Because experience doesn't come labelled, sadly. Wisdom comes from experience.

But so does PTSD.

So being able to work out which parts of your experience are reusable learning points and which were situation specific is not a pleasant post mortem but it is a valuable one.

Can You Be Too Early by Degrees?

The hardest thing to accept about timing is that, if you are too early in the technology adoption cycles or the regulatory change curve, it does not happen by degrees, especially if you are a startup with finite funds. Timing, in those cases, tends to be binary and lethal. 'Timing is the most important factor in everything we do' according to Mike Cunningham. He is speaking from experience as his neo bank venture in the GCC[12] failed to take off and, with hindsight, timing had a lot to do with it. 'With Bank Clearly[13], we were just too early. Too early for the regulators who were reluctant to entertain the idea of a neobank in-region… too early for investors who were not backing such long-range ideas in-region yet at the

> **Mike Cunningham, CEO at 77 Ventures**
> Formerly Chief Strategy and Digital Officer at Banque Saudi Fransi (BSF), CEO Bank Clearly and ex Barclays Emerging Markets

---

12 The GCC (Gulf Cooperation Council) a regional, intergovernmental, political and economic union comprising Bahrain, Kuwait, Oman, Qatar, Saudi Arabia, and the United Arab Emirates.

13 https://www.fintechfutures.com/2017/01/new-digital-bank-coming-to-middle-east-bank-clearly/

time. Nothing was ready where we needed it to be. Now you see licenses granted more easily, investments for that kind of venture more forthcoming.'

I feel frustrated just hearing this. But Mike is more philosophical about it all.

'I would do it again. I still have the flame inside that refuses to go off. My wife would say *'what are you doing'* but it's true. The need to do something big doesn't go away. That's how I joined BSF.'

Fun fact: I actually met Mike when he was with Clearly and I worked for QNB, the biggest bank in the Gulf region. We didn't get to work together then, however. But I got to work with him a few years later, when we was with Bank Saudi Fransi (BSF) and I had returned to the UK to work for 11:FS.

'I had a job in a big bank back in London all signed up' he recalls, around the same time I was making my own return journey from the Gulf back to London. Only he changed course and went back to the GCC. This time in the Kingdom of Saudi Arabia. 'I chose to take on the BSF role. Although it was a corporate job, I was driven by the same drive to do something big. Not big in terms of the title or the money but big in terms of impact. I had the big job ready to go and I couldn't bring myself to look forward to it. It was a great job on paper. I just couldn't bring myself to do it. When BSF came along and asked 'what do you want to do' my answer was immediate: I want to have an impact.'

That word again.

But also the unspoken counter-ballast: I want to have an impact and I now know a thing or two about what to do and what not to do, how to do it and how not to do it. You won't be surprised to hear that all the learnings of Clearly were problems Mike solved for BSF early on. Including making sure that the solution they were building was not ahead of its time in terms of either regulatory readiness or market appetite.

> The problems that break you on your first rodeo tend to be the first things you control for in your second.
>
> Including ensuring you are not too early for your market: in terms of your buyers or the regulator.

Were these early wins followed by other problems? Of course they were. But he got to those faster, for what it's worth. And yes, yes we will speak about them soon. Cliffhangers galore. But we would be doing ourselves a disservice if we didn't answer, definitively, whether exogenous factors such as timing could be the death of your entire endeavour. And there is compelling evidence to say yes.

And yet.

True though it is, there is nuance here. Remember Funderbeam's Kaidi Ruusalepp from the first chapter?

Kaidi's mission with Funderbeam, when the business started, was to change the culture of an entire industry. They were first, they were alone, they were going against the grain. And they were using a new technology. It was all by design. But that doesn't make it easier.

'We wanted to create transparency in the secondary markets in private assets (mainly startup investments) where you often don't know who the seller is, not even mentioning other information about the deal. We wanted to democratise the market with our solution. But that's not what the industry wanted.'

Remember Teun van den Dries in the previous chapter? Describing how his first business, Officerank, wanted to solve a problem, but the people he was trying to solve it for didn't need it solved? Because it wasn't a problem at all for them?

Kaidi faced the same resistance.

So the business pivoted to a place where their mission and the market need overlapped. 'We are still working towards creating liquidity and promoting transparency but within the comfort zones of the investors.'

But this wasn't the only thing that Funderbeam had to take stock on. Because they were early in one more major way. As if creating transparency in an opaque market wasn't a big enough challenge, Funderbeam chose to drive its mission using technology that was very early in its adoption cycle at the time. 'We were ahead of our time with that as well' recalls Kaidi with a wry smile. 'We built everything on the blockchain in 2016. The market didn't need blockchain though, especially in asset classes that were not tokenised. The market wanted access to startup investments and liquidity. The underlying technology was not the key element. You get to know these signs "post-mortem" as all pioneers do.'

The lessons of the first rodeo, so to speak.

'In a way it is a miracle that we survived' continues Kaidi. But was it? We will speak about what happens next (I KNOW! Another cliffhanger, isn't it fun?).

It is clear that being too early is a thing. If your market isn't ready for you, your solution or your technology then you have to change or perish. Changing and navigating those challenges is hard and not everyone makes it. The tenacity, reflection and action that followed in Kaidi's case and so many others (there's a section on pivots, hold on till then) is not a miracle. It's a sign of a team that had a way of reflecting on the feedback the market was giving and acting on it and a sign of having or seeking and using resources to either bide their time or iterate towards something that wasn't too early.

The Journey Needs to Start in Your Head

That's Trygve's answer to my questions about timing as a factor of success. Trygve is the Lead Architect for DNB's Corporate Banking division, a friend and officially my favourite Viking. If you are now thinking 'I don't know enough Vikings to have a leader board of favourite Vikings' all I can say is you still have time to make better life choices that include more Vikings. But back to the serious conversation.

Trygve has led a variety of transformation programmes inside the bank. He has seen the creative side of innovation... the messy part of building new things and the tensions technology companies need to resolve on their own journeys.

He has seen it, warts and all, and his view is that, in order to get to an innovation effort that has some probability of success, you will need to have started somewhere entirely different. You have to accept none of this is linear. And you always react to exter-nalities in a million small ways each day. So effectively he believes that my point about 'this not being the first rodeo' (which he agrees with) disproves my point about timing being an exogenous binary factor of success (which he disagrees with).

Trygve Aasheim, Lead Architect Corporate Banking, DNB
DNB ASA is Norway's largest financial services group

Thanks a bunch.

To be fair, he didn't put it like that and it is important for you to hear the other side of this argument. Because his main point is hard to disagree with: all of this work, be it in a startup or in a corporate, starts as an idea. Why you want to follow this idea, what drives you, what right of success you have (and what lies you may tell yourself in the process) is part of the journey that comes next.

'Innovation with a high probability of succeeding requires grit, determination and willpower' continues Trygve. 'None of those can be found automatically in a forced setting. Or you might find those [traits], but not necessarily linked to the right idea or activity.'

So actually getting to the place where the idea meets those characteristics needed to make it a success is a challenge in itself. What comes next is a non-linear dialogue with the environment around you. So the timing of your idea can't surprise you. The clues are there. If you are paying attention.

If you follow the idea because you believe in it then the rest is about hard work, resource man-agement and time. Not timing, you notice. But time. Spending the time. Putting in the time. So timing becomes a backdrop for Trygve. A factor but not a catalyst.

Bond AI's Uday Akkaraju agrees: 'yeah, sure, luck will play a part. 3%? 5% of your journey will need the stars to align but it is not more than that. It is not the main story. It is a process anyway. There are a series of milestones and only

> Innovation with a high probability of succeeding requires grit, determination and willpower.
> None of those can be found auto-matically in a forced setting. So actu-ally getting to the place where the idea meets the characteristics needed to make it a success... is a non-linear dialogue with the environment around you.
> *Trygve Aasheim*

one or two will be a tipping point but every step mattered in getting you there. Holistically, luck plays a part for sure but there are so many milestones and so many small moments that matter and you can get them right or wrong and not impact the whole story in one moment.'

Nektarios Liolios, co-founder and CCO of Radish, also sees 'luck' as the banner we put over a multitude of sins that may be much closer to our control than we care to admit.

He's in the Trygve camp: not buying it. 'I don't buy into product market fit or timing as reasons for failure that are disconnected from people' he says. 'If you dig, you will find people who disagreed, some voices that were louder than others and maybe drowned out conversation… you will find lack of alignment that led to certain

> Luck will play a part in your journey but it is not the main story. It is a process anyway. There are a series of milestones and only one or two will be a tipping point but every step mattered in getting you there.
> **Uday Akkaraju**

decisions. That's not timing. That's people. I have seen hundreds of startups[14]. If the team have a way of navigating their differences, they will build a thing. It may not be the thing they set out to build. But they will build it.'

And that is a very interesting nuance because it doesn't deny that timing matters, that it may put tension on the team and business, but if it's the right team, timing won't kill them. Especially as, to repeat Uday's point, the reality check is rarely a single, pivotal moment.

> I have seen hundreds of startups.
> If the team have a way of navigating their differences, they will build a thing. It may not be the thing they set out to build. But they will build it.
> **Nektarios Liolios**

Being early undeniably puts pressure on a team, particularly if you have to either create a market or wait for the market to mature and catch up with your product. But that is only a problem if you can't afford the wait, ultimately.

I Got Time

We always assume that one can't afford the wait. We always assume that the wait was not part of the plan. The difficulties of being first and the uncertainties of being early are undeniable, but what if you actually banked on being early and waiting for the world to catch up?

---

14 Nektarios was a co-founder of Innotribe at swift, co-founder and CEO of Startup Bootcamp Fintech and a board advisor to a dozen startups. Saying he's seen hundreds of startups is really not an exaggeration. It may even be an understatement.

'We have learned that there is a considerable competitive advantage to being early' says Bianca Bates[15], speaking about some of Cuscal's plays in Australia. 'For instance. We were first with real-time payments in Australia. Did we make money early? No But because we were early with this, we now have the expertise and the client sign-up to drive substantial growth. If we had sat it out, this opportunity wouldn't be ours.'

Going early intentionally can be a conscious investment in your future. If you have the money to wait, being early may be an extremely astute strategy whereby you build ahead of the competition, create a market and capture the benefit when it matures. It takes time, it takes resources and

Bianca Bates, Chief Client Officer and Deputy CEO, Cuscal
Cuscal Limited is an Australian company that provides payments and data solutions to Australian Banks, credit unions, mutual savings banks, corporates and Fintechs.

it takes leadership but it also proves that being early is not always an accident It may be a conscious doubling down on the learning and experience that you know you will need later. That intentionality is a leadership decision. The money you need to make it happen is actually secondary to the ability to determine where you want to play and go for it. 'The ability to back your own vision, ultimately, entails making a commitment from a leadership perspective' continues Bianca.

'The board and exec have to be behind such an idea and open to what getting it done looks like. The big strategic plays can't be 'bottom up' ideas. Our competitors who decided to wait until the business case fully stacked up, for instance, now have a huge disadvantage.' Worth digesting that for a minute.

> The ability to back your own vision, ultimately, entails making a commitment from a leadership perspective.
> *Bianca Bates*

Being early is expensive. And if you need or want early results and immediate proof points, either because you don't have the budget to wait or because your leadership isn't convinced by its own conviction, then being early can kill you by default. But if you are clear and committed, then the 'spend' is for a reason. If you are intentional then being early is a go to market strategy. And the time horizon pays off.

Move Fast, Hold Tight, Expect Delays

The idea of being aware of the time horizon the space you are entering requires in order to mature is poignant, as we enter realms of greater technological complexity.

---

15 Since we spoke for this interview, Bianca has taken on a role as Chief Customer Officer of Smartgroup Corporation.

When I asked Zor Gorelov who, as you recall, works in the magical world of AI, what he expected to be the hardest thing when he started Kasisto, what he had to say puts the question of 'too early' on its head. Because someone has to work on the thing, so that the thing matures enough from a technological perspective so that it can start being too early from a market perspective. Not everyone is here to capitalise on the market opportunity of new technology. Some folks are here to actually invent the blasted thing.

> Being early can be intentional: to create a defensible competitive moat or because you want to be pivotal in the evolution of an entire domain.
> To do so you need to back your convictions. And fund them.
> Being early is expensive.

'What we expected was going to be the hardest thing turned out to be true' reflects Zor. 'Our vision was to use AI to democratise financial services and help users to make better financial decisions. It is what we set out to do ten years ago and conversational AI is *still* seen as "new" today'[16].

That is not a surprise. It's a long road. The company is ten years old and we are coming into a transformative moment with Generative AI now. People are beginning to see the art of the possible: moving away from prescriptive AI where everything has to be written down manually, coded to a new paradigm.'

When Zor says 'this is not a surprise' he means they came into this fray expecting things to take a long time. Being early was kinda key if you were going to be pivotal in the evolution of a whole technological domain. And it was intentional, in Kasisto's case.

'AI-powered financial advisors will become reality. It will be possible for them to give truly independent and unbiased advice' continues Zor. 'We are not there yet. We are still in a world of labour augmentation but that will shift. Artificial General Intelligence will take many more years to achieve, but what I call AFI or Artificial Financial Intelligence is within reach. Although, ten years on, we are not quite there yet. And

> Kasisto is a spinoff from Standard Research Institute, SRI International, the same AI lab that created Apple's Siri.
> Our product is called KAI.
> We described KAI, as Siri's older cousin, the one with an MBA in finance.
> ***Zor Gorelov***

still there have been times when I thought we were too early. Even though some technology core deep-learning algorithms the industry uses today were invented in the 1980s... we have come a long way and have a long way to go.'

---

16 This conversation took place in 2023 and remains true at the time we are going to print.

It is a sobering thought.

When we speak about things being too early, we always mean in terms of commercial horizons. Return on equity. When do I get proof that this thing works, when do I get my money.

But some ideas and some technologies need you to spend the time. Not to wait. But to work on them for a longer period of time. If that's not your bag, then maybe this is not your domain. This is me speaking, not Zor.

What Zor had to say was this: 'Kasisto is a spinoff from Standard Research Institute, SRI International. We were founded in the storied AI lab that created Apple's Siri, ten years ago. We were incubated at SRI post Siri and decided to apply its leading edge AI technology to the banking sector. Our product is called KAI. We described KAI, as Siri's older cousin, the one with an MBA in finance. KAI's conversations are only as good as the data (transactions, payments, spending and investment history etc., it is able to access so the hardest thing was persuading banks to give us access to the users' data.'

That's not a 'too early' thing.

That's a *banks getting out of their own way* thing.

And I don't mean that in a dismissive way. But when talking about timings, the readiness of the technology is a consideration, as is the existence of a market for your product. And we already

> I heard the phrase 'I got lucky then' so many times.
> From the very people who kept going the ten times before the time they think they got lucky, when they didn't hadn't gotten lucky.

talked about the fact that often you need to budget time for evangelising and doubling down to create said market. But even after all that is done, there is another timing consideration and that is the process of buying. When selling to FS players, sales cycles are long and approvals are esoteric. The patience it requires to get anything done with banking clients is in many ways the story of *Bankers Like Us*.

But whichever way you look at it, timing your business, developing your offering, forging your market and hand-holding your prospects into becoming clients: there is a lot going on here, all of which takes a lot of time and effort and quite a few variables that are not entirely in your control.

'There is always an element of luck in it all' reflects 10x's Antony Jenkins. 'But I would argue tenacity has more to do with it. Is it luck, after all, turning up with the right solution at the right time? Or is it availing yourself of the opportunities that present themselves? Making the most of what you have?'

Most of the folks I interviewed in this work attribute a lot of their own success to luck. None of their failures, mind, and everyone was very open about using the F word. Owning up to mistakes. Absolutely owning up to things that didn't work out.

And every single person put the things that didn't work out down to choices they made (some they would make again, in the same context and under the same circumstances) and some they would not, now they know better. For the avoidance of doubt, I am fully aware that there is selection bias right there. I've been doing this work for a long time and I have met more than my fair share (a truly fair share being 'none', all told) of the arrogant banker or founder who is fundamentally unteachable because all the bad stuff that happen to them are perceived as circumstantial and all the good ones are seen as being down to their genius and leadership. I specifically and intentionally sought out the Other Guys for this work, as you already know. And what they saw was teachable moments in failure and an element of luck in success. I respect that deeply.

I heard the phrase 'I got lucky then' so many times. From the very people who kept going the ten times before the one time when things worked out. The very people who kept going when they didn't get lucky. And that is the message, after all. But there is more here. There are circumstances that will push some people to give up and some people to focus more. It is tough but it pays dividends if you are open to the teachable moment. And that teachability and ability to take the hints the environment gives you is key to many choices you make as a leader but above all the choices you make about timings. When to hold on, when to double down, when to pivot, when to call it quits.

And it is particularly important when you discuss the possibility of your idea having been too early. I guess it's fair to say that 'too early' is relative. To your runway and the realities of the thing you are trying to prove. To your appetite (to Bianca's point regarding Cuscal's strategy on being early) and your exogenous considerations. There are no hard and fast rules other

> Being early is never relative and always tied to your runway, appetite and strategy.
>
> Being delayed by contextual factors and exogenous events (such as war or a pandemic) can be absolute and absolutely fatal to a business.

than life will throw curveballs and you will have hard choices to make. How you navigate those choices determines what happens next, obviously. And every time you have navigated choices like that helps the next time you encounter them (the rodeos, again). The tenacity Antony speaks of. The entrepreneurial spirit.

But it also helps with one more thing: recognising the hand you are dealt and reading the signs your context provides you. Sometimes you can choose that context and sometimes you can't. Either way, reading your context is key. Whatever you choose to do, you need to be aware of all contextual limitations as they apply to you or to the gifts the context unwittingly gives you.

Let's turn to each of those in turn.

The Privilege of Context

My good friend, the wonderful Dr Louise Maynard Atem wrote a piece a few years back about how situational context is not 'created equal' so to speak. In a heartfelt and moving piece[17] she raises two very valid points. Context matters because it affects our lives directly and indirectly. Context does not affect us all the same and although some aspects of our context can be controlled by interacting with our environment or through components of our identity that are in our control to conceal or reveal. My accent, for instance, is

> The context in which you operate will affect your business: regulatory landscape, market, geography, moment in time...
>
> And the way the context perceives *you* as an operator will affect your business. And it won't do so equally.

something I can try to mask. My sexuality is something I may choose to not disclose. My skin colour, is not.

It is obvious perhaps but merits repeating.

In the context of business, *your* context may be choosing to open your business in a country where the regulatory framework is friendly to startups or supportive of the technology you choose to use (that is context you may choose to control). Your context is also the wider socio-economic situation you operate in: Covid striking and hurting or helping your business (we will turn to that in the next section). That context is not in your control and although it will hit everyone equally, it won't *affect* everyone equally. And being alert to how your context affects you is key to building a successful business. And although this is a section about how timing creates context, I cannot avoid digressing for a minute. Because that context is not affecting us all the same. Because there is an elephant in this here room. And that elephant is diversity and access. Do. Not. Groan.

It has to be said. It was to be talked about because it has to be accounted for. This work is hard. Always and for everyone. I think we have made this point already and will carry on making it for the remainder of this book. And yet for some, it is even harder. Contextually speaking.

It has nothing to do with timing, you may say. And you would be right. But it has a lot to do with the context in which you operate and build a business so bear with me. Because we talked about controlling all the things you can control in this very hard journey. And this one is a tricky one to control and one I hope you may choose to fly in the face of. But it is not one you can ignore. And here is as good a place as any to talk about it.

---

17 https://www.womeninidentity.org/articles/the-privilege-of-context

'Female founders in Europe raised less than 2% of the capital invested by the male teams doing the investing[18]' reflects Kaidi. Starting a new business is hard. Getting funding is hard. Navigating the pitfalls of change is hard. But it is not *equally* hard for everyone doing it.

Just…

Remember that.

'Imagine you have a son and a daughter and you give them the same task… say… to open a candy shop. Then your daughter gets two pieces of candy from you as an investment, your son 98. That's the story we are talking about. There is definitely an element of people running towards the familiar and the investors tend to be men, but the way we've been working so far isn't working' and by that Kaidi doesn't just mean it isn't working for half of society. She means it isn't working very well at all.

> Female founders get 2% of investment.
>   Imagine you have a son and daughter and you task both with opening a candy shop.
>   Then your daughter gets two piece of candy from you to get her started and your son 98.
>   That's the story we are talking about.
>   ***Kaidi Ruusalepp***

The way capital has been deployed over the last decade and a half across fintech has not been conducive to building sustainable businesses. That is not because VCs have mostly backed male founders. It is because of how VCs measure success, a topic we will speak of again very soon, the two ills are simultaneous and compounding rather than causally linked. The point remains however.

If anything, the point should be self-evident: changing the injustice of a system that isn't working all that well for anyone *anyway* shouldn't be a hard sell. And it's not just that it isn't delivering results (which it largely isn't), the funding habits of the past decade also failed to encourage focus on the right things.

Remember when we talked about Pismo's year of whiteboarding and how they didn't spend that time thinking about how they will be successful but rather what

---

18 In case you are thinking… this can't be true:

The world economic forum confirms the number, https://www.weforum.org/agenda/2023/12/how-we-can-close-the-venture-capital-gender-gap/#:~:text=One%20area%20where%20women%20are,cheque%2Dwriters'%20are%20women

As do startup resources:

https://startupsmagazine.co.uk/article-only-2-vc-funding-goes-female-and-ethnic-minority-founded-businesses#:~:text=Articles-,Only%202%25%20of%20VC%20Funding%20Goes%20to,and%20Ethnic%20Minority%20Founded%20Businesses

As does the British private equity and venture capital association, www.british-business-bank.co.uk/wp-content/uploads/2019/01/UK_VC_and_Female_Founders_Report_British_Business_Bank.pdf as does… every resource out there.

kind of business they want to be? The opposite of that, as Lizzie Chapman described in the last chapter, is usually how most founding teams operate. Pushed down a tunnel vision of chasing success and measuring success in terms of itself.

'*Success at all cost* is the prevailing god in the industry and capital feeds the god. For as long as this is the most important thing, the customer doesn't come first' explains Kaidi.

> If the way we currently do things gives 50% of the population 2% of the pie and fails at a rate of 95%... the case for change should be self-explanatory.

So we don't need to do better and do differently *just* to not leave half of the population out in the cold, we also need to do it because what we are doing now is not working all that well. From an outcomes perspective. Because the way we choose which startups and ventures to back, leads to 95% failure rate as we already saw. And of course correlation doesn't imply causation but you would be tempted to look into all variables wouldn't you? If we didn't accept that staggering failure rate as inevitable, what may we do differently in the way we select, support and measure success for our founders?

Just saying: right now, what we are doing isn't working. So change is advisable.

Until such a time as change is forthcoming though, if you are really looking at the patterns for success in the world as we now see it, then, sadly for me, I have to call it: being white and male helps. Not because you are any better (sorry boys: you are not. You are equally good, which is more than good enough). But because you are going to get 98 candy to my two and that just increases your chances, doesn't it. It definitely makes you more resilient to whatever other contextual factors are affecting us both equally and at the same time.

'I spent so many years saying there is no prejudice in FS. I would look at my own career as a woman as proof that there is no prejudice any more' recalls Lizzie Chapman.

And then she became a founder and 'I watched companies with no woman at the helm in our space raising more, faster at higher valuations. And VCs wouldn't even hide the reason. We heard things like *I hope your husband helps with the business* or *how will you as a white woman hire and manage Indian men.*'

Lovely.

And look, everyone has a horror story or ten from encounters with VCs. And Lizzie acknowledges that readily. 'It is hard to raise money anyway. And I believe women generally raise less at higher dilution which compounds and hurts over time.' Sadly Lizzie is right. In January of 2023 TechCrunch put the overall share of fintech funding that went to female founders at 1.9%[19], down from 2% the year

---

19 https://techcrunch.com/2023/01/18/women-founded-startups-raised-1-9-of-all-vc-funds-in-2022-a-drop-from-2021/

before[20]. In fact, as a Harvard Business review article from 2021 points out even though VC funding for fintech has been increasing, the share of it that goes to women-led businesses has been dropping year on year having reached the dizzying heights of 2.8% in 2019[21].

> Women are so few and far between in the industry.
> So if you fail, you fail so much more visibly and dramatically than the men.
> **Lizzie Chapman**

That was sarcasm. Just in case you missed it.

And because women are so few and far between in the industry, 'if you fail' points out Lizzie, 'you fail so much more visibly and dramatically than the men. If you fail as a female founder, you get invited to speak at industry events about failures. Not about your successes or your next venture. Or your lessons learned.

Nobody asks the men to do this self-flagellation the same way'.

No. Men who fail and go again are celebrated as gritty and resilient serial entrepreneurs. Women are failed founders.

'And you keep getting the narrative *women are so emotional* continues Kaidi 'and you think… What is wrong with that? Emotional intelligence is highly expected in leaders. What's wrong with caring about talent? Male founders are often lunatics and nobody calls them emotional. We need balance of age, gender, religion across the board' for better outcomes.

'The experience has been eye opening' reflects Lizzie. 'It is just a tougher journey if you are a woman but I guess we all loved the journey enough to go again.' Yes dear readers: another lunatic who went again. 'And the pain and the struggle is part of it' continues Lizzie. 'The *are we going to make it* pain. Would I do this again? Of course I would. In fact… I am. I needed to rest and recoup but yes doing it again was a given. Ultimately it was a lot of fun.'

The Missing Rung Problem

As I said in the last chapter: these change-makers are made of sterner stuff. I would *definitely* be tempted by the piña colada on the beach by now. But not Lizzie. She is doing it again. Knowing everything

> Female founders are given survival capital rather than risk capital.
> **Kaidi Ruusalepp**

---

20 https://www.bloomberg.com/news/articles/2022-01-11/women-founders-raised-just-2-of-venture-capital-money-last-year?leadSource=uverify%20wall

21 https://hbr.org/2021/02/women-led-startups-received-just-2-3-of-vc-funding-in-2020

she knows from the last rodeo. The knowledge is not putting her off. But she is forewarned and therefore forearmed.

Which is just as well.

Because it's not just that women raise less (although they do).

It is also that the capital they raise is a different kind (and we will turn to why this matters in the next chapter). 'Female founders are given survival capital rather than risk capital' continues Kaidi 'and it is a case of 2x return… but we have to count the pennies to get to the same outcome. You get funding to build a product and once built, instead of starting to sell it, you run out of funding and are forced to fundraise.'

It's not a glass ceiling. It is a missing rung[22].

So actually scrap what I said earlier. Being male and white helps with early survival statistics. But for success against the odds, it helps if you are a woman or person of colour… still standing. It is a testament of exceptional resilience even among those most resilient.

Yes I am being facetious. But only slightly.

And I know you know all this stuff but it is important to stress that in this mix of hard things done the hard way, the landscape is even harder for some.

And *that* sometimes is the very reason why people keep going.

'I was passionate to solve a problem' recalls Joel Blake.

The missing rung problem. The closed door problem.

'My first business was a recruitment agency helping ethnic minority candidates from Russell Group universities get good jobs.' It was a problem Joel understood well from lived experience. This passion is key. But it does not a business make. 'What I needed to do was understand why this is a problem beyond my emotional starting point. I knew it was a problem because of the experience I had had looking for a job. But that knowledge isn't enough.'

The business did not survive.

Joel Blake OBE, Founder and CEO of GFA Exchange

NED and advisor to, among others, Taranis Capital, Chairman of the Board of Trustees of Employability UK.

Joel was granted an OBE in 2016 for services to business support and enterprise

> The deficit model around diversity and inclusion, the pity-first mindset is not evidence-based.
> *Joel Blake*

---

22 If you have no idea what I am talking about… see here https://www.forbes.com/sites/kimelses ser/2019/10/15/new-leanin-study-the-broken-rung-keeping-women-from-management/?sh= 20377a5b7803 but also… where have you been over the last few years? Under a rock? This study came out in 2019… do keep up.

But the entrepreneur did.

Joel went on to co-found an SME lending firm. We will speak at length about this firm's business model in a later chapter. What you need to know for this exercise is: the business succeeded. It was profitable. It scaled. But in order to scale and still meet its expenses it had to make hard choices. 'We were helping our business grow but saying no to three times the loan applications that we were saying yes to. And when we dug a little deeper, we saw that we were being really narrow, we were hunting down our management fee. Our business was becoming lucrative but who were we saying no to? The same people everyone else was saying no to. Disproportionately women and minority-owned businesses. I was not comfortable with that. So I left and started GFA.'

GFA Exchange is risk management software with a twist: it helps lenders find the most suitable businesses for long-term growth while giving a holistic view of the diversity, inclusion and profitability metrics of their portfolio. It doesn't help minority or female-owned businesses get access to finance, it helps the numbers do the talking and the numbers don't lie: diversity is good for business. This is not their pitch, this is me talking.

> I was passionate about solving the missing rung problem. The closed door problem. Knowing the problem from personal experience is key. But the passion is not enough to build a business.
> **Joel Blake**

But Joel's aim is to 'build an alternative credit risk model for the market. Become the single destination for those who want to get a view of a business' performance for a loan or as an investor in a business and sector agnostic way.

And I want to achieve this within five years.

Personally, success is making inclusion an equitable idea in the marketplace. I want to get to a place where we have objective and accessible data that shows real benchmarks on a pure evidence basis. We are bringing equality into a highly inequitable space.

I am personally not interested in yachts and big houses. When you are dead and gone they don't mean anything.

> Society puts value on how much money you have. But we have it all wrong: it is about the value money brings.
> **Joel Blake**

What is your legacy? Society does place value on the amount of money you have but we have this all wrong: the focus should be on the value money brings. We have this wrong and I don't see why we can't fix it. With numbers only: everything else is subjective and of course there are biases in how data is used but give it enough time and perseverance and then *you can evidence the evidence*.

And there is consistency and equity in a fair, data-driven process. In my business, for instance, we focus on inclusion but we don't drive it, *your* business does.

The deficit model around diversity and inclusion, the pity-first mindset is not evidence-based. The numbers don't lie. The data will show where your gaps are, what your business needs to do in order to improve your health and performance as a business. Not just your diversity score. All the metrics that feed into the performance that a lender or investor wants to see. And as a lender, you can see your impact on businesses and also see that impact across your portfolio and benchmark yourself against your peers in the market. We offer the different level views to enable really seeing how these factors affect performance.'

I am getting a sense of 'bring it' while chatting to Joel. Even though he speaks of data, objectivity and inclusion as an outcome of good business performance. He believes an equitable world is a better world and a better performing world and is doing what he can through his business to make the change. This is where he has chosen to have an impact. And he is not alone.

'We have a responsibility', stresses Kaidi. 'We are hoping for a new and open-minded generation to follow ours, but our generation has to lead the charge and we have to take the hits.'

> We have a responsibility.
> If we are hoping for a new and open-minded generation, our generation has to lead the change and take the hits.
> *Kaidi Ruusalepp*

Please stop and absorb this: we are driving the change by taking the hits to make it better for the next generation. Please remember that when you read these pages. Especially if you won the birth lottery and situational context is kind to you. This journey is hard for everyone but it is infinitely harder for the brown faces in this group, for the women in this group.

It just is. It sucks. And it is a lived reality we need to be aware of when talking about what motivates our leadership teams, accelerates our economic drivers, inspires our founders and innovators; what impacts and affects them. Some experience the world differently.

We don't need you to feel sorry for us, by the way.

But we need to be aware that the playing field isn't even

We need all of us to acknowledge the world is unequal. That is a fact. But not one we accept as an inalienable truth. Everyone on these pages is fighting to change these facts. And things are moving.

'A lot of ideas (such as inclusion, diversity, financial inclusion) didn't exist 50 years ago' flags Maha El Dimachki, now with the Bank of International Settlements in

Maha El Dimachki, Head of Department, Early and High Growth Oversight, Financial Conduct Authority

Since we spoke, Maha as joined the **Bank of International Settlements as the Head of the Singapore Innovation Centre**

Singapore but, at the time of this interview working with the Financial Conduct Authority, in London. 'Now people care.' Now we just need to align caring to do the right thing with financial returns which, just like magic, is better aligned anyway: equity brings better financial returns. Whaddayaknow.

Until that alignment happens, we will keep fighting. And going again. As many rodeos as it takes. And hope that occasionally, life won't throw curveballs, but lemons.

My little hiatus on the privilege of context is over. But there is one more, one last thing to say about context and that is sometimes things that are entirely outside your control such as the timing of global events changing the context of business for everyone, may just play right into your hands.

When Life Gives You Lemons

We spoke about first times and hard times, we spoke about bad timing and unforeseen exogenous factors. Decisions and trade-offs being forced upon you before you are ready for them. A common story, that. But it's not the only story. Exogenous factors create opportunity as well as tension and the general sentiment among the wonderful people I interviewed was 'when history is trying to help you: let it'.

When I asked Teun van den Dries what helped with the success of Geophy – and after really hesitating in visible discomfort at my use of the word *success* – he reflected 'the hard work and the good idea are not enough. It takes dumb luck and random support from people'.

If you remember from the last chapter, in 2016 both Teun and Geophy were broke and in debt. And randomly, in the midst of this all, an invitation comes to join a Fannie Mae[23] showcase. It was a mistake. Fannie Mae was a perfect

> If you find that fate is conspiring to help you... let it.
> Unforeseen events create opportunity. When they do: seize it.

partner for Geophy apart from one small detail: they are a US entity. Geophy was, at the time, a Dutch company with no subsidiaries, presence or plans for a presence in the US. They were contacted entirely by mistake.

A magic mistake[24].

'At that point, I had never even *been* to the US' reminisces Teun who practically lives there now. 'We got on the list accidentally, put there by someone who thought we were a US company and didn't check.'

What do you do, when life gives you lemons?

---

23 The Federal National Mortgage Association, commonly known as Fannie Mae, is a United States government-sponsored enterprise and, since 1968, a publicly traded company.

24 If you are wondering what I mean, feel free to read this: https://www.fintechfutures.com/ 2020/08/magic-mistakes-and-how-to-make-them/ where I explain it all at some length.

'I had to borrow cash for the ticket to fly to DC' he recalls. He was broke, remember? But he borrowed money and he went. Last roll of the dice type thing.

And while he was there, pitching Geophy, he was asked 'if I give you my data, can you build an AVM[25]?' 'Could we do it yet? No... Were we able to build it? Probably... Did we say yes? Well... Yes.'

Did they build it? Also yes.

I want to say 'and the rest is history' but it wasn't so simple. A break came. A break that saved Geophy from the brink. It just gave it the chance to fight another day and sometimes that is all it takes because only the end is final, everything else you can fight for.

This opportunity to work with Fannie Mae of course didn't even go near to solving all the company's problems. Product market fit remained a work in progress but with a contract and a first round of funding, the switch happened: 'Geophy became a US company, with a new basis and a new price point.' A pragmatic decision that set in train a series of events and pragmatic decisions leading to Geophy's exit to Walker and Dunlop a few years later.

This wouldn't have been an option had Geophy not switched its operations, base and focus to the

> A lucky break still requires you to take action, make decisions and work hard towards operationalizing whatever it is you decided to do in order to capitalise on the opportunity.

US market. The opportunity to do so was luck. The pursuit of the opportunity was a lot of hard work. The switch itself was a pragmatic decision, not a strategic one. As was the exit, stresses Teun: a pragmatic decision. Maybe that is what entrepreneurs mean when they speak of luck: their ability to make the most of opportunities as they arise, in the most pragmatic way possible.

'I don't believe in luck.'

Trygve Aasheim, my favourite Viking and DNB's VP for Product Management, Architecture and Engineering Practice in Corporate Banking and International sees things differently:

'Luck inherently says that there are things at play that are outside of your control, superstitious types of things. It also implies that you need a level of faith and sort of "wait and see" type of mentality. And I don't like external attribution. I believe that most circumstances can be identified and controlled, at least indirectly in that you can know about them and work with them even if you can't change them.' So in this context what Teun looks at as dumb luck is just circumstance that he made the most of.

---

25 AVM is an automated valuation model: a computer algorithm that uses available data to estimate a home's value.

And although I agree with Trygve philosophically, I like the humility of teams who look at their hard work and success and acknowledge it doesn't all boil down to genius.

'You often don't see "luck" as it happens to you' reflects Enfuce's Denise. 'But the reality is some big ticket moments hit and they are huge.' Monika concurs: 'When Covid started and the military were on the street in Finland… We had no idea how it would affect us. Would we grow or die? We grew but you don't always know how it will play out and definitely can't anticipate certain things. Same: when the Russia-Ukraine war started. If we had gone global just before, it would have hurt is. There are moments in time that, if we had been blinded or if they occurred slightly later, they catch you more extended… more exposed' and similarly there are moments where you took a gamble and the world shuffles to land exactly where you need it. You still need to do something to capitalise on the opportunity of course.

> Whether life gives you lemons is outside your control.
> But if it does give you lemons, you are not done.
> You still need to grab them and squeeze them.
> Lemonade won't make itself.

If life gives you lemons, you still need to grab them and squeeze them. Lemonade won't make itself. So maybe it's less luck and more the context created by timing. We spoke about being too early and opinions are divided as to whether that is a binary impact or just a factor that may accelerate or delay what would happen anyway.

I like the idea that good businesses, good ideas and good people will flourish anyway. Emotionally, I am drawn to that idea. But I also know that exogenous factors present you with opportunities or challenges that, if they hit at any other time, they wouldn't have had the same effect. Positive or negative. You can never separate what happens next from good leadership, but even the best captain has to react to the weather.

And sometimes the weather is more clement than others.

The Same Sun Shines upon Us All but Warms Us Differently

As I was working on this book, a high interest rate environment and low investment appetite created a context in which most of the fintech world groaned and withered on the vine. In this context, Flagstone, a wonderful business I had the privilege of sitting on the board of, soared.

Why?

It is a cash savings business so fundamentally its business model benefited from the interest rates.

> There are fundamental building blocks for a growth business: a large addressable market with a clear need for what you are building is key.
> **Simon Merchant**

Interest rates soaring was bad news for a lot of businesses either directly or indirectly but for us it was good news.

A bit of luck, you may say. And you would be right. The business was not designed in the hope of high interest rates. But life gave us lemons.

What wasn't luck was the timely and focused decision-making that followed. The leadership team saw the opportunity and made the most of it. That part isn't luck. Ultimately, you could argue that what happened for Flagstone during a period that was hard for most businesses was a contextual accelerant for a business that would have succeeded anyway.

Simon Merchant, CEO of Flagstone, who you met earlier, admits that luck and randomness are always in play, but 'there are fundamental building blocks when building a growth business: a large addressable market plus a clear need for what you are building. My first business had neither of those! I had a small market appeal that was *potentially* lucrative so everyone wanted to talk to us. It took two and a half years to realise the difference between a product that is nice to have and a must have product. That's when we pivoted and we saw an immediate difference in reaction. We went from good conversations to conversations around *when can I have it* and *how much does it cost*. So: you need a large addressable market to succeed.

Then you also need a growth mindset: a conscious desire to learn new things and accept that you don't know all the answers. That comes with an acceptance that you will be wrong. And with that comes the realisation that, even though you will be wrong, you still need to make decisions. You can't postpone making decisions in the fear of making the wrong decision because, in not making a decision, you have made a decision. So make decisions fast. If you are wrong, your speed gives you the option to make another decision and a better informed one. You need to be able to tell yourself you are an idiot occasionally: confidence and humility can coexist. And an awareness of your own limitations is key. You see a lot of people who believe in their own bullshit.'

In the context of the world conspiring to help you, this of course means that life may give you lemons and you may still mess it up. You may miss it or ignore it or delay acting because you don't feel you need it or fail to do the work needed to make the most of the opportunity. Flagstone came out of the era

> You need to accept you do not know everything and will be wrong at times. And you must make decisions anyway because not making a decision is in itself a decision.
> **Simon Merchant**

of high interest rates having navigated the opportunity exceptionally well. That was not a given. Not everyone in the space did that.

Equally, life may throw you a curveball that no amount of good leadership can avoid. There are undeniably events that affect everyone at the same time. But not in the same way. When the war in Ukraine started, for some of us it was an unfolding humanitarian issue and for others it was their homes on fire and their brothers dying each day. From a business perspective, for some it was just another 'tailwind' to add to the macro-economic considerations at work, while for others it came with the practical implications of business models relying heavily on engineering teams in Ukraine and Belarus. Business models that overnight became non-viable and full of risk.

The impact of the war on businesses was very different depending on who they were, where they were and what choices they had previously made. A wave appeared that was just the right size and shape for some and a tsunami for others. Whether you successfully ride it or not is of course a matter of choices, actions and talent deployment. But you can't deny that world events hit everyone simultaneously but not equally.

A Global Crisis, A Business Opportunity

Let me start by saying I personally believe Brexit to have been a terrible idea, badly executed. I do not know what OakNorth's founders think on the matter. And it absolutely doesn't matter because irrespective of their views, the sequence of events presented them with an amazing set of opportunities that they were quick to grab.

Irrespective of what they thought, what I know for a fact is that OakNorth was a business that found Brexit created opportunities that could not have been foreseen when they started their journey in 2015, with the vote still a year away and not a driver of growth they were counting on.

Not only were they not anticipating this vote. They actually had no way of anticipating what it would mean for them when it happened. In fact, when the referendum took place and results came out, amid the shock of everyone in the City going 'what just happened'. Valentina Kristensen recalls, the question on everyone's mind was 'what does that mean for us? It was not a problem that we anticipated... it was not something we had planned for... and in the end it became a huge opportunity.

> No single factor ever holds answers for a success or failure. But the best entrepreneurs pay attention to events around them.
>
> They don't underestimate threats they do not ignore opportunities.

The loan book was 98 million at the time of the vote in June 2016... 300 million by the end of that year. The timing turned out to be in our favour.' SMEs needed more support than ever. And they needed the support from a home brand.

Fast forward five years: January 2020, the UK leaves the EU and then Covid hits. Another shock event nobody could plan for. Another squeeze for SMEs. Another reason for SMEs to need help.

And yet again OakNorth sees the numbers rise: 1.1bn of new lending in 2020, 1.8bn in 2021. For a business like OakNorth, the economic strain of the pandemic brought an increase in the need for loans. Businesses needed help of the kind OakNorth offers. The crisis offered an opportunity and a validation of the business model and solution offered.

Obviously two history-altering events (Brexit and Covid) were not part of the business plan and they turned out to help but, as co-founders Rishi Khosia and Joel Perlman always say to the OakNorth team: 'The best entrepreneurs thrive in turmoil.' Maybe that's because Trygve is right and there is no such thing as luck. And maybe it is because the best entrepreneurs pay attention to what is happening around them and adjust accordingly.

'When you look back, it's hard to know what is a factor in your success that wouldn't have otherwise happened' points out Mettle's Ken Johnstone. 'For instance, Covid was an interesting time for us. A lot of people were furloughed and those who were not had more time with long commutes gone and nothing else to do. So we saw a big spike in side-hustles. People started new businesses (or started accounts for businesses that they were already working on) for side gigs.'

It was not a make-or-break situation but it definitely created an accelerant.

> Historic events such as Covid, Brexit or a war will affect every business.
> Whether they will accelerate your growth, derail you, slow you down or force you to revisit your entire business model has nothing to do with whether the events are good or bad in themselves and everything to do with your business.

That is a common theme. Those dramatic events are noticed not least because people pause to reflect on how this may affect them. Joel Blake, for instance, believes that Covid would have been make or break for his business if it had come either earlier or later. 'Covid came at a stage when we could survive it. Any earlier or later and it could have killed us.' Any earlier, the idea was too ethereal, too abstract. It would have withered on the vine. Any later, the commitments already made would mean that time and money would run out. 'Having gotten the validation and being at a moment where the business was not commercial yet, we could take the time to listen. We could take the enforced downtime to listen to what the market needed.'

The reality is, no single explanation ever holds every answer. No single factor ever causes success or failures. Businesses are complex beasts and no one thing ever holds all the answers. A good leader 'listens' to market feedback. Sometimes it is delivered in big dramatic gestures. Sometimes it is subtler. But it is always invaluable. And the impact of exogenous events is always undeniable. Covid (still top of mind for everyone as I was researching this book) was a factor everyone contended with for better or worse. For some, as we saw, it was an accelerant. For others a deccelerant. For Funderbeam, a company based on 'the power of the crowd' Covid meant that 'people were locked in. Those who had some extra money had nowhere to spend it so we saw a boost in crypto investment but also investments in crowdfunding platforms. Then the markets went shaky, the war in Ukraine started and retail investors became understandably super cautious. People would keep their money under their mattresses.' The corresponding pressures on her business were both con-siderable but also a data point in itself.

What followed was a pivot. I know I said there is a whole chapter on pivots. And there is. This isn't it: consider this a sneak preview. Is exogenous pressure leading to a pivot the same as life giving you lemons?

You tell me.

'Our pivot and change in business model was crucial for us to attract €40m investment by VentureWave in May 2023 and enter the institutional and later stage startup market' reflects Kaidi. Success often appears inevitable once it has been achieved.

But how a leadership team reacts to those critical juncture moments, the luck and the crisis, the contextual pressures and opportunities is not inevitable. So when we speak about luck it is always with that caveat in mind: what life throws your way isn't always in your control. What you do with it is.

Always within reason, of course.

A friend of mine had just opened a beauty business as Covid hit. There was no opportunity for a beautician in lockdown. It was a blow. Her business couldn't go online. It had to wait and hope for the best. The same lockdown accelerated success for others. It didn't make it, and that's the point.

Jasper Martens, CMO PensionBee
PensionBee gives customers control of their retirement through day through a service that allows to combine pensions, contribute and withdraw

For the wonderful people of PensionBee, Covid brought about a major opportunity for change. I briefly mentioned them in the last chapter as an impact-driven business that sees itself in terms of decades' long planning horizons.

So their plan to IPO shouldn't surprise anyone. That's what businesses who intend to stick around often plan for. Only, this one plan, didn't go according to plan. In fact, it came about much sooner than anyone anticipated.

When lockdown hit, everything started moving faster than planned and, although the company was growing anyway, everything accelerated. 'People were closer to the admin drawer' reminisces Jasper Martens. 'People were locked in and locked down. Working through personal admin was weirdly something people could control in the midst of an unprecedented crisis. Sorting the admin pile out was good for people's mental health. We saw an increase in activity and we doubled down on it.... That's the angle we took: do your admin. The papers are one metre away, put it all under control. We took advantage of advertising rates, drove the point home and we saw massive customer growth. The decision to go public was made in November 2020. In April 2021 we were listed. We did our IPO video with lockdown hair but the energy was there: we saw the opportunity. We went for it.'

So fine, Trygve is right. That is not luck.

It's life and lemons and whatnot. And leadership. And nuance. Because although accelerated growth actually meant that there was good reason to go faster after an IPO, that wasn't the only thing changing with lockdown.

People's 'aha' moment when they start working out what they want from their pension normally, or rather pre-pandemic, came around the age of 42. During lockdown and through the changes and pressures it brought, that moment came forward to about 38. People were beginning to think about old age and, let's face it, their own mortality at a much younger age given the context we were all living in and through.

> Businesses need to be alert to the world around them.
>
> The macro changes and the opportunities they bring.
>
> But also the impact they have on people: our communities and customers whose needs, realities and 'aha' moments shift according to major external events too.

Staying in tune with those changes was key for a business like PensionBee. As was enabling the team of beekeepers (yes: I know, it is the best name for customer success teams. I love it too) to stay close to the needs of people twice their age. Because PensionBee is a young team. At 46 at the time of writing (Jasper and I are exactly the same age and wearing it very well thank you very much), he is one of the oldest people in the team. Understanding the needs of people who aren't like you is key. Understanding how these people change is key.

And it is hard.

Maybe this de facto realisation makes the beekeepers vigilant and aware to changing contextual factors. That in itself is a strength. And although I have argued myself away from my original notion of 'luck', I can't let go of the power of context. Because there is no denying that unforeseen factors are always at play.

And they don't always need to be negative or dramatic. It could be a rising tide that lifts all boats.

Engaging with Extreme Events

For ING's Simon Boonen, the world changing around you is important to notice even if it doesn't affect your organisation as much because of its size and stability. Bigger ships can weather most storms and all that. It also means that big organisations have the option to ignore the direction of the world for a very long time if they so choose. It is possible albeit irresponsible. Because the context in which you do business will catch up with you eventually.

And the world has been changing for a while and it changed even further around the pandemic and it would be naive to assume that a big corporate like ING is immune to the impacts of this change.

In fact, Simon finds that although the conditions didn't create a defining 'do or die' moments, the change created conditions ripe for accelerated innovation adoption, introduced some new challenges but also created new imperatives such as a greater focus on sustainability. 'Now ESG isn't a side show' points out Simon. 'Health, the planet's health as well as our communities' health, has stopped being abstract. So innovation is a means to addressing these challenges *as a bank*. As a global player looking at global issues. We look at what we can do to contribute, to make the transformation inclusive, to ensure we leave no-one behind and leave the world better than we found it. Social and environmental impact – being conscious about energy use, for instance – articulating issues around social wellbeing… that's a planetary challenge. Given the mindset we have, this is the next aim.

> Big organisations can weather most storms.
>
> That means they often have the option to ignore the way the world is going.
>
> But it is responsible not to.

Take what we learned from the time when we engaged with innovation in the early days when the focus was on creating awareness and making the bank better at applying itself to global problems. From an MVP to global wellbeing issues… it's all about focus and consistency in your approach. It sounds simple. But it is not.'

Frankly, I don't think it sounds simple at all. It sounds responsive and responsible, though. It sounds like a big global player paying attention to the context they are doing business in and responding to changing needs, priorities and imperatives. 'As they should be' you may be thinking. And I would agree. But it is not universal so it is important to flag that it is possible and share what it looks like when it happens for the avoidance of doubt.

That's how I see the digital wave Greece has been riding recently, incidentally. As an entire economy *finally* responding to the way the world is going.

A Taste of Home: Greece's Digital Rebirth

Before I go any further, let me say for the non-Greeks amongst you, that politics in Greece is deeply divided (think sectarian, or think of it in terms of football teams to understand the visceral way in which people align to their

> Capital controls in Greece is a good example of how extreme events catalysed people's behaviour: in the public and private sectors.

respective sides) so I am making a deeply controversial statement here by acknowledging that the team that isn't the one I naturally support has not only done a good job but also galvanised society in a way that is a delight to see. I am proud of it. So allow me a moment of self-indulgence here.

As a Greek citizen living in the UK since the mid-1990s, I have spent a long (too long) period of time being put on the spot about things happening or not happening in Greece. Oversimplifications, flippant commentary and click-bait news coverage didn't help. So, usually, over the years, when people clocked I was Greek and started talking about whatever it is they had heard about the motherland on the news, I tended to brace myself for the unpleasant conversation. I assumed an a priori defensive position expecting to be mocked about tax evasion even though everyone I know at home is crippled by huge tax bills; or taunts about an ailing economy even though it was my friends and family that struggled to find work or, frankly, live in said economy.

A creaking, Kafkaesque bureaucracy prone to corruption, error and delays. The jokes were never-ending. So I would get the jibes and try to keep the balance between picking a fight nobody but me was interested in and giving people a lecture about a topic they didn't care to understand. I ended up somewhere in the defensive middle. 'Yeah I know… but… it's not so simple.' You know how it goes.

And then something really weird started happening.

Greece started doing better across the indexes that are visible abroad. The economy stabilised, the response to the rise of the Covid epidemic was decisive and digitisation started picking up serious steam. Not all was perfect. Not all was rosy. The political debates raged and often rightly so. But for me, coming in and out of the country at irregular intervals with detached but loving eyes, there was no denying that e-government was now a thing. Digital identity. Digital processing for pensions and benefits that went through in minutes when normally it would have taken months, unless the file was lost in which case it would take years.

Greece was *changing*.

Now in my travels people would say 'hey what's going on in Greece' and I would feel my shoulders tensing and my face getting ready for the 'it's not so simple' response, only they continued with 'it's amazing'.

George Kostopoulos of Piraeus Bank contextualises this change more succinctly than I ever could: 'Greece is an example of how extreme events triggered fundamental changes in people's behaviour.'

Ten years of change brought to you courtesy of two unrelated, catalysing events. First, capital controls, introduced in June 2015 and not fully lifted till September 2019,

> **George Kostopoulos, Senior Manager, Piraeus Bank**
> Head of Innovation Center & Alternative Channels, Retail Banking & Distribution Networks

forced Greeks to start using debit and credit cards more than ever before because cash withdrawals were heavily limited. Then Covid hit with prolonged lockdowns that meant Greek consumers were forced to use ATMs and debit cards for their daily transactions as bank branches were closed, whilst e-commerce became vital. This was a harsh introduction to the digital world, as George rightly points out, but it led to significant and lasting changes to both customer behaviours and digital capabilities.

'The Greek government played an important role towards digitisation, by incorporating numerous services that were performed online or with mobile apps. From the extensive use of QR codes (e.g. vaccination certificates) to video-calls with the tax office employees. Consequently, the banking sector, along with fintechs and neobanks that operate in Greece, are now benefiting from the digital environment that the Greek government has established. For example, during the Digital Onboarding process that can be completed through Piraeus Bank mobile app (winbank), all customer's data is retrieved through gov.gr/KYC.

The procedure is completed in just 15 minutes.

In 15 minutes, the customer has a new banking relationship (checking or savings account/ debit card/ e-banking credentials) and the Bank has all the necessary data to create a customer profile, in order to offer personalised products and services. In addition, the procedure is fully accessible to people with hearing impairments, as the Bank's employees that verify the identity of the customer are trained in the Greek Sign Language.'

And that is not all. This fully digital onboarding is the only one (so far) in Greece that is fully paperless. 'All data is retrieved from gov.gr/KYC and uploaded to the Bank's systems, thus enhancing ESG metrics.' If you love this insight... just you wait till I get to tell you about Piraeus Bank's accessibility branch... (Yes another teaser... I need to keep you engaged don't I?).

The reality that George describes above affected everyone. Everyone had to react to it somehow. Not everyone invested in the same things or reacted in the same way. Maybe this is the point. It's not luck. Because if it was luck more people would do the hard yards. It's about picking your moment. Or not picking your moment.

Serendipity, Lady Luck's Favourite Cousin

When I posed the question about the importance of luck to Thought Machine's Gareth Richardson, his view was it matters a lot and not at all. Of course 'external factors were clearly important. If money wasn't around, we would have had to have built differently. But we would have still built'.

Gareth was part of the Rule Financial team that exited to GFT. By the time he completed that journey he was burnt out and exhausted but also wiser. Second rodeos and all. In an industry where companies were, at the time,

> Although landing a marquis customer when you most need them feels lucky... is solving a real problem in a way that resonates really... luck?

burning cash like crazy, Gareth had seen enough not to be seduced by that. 'Thought Machine was clear to me: right team, right product goals. I believed the market was there, if it could just be tapped in the right way, and was lucky that I knew some people on the inside. But that is how relationships work. That is how things work.'

That's how life works.

Thought Machine landed a major deal early on with Lloyds Bank in the UK. If you are in core banking you know all about this (and were probably green with envy at the time, I know I was). If you are not in core banking what you need to know about this deal is that it came early enough to create a positive wave in terms of credibility and viability for the Thought Machine offering. 'Were we lucky to get Lloyds?' reflects Gareth. 'Yes, because our product was not ready. Or not… because the business need was clear, they had that need, and we had enough to show we would address it. Plus the size of the problem and lack of solutions in the industry meant that they were willing to experiment, work with us and wait for the solution.'

Remember Mox and Deniz Güven? Mox is a Thought Machine client.

'Was it lucky that Standard Chartered Bank set out to build a digital bank in a way that was customer-first and defined financial product requirements that put almost every product already in

> Saying no to opportunities that will take you off course, strain your resources or distract you is as important as grabbing the right opportunities when they appear.

the market out of contention?' continues Gareth. 'Or is it proof of an underserved market and correct product market fit hypothesis?'. Of course capitalising on that opportunity took a lot of work.

Similar to the experience Daniela described for Pismo (a direct competitor of Thought Machine's actually so facing similar market challenges), 'we have had to take people on the journey and show them things they didn't know' recalls Gareth. 'Cloud usage for a critical core banking system, was something the industry was very sceptical and nervous of… speaking of real time services in a "batch" world' and that was before they got to the part about explaining the specific nature of their own product design choices. Was it lucky that it resonated? Was it luck that the problem they were solving was big (Simon Merchant says no)… and that they way they were solving it resonated?

Gareth believes it's not.

Especially as, for every story where a customer was a great fit, there are many that weren't and more than a few that you had to walk away from.

And although you always want

> When it comes to navigating opportunity, the 'Will Not Implement' portion of our roadmap is as important as what we will do.
> **Gareth Richardson**

to be customer-first, saying no to customers is one of the hardest but strongest things you can do in order to stay focused. 'We have had to hold the line on what our product does do and doesn't do – because the scope of a core banking system has traditionally spilled into areas it never should have. It has made us say 'No' to customers when they have asked us to develop a specific feature or area. (Sometimes getting it wrong and having to backtrack later but mostly have held the line on major areas.) The 'will not implement' section of our product roadmap is as important as what we will do.

We said 'no' to some smaller bank prospects at times, especially in the early days. We needed to make sure that we had a roster of the largest banks solving the hard problem, because there is a view in the industry that if you can serve the smaller banks you can't serve the larger banks. We had to make ourselves the most credible in the industry for our chosen market.'

As I've said before, success once achieved seems inevitable but the hard work towards the right things (and saying no to the wrong things) is neither inevitable nor easy to navigate as it is happening. Saying no to customers is a very hard thing to do. Often the right one, but hard nonetheless. It's in the same bucket of 'hard' as taking the time to think through things when money is short. Counter-intuitive but ultimately the right thing.

Sometimes.

Because saying no isn't always heroic. And it isn't always right. Sticking to your guns is not a 'by default' position. Sometimes it's short-sighted. When I asked Dharm Mistry about this, he thought back to when he and his team created the world's first multi-channel, online voting system, running on eight devices.

It was shown on Tomorrow's world[26]!

And it got interest from several governments, albeit no buyers at that point.

But these were the .com days. The world was getting out of hand. Silly ideas and unrealistic expectations. The bubble was getting bigger and bigger and we all know what happens to bubbles. The writing should have been on the wall for anyone to see. But people often only see what they want to see.

> Maybe there is no such thing as luck. But there is definitely such a thing as serendipity… and proactive, context-aware decision-making.

'In the midst of all this, our business got £20 million of funding on £15 million of revenue' recalls Dharm. Which is brilliant.

But these were heady .com days 'so the advice was that valuation will go up by a million for every person you hire… so the owners went on a hiring spree.' And then, true to the hype, they actually got a cash offer for the company for over 100 million. That's 1999. And saying no the first time round seemed like the best idea anyone ever had. Because look at the second offer we got through, right?

Piña colada time: sell up, cash in, bask in your own glory.

Only, the CEO got advice from Lehman Brothers (remember them?) to turn the 100 million offer down as 150–180 million was within reach through floatation. Taking that advice was not inevitable. The CEO had a choice. The CEO chose to

---

26 https://www.youtube.com/watch?v=KR8Gu6ZEU2A

say no *yet* again. To take the advice, to give in to greed, to believe that the conditions around him would never change.

'We never got that' recalls Dharm. 'The company was eventually sold in a fire sale.'

Was *that* luck?

Although the external factors were obviously at work, ultimately the things you choose to do and not do are a matter of leadership. Everything, in fact, is about serendipity and proactive decision-making.

Ultimately, events big and small will present you with challenges and opportunities. Those are not the same for everyone. The nature, size, age and prior choices of your business will determine whether the same event is good news or bad. But even an opportunity open to many is not seized by all.

The moment will come. What you do with it, is a people problem.

You may get lucky in that the journey gets easier than you had planned for. Or you may get unlucky and still do well. Or Trygve is right and there is no such thing as luck. No matter which way you look at it, whether something is an opportunity in the first place and your ability to make the most of it equally depend on the business you are in.

So maybe it's time we talked about the fundamentals. The stuff in your control. The ship you have built for yourself and are sailing in when opportunity or disaster strikes.

But first…

Your Call to Action

- Be alert to external factors: when the universe gives you feedback, take it… when serendipity helps you… let it.
- Don't be afraid to pivot to capitalise on a big opportunity.
  And don't be afraid to say no to distractions.
- Knowing the difference between a valuable pivot and a distraction is leadership, not luck.
- Be prepared to say no when it helps you retain focus but be mindful of saying no because you believe in the endless providence of the universe.

Chapter 3

Getting the Basics Right or 'You Just Pointed at All of Me'

What's Wrong with Me?

What is wrong with me, or words to that effect, asked Hiccup? Yes, the guy from *How to Train your Dragon*. Yes, the cartoon.

The weapons master didn't quite respond; he just grunted and gestured at him. A sweeping motion across his entire person. 'You just pointed at all of me', Hiccup cried in despair. Which is what you are about to mutter at me when I list out what I mean by 'the fundamentals' to be discussed in this section of the book.

Here it goes: The first couple of chapters identified things that successful change-makers have or are that are important but largely outside your control (even though being aware of them actually helps towards some control). In the next few chapters, we double down on the things successful change-makers *do*. Which is great. The things we choose to do are ultimately a lot more in our control than character traits, external factors and formative life experiences. The things listed in this section are things you can immediately apply if you so choose.

And there is more good news as *there is* a pattern of key, foundational, fundamental things that you need to think about and get right early on. There is a little list. Isn't that great? Now, a list creates a sense of finality. On the surface, a list sort of

DOI: 10.1201/9781003395577-3

means that everything *not* on this list can wait, which is entirely true. It also means that none of the things on this list can be left for later, which is *absolutely* true.

In fact, one of the common mistakes we see in failed ventures, failed businesses and stalled transformation efforts is *exactly* the belief that one of the below things can be treated as optional and dealt with at some later date and not right out of the gate. And it can't.

That is the lesson of this section: all the below four things need to be done, they need to be done at the same time, they need to be done right and they need to keep getting done. We will dedicate a chapter to each but the main thing to remember here is you don't get to choose. You have to do them all. There is a long list of other things you also need to do. Some at the same time, some can wait for later. Out of that longer list, these are the burning ones. And the winners are:

1. You need to get your product, its target addressable market and their fit right and keep getting it right;
2. You need to get your business model (including my favourite topic of cost to serve and price point mathematics) right for your target market;
3. You need to get the people aspect of the equation right: talent and culture cannot be addressed as an afterthought;
4. You need to work on your process for negotiating trade-offs inside your business as you try to do ambitious work with limited resources in time, cash or team size/talent. This process has to be clear from the outset and not reinvented every time you need to navigate a decision.

   You will never have enough time and money to do everything and hard choices will need to be made. Often. How do you make them? (If your answer was *I am the boss, I call the shots*: keep reading. You are wrong but there is time to realise that).

Looking at this four-item list, you are probably thinking: this is *everything*. And maybe you are not totally wrong.

You are a bit on the exaggerating side. It's not everything-everything. I don't have tech choices and partnership models and fundraising trade-offs and incentive structures and a whole host of other, very important things in there. But I do concede that the fundamentals are *a lot*. Building a successful venture is not easy. And although a lot of people make a lot of mistakes and still somehow survive against the odds, many do everything right and still don't. The fundamentals are necessary but not in themselves enough. But they are in your control.

So it is important, if you are starting on this journey yourself, to at least try and manage all the things in your control. Even if it is a lot. And it comes with a lot of hard work. No silver bullets, no easy answers, but actionable ones, if you choose to listen to the lessons learned by those who did all this work before. More than once.

Before we go into the detail, I need to stress again that the fundamentals are key and they are *all* key. I was tempted to build up to a denouement that says at the end of the fourth section that the four things outlined above are all key, that these here things are fundamental because you don't get to trade-off between them or choose which one to do or do them sequentially: you need to get all of them right and keep ensuring they stay right... mic drops... I exit.

But it's too important a point to save for a dramatic chapter finale. You may miss it. So instead, I will say it a lot throughout this section, in the firm belief that repetition aids learning.

> To succeed in building or changing a business you need to do a series of hard things all at once. You don't get to choose. You need to do them all.

In my research, interviews and, frankly, personal experience, in the pursuit of long-term sustainable success in a business (whether it be young and fledgling, established and thriving or mature and transforming), getting these four things right is non-negotiable and, frankly, the failed businesses, the failed transformations, the failed ventures have almost always made the cardinal error of thinking they can leave one of the four 'for later' when they were working towards the fundamentals.

That's like your five-year-old insisting a potato chip is a vegetable and they don't need to eat their greens. Nice try Tommy. Now eat your peas.

For Some... The Ship Runs Itself

There is a small caveat to this statement. Ok, not very small. But a caveat nonetheless.

Although everyone needs to eat their vegetables and keep an eye on the considerations above, the urgency surrounding some of the work is felt more keenly in newer ventures. An established venture basks in the glory of successful growth achieved by people getting this balance right before, and achieving scale that creates its own challenges, of course, but creates a certain degree of stability. So, although some of the challenges, lessons and opportunities discussed in this book are universal, no matter the type or size of your venture, others have a different kind of urgency, depending on where you sit on the size spectrum. Product market fit for instance is, of course, a consideration for all businesses, but the reality is, it's only on fire for cash-strapped businesses.

Speaking to Arthur Leung, CPO of Shawbrook, who has experienced working for giants such as Barclays and tiny startups when taking their first steps, he observed that once you reach a certain scale, product market fit becomes binary. It is a life or death consideration for early ventures and young companies, but once you have it and manage to achieve scale – and you can't have scale without product market fit – then losing it, although possible, it is gradual and slow.

So, once you have it, product market fit stops being a consideration. 'Even when established entities need to change dramatically and reinvent themselves, it is rarely about *that*' reflects Arthur. You need product market fit to achieve scale, but once you have it, 'you can be hit by a torpedo and still keep going' he reflects. 'For a scaled company such as Shawbrook, there is no worry about product market fit. We are not complacent. We know we need to change and evolve but we also know what our business model is. We can focus on keeping our culture up so that people stay hungry etc. but we don't lose sleep over finding our place in the market. Having product market fit allows you to evolve differently'. It means that the world isn't on fire the same way. Your existence is not at risk day in, day out, but it also means that 'you can't pivot any more. You have your place in the market. You need to make changes and keep things fresh and relevant without changing direction because you have people who love and use your product.'

> Even when established entities need to change dramatically, they rarely need to worry about product market fit.
>
> You need to have that to achieve scale and, once achieved, it is hard to lose.
>
> You can be hit by a torpedo and still keep going.
> **Arthur Leung**

Which is important for two reasons: you need product market fit to get scale (which gets you the prize you started off for: a viable business), but once you have it, you are sort of stuck with it, so to speak. Reinventing yourself is hard. It's also destabilising. So your window for doing it is limited.

'You know the advice you get when considering a job change? That you can change your function,

> You can't change your culture, product and tech all at once. You need some stability.
>
> That's why founding teams become so important: in the absence of product market fit, they provide continuity.
> **Arthur Leung**

industry or geography but not all three at the same time?' reflects Arthur. 'The same applies to companies. You can't change culture and your tech stack while still looking for your product market fit. You need some stability. That's why a founding team becomes more important than the idea, often, because in the absence of product market fit… they offer that continuity.

As you grow and become more established… that changes of course and you can change leadership. But you need to have achieved stability in something for that to be "survivable". Which, funnily enough, is a problem many fintech companies are facing right now. They are coming of age now, having been around long enough to acquire legacy. How they deal with that may give them a taste of their own medicine.'

Eat Your Greens: Product Market Fit 101

So, getting product market fit is the key to achieving scale.

So, to state the bleeding obvious, it is important. And once you have it and have scaled, you are sort of stuck with it. It is not only your shield and your stabiliser but also the millstone around your neck. So what I am trying to say is: focus on it and get it right.

If you are thinking that there was a time, in the not so distant past, where getting scale had nothing to do with product market fit, you would be right. Until recently, you could get *seriously* big with VC money and the right attitude. After a series of burst bubbles, court cases and market contraction, that narrative has shifted considerably. The global economy has been hit by a series of events that mean that everyone, everywhere is experiencing pressure. A period of contraction and introspection has hit the global economy and it has affected everyone and everything. Humans have seen the cost of living shoot through the roof. Companies have seen funding dry out.

> Product market fit is necessary for scale.
>
> In an era of reduced funding and economic contraction, getting this right is existential.

'Things have shifted' observes Liz Lumley, deputy editor of the Banker and affectionately known as 'the Godmother of fintech' across our industry. 'Recently with high interest rates, banks have been making money hand over fist. People will be defaulting on their loans… banks are about to become evil again, in the eyes of the public. But internally also a bank that makes money is a bank where innovation loses its energy, tech goes back to being a cost centre and innovation is no longer sexy.

So banks will spend less…' they will invest less. In proofs of concepts, experiments and early stage ventures. They will also generally do less. Change-makers inside the banks will find themselves going uphill again, finding funding and headspace hard to come by *again*. 'That will have an undeniable effect on the ecosystem' continues Liz. 'There will be a contraction. But those who should survive, will.'

I am not starting the section with this statement to depress you. I am doing it to scare you. Product market fit (i.e. the topic of this section and the one immediately after, on pivots) and a business model that essentially shows you have worked out how to get to profitability should have always been important. But during the heyday of easy funding, they were often relegated as themes secondary to growth. All I am trying to say is: those days are over.

Sunny Days Are Over

Given everything going on in the funding market, getting your product and pricing right are now absolutely non-negotiable. But that absolute urgency only applies to startups, I'm afraid. Because banks and other scaled, 'legacy' financial services institutions already have product market fit, for all their faults. They already have scale and profitability. Change and adaptability are options for additional growth or protection of their current success but they are not binary.

And as Liz rightly points out 'there are certain things that banks are just better at than startups. Diversity is one. Understanding the mechanics of profitability is another. Startups often don't include profitability in the playbook at all. Innovation inside banks was initially the same. Growth was seen as more important. And look at Uber or WeWork.' That model is not working. Party is over.

So for any startup and any new venture inside a bank, this section is key.

'Now we will enter a period of consolidation' continues Liz. 'Things will be bought, consolidated together or copied. The mentality of "your money is safe in the bank" will reappear and there will be a retraction. It doesn't help that some of the neos have had AML issues, folks lost their money in a really public way. So in this new period, banks will be flush...

> Startups often didn't include profitability as a consideration in their playbook.
> Innovation inside banks was often the same.
> That era is over.
> *Liz Lumley*

VCs will be tight... there's trauma ahead. People will have reality handed to them.' As I said, I am actually *trying* to scare you. I hope it's working.

I am trying to scare you into realising that product market fit is extremely important to get right, even if you feel as you are getting started that the pressure to furnish proof points won't touch you for a while. Because, if you feel that, you are wrong. And before you say 'nobody is that naive any more'... as late as April 2024 I received a deck from a founder, who had no technical co-founder or technical knowledge themselves, so they had no way of knowing whether the proposed product could work, what it would take to build it and how complex that would be. I received the deck with an ask to endorse and provide introductions to investors. And when I challenged the founder with the above observations the answer was 'Dropbox didn't have a working prototype when they started and they were fine'.

So, my point is: there are people who still need to hear the basics as we are not learning as fast as we should and part of the reason for that may well be that it has been easy enough to blag things for long enough that we forgot it is not normal.

'Barriers to entry for new players [in the financial services market] have been lowered over the years' observes Maha El Dimachki. Maha heads up the

BIS innovation hub in Singapore, but at the time of our conversation, she was working for the FCA, the UK regulator and her vantage point remains second to none. 'Money has been available and "digital" comes with lower overheads so it is easier to enter the market. Regulation has, of course, also helped with this. This has been a deliberate move on behalf of the regulator: creating a space for startups to creatively disrupt the market. That doesn't mean that everyone can scale up though: there is a whole raft of different things that impact viability and success. In the digital age you can scale at the blink of an eye if the ingredients are there but what those ingredients are is the million dollar question. Now, the focus is shifting. The market wants to see economic growth. Contributions to the economy, how do you achieve that?'

The consensus seems to be universal: start by solving a real problem.

Find a Problem Big Enough to Be Real

In order to build a viable business, you don't just need product market fit in general, but 'product market fit for a problem that is big enough to be real' says OakNorth's Valentina Kristensen.

OakNorth knew what problem it was there to solve from day one: the lending needs of smaller/ earlier businesses. *How* they went about solving it was multifaceted and kept evolving. Some ideas worked the first time, others didn't. The market they were trying to 'fit' was known, is what I am trying to say. The product was tweaked to get the fit right. That is normal. There is no one

> If we build a startup that can become an incumbent…
>
> A business that will still be here after we have left this earth… isn't that something?
>
> To do that… you need to solve a problem that is big enough to be real.
> **Valentina Kristensen**

way to get your product built, and it will never be linear. That said, that there is a right way round and a wrong way round when it comes to building a product. Starting with the product you wish to build and then looking for a market is not only extremely appealing but also very risky. Starting with the problem? This is the right way round. Because starting with the problem will guide your feature development.

For instance, for OakNorth 'rental payments being part of your credit score: that is a no-brainer idea. It fits what we are trying to do. Our mission is to lend to entrepreneurs differently' so everything that fits in with that and promotes that can stay. The problem statement becomes a powerful filter. If you have it. 'There are a lot of fintech businesses out there' muses Valentina 'where it's not obvious what problem they are solving.' Or for whom, as we already heard from Geophy who felt really strongly about the problem of data asymmetry but the people they proposed to solve it *for* actually didn't see it as a problem at all. So make sure the problem you are solving is indeed a problem. And not only that, but a problem big enough to have a market big enough to sustain a business.

Then focus.

Continues Valentina, 'it is important to not get distracted: you need to make your proposition 10x better than the alternative, to create a competitive moat as we want to be the de facto choice for scaleup businesses seeking debt finance. If we can build a fintech that becomes an incumbent, isn't that something? It is better for us, better for the customer... if we achieve this and build a business that will be here long after we, our team, have left this earth, isn't that an amazing thing?'.

Yes it is. It is amazing.

What it isn't, is accidental. 'Our founders wanted to build a business that solved a real problem' continues Valentina. 'Of course we were very scrappy at the beginning. We spent an average of 35k on marketing every year until 2022 (we hired our first marketing director and started building a marketing function in October 2021 – six years after launch). But you know what we had? Product market fit and a customer-first mentality. Entrepreneurs recommended us to each other.'

You are nowhere if the people you are solving a problem for don't rate your solution. But equally, you are nowhere if the people you are doing this for change, their needs evolve and you don't. Getting product market fit is hard. Retaining product market fit is also hard. It's not a one and done thing until you achieve serious scale.

It Starts Hard. Then It Gets Harder

'All of it is hard' reflects Ken Johnstone, Chief Product Officer at Mettle. 'And the longer you succeed, the more is at stake and the pressure keeps building until you really break through to self-sustainability. It starts hard and gets harder and that is as it should be.'

For the avoidance of doubt, I am still trying to scare you. But it's the good, healthy, I-can-learn-from-this type of fear I am going for. Product market fit is not an elusive concept. It is a very specific pursuit, and it requires intent:

> When you know what business you are in and have a strategy, you realise that every sector is busy and you need to find what makes you competitive.
>
> Once you have that focus, to move forward, you need organisational congruence: everyone needs to be pointing in the same direction.
>
> **Ken Johnstone**

'The genesis story for Mettle is that digital banks started popping up and the RBS/NatWest leadership felt that *we should do something similar to help lower the cost of customer acquisition*' reflects Ken. It was not a technology play, at first. It was a go to market play leveraging technology. 'This decision to *not* start focusing on the tech was very conscious' continues Ken. 'We decided to focus on solving real problems for real clients'. The tech stack to be used in pursuit of those solutions was an important but secondary consideration.

'We also set ourselves up differently. We knew that we needed to align on compliance and policy but we were a bank within a bank from the get-go and we were separate. And the focus on the problem rather than tech was clear in the choices we made: we used consultancies to get off the ground early. We hired externally. We set off clearly looking for our competitive angle. When you know what business you are in and have a strategy, you realise that every sector is busy and you need to find what makes you competitive. And once you have that focus, to move forward, you need organisational congruence: everyone needs to be pointing in the same direction. You can't do everything. You need to focus. And you need the whole organisation to be focused.

We decided to focus on customer engagement as our first proof point. When we had proven product market fit, then we could scale.

To do that you need to focus as the pressure to be 'all the things' is always there. You need to actively *not* give into it. When we got confident about product market fit, the cultural transition to *ok we can now scale* was hard. It meant deciding to delay certain cool things that were on the roadmap… it meant changing gears. The next phase was starting to monetise. Hard again.

Moving away from the place where every customer is a cost to every customer being a source of revenue. We were conscious we had to forego revenue for a while and now we were changing gears and coming out of that phase. We knew we had a solid product and saw the first signs of revenue coming in so we were on the next phase of the journey.'

> You cannot do everything. The pressure to be 'all the things' is always there. You need to actively not give into it.
> **Ken Johnstone**

Product market fit is exactly that: a journey. Getting one step right only guarantees that you can get to the next step. It doesn't guarantee that you will get to the destination of being a scaled business. The journey itself requires focus and intent, and it requires you realising *when* each phase is done *enough* for you to move forward. In itself a hard thing especially when you are passionate about the problem you are solving. Perfection is always tempting. But being realistic about when to double down and when to move to the next step is key.

Retaining Fit in an Evolving Market

Remember in the last chapter, when Jasper from PensionBee was describing how the pandemic altered the way their customers approached the questions around their pensions… and the time in their lives when they may do that? Obviously the pandemic was a dramatic event, but shifts come all the time and most often don't signpost themselves. But staying in tune with your customers' needs is what product market fit actually looks like. And inside PensionBee there are people whose job it is to do just that.

The Beekeepers (I know I already gushed over how much I love this name but… really… I double-dare you to try and find a better name for a team of customer success managers) need to stay in tune with the demographic they are here to serve. 'Digital adoption moves extremely quickly' notes Jasper. 'Adaptation to digital tooling is accelerating. Trust, however, moves to a different timeline.

That is slower.

For a consumer brand, realising those two different timing curves is the most important thing. Trust and inertia cannot be sped up. We are on the right path to becoming a primary provider. But we need to give consumers the time they need. If you got pensions to transfer, you want to do some more research before you do. I would… and we see our customers doing exactly that.

You can observe that behaviour as part of the onboarding/sign-up journey. They check the company's performance and reputation.'

That's what product market fit looks like: *caring* to know that, respecting that. And doing something about that. In that order.

So knowing what problem you are solving (check), who you are solving it for (check) and what other options they have (check), how the people you seek to help are changing (check, they may be on an accelerated digital savviness journey but they will trust you when they trust you) and giving them the proof points they need (check). Each step is distinct and interlocked and all of it is an intentional journey. Nobody stumbles into this. Contrary to the popular stories of geniuses in garages innovating in a void in the time it takes to play an uplifting power ballad over a montage of toil but no market verification.

> Digital adoption moves extremely quickly. Trust moves to a different timeline. That is slower.
>
> For a consumer brand, realising that is the most important thing. Trust and inertia cannot be sped up. We are on the right path to becoming a primary provider. But we need to give consumers the time they need.
>
> **Jasper Martens**

Jasper continues: for a consumer brand being a *recognisable* brand helps. People seeing TV and billboard ads. Seeing our name on the front of a football shirt[1]: it creates emotional certainty. '*These guys are not going away.*'

PensionBee's early customers were the older end of the digitally savvy demographic. That's a solid proof point but too narrow for a B2C brand. 'Once we were on TV, the average age of engaged customers went up steadily. As we started advertising on commuter rail, daytime TV, we could see the average age continue to rise. And there is a direct correlation in real time. You advertise during the Great British Bake-Off[2], you need to increase server capacity that evening. We see those spikes. But we also know there are certain parts of the journey that you have to let mature (such as the number of consolidated pots, for instance). You can't speed it up and that is why my job is so interesting. Because it has changed: it is now a different ballgame.' Hold onto this thought, by the way. We will be needing it later.

Product Market Fit Hacks #1

Find Your Problem. *Then* Solve It

The hack is sales traction, of course. Duh.

But how much is enough to say you have product market fit? When do you call it? In Chapter 1, we came across Bond AI's Uday Akkaraju who feels that product market fit isn't the right metric for him but rather whether the problem he set out to solve… is solved. Or at least smaller than when he started. Although it is hard to measure this, the first big question about product market fit is actually whether the problem you are addressing is real enough, large enough and whether you understand it enough. Although it is absolutely possible to make a lot of money with passing fads, that is more likely to work in fast fashion and consumer goods. Less so when technology

> When do you know you have product market fit?
> When the people the problem is being solved *for*, find that the solution solves their problem. *And* are willing to pay for it.

---

1 PensionBee sponsored a football club known as 'the Bees'… yes yes, before the sponsorship. That was the whole point. https://www.pensionbee.com/press/pensionbee-2-year-deal-with-brentford#:~:text=As%20the%20Official%20Sleeve%20Sponsor,the%20growth%20of%20these%20teams

2 For those not living in the UK or not watching broadcast TV… the Great British Bake-Off is a competitive baking TV show (at the time of writing it was in its 15th year) that has over 4 million tuning in routinely for many of its episodes.

 Yes… I know. Competitive baking. It is, it turns out, a thing. And evidently it has product market fit.

needs to be designed, built and deployed. So a real problem, basic as it sounds, is a key starting point. And, to find a real problem that isn't being successfully addressed already, in our saturated markets, you need to look for a hard problem or a new problem. Something only addressable through the art of the recently possible or something very thorny and hard to do.

'We don't worry about the problem we are solving going away' reflects Radish's Nektarios Liolios. Their mission is to facilitate access to lending for communities that are historically underserved because they are considered risky, unprofitable or their needs are not understood. 'We are currently working with ex cons on ways we can give small loans to break the chain of reoffending. Imagine, someone comes out of prison… relationships often have broken down and everything they need to do once they are out *needs* money… getting a job requires an address… even seeing their kids requires an address. For which you need a job. To get a job you often need some money to get started. For instance £800 would enable you to go on a course to become a lorry driver or buy a set of knives to start out as a cook. The chances of reoffending reduce drastically if you can get into employment. This is not a popular problem. But it is a huge problem. For the people coming out of prison and for society. We want to solve this.

And *yes* we need to find ways of measuring impact as well as building a sustainable business but now, a year in, we are measuring success for each stage. We need funding to get to our regulatory application and we need to get a first loan out to someone. The day we do that? That's success. The day when a gay couple can afford surrogacy thanks to a loan we facilitated? That's success.'

A real problem. Big enough to matter. And even that is not enough. Because finding it doesn't give you product market fit, as we already said. Sadly Radish is no

> We do not worry about the problem we are trying to solve going away: We are trying to solve a problem that is huge and most won't touch it because it is considered risky and unprofitable.
> **Nektarios Liolios**

more. The problem they were trying to solve is still very much there, waiting to be tackled. So when the next Radish comes along and tries to tackle the same big problem, when will they know they have product market fit?

It will be when the people the problem is being solved for, find that the solution solves their problem *and* the economics of the entire operation stack up.

To get there, changes and pivots may be needed (I am not speaking about Radish, that's everyone), and we will get to that in the next section. But solving a real problem for people who want a solution is the first test.

Because what happened to Teun and his team during the early days of Geophy is not an uncommon story for many early fintech innovations: creative technologists looked at the world and found inefficiencies and redundancies and deployed solutions of great elegance to address them. And flopped. Or hit a wall. Or ran out of steam. Or were met with deafening silence.

Because the people who were expected to pay for those solutions were the very people monetising the inefficiency. Or, less dramatically, the people this was for would welcome a solution but wouldn't necessarily pay for one. So the problem you are solving needs to be a problem that the folks you expect to pay for it want solved enough to be willing to pay.

The good news is that getting this wrong isn't terminal. We will be talking about pivots soon. Which is what good entrepreneurs do when product market fit proves elusive or not quite right. But realising you need to shift is often uncomfortable. Because you *want* your original idea to work and that passion may actually become an obstacle.

'Someone, in the early days, gave me £15k to run an MVP for GFA Exchange' recalls Joel Blake.

He took it. Of course he took it.

He was so passionate about the work and here is someone willing to back him. *Of course* he took the money.

The next step should be the easy one now: he had the idea, he had the passion, he had some money. Now he just had to put it together. This should be easy, only it wasn't.

> It is not enough to find a problem or inefficiency, especially if the people you expect to pay for your service benefit from the inefficiency.
>
> Find a problem your customer wants solved. Not one you enjoy solving.

'It failed miserably. *Because* I was so passionate about the problem I wanted to solve, I thought I had validated it, so I didn't spend any time *actually* validating it. Plus I didn't take time to unpack what I was doing in terms of what it meant in the tech space. Someone wanted to take a punt on me. The money was on the table. I should have said give me three months to work out the kinks and come back to you. But I didn't. This individual and I met serendipitously, our values resonated and he was willing to back me. He mentored me and said *I love what you do, here's some money to get started*. I took it. And it failed. But in that process I worked out the kinks. I worked out the things that needed to be worked out and that made me realise the importance of market validation being woven into your process.' So he didn't fail. He just learned the hard way that product market fit isn't about disruption or vision alone. It's about finding something people are willing to pay for. Solving a problem for the benefit of your customers and your business.

Finding a Groove Is Not Just for Startups

I know I said that product market fit isn't an existential concern for corporates and I stand by that. But that doesn't mean that they don't have the opportunity to seize upon a moment, a changing need or an opportunity to create something new that answers that need. It is not frequent but it happens. It is why ING, to borrow their phrase, succeeds or learns but doesn't fail. And it may look like a product adjustment, a new venture or a twist on something very familiar like the bank branch.

I don't often have occasion to swell with pride as a Greek citizen so please indulge me here for a moment while I wax lyrical for a bit. Because the first time I walked into Piraeus Bank's accessibility branch, I had to go through the whole 'there is something in my eye, I am not crying', routine.

Banks the world over are closing branches at a steady, irreversible rate. Banks are also *terrible* at thinking about 'outliers'. Users, communities and behaviours that are not statistically significant as profitability drivers are almost always an afterthought.

Inside banks products are designed and problems solved for *average* behaviours. A bit like how safety features in cars are designed for 'average' bodies which turns out it means men's bodies[3]. Or a world designed for bodies with no accessibility constraints. That is sadly true in most places and in my native Greece, it is blatant: ramps are rare and often blocked by illegally parked cars. The pathways for the blind built on pavements often lead into walls or trees. It is dangerous to say the least to try and navigate our cities if you have the slightest impairment. So disability becomes invisible in Greece because public spaces are inaccessible so people don't use them. By making our public spaces inhospitable for people who are partially sighted or mobility impaired, we effectively perpetrate a huge injustice. So where does banking come in?

So glad you asked.

'It is common practice across all banks worldwide to shrink their branch network and hence reduce their operational costs especially as digital literacy is thriving' comments Piraeus Bank's George Kostopoulos. But what about those who are not digitally savvy? 'Especially those customers aged above 60'.

> We have video-tellers trained in Greek Sign Language, braille signage, lower displays and booths helping wheelchair users perform their transactions with ease and extended working hours.
>
> The results? Ten e-branches have attracted more than 25,000 customers each, decongesting traditional branches with a significant lower operating cost.
> *George Kostopoulos*

> When looking for product market fit, looking at those not serviced by others is always an opportunity. So, in a digital economy, what does servicing those excluded look like?

---

3 If you are interested have a look at https://www.theguardian.com/lifeandstyle/2019/feb/23/truth-world-built-for-men-car-crashes and if you want more, pick up Caroline Criado Perez's exceptional book *Invisible Women: Exposing Data Bias in a World Designed for Men* (published by Henry B Adams, 2019).

What happens to those who are visually impaired? Or need more help navigating their options than can be provided by self-service?

Branch closures are 'causing exclusion from daily transactions and serious fraud-related risks. So a "golden mean" has to be found in order to balance digital banking and the traditional approach'.

How do you do that?

'In Piraeus Bank we analysed and researched the landscape, trying to identify the special needs of the customers (new and current), to build the best possible branch that will be able to offer specialised banking services in a modern and evolving environment. Moreover, we took into account that about 10% of the Greek population are persons with disabilities, whilst even more face mobility limitations either permanently or at some point in their lives (the elderly, someone with an injury or while pregnant).

Notably, the World Health Organization (WHO) describes barriers for the disabled as being more than just physical obstacles and defines barriers as: "Factors in a person's environment that, through their absence or presence, limit functioning and create disability. These include aspects such as: a physical environment that is not accessible, lack of relevant assistive technology, negative attitudes of people towards disability, services, systems and policies that are either non-existent or that hinder the involvement of all people with a health condition in all areas of life".

With all these aspects in mind, the redesign of a traditional branch to a more modern and accessible one was not an easy task. So far, in Piraeus bank we created ten e-branches that combine digital services, self-services machines, advanced accessibility services and extended working hours. For example, there are no tellers at this type of branch, but colleagues who can help you use the technology or have a consultation with you in a private nook or room to give a better environment to work. There are screens that black out when you connect headphones and prompt

> The accessibility branches catered to segments of the population who normally don't have access and did so with lower operating costs than traditional branches.

the system that you are visually impaired and video-tellers who are trained in Greek Sign Language in order to support people with hearing problems. In addition, the Video Teller System provides braille signage for visually impaired customers and is placed at a lower level; helping the wheelchair users perform their transactions with ease.

The results were remarkable and these ten e-branches have managed to attract a significant number of customers making more than 25,000 transactions per month for each e-branch, decongesting, at the same time, the traditional branches with a significantly lower operating cost while, the customers are simultaneously becoming trained in this phygital (physical+digital) environment.

So far, the combination of innovative thinking and cutting-edge technology helped us surpass major obstacles and drove Piraeus Bank towards the next phase. This was the launch of a new branch model that combines state-of-the-art self-service machinery and high-quality advisory services. In addition, these new branches incorporate assistive technology for people with visual, hearing and mobility disabilities. Indicatively, the customers with visual disabilities that use an ATM can perform all the basic transactions thanks to a special software installed, which offers audio guidance when the user plugs in a headphone.

Piraeus Bank is aiming to bridge the gap that digitalisation brings in certain customer types, enhancing at the same time accessibility and inclusiveness. These two factors are core to the Bank's strategy as they bring together the human aspect and the digital aspect, resulting in a "phygital" approach towards the offering of products and services to Piraeus Bank customers. This firm commitment is established through the expansion of the Virtual Teller System network to more branches, in order to serve more people with disabilities and tackle digital illiteracy. In addition, Piraeus Bank's management decided to change all credit and debit cards and print new ones that incorporate braille signage stating which card is debit and which one is credit, making the payment procedure easier for people with visual impairments. Piraeus Bank's main objective is to spread the message of inclusivity throughout Greek society and raise awareness, as the new cards are issued to all customers.'

I am not crying. You are crying.

Or you may be irate. You may think this isn't the right way of solving the problem at all. To which I say: great. You have found a problem big enough to warrant a solution and if you think you can do better, then welcome to your entrepreneurial journey.

Product Market Fit Hacks #2

Everything Has a Price. But What Is It?

If the story above didn't give you the warm and fuzzies, there's something wrong with you. But I hope you noticed that the endeavour wasn't about the warm and fuzzies. There was a business driver at work: nice and inclusive as it all was, it has lowered operating costs and increased servicing efficiency

> You cannot have product market fit without product-pricing fit.
> If your pricing doesn't work, you don't have product market fit.
> **Simon Merchant**

across the branch network. The initiative has financial benefits or, let's face it, it would just be a marketing play. And although it has marketing value (and that doesn't make it shallow or fake, it just makes it realistic), that's not all there is to it.

In fact, it could be a marketing play and that would not be a bad thing. Rabobank and ABN AMRO in the Netherlands organise home visits for the elderly. That solution neither scales nor does it support increasing digital literacy. It just supports a demographic that, frankly, isn't growing. That support may have zero financial upside, *but* it means a lot to customers and employees. And that is not nothing. It has considerable albeit non-monetary value. But the accessibility branch network for Piraeus isn't just marketing and its value is monetary as well. It is a commercially viable decision that solves a problem. And that commercial part is key. Because without it, your product is a nice gesture that you can afford to make as you fund it from profits elsewhere, or a very expensive hobby at worst, if said profits don't yet exist.

So, getting the solution right is not done until you are monetising it. Which means that a big part of getting the solution right is pricing it right.

'You cannot have market fit without pricing fit. You don't have fit if the price isn't working. Your unit economics have to work' agrees Simon Merchant. 'Over the last ten years the VC world has lost the plot and forgot that basic fact' he reflects, thinking about all the businesses that were declared unicorns, runaway successes without having reached either profitability or a clear understanding of how to get there. 'But that was never the real world. In the context of 200 years of investment, this represents ten years of anomaly. Businesses founded and funded in the period of free money with unit economics that made no sense will suffer as that period is over.'

The economics need to work in a very fundamental way: if you have found a problem that is real and the people you are solving it for want it but don't want to pay for it, or only way to pay for it less than it costs you to deliver your solution, you don't have product market fit no matter how many people are willing to use your services. Besides. Getting user traction can be misleading.

> If you have found a problem that is real and the people you are solving it for want it… but don't want to pay for it… or only want to pay for it less than it costs you to deliver it… then you don't have product market fit.

'In a market like India' reflects Lizzie Chapman 'with a huge population you could fairly easily launch something that finds a million people who need it before long. That doesn't prove product market fit. And you don't have product market fit, no matter how many users you have, until you have pricing market fit'.

And that is not just for India. That is a universal fact: if you can't get the pricing right, you don't have a product. 'If you think about it' continues Lizzie 'the Goldman-Apple breakup isn't about product market fit but about pricing[4]. At Zest

---

4 Lizzie and I were speaking in November 2023 when this news was fresh. If you don't remember that this partnership existed, let alone that it ended, here it all is: the greatest PR coup in finance ultimately played out in terms of pricing, margins and cumulative operating cost considerations https://www.cnbc.com/2023/11/28/apple-is-trying-to-unwind-its-goldman-sachs-credit-card-partnership.htmlhttps://www.bloomberg.com/news/newsletters/2023-12-03/apple-to-drop-goldman-sachs-for-apple-card-chase-bank-is-ideal-replacement-lppjbe7z

we got product love early, and then we got bank love early because we gave them a solution that was so easy to implement. We were good at making this easy for them.

We realised in hindsight that we were good at this'. So what went wrong? Because everything here suggests Zest was getting all the ticks in all the boxes. And yet... Zest couldn't make ends meet. Why?

Arguably because they were early in the journey and the curve and they were taking the hits and getting the learnings for the rest of us to benefit from. 'During the time of struggle' recalls Lizzie 'we put our prices up and didn't see impact on customer volumes'. That is a learning that would have been useful earlier perhaps but it is a daring thing to do, putting your prices up. Especially when you don't have to because you have investor cash.

In a very different geography, an interviewee subject who was

> If your growth is backed by investors, what they consider a growth metric becomes what you measure. So it defines what you do.
>
> When that tune changes, you hope you are given enough time to adjust to a new reality.

facing similar existential pressures and asked to remain unnamed had this to say about pricing. 'We had investor cash to subsidise growth and the investors themselves looking at adoption numbers not profitability as their metric of choice. When that tune changed, it was too late to turn things around but we put our price up by 50% and clients didn't complain. We hadn't done it sooner because it hadn't seemed to matter. But had we done it, it may have saved us.'

These two companies are not alone in finding the hard way that clients are often prepared to pay more, or considerably less than where you have pitched your business. And finding that out early is the only way to survive the lesson. 'I would advise now' reflects Lizzie 'think about your pricing if you think you already have product market fit, especially in credit. In credit pricing *is* the product'.

Wise words. But getting the pricing right is hard. Balancing what it costs you to get your service to market and fuel your growth... what your customers are willing and able to pay and how to add profit in the mix is hard enough and when you are launching a service or product that can't be benchmarked against incumbents, the work is harder.

Putting a Price on Things

'We had no choice from the get go but to be profitable' is Monika Liikamaa's answer to my question about how they approached their pricing. 'We set out taking a different route into this world and we intentionally set out to build a business that would survive on its own and scale'. In other words: not for them the ridiculously subsidised pricing for early adoption that some of their competitors used to lure customers.

But that is not all.

'We were very mindful from the start of what it took to succeed' continues Monika. So, they didn't have heaps of free money to fund growth (partly because, as I am sure you recall, they were offered it and turned it down knowing full well it wasn't free and it came with a heavy price to be paid in the future). So they were not able to fund a low price like many VC-backed firms do, to achieve early traction. But more to the point, they didn't need to mess around to find out what was actually a low price and what would the right price be. They knew what the service needed to cost.

> When it came to pricing we had an unfair advantage: we had done this before so we knew what it cost to build and therefore knew how to price.
> **Denise Johannson**

'We knew what was critical for success and at which phase of the journey it was critical', continues Monika. 'We had the unfair advantage of having a background in this' says Denise Johannson 'we knew what it would cost to build and what it would cost to run. The headcount we needed etc.'.

'We saw VCs inject money in competitors' recalls Monika 'they used that money to try and beat us on price. They have now been bankrupted and there is no more free money.'

I am still trying to scare you, in case you are wondering.

Thankfully, this is one of the many ways in which being on your second rodeo helps: you know what it costs to build the thing so you are better informed in pricing the thing.

But what happens if you haven't done it before? Or if the thing you are doing hasn't been done before?

Thinking back, Gareth Richardson recalls consulting firms having a go at Thought Machine for its pricing strategy compared to the incumbents: 'We had consulting firms telling us we are killing the market. And we knew that we needed to scale for [our price point] to play out. But we also wanted transparent pricing. Charge per account, flat licence rates as that will bring the longest term value. Ideally play for the long term, which in core banking is 25 years+.

This model doesn't work without investors willing to fund that period towards product maturity and until the banks are ready to put volumes through.

With hindsight, it has had a somewhat drawbridge effect for us. Timing had a part to play here.

In the current market, Investors are no longer willing or able to fund that kind of strategy. That plays against anyone entering this market now in the way we did.'

There are two parts to this that are important.

The first is that, no matter how you price, there is a window of time where you are not yet profitable but heading towards profitability. For Thought Machine (and all core banking players) that window is bigger and longer as you are building a very big thing, selling it through slow sales cycles to people who usually tread cautiously. If you choose to price low then your break-even is possibly further away. It may be intentional but that doesn't make it easier.

> No matter how you price, if you are new there will be a time when you are loss-making. How long that period is has to balance your cash reserves (how long you can realistically wait) with the price that you believe is right to clinch product market fit.

And however you choose to price, the proof point of product-pricing fit comes after product-market fit. *How soon after* is something you need to be cognizant of.

The second thing is that, just as product market fit doesn't emerge fully formed: it comes in stages, as Ken Johnstone already described and it may require pivots and big changes as we will see shortly, so does pricing.

'Product market fit was never a problem for us' continues Gareth. 'Product pricing fit is an evolving conversation. Where we are now (speaking in Q1 2023), I expect we will go through some dislocation as the industry gets weaned off free cash and meanwhile our biggest challenge is to continue to increase the big banks' confidence to move all their inventory across to our system. An initial go-live is one thing, but moving the whole bank to the cloud has proven to require a larger build of confidence at the bank C-level than we expected, which changes the time horizon and in turn affects our pricing and funding dynamics. Of course with transparent and equitable pricing, your pricing mechanism may be the same across all clients but the scale of each bank is very different and realistically not many have x million customers in the first place. So finding the right product pricing fit will continue to be a journey for a while yet.'

And therein lies the lesson.

Getting the price right is a journey. To get it right, you have to go on the journey and by that I don't mean you have to put one foot in front of the other and hope for the best. I mean you have to set out to intentionally test your assumptions out and find the answers you don't already know.

You start with formulating some hypotheses about market acceptance, reflects Kelvin Tan.

You benchmark against competitors, of course. You assess what the baselines are in different geographies. *Then* you go out there and validate these hypotheses.

So far that may sound sensible but it is quite a lot of work, by the way. And Kelvin isn't even done.

'Validating these hypotheses, for us, involved determining the right pricing, working backward to establish costs, accounting for custom pricing in various geographies. If we overestimate market appetite in lucrative regions, adjusting the cost structure becomes essential to protect margins. This can involve finding cost-effective methods and optimising the balance between cost and technology.

While benchmarking against competitors is an approach you may choose to employ, testing pricing strategies in the market, gauging reactions and evolving based on conversations and feedback is crucial and non-negotiable. Adapting to market responses is an ongoing process, acknowledging that there are no definitive answers. Testing assumptions is imperative.'

Kelvin Tan, CEO of audax

Audax is a digital banking solutions provider enabling banks to modernise for scale at speed & pursue advanced digital banking models, including Banking-as-a-Service and Embedded Finance.

Previously Managing Director at Standard Chartered nexus.

Not assuming you know best is always excellent advice but the reality of Kelvin's approach is twofold: you need to do the work to build the hypotheses (no finger in the air for the love of god) and then you need to test and *adjust* accordingly which means inevitably that if you have overestimated the market's appetite for your product or the market's willingness to part with as much cash as you need, then you need to adjust your cost base. You need to put in the time, do the work, allow your hypotheses to be challenged. Allow yourself to be wrong.

That part, by the way, is where most startups fail.

'Ultimately, businesses fail because they run out of money, not because they made a wrong move' reflects Antony Jenkins. And how do you run out of money? By spending more than you make. Captain Obvious reporting for duty here, but if you recall the heady days of the .com era and the early, fat years of fintech VC investment, spending more than you made was how the cool kids did it.

> To get pricing right you need to make hypotheses… benchmark… and validate.
>
> Once you determine the right pricing, you work backwards to establish costs. If you overestimate market appetite, you need to change your cost structure to protect margin.
>
> You do not start with your cost.
> *Kelvin Tan*

And ultimately, isn't that what venture capital is for?

The answer is of course: no. Venture capital is there to start you off when you don't have revenue and fuel growth faster than you could organically achieve. But the idea is that the revenue curve will catch up. It often doesn't. Either because your product is not as needed as you thought it was. Or because your pricing is wrong for your market. Or because you got comfortable spending money you didn't earn and got carried away.

Understanding the price your market is willing to pay for your product goes hand in hand with controlling your cost base. Understanding your cost to serve at a unit economics level and keeping it clean and under control. Of course, in financial services, the economics rarely work unless you have scale. But you shouldn't strive for scale without understanding or control over your unit costs and hope it all comes out in the wash. Because it won't.

Product Market Fit Hack #3
Go Big or Go Home

Solving a problem for a market that wants it solved, and doing so in a way that the market responds to *and* is willing to pay what you need them to for it, is not an easy feat and it is, all things told, a solid start. But it is not enough and you are not home free yet.

Because, in financial services, no product or service can perform economically without scale. How big that scale needs to be depends on what you are solving for, your cost base and price. But whatever the benchmark is, scale is needed. And the danger of losing that early 'fit' as you grow is real and present.

> Keep your product simple. Don't get carried away.
> Bells and whistles are not needed unless you are in the bells and whistles business.

'With hindsight' reflects Lizzie Chapman 'our best products were the least *producty*. Seamless, frictionless, white-labelled. No product there, really. Being intellectually honest with yourself is key: we thought we were product geniuses. But the customer doesn't care. Simple works. Don't get carried away.

We had a winning product from the start.

As we scaled, we kept needing to evolve the story: you can't say to investors *the product works, give me money to get to break-even*. And we had foreign investors going *Klarna did this or that* so we complicated our product in order to emulate European ideas that were not fit for India in order to be able to raise the next round. At the end we chopped everything excess, everything that had been developed in this manner' and, if you recall, they increased the price. 'We became profitable at the very end. But it was too late.

Having early product market fit may have been a problem after all. If it had been harder, maybe we would have come at it with more humility. Maybe that early traction is not a good thing' says Lizzie. A cautionary note from one of the industry's best: if you have found the formula of what you are solving for, hold onto it in its simplest form. Scale doesn't need bells and whistles unless you are in the bells and whistles business.

And you may well be. But even then, you should take Lizzie's advice and not over-complicate your solution once you've worked it out. You don't need to be all the things. Doing more doesn't make you bigger. Doing a little of a lot may prove early traction but doesn't translate. Scale most definitely isn't the inevitable concomitant of traction: it is its own animal and it requires focus.

> Don't over-complicate your solution once you've worked it out.
> Don't try to do all the things and be in all places at once.
> Scale isn't the inevitable concomitant of traction: it is its own animal.

By the way, you don't need to be in all the places, either. While we are at it. Growth and scale inevitably bring with it questions of geographic expansion (or cross vertical expansion). You can't fake it till you make it so not doing all the things on the way to achieving scale is important. The adage of 'if you build it, they will come' doesn't always work. Don't build the bones of the animal you hope to become and hope the flesh will come. Focus. Don't try to do or be everything. Not trying to be in all the places as once is *as* important. Even if you could or eventually should.

One of the folks interviewed for this book was in the process of cutting one quarter of their workforce when we spoke and would rather stay anonymous for reasons anyone who has led a redundancy round would sympathise with. 'FTE reduction' is a process that, no matter how you do it, is hard and harrowing on the people, ugly for the organisation and noticeable to the market. No matter how well you execute it, there is fall-out: practical, emotional and reputational.

'There are no two ways about it' he reflected (asking to not be named). 'We got cocky. We had gotten our calls right for the first 3 or 4 years, product success in our home market came fairly easy. We raised a large series C in the name of geographic expansion because we knew VCs liked that. We opened offices in three geographies *at the same time* and… let's just say we got it wrong. 18 months on, zero sales across the new offices and dipping sales in our home market, culture tensions and a cost black hole. We are retracting now. Closing the offices, firing everyone [in the new geographies] and licking our wounds for now and the home market will be our focus whether we like it or not, as that money is now gone.'

So it pays to think about these things before you go all in. Be more Kelvin, essentially. Take the time to work things out and trust the numbers.

For Kelvin, the problem audax is coming in to solve is unaddressed complexity. The complexity of emerging technological capabilities and associated business models that many financial institutions refused to address as it emerged, and now there is too much happening too fast. And that problem is huge, it is global and it is pressing.

'I firmly believe that financial institutions will require new
digital frameworks alongside their
existing ones, complemented by
fresh talent possessing the skills
to navigate the evolving landscape
of technology. Following 15 years
of financial institutions operating

> Your target addressable market (TAM)
> needs to be big enough that, even
> if you only capture a fraction of it,
> that fraction is big enough for your
> business to succeed.

with conventional technological infrastructure, combined with the need for banks
to enable scaled digital banking models, an opportunity has arisen to monetise what
we developed with Standard Chartered nexus' reflects Kelvin Tan, who was MD of
nexus inside Standard Chartered Bank and is now CEO of audax, the next generation of thinking in this space.

'Audax is designed to cater to other banks and financial institutions seeking to
modernise their technology for scale, which is already gaining early traction. The
Total Addressable Market (TAM) for our venture is potentially immense, estimated
at USD$440 billion till 2030 (BCG & QED Investors, 2023). Even if we were to
confine our focus to Southeast Asia and the Middle East, where there are 400 banks,
we have made significant strides. In the eight months since our market entry, we
have established a pipeline with over 50 banks expressing interest.

What sets audax apart is our fully integrated offering. While we may compete with vendors operating at different levels of the technology stack, there are
few comprehensive solutions available in the market. Of those, only a handful have
demonstrated success with tier 1 banks in multiple jurisdictions. We possess the
credibility of having delivered for an established institution and the speed and flexi-
bility of a fintech, positioning us uniquely in the market.'

Is that big enough for ya?

Thought so.

Things You Didn't Know You Needed

So, you need a problem that is real enough for a market that is big enough. Got it so
far? Because we are not done as *big* doesn't automatically translate to 'willing to buy'.
So, even though your TAM may be huge in potential, if your potential customers
are used to poor service, fewer options or have already some commitments solving
the problem in a different way, you have work ahead. Also, if what you are doing is
not how things were done before, you may need to bring the horse to water so to
speak. In that sense, achieving scale may be less about your ability to deliver, and
more about your ability to build demand. Which is a step towards sales traction but
may not look like it up front.

In fact, creating demand for something that didn't exist before you came up with it may look like forgoing short-term revenue which, let me tell you, is the most counter-intuitive thing of all when you are building a business.

'As recently as 2022' notes Joel Blake reflecting on his own business 'I could see a lack of conversation between and within banks around inclusion. Or rather, the conversation that was happening still had a competitive edge to it. So when we

> I made a conscious decision not to make money there and then: instead I brought the conversation into the room to create a longer term solution.
> **Joel Blake**

got a chance to sign a deal with NatWest for £120k I requested that we do it as partly a charitable donation: we would use the funding to create a *not for profit* body for the industry to start addressing this topic.

To get to that point, I was given access to the board, I was given the opportunity to bring the conversation into the room and I made a conscious decision not to try and turn this into a consulting opportunity. I made a conscious decision *not* to make money right here, from this access even though I could have. But I knew that there was a need for a longer term solution so this first payment became phase one of a one million pound deal with a long roadmap ahead. Now we have a *not for profit* body that GFA-the-business owns. We have set up governance to make sure the ownership structure is clear and managed ethically with no conflicts of interest as I own them both, but of course the implication is that the awareness raised by the not for profit is the best sales engine for the GFA product. The not for profit is a beacon that becomes a sales channel because it raises the issues that need addressing.' *Patience, you must have*, as it turns out, was good advice.

If you are reading this thinking, that's alright for Joel but this is a very hard thing to do when money is what you need and money is on the table, remember that he has learned this lesson the hard way. If you recall, by the time this here rodeo came along, Joel had made the mistake of taking cash too soon

> If you are building something that didn't exist before, your ability to deliver is secondary to your market's awareness and willingness to consume it.

and learned from it. He had learned the hard way, the difference between money and value and how delayed gratification may connect the two. Taking the money early on seems always like an obvious solution to scaling for product market fit. Get the money, fuel the growth. But firstly, as we will see in Chapter 4, money always comes with a catch and funding growth can be dangerous; and secondly, if you are trying to scale something that wasn't there before, your ability to grow is secondary to your market's awareness and willingness to consume what you do.

So sometimes you need to help build the demand before you meet it.

'Product market fit concerns are always on your horizon. You would be a fool not to worry about it' stresses 10x's Antony Jenkins. 'Product market fit is a requisite for success but it is not binary. In a world where change comes at us at great speed, maybe the product creates the fit. Product functionality is a commodity, after all. You can flex along the way.' One of 10x's biggest competitors is Thought Machine and, funnily enough, Antony's pronouncement reflects the choices they made on their journey as well. Although, rather than being early and creating demand like Lizzie Chapman and Zest money did, Thought Machine played around looking for a problem big enough to matter and new enough not to be solved yet. They didn't start with a problem statement. They went looking for one.

'Paul[5] chose to work in FS because of its data richness' recalls Gareth Richardson, Thought Machine's COO.

'He wanted to build something that was mission critical *and* do so with the massive web scale technologies he, and the founding team, had used at Google. We didn't actually start looking at the core [where the current product plays.] We went looking for the

> If you want to sell to a particular type of demographic, you need the credibility of having already done it.
>
> To get there takes patience, hard work and constant adaptation so that the thing you are selling is something they will buy. Not would or could. But can and shall.

biggest problem. We played around with a PFM for high net worths... a trading platform... a pricing tool for the housing market... we have five or six pivots as we were trying to see where the problem was in the market. We would bootstrap a basic POC so see where the pain was.

In 2014 we were playing around with machine learning for spend analysis and categorisation with a sponsor bank. We went to put the POC live, but it was impractical: the bank liked what we had done, but they couldn't put it live as they couldn't feed it real time data, it needed humans cleaning the data over several weeks for each batch of data.

This happened twice. And both times we were told the data was locked within the core/s. On the back of that, we built Vault. We started with two engineers on it.

The mission was: go figure out what this core banking thing is. 2015 was a major pivot. That's when core banking became *the problem* we were going to solve. Always wanting to solve the problem for the large incumbent banks, but initially targeting the nascent fintech banks with a notion of a bank in a box, thinking to service startup banks looking for full stacks. However, as initial prototypes were being shown to the wider Banking industry and new executive team members came onboard from traditional finance backgrounds, we honed in on that the genius was in the middle.

---

5 Paul Taylor, CEO and founder of Thought Machine.

Taking inspiration from several concepts from other industries or players; mirroring the "headless" notion from the enterprise "headless" Content Management Systems, adding real time, API-first, Cloud native concepts from Google, aligned with a comprehensive configuration system, inspired by the smart contract notion from the Ethereum White Paper.

It helped that Standard Chartered, SEB, Lloyds plus other big banks expressed interest. Those big name banks are the prize in core banking after all. If you are targeting that market, you cannot get the credibility if you go to market with only small guys on the platform. So we started focusing on a few key logos: what does it take to land them? What do they need? How can we serve them?

We have gone from there. And we have the right team. We went engineering-first so we have "good bones" for growth. Commercial and compliance etc. came later. In fact we didn't scale the sales team for a while because the product sold itself: the market found it, frankly. We spent a lot of time talking to journalists and bankers, we made a lot of connections and a lot of the market was coming to us to see what we were doing. So the product and problem statement sold itself and got us the second conversation. In the last decade or more, few people have tried to take out mainframes, for obvious reasons, so nobody else was trying to do what we were doing at the time so that created interest.'

Don't Drink the Kool-Aid

'At the start everything is hard and there is a relentlessness to it. But at the same time, at first, everything is possible. So you need discipline' reflects Antony Jenkins. 'To stay disciplined, you need to strike a balance between what you are trying to achieve and being flexible and learning from other people. You need to identify the problem you are trying to solve and make sure your solution is better than that of other people's. But equally you need to remember all the things you *don't* know and never get caught up in the hype around yourself.'

You need to keep an eye on the competitors, because they will be keeping an eye on you. And you need to keep an eye on yourself: not drinking your own Kool-Aid so you don't become blind to the inputs the market is giving you.

> As an entrepreneur, success is about the mission. Ultimately you may or may not make money and whether you do or don't may have no impact on whether you achieved your mission.
>
> **Antony Jenkins**

The team building Mox in Hong Kong, for instance, was made up of people who had done this before and led by Deniz, who we met in Chapter 2, who had also done this before. It would be easy to just assume they knew exactly what was needed, they didn't need to test, research and sanity-check their assumptions. 'Hold my beer, I got this' territory.

And yet, in order to deliver meaningful and differentiated products to clients, the Mox team didn't rely on what they thought they knew but rather engaged in extensive ethnographic research.

Every aspect of the business would come to be connected to the needs of customers identified through this work. But also the process meant that every stakeholder was sighted, aware and aligned with these intentions, at first, and then the learnings and then the resulting actions. That alignment was key both for the service-led approach the team intended not only to take for product development but also to deliver a profitable business. And yet getting that alignment, investing the time in research is not always seen or felt as time well spent at the early stages of a venture. People want to see progress and, although this type of work is foundational, it is often not seen as such. Having done this before, surely, you know what you need to do next, is the implication. So it takes a certain type of courage to take time at the beginning of a venture to do work that doesn't register as 'progress' on anyone's burndown chart.

And there is humility in this process. Which is the thing I want you to take away from this.

Accepting that you may not know it all already or that the knowledge you have, valuable though it is, may not translate like for like is as important as the experience and knowledge itself. And this humility needs to stay at work because, as an entrepreneur, you not only need to constantly seek your own blind spots but you also need to accept that creating a viable business and fulfilling your mission are, sadly, not the same thing.

'I live my life in a state of constant dissatisfaction. It is not an easy way to live' reflects Antony Jenkins. 'You need to be resilient and tenacious. Ultimately these are the most defining factors of success. Because, as an entrepreneur, success is about the mission.

> As an entrepreneur you need to constantly challenge your blind spots. Especially as fulfilling your mission and building a profitable business are rarely coterminous.

Ultimately you may or may not make money and whether you do or don't may have no impact on whether you achieved your mission.'

Hold onto that thought, by the way. Not because I will come back to it later but because it is absolutely true: you may succeed at your mission and fail as a business. If your aim is to do both, then there are a few things you need to be mindful of: 'If I look back now [at Zest Money] and think *we failed*, our bank clients beg to differ' recalls Lizzie Chapman. 'They tell me that we built the best BNPL stack in the market. Maybe the business failed but not the product, not the technology, not the team.' It is a crushing thought, that sometimes you have to compromise on the reason why you are doing things in the first place, to get the business traction that will allow you to keep doing the thing you are doing.

But that is exactly the lived reality of entrepreneurship. And because success is not linear, the way there entails a lot of retracing steps, trying different ways to get to wherever you going and, of course, that time-honoured startup staple: the pivot.

Here We Go: PIVOT, PIVOT

If you didn't just 'hear' this in your head in the voice of Ross from Friends, I don't even want to know you. And come to think of it… I don't even know if they got that couch up the stairs in the end. They must have, right? What I *do* know is that when you say to a normal person 'pivot' they think 'Friends'. When you say 'pivot' to the rest of us fintech geeks… we heave a big sigh and think about beloved product features that never saw the light of day. We think about hard work and 'I told you so.' For us, a pivot is part of the fintech lexicon and with good reason. Because almost no product you know and love today started exactly how you know it.

> Dare to pivot on your original idea
> **Jasper Martens**

The most famous pivot stories are radical (Slack starting life as the chat function of a game that never made it because investors homed in on the chat) but reality tends to be more mundane.

Sometimes the changes are a bit of a cha-cha-cha. A few steps forward, a few steps back but always heading in the same direction. Monika Liikamaa says 'Enfuce does exactly what we set out to do. We set out to be the best… we messed around a bit… found out what we are best at and have focused on that. On not ever becoming average.' But the road there was not linear. Enfuce set out to service banks but 'when we couldn't attract big banks at the start' reflects Monika 'we had to get customers elsewhere. So we did. Now we are focused back on our original mission and we are better able to do what we were born to do than we were in years two or five.' Denise concurs: 'we have taken the necessary routes to grow and now we are back to our roots. It's where we have been heading.' It just wasn't a straight line. It never is.

> History is written by the winners so the stories of what actually went on inside tech companies is streamlined: there were many close calls that happened behind closed doors.
> **Arthur Leung**

Sometimes, the changes you have to make are ones of degree. Other times more dramatic. But the need to iterate on your original idea is a universal experience. Although not everyone responds to it equally well.

When Jasper and I started chatting about PensionBee in the context of this book, I asked him what were the critical points of a journey that took them from being a startup to having billboards the size of houses in mainline train stations. He was unequivocal: 'First of all, dare to pivot on your original idea. When you are at the start of your journey and you have a great product or idea... dare to change it when you get first responses back from your target customers to make it better. For example, when we started PensionBee, we would find and combine pensions for you. However, the main pain point of our target customer was transferring them easily. Can you make combining pensions simple?' That's what the market wanted. And PensionBee listened. If you want a business that gets product market fit, is the lesson, listen to the market.

Listening to market feedback is not a widely shared trait among finance professionals, by the way, who often believe they know best[6].

Which is why product market fit often remains elusive. Because often founders and business leaders don't take no for an answer. Even if the market says it really, really loudly. Founders often believe that their vision is the North Star they need to follow and market feedback is part of what we mean when we say that the work of building a business is hard. But it isn't. Building a business is hard even if you take the market feedback and change accordingly. If you don't take that feedback, building a real, scalable business that will survive the test of time is not just hard but unlikely.

And yet for a very long time we have fed the popular myth and surrounding narrative of the Founder Against the World, standing tall, sticking to their guns even when things seem desperate. This trope was so popular for a while as to become blinding to the simple fact that only success could ultimately help you tell *focus* apart from *pig-headedness*. With hindsight, spectacular failures (and associated court appearances in many cases) should have been the reality check we all needed. Watching Elizabeth Meriwether's miniseries 'the Dropout' chronicling the rise and fall of Elizabeth Holmes of Theranos makes your skin crawl if you are honest with yourself and remember the adulation before the fall. She was the undaunted 19 year old who was told her idea couldn't work because the science wouldn't work but she wasn't put off, she wouldn't be kept down, she dropped out of school and she showed them.

Only she didn't.

The science couldn't work, as it turns out, and she is doing time now. Because believing in your own hype and faking it till you make it is, as it turns out, a terrible idea. And although terrible for all involved, this narrative has been pervasive.

'How do you balance that narrative of relentless determination and need to focus and control... with the inevitable need to pivot?' asks Shawbrook's CPO Arthur Leung. 'My personal experience working with founders and seeing unicorns is that we, as an industry, need to recognise that there is an unreasonable degree of optimism

---

6 Yours truly wrote an article about this very topic in 2022 https://www.fintechfutures.com/2022/09/the-designer-the-surrealist-and-the-potted-plant/

required for this work that is not natural or inherent in most people. You could easily say these folks are delusional and sort of need to be to carry out this work. And you see this trait in both successful and unsuccessful entrepreneurs. The balance between determination and knowing when to give up is not clear. And we have all seen it done… not well. But history is written by the winners so the many versions of what *actually* went on inside tech companies are streamlined and, in reality, it is very rare to know the kodak moments as they happen behind closed doors and there are *many* close calls. It astounds me how steadfast and strong some CEOs are despite where the market goes, where usage numbers go and who knows what happens in five years? Maybe they will be vindicated.'

Arthur is right.

We are between a rock and a hard place because, without relentless optimism and an ability to bounce back despite how hard it is, people can't do this work. But this relentless resilience may make these very same people immune to

> An unreasonable degree of optimism is required for this work that is not natural for most people.
>
> **Arthur Leung**

feedback – be it from other folks or the market. We know that products and digital transformations often fail because the people at the helm are often wilfully blind to feedback. Ultimately, the very thing that makes you good at this may be what kills you. Which is why pivoting is a superpower: knowing when to blink is not obvious when resilience is the name of the game.

Feedback: Not Always Friendly, Always Your Friend

What should you do when the market points you in a particular direction?

'You pivot your proposition' states Jasper unequivocally. And when PensionBee did exactly that, 'conversion rates doubled. We knew we were on the right track.' The numbers don't lie.

Of course making changes like this is hard, both emotionally and materially as they may entail changing operating models, your actual product or go to market strategy. 'You can make those decisions more easily at the start as they will become harder as your business grows' concedes Jasper. But no less important.

Especially for a mission-driven business, what you are trying to achieve needs to be more important than the specifics of the product. It shouldn't become a sacred cow. The product should be nobody's baby. The mission should be everybody's. But that is hard when it comes down to the actual experience of doing the work. It is hard and therefore important to point out what it being done well looks like. So, for PensionBee, the mission is 'we want to keep things simple so people can enjoy a happy retirement.' That is the part that should be non-negotiable. *How* is fungible if it achieves the aim.

So, they pivoted. It worked. They are growing and now, Jasper continues, 'we want to become the pension provider of choice for UK consumers, not just a consolidation partner. Start with us in your 30s and stay. We are on track to make the business profitable. We want to make it a mainstream brand. We won't settle for less.'

To achieve that, you need to be constantly changing in line with the needs of your customers of course. You need to keep listening to the market and evolving with their needs. Which is not always easy but at least we know it works. Since having this conversation PensionBee has been achieving key earning milestones, started its US expansion and at the time we went to press was on track for a full-year profit in 2024[7]. And pivoting on the original 'how' to keep servicing the mission was partly how that was achieved.

But success always seems inevitable once it has happened, hindsight being 20/20 and whatnot. So I asked the obvious question: Was there resistance to the change? Jasper's answer was no. That, as we will soon see, isn't always the case although if you are making a change because the market data suggests you should, debate is pointless.

'When you've got the data in hand' reflects Jasper 'there should be no resistance and the team, including co-founders, were no obstacle to grow the business in the right direction. We often talk about *leaving ego at the front door*. When you have that environment, you can truly drive product innovation.' That is a culture trait that we could all use to be honest.

And you need to continuously drive product innovation because the product needs to keep pace with your community, it needs to address the needs of a wider community and also stay relevant as you grow. Each problem to be solved requires shifts and changes.

> When you've got the data in hand, there should be no resistance to change.
> You cannot drive product innovation unless you leave ego at the front door.
> You need to leave ego at the door in order to drive product innovation.
> And you need constant product innovation in order to keep in touch with what your market needs from you next, as you grow.
> **Jasper Martens**

'When we got bigger' he continues, 'the next thing that drove conversion rates up was finding an innovative way of dealing with hundreds of different pension providers (yes 100s!). We knew they would not change *their* ways so we had to tailor

---

7 https://www.marketwatch.com/amp/story/pensionbee-expects-profitable-year-rapid-growth-in-u-s-813f3c40

and innovate the way *we* deal with them. That means what you built is complex but effective. It's also why many that have tried to replicate us, struggle to make it work for them. Transferring pensions is not new but it is hard if you want to do it effectively and at scale.' Jasper's point is extremely poignant: you pivot and pivot and pivot again. That's what being a challenger brand means. But those pivots are exactly what it says on the tin: they are adjustments, not departures.

It is funny because if you look up the definition of the word pivot, as a verb, it means to shift or oscillate around a central axis or point. It's a sustained range of motion. A secondary meaning, however, is offered as 'to completely change the way you operate in a business context'. I don't like that definition. The whole point of a pivot is you hold onto some central tenets and shift around them. There is a different word for changing everything completely. A pivot is not about that. A pivot is what you do when you come into this work with a vision, a few hypotheses and an early version of your product and discover that some of that doesn't work.

Keep Changing Until You Speak Your Clients' Language

I spoke about pivots with Christian Nentwich, Founder and (at the time) CEO of Du.Co. Christian and I have known each other since the early days of Du.Co (founded in 2013), and I have been an unashamed card-carrying fan of his ever since.

Also the business'. But mostly Christian's.

Du.Co started life as a software project, remembers Christian.

'How do we help business people drive work and harness insight without code? That was the problem statement. A co-founder and I had had a joint vision about this, and we were on our way. Although the co-founder exited around series B, a lot of the early team are still with us. Employee number one is still with us. So is employee number three and many others. When we started, we thought that the hardest thing would be the problem itself. Reconciliation happened between systems… hard-coded… and thousands of spreadsheets. Our original aim was to go after the spreadsheets.

Imagine trying to sell SaaS in 2013. It was hard.

So we pivoted.

Christian Nentwich, Founder and CEO Du.Co

Du.Co is a solution that enables users to consolidate, standardise and reconcile any type of data for operational efficiency, business agility and strategic decision-making.

We sold to some non-bank brokers first to drive the change and brought in some deals. Two years in, we had 20 clients and some seed and Series A investment from Euclid Opportunities. A financial investor with a strategic angle which was a great help.

But we didn't have a business pitch yet... not really. We didn't have product market fit yet. And the sales cycle to large firms was our biggest challenge. The feedback loop was slow. And we couldn't yet articulate the problem we were solving, who we were solving it for, exactly where the cost we were taking out was.

> If you are solving a problem in a way that is early for the market you may need to pivot, bide your time, and pivot back when your market is ready for you.

We had zero product marketing at the time. We tried to scale through sales but we didn't have a playbook yet. So I had to drive a lot of the sales myself. Revenue increase, metrics and understanding and a track record actually came together at the same time. Plus by the time we are raising our series B in 2017, SaaS is a thing.

It is relaxing to be using vocabulary people finally understand. And our investors were supportive of the pure SaaS model. But pivoting to that meant turning revenue away.

A supportive board is key to be able to do this. And we have had a good board every step of the way: with knowledge and understanding of the needs of a scaling business and capital markets. And they understood the aim of the business, the problem we were trying to solve.'

This, in so many ways, is the other side of the timing question we addressed in the last chapter: you pivot, you adjust. You bide your time.

> Your pivots may mean that you need to turn a certain type of revenue away in order to focus.
>
> Make sure your investors understand that.
>
> Make sure you understand that.

Either to take advantage of a beneficial shift in your operating environment, or in recognition that you may be early and need to survive till it is no longer early.

Du.Co didn't shift away from being a SaaS solution exactly, but it did shift the way it went to market and the type of clients it approached, until SaaS was not an impossible proposition for financial services any more. The problem they were trying to solve for, however, remained constant: 'The way the industry approaches data is so disparate and manual. The compounded effect of this is so wasteful you can't even begin to quantify it.' That is what Du.Co is solving for. Around that, shifts, changes and evolution are par for the course. Sometimes a pivot is the only way to survive. But it is a nuanced balance. 'My advice would be' cautions Christian 'if you have product market fit, stick it out' don't pivot any more: wait. Things will come round.

'We have been kicked out of sales processes only to come back three years later and win.' It is indeed a long game.

The Fine Line between Vision and Obstinacy

So how do you know?

How do you know when to wait and when to pivot? When to double down and when to take the hint and make a change? Knowing when to adapt and change and when to dig deep is, unhelpfully, the knife-edge on which this rests. Getting it right is what makes you good. And there is no hard and fast rule on how to get it right, but it helps to know that you need to forever be asking the question. You are less likely to miss it then.

Soups Ranjan, Sardine CEO, who named his company *Sardine* because it is designed to stop fishy behaviour (don't you love that? I love that) recalls that he set out to build the number one company anybody thinks of when they think about fraud. 'We wanted to become the verb, so to speak, as google did for search engines. We set out to build lego blocks for fraud and compliance.

We have found good product market fit and are scaling well across industry segments. We want to build a long lasting business and to do that we have to keep scaling without burning too hard.' But getting here was neither easy nor obvious.

'The hardest thing at the start was how do you acquire your first set of customers and how, frankly, do you build a fraud engine when you don't yet have data. The first set of customers break that, but to get those we had to get very creative. And I am not a natural sales guy. I utilised my network (having led fraud and AML teams at Coinbase and Revolut) I reached out to folks I knew to see if they needed those services. I activated the alumni group. Then, when people reached out to hire me as head of fraud... I offered them the product.

> Pivoting doesn't mean fundamentally changing what you are trying to do. But it may mean fundamentally changing the manner or order in which you build things or how you take them to market.

Before Sardine, I used to run a meetup called Risk Salon for heads of fraud and compliance which had grown to over 2,000 leaders. I reached out to them. And as I reached out to folks, I realised that at first the idea didn't resonate.

I had a lot of feedback all about how it wouldn't work or how they had already built or bought something that solved that problem. To sell what we sell, you have to catch your buyer at the right moment so we decided to go down a really modular path: to multiply the opportunities and also to home in on the question of what are the things you really wouldn't want to build yourself as a client? Device telemetry, for instance.

How you hold your device, type or swipe as ways to detect fraud. An in-house risk team would not have the means to build telemetry like that so it became the first building block we decided to build.

It was not a big pivot and the direction we were going in did not fundamentally change but the order in which we went about things did change. We knew we would build device fingerprinting but didn't intend to start there. After the first hundred conversations we realised we had to do it first.

You have to be super adaptable. Frankly, it is presumptuous to solve a problem the market doesn't need solving. So you need to be adaptable to the needs of the market.'

And those needs keep changing. Sometimes as the market matures and sometimes as it reacts to exogenous events.

In the previous section, we talked about how exogenous factors including the change in investor behaviours the war in Ukraine brought about, put pressure on Funderbeam. Kaidi Ruusalepp reflects: 'the war in Ukraine started and retail investors became understandably super cautious. People would keep their money under their mattresses. This level of caution was partly why we pivoted our business away from a crowd-focused play to being an infrastructure provider for private investor networks and institutional investors that are booming because the prices right now are attractive for those who have capital and want to build a portfolio.'

> It is presumptuous to solve a problem the market doesn't need solving.
> **Soups Ranjan**

That makes sense.

You are still solving a problem that you understand and believe needs solving for a market that wants your solution. It makes a lot of sense... from the outside. But calling it, from the inside, is always a complicated decision. And an emotional one even if the data shows you, as Jasper said, that this is The Way so to speak. I asked Kaidi how hard it was for her to make this change. She answers with a smile: 'Not hard once the decision was made.'

Executing the pivot was the easy part. Making the call to change direction was the harder part. 'Pivot decisions as such are always hard' Kaidi reflects. 'I am the founder, the largest shareholder and conscious of the responsibility that comes with people investing in the business because they trusted *me*. So my job is to create a sustainable vision not pursue a dream no matter what it costs.'

Leadership, folks. That's what it looks like.

Kaidi continues: 'Of course it is hard to communicate to the "crowd" that you are not going to service their needs the same way any more. That you will keep custody and services and not close the accounts they have, but the focus of the service will be different. And it is also hard to face into the team and realise that for the pivot you need a different team, different sales force, different size, different back office.

From a tech perspective though the change was minimal. The same infrastructure largely with slightly different branding.'

This is key. A pivot isn't always just another way of getting the same Friends to take the same sofa up the same stairs. Sometimes you need to make changes to the product, sometimes to where you are taking it, as Christian discussed, and sometimes you need to make changes to the people on this journey.

It is not romantic.

But it is essential.

As for the emotional side of the change, it *can* often be hard, but it shouldn't be, reflects Kaidi: 'you see something is not working... you change it. And now we have a different business model and frankly lower risk exposure.' The loyalty and support of investors and shareholders were key in this process, stresses Kaidi. So was *not* getting early traction. 'Given our early entry in the blockchain and crowdfunding world and looking at our competitors back then, it is good we didn't succeed and become a great size early on. If we had, I'm not sure we would be where we are today.'

The option for a pivot would not have been available in the same way and then the company may have failed, rather than changed.

A Dollar Burning a Hole in Your Pocket

Although I personally have faith in Kaidi's leadership abilities, the point she raises is valid. The options you are presented with within a shifting context are not constant. They have a lot to do with your size, agility and reserves of cash. And that will have to drive a lot of decisions, ultimately, because it colours your options.

Dharm Mistry reflects on his own entrepreneurial journey over the years and acknowledges that he has had to scrap products in his time.

> Everything in a startup is about cash flow. If you can't see the next six months, you can't afford to do whatever it is you are thinking of doing.
> **Dharm Mistry**

'Everything in a startup is about cashflow, if you can't see the next six months, you can't afford to do whatever it is you are thinking of doing. Any less than six months and you don't have time to manoeuvre. If feeding your product roadmap becomes a luxury then you need to think.'

Think about your options, think about your next move, think about your business viability. So what does that mean in real terms?

To Antony's earlier point, if for whatever reason your original idea isn't working as fast as you need it to for the money to not run out (and you appreciate that is not an absolute number, it is *absolutely* relative to how much cash you have and how quickly you are burning through it) then you have no choice but to pivot.

Now you are probably thinking 'that is not true: you have the choice to raise more capital' and you do. And for many years that is exactly what most founders did: doubled down, raised more and spent more. Because it was an available option, even if it wasn't a sensible one.

In her 2023 book *The Great Crashes: Lessons from Global Meltdowns and How to Prevent Them*, Linda Yueh paints a picture of the boom and bust of the .com era, the easy money and the reckless way in which it was spent that is stark and scary, largely

> You have to listen to the clients rather than try to educate them. But founders who have too much cash may indulge in exactly that.
> **Dharm Mistry**

because it played itself in exactly the same way (albeit in a slightly more long drawn out timeframe) in the fintech space a decade or so later.

But as we said, the era of free money is over and your investors increasingly will see your lack of traction for what it is. And if you are lucky, they will back your pivot. So you will have to make changes. And this is not the same as doing things differently from the outset. A pivot may entail taking an option you considered and didn't pursue at the outset of your work, but going down that path once something else was attempted isn't the same as getting it right the first time. Not because of some cosmic scoreboard but because you don't have a blank sheet of paper anymore. A pivot is hard, notes Dharm, *because* you are in the middle of running things, you are mid delivery. So you have to change things that are already in flight *because* you are running out of viable options.

So there is more to manage. Operational complexity, talent, resource deployment, emotions, clients, commitments, learned behaviours. You need to challenge and change all of those mid-flight.

That is hard. But it is necessary: 'You need to listen to what the client actually wants. Founders who try to educate customers despite what the customers say they want are barking up the wrong tree. And of course you may find yourself indulging in exactly that, if you have too much money. Because if you have it, you spend it.' Again, we are on a knife-edge: the balance between generating demand for a new product and accepting that the market isn't lacking information about your product but interest in it. If a customer doesn't want your product, the choice to keep 'courting them' until they change their mind is there for you. But it is an expensive and arguably foolish choice. If you don't have that option, continues Dharm, 'if you think about what you need to do in order to make the money last till you are on your feet as a business, then you spend very differently.'

And that discipline is hugely valuable.

In fact, for Sardine CEO Soups Ranjan, his reflection on what he would have done differently with the hindsight he now has is that he would have raised less. 'If I went again, I would try to see if I could do even more with less capital.' Because managing your runway sharpens your focus.

Which is, of course, the reason that this section includes zero big bank examples. Because as Bianca Bates rightly explained in the previous section, a big entity has the option to deploy capital in order to establish and hold a beachhead. They still need product market fit but they don't worry about running out of cash.

Which is both a good thing and a bad thing.

At least keeping an eye on your runway is a ticking clock that is hard to ignore. It creates urgency that can be very healthy when trying to retain focus and tempo.

> If you think about what you need to do in order to make the money last till you are on your feet as a business, then you spend very differently.
> **Dharm Mistry**

When you have both *existing* product market fit in your main organisation and access to capital, it is as easy to burn it, as it is to sit on your laurels and not do a thing. A different problem altogether, but a real one especially as most large organisations are reluctant to go early. And yet, even for a big organisation, doing something new requires the same sensitivity around retaining focus and not being blind to market feedback. And although a big organisation will rarely need to worry about running out money, having money and choosing to deploy it aren't quite the same thing.

You've Got to Know When to Hold 'Em, Know When to Fold 'Em

Full marks if you recognise this as the chorus of Kenny Rogers' song 'The Gambler'. No marks if you think that deciding whether to pivot or double down is a roll of the dice. I have said 'this is leadership' so many times already I am boring myself. But I will keep saying it because that is the ball game. It's a set of decisions that are neither obvious nor risk-free but need to be specific, consistent and aligned to your purpose and strategy, otherwise it's not leadership, it's gambling.

A pivot should come when the market is giving you a reality check that your original assumptions are not working out as planned. It shouldn't be the thing you resort to when you lose heart. That is particularly significant to remember when you are intentionally early

> Being early comes down to money: Having it. And being willing to deploy it.
> **Bianca Bates**

with an idea or venture. Because this work is hard anyway and you will have days when you wonder 'what am I doing' especially if you are intentionally early. So you will need to remember what is what. You need to have clarity of focus and yet be receptive to feedback.

I know it's hard. It's meant to be.

Ultimately, the consistent theme so far is that you need to choose a market you wish to serve then listen to its needs. You need to pick a direction you believe is the right one, then do the hard work of getting to where you are going. None of this is easy and balancing focus with the ability to change is impossible for most people. But not for all.

'We have three themes that we believe are enduring' says Cuscal's Bianca Bates.

'Digital (ten years ago that was called Mobile); Data and Real Time.

We believe these are the important themes for Cuscal and discretionary effort, product development and investment makes sense for us in these areas. Anything out of these themes is questioned and sometimes not pursued.'

What does that mean when the chips are down?

It means that Cuscal backed :86400[8] at a time when digital banking was early and no real 'runaway' successes could be pointed at for comfort. The decision to do it aligned with the themes identified as enduring. Then 'it all came down to capital and money actually, because we had it and we were willing to deploy it. It was an interesting balance.

[The :86400 team] didn't have to make desperate decisions because the option to fund them was there. So they didn't need to make desperate choices to descope or compromise' like a 'normal' startup would. 'We had a clear idea of what it was we were building from the get go' continues Bianca. 'We wanted a bank that put the customer first. That had a truly

> Sometimes running out of money is a proof point that change is needed.
> Being well-capitalised means that you don't have to pivot or descope things out of desperation. But it doesn't mean you shouldn't pivot or descope things: it may still be the right thing to do.

digital experience. Of course you want to sell products that make money but you do that through insights and budgets that help people look after their finances. Before making a home loan available, for instance, we offered an energy switching service. A nudge saying *hey you may be missing a payment here or you may be missing a special rate there. Do you want to do something about it.*

A bank doing the right thing by its customer.

We felt that if we could show digital capabilities in a digital bank, we could learn what good looked like, then bring it into the main bank and show our own clients. We had innovations inside the bank that clients were reluctant to pick up before

---

8 :86 400 (the number of seconds in a day) was an Australian neobank founded in 2019 by Robert Bell and Anthony Thomson and majority owned by payments company Cuscal. It gained a licence to operate as an authorised deposit-taking institution in 2019.

In early 2021, it was taken over by National Australia Bank (NAB) and merged into its UBank subsidiary.

:86400 did a similar thing. It was a university experience in working out what good looked like and then bringing it back to the main business.'

Bianca sees this set of decisions as coming down to money. Which is absolutely right, of course. But it also all comes down to leadership. Because having the money is key. But many big banks have the money. It is literally what they are made of. Having the money isn't the differentiator here or everyone would have done what Cuscal did.

Choosing to deploy the money in the service of a particular strategy is the differentiator for Cuscal. And for :86400? Having the discipline to pivot where needed and listen to the customer feedback when required, despite not having the sobering factor of running out of money in play.

':86400 knew what the problem statement was for the client and could release quickly and meet the need. But equally, they had the discipline that, if the client didn't like a feature, they would spend no more time on it. Speed worked both ways' confirms Bianca.

And we now know that :86400 is a success story. Part of the lore of Australian digital banking. They were bought by National Australia Bank as part of their series B and the rest, as they say, is history. But that was *not* known at the start of the journey and that is important.

Cuscal were willing to back their own strategy and know that, success or failure notwithstanding, the experience will teach them a lot. And it did. And part of what it taught them is that, if you listen to the customers, you will build a product people want. And what people want may not be the fancy thing many innovators want to build. People actually want simplicity.

> Knowing when to stop trying, when to pivot and when to sell are not obvious decisions. But they are critical.

'The customers want you to get the basics right' notes Bianca: 'Account aggregation. Categorisation. Rollup substitutions. We thought clients would want really tricky things but what they loved the most was the simplicity.'

Jasper from PensionBee agrees fully, by the way. This is not Big Shop wisdom. It's product market fit wisdom.

'There is a lot of cool stuff you can do' notes Jasper 'but if you can't add a beneficiary to your pension, you don't care about the cool stuff. You need to get the *boring* stuff right. For instance, we doubled down on risk frameworks early'. The important over the shiny.

Innovation is great. But market traction and a focused business are greater.

Which is also the story of why Cuscal sold :86400 when they did even though it was a success.

'We were just getting started when we had the opportunity to sell :86400' reflects Bianca 'but the reality was that we had learned how capital intensive a successful startup that is actively lending *actually* is. And successful though it was, :86400 was ancillary to the main business [of Cuscal] and a diversification. But actually their success made them a complication for some shareholders, so to sell at a good return before ploughing more capital in was a solution and in itself a huge success.

Then the challenge becomes how do you retain the learning mindset?.'

This seems so obvious when abstract. But in the weeds of each decision, how do you know when to go big and back your vision and, having done that, take the hint to pivot, double down or stop trying?

'There is complexity to decision making' explains Bianca.

> Given how decision-making is risk-managed in big banks, once you have committed to a decision... the option to stop is not really there.
> ***Bianca Bates***

'In a big organisation, big projects tend to be lifecycle-managed. They represent necessity with added opportunity. So there is no turning back for projects like that [once they are rolling] because you use an inevitable, wider lifecycle need to drive change. You may want to be flexible around the change work but because the process is triggered by a system reaching end of life, there is no turning back.

So you lock yourself in.

For big banks, once you are in the process, the choice to stop is not there. When you are working on a pure strategic play that is different. And we have had situations where we experienced strain: clients not happy or delivery not going as planned with a brand new thing. In those situations you do have the option to stop but if you have strategic vision and you believe in it, you keep going.

The hardest thing of it all is that all this is happening while your plate is full with BAU work. Additional challenges (such as the Covid epidemic) create situations where progress occasionally requires brute force from some great people. The whole organisation relies on people to get through the impossible and your mission as a leader becomes motivating these people to stick with you.'

Leadership, ultimately, is what it comes down to, whatever your size or the challenge you need to navigate. Ultimately, deciding when to pivot and when to double down may be a slightly less existential question when you have money to deploy but it is no less difficult. You double down on the wrong thing and your board and shareholders will have something to say about it even if you can afford it. Making the call is, you got it, leadership.

A Small Change Is Still Change

Zor Gorelov reflects on those pivotal choices.

In the context of Kasisto, playing in the AI space before it was commonly understood, before it was the household topic that it has become by 2023 when Zor and I spoke in the context of this book, managing *timing* has a different quality to it.

'It is still early in AI' reflects Zor. Even after ChatGPT became a household name. It is still early in general and it is definitely early in terms of AI adoption in our industry. 'A lot of things still need to happen for these AI assistants to reach their full potential in displacing bankers. We need to find ways to enrich large language models (LLM) with common sense and human values. We need to find ways to move towards models hinging around human values, systems that can think and act like humans. My own interest in AI goes back 30 years. I worked on some of the early projects as a software engineer, language models were small back then but the computers used to run them were large. But I believed then and I believe now that conversational interfaces are more natural than GUIs for users.'

> When you decide on a change as a leadership team, one of the hardest things is to get the employees to consistently change what they are doing each day.
> **Zor Gorelov**

So Zor was a believer and a builder. And *he* was early consciously and by design. And although *it* is still early, we have reached a pivotal moment in the evolution of this technology and Kasisto had to react to that inflection point when it came. That wasn't a pivot. It wasn't a re-think. But it was a realisation that a gear change and shift in focus was needed as the world was itself changing gears when it came to AI.

And even though this was always the plan, the shift itself is never easy.

'Now, as Kasisto is transitioning to build generative AI products, the hardest thing is convincing people to start the transition, adopting and embracing this new technology. Not a pivot as such but part of the company's continuous evolution and adoption of new technology. We are evolving away from the "prescriptive" to descriptive or Gen AI systems. And this transition isn't just about tech but also compliance, copyright, PII etc. We saw this Gen AI transformation in business and had to decide that there was no plan B. We had to go all the way and the board and investors came on that journey.'

> A pivot that is 100% right for your business will ask good people to stop working on things they believe in. It is prudent to expect resistance.

Arguably, they should have expected it.

'The hardest thing was to get the employees to change what they were doing. We needed to be patient, deliberate, to make sure my army follows me into battle and believe the battle can be won. This takes time.'

Taking the time to ensure the decision you made is fully carried through is part of the process. So you need to make the decision knowing you will need to take this time to embed the change and convince your people even if the change is very small and glaringly the right thing to do.

It's leadership because you need to explain the vision to your board and how doubling down and focusing aligns with the mission and, simultaneously, you need to appreciate how your team understands and experiences this doubling down. Because strategic focus at the top of the house may bring small shifts, seemingly, at the functional, organisational level. But even the smallest shift is experienced as disruption. People will be asked to stop working on things. Things they were giving their all to, until five minutes ago. They may not like it. They may be slow in the shift. They may be reluctant or they may resist in the hope that the new direction won't last. As a leader you need to absolutely understand how your teams will experience those shifts and be sympathetic to the reasons behind reticence or resistance.

Zor knows it: 'We spent time believing what we used to do is important. And maybe it was, but things changed around us. So I had to convince people that whatever change we make is thought through. And as important [as what we were doing before]. This takes time. But you always need to change. You win by changing as the world changes.

We were already working on generative AI. Doubling down was the change: investing more and putting *all* effort into it.' It is a change of degree rather than a pivot. But try saying that to the person whose project and work was deemed outside the focus area.

It is hard 'but we did that extremely quickly. Our banking customers are supportive as well: generative AI is changing the world around us, I have had a couple of dozen meetings with banking execs on this. Big banks are looking hard at it. Hundreds of jobs are being created to look

> Any change (be it a pivot or a doubling down) will face some resistance as a combination of habit and belief getting in the way.
> **Zor Gorelov**

at large language models. Smaller banks know they don't have the resources to do things on their own and they need to understand how this shift affects them. It's a hard transition for some but we are helping them, this is new for many but for us, this is a path we were already on.'

This is hugely significant. A pivot is a dramatic word. What Kasisto did was not a pivot. It was doubling down on something they were already doing. And it was the right thing to do. But it was neither an obvious decision, when it was made, nor an effortless decision to implement as even the doubling down requires teams to change and 'a combination of habit and belief get in the way' as Zor explains exactly because 'we spend time believing what we used to do is important'.

This is extremely important to remember as a leader. A pivot is, maybe too 'final' a word. Too dramatic. Maybe changing and shifting and adjusting is what every business does. The ones that don't, die. But neither the shifting is obvious nor does the adjusting come without challenges. To do both is… come on all together now… an act of leadership.

'We have always tried new things and will continue to do so' reflects Valentina Kristensen when I asked her about OakNorth's experience with pivots. 'We don't do a song and dance about it. We see what works. We move on from the things that don't. For instance we tried to offer mortgages and quickly realised that we understand entrepreneurs and their atypical sources of income but the market for mortgages is very different and we couldn't make our assumptions work. We stopped. Making the decision to stop was not hard. If you are willing to try it, you have to be willing to kill it. You also have to be willing to revisit when the time is right. The question is how long does it take you to commit, to make a decision to either try things… or kill them when they are not working.'

I have nothing to add to that. 10/10. No notes.

You will be pleased to hear I am done, for now with product market fit and pivots. I appreciate that was a lot and we are not even halfway through the fundamentals yet. So a little recap may be in order.

> The decision to stop things that aren't working shouldn't be difficult. If you are willing to try it, you should be willing to kill it.
> *Valentina Kristensen*

Your Call to Action

- You don't get to trade-off between the fundamentals of your business. You need to get product market fit, cost to serve, culture and your mechanics for negotiating trade-offs right and keep getting them right as the world changes around you.
- You can't get product market fit if you are trying to be all the things to all the possible customers. Focus.
- Getting pricing market fit is as important as getting the product right. In fact, it is part of the same process: if your market likes your product but isn't willing to pay for it in line with what it costs you to produce it (plus margin) you have a problem.
- Find a real problem that you understand to solve. That is two things: make sure the problem is real. Not hypothetical. Not simply interesting to you. But something actual paying customers experience. And make sure you understand it well enough to solve it.
- Realise that changing as required in order to achieve a purpose is marginally easier for a mission-driven business. Because they tend to know the problem they are solving and are willing to flex on the shape of the solution and the economics to achieve it. They pivot around principles. Not pet technologies or valuation wishes.
- Having no product market fit won't kill you per se. Burning through your cash runway or your shareholders' goodwill while not achieving traction is what will kill you.

- Deploying capital to gain and retain a beachhead is an option. Few take it because it takes leadership guts *and* cash, both of which can be in short supply. But being early can be a conscious choice and a strategic advantage.
- Deciding to pivot cannot be emotive, it cannot be everything and it cannot be vague. Ultimately, you will have to do it again and again and again as you grow, and the world throws you curveballs.
- Make sure what you are pivoting around is well understood. Not everything should be up for change. But most things should. Make sure you and your team know which is which.

Chapter 4

Unit Economics for the Home or Why You Should Be Ashamed to Admit You Don't *Actually* Know Your Cost to Serve

A business model is a business' plan for making a profit. Yes, I know you know. But bear with me. Business models are a bit like flossing after brushing your teeth. Everyone knows what they are for. Everyone knows they are good for you. Not everyone does the thing. Every single business I have ever worked in knew what a business plan was for and yet they all singularly failed to produce a business plan that was what it says on the tin: a plan. Not a set of abstractions but a plan for the business to actually follow.

As the song goes, what would Brian Boitano do, if he was here right now? He'd make a plan and he'd follow through, that's what Brian Boitano'd do[1], the *following through* being the critical part. But rather than doing what Brian Boitano would do, most businesses create business plans as artefacts, not statements of intent. The plan exists but it is more of a hygiene exercise for investors, auditors or analysts. Documents are *always* produced and shared, but they are often more window dressing than substance. Too abstract to be useful.

There are many tools and books and canvases and theories on how to put together a business model but, fundamentally, even if you use no science and just write down

---

1 Yes yes. Southpark, the musical. And yes yes, earworm. #sorrynotsorry

DOI: 10.1201/9781003395577-4

what you are trying to achieve, what you have by way of resources (people, money, technology), your known dependencies and assumptions, plus your next steps for a period of one to three years, on the back of an envelope, you are off to a good start. Provided you are honest about what goes in it, you reflect on the gaps it highlights and you are thoughtful in how you amend your next steps accordingly.

The model should spell out your plan. And your plan is no good unless you follow it. This set of haves, wants and configurations of assumptions is your plan to achieve profitability ultimately, not an intellectual exercise. This means that things like what you are selling, to whom and for how much are key (and we addressed product market and product pricing fit before so I won't repeat myself here), things like distribution models and partnership strategies are key and should be in there, as are things like costs. Cost is not what you end up paying for as a side effect of building your venture. It is a key driver of your work and your thinking around your cost base should be right there. In your plan.

> Most big banks know their cost base but can't always itemise unit costs, cost to serve particular segments or total cost of ownership for particular systems.
>
> Startups think that, by extension, they can be vague about those numbers too.
>
> They cannot. And increasingly neither can the banks.

Running and operating costs, manufacturing (or build costs in our industry's case), distribution costs. Unit costs. And costs to serve. We already saw Enfuce who were confident about what their product needed to cost to customers because they knew what it would cost them to build. We also saw audax going out into the market working out what the customers were willing to pay knowing full well if that number was lower than expected, they would need to flex on their cost base. If this sounds obvious, you may be in for a little surprise.

Fun fact for you: most banks don't know what their unit costs are and can't really work them out. Most businesses are terrible at working out what the total cost of ownership is for clients using their services. And many businesses don't really know how much money they will need to get from A to B. And if you are thinking that banks seem to be getting away with it just fine, as did startups in a world of free cash. You would be right. But that doesn't make it right.

So. Do better. Do the math. Know your numbers. And control them relentlessly.

What Does It Cost You to Exist?

Remember when Lizzie Chapman was describing how part of the challenge Zest Money faced was that it underestimated how much time and money it would take to disrupt the credit industry? They expected it to be expensive and cumbersome. They *expected* it to take years and tens of millions. But it was not tens, it was hundreds.

Lizzie is rare in her honesty, *not* in facing this kind of problem.

I remember working for a very large bank, inside a business process re-engineering division (it was a long time ago but not much has changed to be honest) and my boss went on an absolute crusade to work out the bank's cost to serve.

> Historically, investors have doubled down on the potential size of the target addressable market rather than the cost to get to live... or the cost to operate.

I don't know what was a bigger eye-opener for me at the time: the fact that nobody actually knew what it was, or that nobody cared. Things worked on the whole. At a macro level, we had a full view of our economics and, if need be, large levers marked 'cost cutting' could be pulled. They may have lacked nuance but they were effective. They may have lacked finesse but they balanced the books. Like the time another bank stopped ordering biscuits for internal meetings. For a global organisation, that was a saving in the millions. To employees it spelled disaster. Not because they lost their sugary treats but because the feeling was that if you can't afford a $5 packet of store-bought cookies, things are bad, right? Or when the sales team of a big broker dealer was 'rationalised' by one-third and their targets went up 50%.

We have all lived through those cost-adjustment exercises and we can agree that they are effective in that they keep the ship running but they are hardly efficient: they are usually over corrections, they hit indiscriminately divisions that bloated and those that didn't and they guess at cause and effect.

> You need to know what it costs for you to exist because a thriving business can stop thriving pretty rapidly when its cost base is out of control.

Surely, given our armies of super intelligent people and penchant for analysis paralysis inside our organisations, we can do better than that? We can manage our profitability through the double vector of sales and cost to serve? Surely. Right?

Actually, no.

Unit economics are largely scoffed at inside banks. The very idea is dismissed usually. We are not shoe manufacturers, the reaction went. *Why... you don't say, that's me told.* It is not that simple, we were told. Only it should be. If not simple then at least known and knowable.

I don't need unit economics to be simple: I want them to be known. You need to know what it costs for you to serve your different customers because some may be losing you money. You need to know what it costs you to deliver your different products in your different geographies because occasionally you are cross-subsidising and don't even know it. Even more poignantly than that, I need you to know what it costs you to run your organisation because every decision you make (to create a digital product, to build a new division, to compete in a particular market) entails decisions to build new systems, extend the capabilities of existing systems and by extension retain or switch off old systems. But that is not treated as a business decision. And often it is not treated as an economic decision. Even though it is both.

> When I told the Chief Business Officer of a large bank that systems rationalisation is not a tech decision, it's a pricing decision he answered 'no it's not... I don't pay for that... the Bank does'.

When I told the Chief Business Officer of a large bank that system rationalisation is not a tech decision, it's a *pricing* (not to mention an operating risk) decision he answered 'no it's not... I don't pay for that stuff, the Bank does'. And technically he is right. A central cost does not appear in his divisional P&L. But he is still paying for it. He just doesn't know how much it is and that is a problem. Just not one he is aware of.

You need to know what it costs for you to exist because a thriving business can stop thriving pretty rapidly when its cost base is out of control. The growth side of the equation can work great while the cost side gets out of control. So you need to be aware and you need to be prepared to do something about it. And that *something* can't always be indiscriminate job cuts.

I am sure you recall Kelvin's pricing validation approach in the last section: you work out what the market is willing to pay for your service and then you manage your cost base to maintain margin.

Do I need to tell you how important that is?

Actually, if you look around the fintech ecosystem and financial services ecosystem alike the answer is yes: I *do* need to tell you because the willingness to manage the cost base actively in line with the price point is extremely rare. What business decision-makers usually

> Cost to serve has historically been scoffed at in FS: venture-backed businesses went for growth metrics as the only thing that mattered... and established businesses often look to the markets, not their own organisation, to balance the books.

do instead is manage cost in line with the topline (if you are a going concern) or in line with a diminishing runway or an agitated board. Which means that they cut rather than manage. Which means that the discipline of seeing cost and profit as part of the same continuum doesn't emerge. The basic mathematics of what running your business costs: what you can possibly charge customers for your services, how that is looking and how long (build cost, volumes needed etc.) would be needed to tip you to profitability is a set of questions every business should ask itself regularly, even if it is established as the variables are never static.

But we don't.

For the large organisations in FS, the reality of our everyday work bleeds into the way we manage our balance sheets: there is a lot of jazz hands, making-the-numbers-dance leveraging, deleveraging and eating our own dogfood when we should know better. This is not a book about why Lehman Brothers collapsed but let's just say that, essentially, an organisation that can *profitably* take a liability off its books learns that they don't need to pay attention to mundane questions like cost bases and gross margins the same way as a manufacturer would.

For startups and venture-backed businesses the reason is different but there is a powerful reason at work there as well.

Historically, investors have doubled down on the potential size of the target addressable market rather than the cost to get to live or the cost to operate once there. Growth at all cost is a mantra we heard a lot, from the people who were bearing said cost. 'Hypergrowth' became one of those words like 'hustle' that were used to indicate you belong with the crowd that gets it and gets the pro-verbial done.

The Era of Growth at All Cost Is Over

Right or wrong, the prevailing winds set the mood music for a long while but now, as the funding environment shifts, that mood is also shifting.

Still, it is fair to say that looking back at the success stories still standing today, they didn't need to be told this (understanding your cost base) is important. They could work it out for themselves, as Simon Merchant points out in the last section. *They didn't need to be told.* And neither should you.

And yet.

I recall speaking to a company a couple of years ago whose monthly burn was higher than their in-year revenue.

> If you have taken VC money, you will report on the metrics VCs want to see: speed of growth, customer acquisition speed, sometimes speed of hiring. Rarely operating costs.

Please read that one more time: they spent every month more than they made in the year. And they were not a 'just founded' baby company. They were in their eighth year of operation, the product build was *going*. Admittedly not exactly to plan other than directionally. They were heading where they had said they were heading, but not as fast and therefore they were burning cash and lacking customer proof points to boot. Which of course had a compounding effect.

At the point of this conversation, their runway was just over a year and their sales cycle about as long as that because enterprise sales are slow and it is doubly hard to sell an unfinished product. Not impossible, weirdly, but hard. Plus at the time of the conversation, the CEO was not interested in talking about operating costs and a workable plan and bloating. He was hiring for acceleration, secure in the conviction that he would have no issues raising the next round of funding when he needed it. I am not guessing here, you understand. I asked. And he said the magic words: I will have no trouble raising. Even as the current funding situation was clearly visible on the horizon, the belief that 'it won't happen to us' was strong.

He was wrong, by the way. When the time came to raise, he found he had overestimated both his ability to raise and the VCs' patience.

> You train your team to believe that growth = success and they become addicted to growth itself.
> *Lizzie Chapman*

'So many entrepreneurs and businesses rely on VC funding to fuel their runway, without focusing on building a sustainable business model' observes OakNorth's Valentina Kristensen. 'There are metrics such as customer growth, cost of acquisition, or indeed valuation that are useful but they are not the most important metrics... unless you are a VC.' And she is right. The market has been long-focused on customer growth as a measure of success. VC-backed businesses reported on speed of build, regularly speed of hiring and speed to market, but rarely on operational costs.

It stands to reason that you will measure what you are asked to measure by the people who gave you the cash in the first place. Because it's their money you are spending, but also because you assume they know what they are talking about. And if you are a second- or third-time founder, observes Lizzie Chapman, you know that VCs operate this way. 'But first time founders see the investors as the experts who have been to this party before and you think they will help you.' Which is absolutely understandable. And if the people who are willing to put money into your business ask you about growth indicators, not cost to serve

> Historically, investors have doubled down on the potential size of the target addressable market rather than the cost to get to live or the cost to operate.

then you trust that they know what they are talking about. It's their money after all. Meanwhile, what you measure becomes what you focus on, as in all aspects of life. You end up chasing product features you don't need as we saw in Chapter 3. So you end up 'doing' what you measure, so you can measure more of it.

You end up over-hiring.

Either because you have the money to throw people at problems without thinking about your structure. Or because you need to hire to meet the growth targets and quality control goes out the window. I have worked with an investor who measured 'engineering onboarding' as a success metric. And we, as a team, were torn between trying to explain to him that it was a terrible metric of progress and giving into working with a metric that was very easy to game. But, of course, hiring like this inevitably leads to firing like this.

'We had been so good at this for so long' said confidentially the COO of a tech unicorn who had just gone through a very public round of cuts. Overall 20% of their staff had been let go, soon after celebrating their hypergrowth targets being met. 'We had been so good and the last 18 months, after the last fundraise it was grow-grow-grow. The investors wanted to see accelerated expansion so that became the name of the game. We hired. And now we are firing almost everyone who came in during that round plus a few more to even things out. It will be ok but it is painful and it has set us back by a year plus the year we spent doing the hiring and firing. We are worse off than we would have been if we left well alone.'

If you are thinking: wait, did you not just tell us this story in Chapter 3, you would be totally forgiven to think so but it is actually a different company. It is just an extremely common situation. Raising money is a constant cycle for startups. Both because you

> Hiring for growth rather than need may leave you worse off than if you had left well alone.

need it to build... and because the fundraise itself has become a metric of success in its own right.

Raising a lot of money at a high valuation is often an unthinking measure of success. And of course, once you have done it, the more money you have, the more you can spend. The more you can bloat. And, of course, the money always comes with strings. The investors want to see what they want to see, so you open offices abroad or hire faster than you can make the teams effective to please them. But that's not the only problem you may create for yourself by being flush.

When you have the cash, you are likely to over-engineer. Because you can. 'You build a Porsche where a mini cooper was needed' reflects one of the founders who'd rather not be named 'and then you are too expensive to run as a business because, having built a Porsche, you don't price it that way. Because the market didn't need a Porsche. And, for a time, it has been *silly season* with investors. They always pushed us to grow faster, even when we knew it was wrong.'

This is a very common theme. Well-capitalised businesses building platforms that are too expensive to run and price themselves out of the market are a very common fintech malady. And that is not all either.

If you have a lot of money and spend it to grow fast, recalls Lizzie Chapman 'your team gets addicted to growth', and this is as significant as everything else here: the entire industry became addicted to growth over any other metric. Cost to serve? What is that? Hypergrowth was where it was all at for almost a decade. The investors expect it, so you give them what they ask for and before you know it, your team expect it too. Because the investors wouldn't care if it wasn't true, right?

'You train your team that growth equals success' continues Lizzie 'and if you have a flat month people walk out because they take it as a bad sign'.

This has been the reality of fintech for so long. And then things shifted and the party was over. In 2022 and 2023, layoffs and contraction have been the name of the game for the tech sector in general and fintech in particular. While the big boys of financial services are enjoying a rare reprieve in the high interest rate environment (banks might as well print money when the interest rates are this high), entities relying on investment all of a sudden find money got very expensive.

Hundreds of companies were laying off hundreds of staff[2] and the trigger events[3] often included a regulatory fine or market shift affecting short-term revenues. There was always an external event pushing things too far and leading to the redundancies. But buried in the explanations in every article and personal story is also a realisation that, whatever the events that transpired were, their main effect was that they shook investor confidence. And that meant that the money tap was turned down to a trickle, if anything at all, and when that money stopped flowing it was impossible not to notice that the business they had coming in, couldn't sustain the shop they had built around it.

That was not a surprise, by the way. Everyone affected knew they were building a business that was not self-sustaining. The fact that it was a problem was a surprise. Many founders in fintech genuinely thought the free money would last forever. Now they know better.

You Don't Start at the End. But You Need to Know How to Get There

Asking an early-stage business what their expected or projected unit economics will be is extremely rare. Or it was, at least, while money was plentiful. Now we are at crunch time, the pressure to understand a business' cost to serve is mounting. What will it take to be successful? What do the numbers need to look like in order to balance the books? Effectively, the exercise Kelvin is undertaking as he road-tests his pricing assumptions, ready to adjust his cost to serve to make it work.

If you've never thought about it, working out unit economics after the fact is next to impossible, reflects Valentina: 'working out what your unit economics actually are when you have millions of customers is hard. Working out what they *should*

2 https://www.efinancialcareers.co.uk/news/2023/07/fintech-layoffs
   https://www.bloomberg.com/news/articles/2023-02-10/financial-technology-workers-slam
   med-by-thousands-of-job-cuts?leadSource=uverify%20wall

3 https://www.americanbanker.com/list/major-fintech-layoffs-in-2023
   https://www.fintechfutures.com/us/category/job-cuts/

be after the fact, even harder.' The amount of hard choices you would need to make to recalibrate your cost base is next to impossible. People often fire folks to balance the books but they rarely re-think their structure and operating model, they just go on crash diets and hope for the best.

For OakNorth, an understanding of that cost to serve was a key consideration from the beginning. 'We have a clear business model and a clear sense of mission but also a clear sense of where our cost base needs to be and where our profitability comes from.

> Working out what your cost to serve is after the fact, after you have clients, is hard. Working out what it *should* be, next to impossible.
> **Valentina Kristensen**

When we started, the measure of success was *will we be able to stand up a sustainable business that uses data and analytics to support the needs of customers, customers that have different realities and needs.* In the context of Covid, for instance, a retail customer may have an awful turn (a couture wedding dress shop for instance would see their sales plummet) or a lucky break (an online retailer of yoga equipment could still thrive), understanding that difference is key. Equally, as we lend to scale-ups, we can't look back to historic data, we need dynamic data that looks to their future.' That was the challenge at the start. And it worked.

So the measure of success now is can you prove the model in a downturn? Can you maintain this approach and cost base and deliver against the profitability assumptions? Looking at OakNorth's performance, the answer is yes and it is probably evident by now that my belief is: to get it right, you need to get it right from the start.

Rolf Eichweber, Royden Volans and the team of OM Bank wrote the most comprehensive unit economics white paper I have seen in my 20 plus year career to-date as part of their investment case for the new venture, OM Bank. Nobody had asked for it, by the way. But they knew it was needed. And, for the avoidance of doubt, this was on top of the mission statement for their new impact-driven bank and on top of the breakdown of their target addressable market, the personas of customers they were effectively doing this for: a deep dive into their needs and current options in-market.

Before they had made a single hire, written a single line of code produced a single wire frame. They produced a cost to serve analysis locking down three significant variables: what their services *needed* to cost in order to be palatable to the target market and true to the mission, i.e. what is the customer willing and able to pay; what their cost to serve needed to be (or what waterline it needed to stay under) in order for the endeavour to be priced right and profitable, because profitability is the key to success; the corresponding partner strategy to make sure those two numbers met in the middle.

At the beginning. At the very start. So it can be a plan to execute against. Otherwise it becomes little more than powerpoint filler. The discipline to do that work at the start is one of the hardest things. So most go for the Napoleonic approach *'on s'engage et puis on voit'*[4] which, in the end, didn't work for Napoleon and it won't work for you.

Ken Johnstone agrees. With Rolf and Royden, not Napoleon.

For Mettle 'our initial objective was to build a digital proposition with lower acquisition costs. A lower cost to serve was a core principle. *How* wasn't clear from the get-go. We had to work that out.' But they started from that. That was the exam question, above all else. Let that sink in.

This Is How You Do It: The Mox Story

Mox had worked out their internal mathematics from the very beginning.

The business *started* with three very clear imperatives tied to its plan towards profitability. You will notice that all three are pretty big, as assumptions go. Not the sort of thing you can think about after you've acquired your first

> In the early days of neo banks the focus was on cool features not sustainable economics. We all thought it was an innovation game we were trying to win.

batch of customers, as Valentina rightly pointed out above. Big, bold, foundational assumptions have to be there as the foundation of the business. You can't retro-fit them.

The Mox three-pronged plan was as follows:

1. Operate through a joint venture (JV) construct (so not the parent bank on its own and not a stand-alone new venture on its own) to accelerate adoption;
2. Lead with lending as a product as that is key to profitability.
   This assumption seems obvious now, knowing what we know about all banks and neobanks (and that is: nobody makes money without lending). But at the time, this idea went against the grain of all neobanks who went to market with lending loosely on their roadmaps *at some point* but no lending capabilities 'right now' or any time soon, really. Because lending is hard. But without it, you are not really a bank, are you? Definitely not a profitable one, at any rate.

---

4 You got me. We don't actually know if Napoleon ever said that. Some say Lenin did, though why would Lenin say it in French is a mystery. The point remains 'we engage, then we see' is a meme, not a strategy. Don't do it.

3. An intention to create a repeatable operating model that would further reduce cost to serve for the parent group when they redeployed it for other ventures similar to Mox in other geographies.

That last part is very interesting because it stretches out the horizon and types of metrics you need to deliver against to consider yourself a success. It complicates the business model. But it also defines it.

> The Mox model was designed with upselling in mind.
> **Deniz Güven**

These are also very clearly intentional decisions in a business model that cannot be thought of halfway through build. You either start going in this direction or you don't go in this direction. So it takes vision, discipline and focus early on. Especially as some of the ideas here were very new at the time and some remain unusual. The JV construct, for instance, was an innovative idea and explaining the rationale of the JV after the fact makes it seem like the most obvious move ever. But it wasn't.

'Collaborating with HK Telecom as a partner provided a significant boost, as they offered their customers a seamless transition of direct payments to Mox and a 5% cashback incentive' recalls Deniz Güven, founding CEO or Mox.

'This allowed us to tap into the payments and invoices of 50,000 customers across six different businesses, opening doors for cross-selling opportunities. The model was designed with upselling in mind while always prioritising service' continues Deniz. 'This approach facilitated the onboarding of additional JV partners to drive growth.

Building a new operating model required maintaining a relentless focus on differentiation across all areas: revised risk frameworks and anti-money laundering (AML) measures. And Mox has, by now, proved its portability.' In short the unit economics proved themselves in a timeframe that is half what any

> When building neo-banks many focused on user experience ahead of profitability. With time user experience became table stakes and the business model was the only real test of viability.

other challenger bank in the world has managed to achieve to-date. I would argue half the battle was won because they took the time to work out what their cost base and cost to serve needed to be rather than hoping it will all come out in the wash. Plus, creating the repeatable, lower-cost-to-serve infrastructure package also worked.

'Trust Bank in Singapore was built with the same tech stack and a similar operating model/partnership with Fairprice (the largest grocery/market of Singapore), thanks to Mox's learnings. Trust bank onboarded almost 18% of the bankable population in less than a year.'

This is why you should have a plan that you follow through, by the way. Excellence is never an accident.

This level of focus is not accidental. And it is not easy to come by. It comes from painful experience. If we go back a few years before Mox, when Deniz cutting his teeth with Garanti Bank in Turkey as well as BBVA's acquisition of Simple, we can see the germination of the ideas behind Mox and the testing grounds where he saw what worked (keep) or what didn't quite work (evolve). He had seen the significance of customer experience in customer acquisition but, by the time Mox came along, he had also witnessed that idea become table stakes and the complexities of standing up a business being where the new venture would live or die.

This is how the first rodeo, so to speak, informed the second: iGaranti Bank, the Turkish challenger, had a separate balance sheet as early as 2012 'with the full intention that the executives would see the digital business as a separate business line. In all the things we achieved, that was the biggest win' remembers Deniz. And a win that he replicated later, knowing it worked. 'We decided to build a new bank outside the main bank. That was not an obvious choice at the time.' It is now a pretty standard model but back then? It was as original as the JV idea was for Mox a few years later.

And as uncomfortable.

But that is the point: in order to do new things, you have to face the discomfort, push through and see what works. And this is a step-by-step process: you can't get to the JV idea without having first gotten comfortable with the idea that your new venture will be outside the main shop. The first rodeo was essential to get here. And there is more.

> The question we were trying to answer was can we attack other markets with our existing operating model? Can we defend ourselves against the real new giants?
> **Deniz Güven**

iGaranti had a separate tech stack, different banking licence, different products and different people to the main bank. And it worked.

'In six months we had 500k customers. People the world over started lifting the model because the experiment had worked.' Another lesson to be replicated showing that the lessons learned on your first try don't need to all be learned the hard way. You learn from mistakes, of course. But you also learn from successes. You learn what worked and how so you can build faster, aim higher and go further next time. As happened here.

But not all was plain sailing, recalls Deniz: 'The problem was that we gave credit cards to customers from day one but didn't *focus* on credit. We focused on cool innovative features (such as QR payments) rather than doubling down on money-making products. We assumed at the time that this was an innovation game.' But it was not.

Innovation alone does not make for a sustainable business. Another lesson learned. By the time Deniz had moved to Standard Chartered and accepted the Mox job the lessons already learned meant he was adamant Mox would be outside the main bank, that it would have its own tech stack, people and processes, that it would lend fast *and* that it would set itself up as a JV.

The interesting thing about people not on their first rodeo is their ability to get you through the first few rounds of challenges without dropping any points, without dropping any points, so to speak. If you let them.

'There was some resistance to that idea as you would expect but I felt really strongly about doing it this way.' This was, for him, now table stakes. Something he knew was needed, not something he felt he needed to prove.

'The question we were trying to answer ultimately was not "can we build a challenger bank" but rather "can we attack other markets with our existing operating model?" Can we defend ourselves against the real new giants especially in the Chinese context.' Essentially can we create a profitable structure with operating costs that are predictable and operating levers that are repeatable?

Mox was never about the cool design. Even though it had a pretty cool design.

It was always about the repeatable operating model. That's a next-order consideration and it comes with fully controlling your economics.

'These are provocative and real questions and I managed to sell the idea internally that we are not actually building a challenger bank but a new operating system for Standard Chartered. So we built every component under the new model. Then, the idea is, you can use it globally. It was never meant to just be the Monzo of HK.'

> It's easy to lose faith in fintech when you look at the boom and bust but if you focus on product and focus on making money rather than growth at all cost, you end up with a different model and it works.
> **Deniz Güven**

The vision was bold but, more to the point, aligned to the business model. And not everything worked first time, as you would expect.

'We made good decisions and bad' continues Deniz. 'We used some unproven solutions and of course when you do that you have to be careful, not everything goes to plan. But eventually you learn and we have now actually transposed the tech stack to a different country (Trust Bank in Singapore) with the exact same model. Which was the original idea: can we create a stack and model that can "travel"? In Singapore the JV partner is a supermarket chain, it's always a local JV, on the same stack and operating model and the intention to be service-first and upsell.'

When Deniz and I recorded this interview, in 2023, Mox was turning four. 'Next year Mox will break even.' Not many challenger banks can claim that they reached break-even in such a short time. Most are going for a decade and can't claim that yet. So it's a big deal.

'The scalability is amazing and the next time we use the model the payback will be sooner. Part of the reason is that we understand that we are in the credit business. You can get a credit card in seven seconds. You can change your limit in four. There was no other bank like that in HK and if you come in and your default turnaround time is always low single digits you can build a portfolio. It takes time but it is a beautiful business and we could break even with half a million customers.

As a VC you would probably push for growth but we are proving instead that a different model works. It's easy to lose faith in fintech when you look at the boom and bust but if you focus on product and focus on making money rather than growth at all cost, you end up with a different model and it works.

> Do you fundamentally understand the business you are entering?
>
> Most neo-banks have played a deposits game.
>
> The neo-banks making money are focused on credit.
>
> Growth will never substitute profitability in the long run.

Banking means credit and wealth products' continues Deniz. 'The deposit game is different and doesn't scale. You see challengers saying *yeah we do have credit* but only do overdraft… it's not enough. You won't make money so you won't be a sustainable business. You need credit cards, you need a full suite of products.

That is where the Mox success story played itself out.

The business model with the partner JV and focusing on real products, like credit. Mox has become the fourth biggest lender in HK.

That's the challenge: if you can build and manage the portfolio, this is a very good business. And of course we made mistakes. Even in the things we were focused on. For instance we could have managed the cost base better. We could have spent less while building. This is important as it impacts the cost model and of course it is key for your business model. The cost base and how you construct that is key to get right at the beginning. It is hard to fix afterwards. And I don't mean the capital side. Of course building a bank is capital intensive. Whatever happens. But you need to look at the business model and the cost base super hard and not conflate the two.'

That is very valuable advice and poignant as it was given in a year when fintechs had to cut deep. Having bloated on the back of VC money and 'growth' metrics, as we discussed, redundancies hit hard. But did the lesson land?

Managing Your Cost to Serve Is a Top of the House Job

We already mentioned the hundreds of fintech companies that cut thousands of jobs in 2022–2023, with redundancy numbers representing big chunks of the workforce and, occasionally, heralding geographic retraction or closures. FinTech

Futures, the industry's most widely read publication, even had a *job cut* section on its website as the news was coming so thick and fast; it was a genre[5]. The job cuts were measured in the hundreds of thousands globally and, if you allowed for bank closures and overall tech job losses to be counted in with fintech job cuts, those numbers get terrifying. This is not a wave you want to be at either end of, truth be told: you don't want to be losing your job in the middle of such a market retraction. But also, unless you are Darth Vader, you don't want to be the one

> The only way to avoid becoming a company that cuts its cost base brutally and publicly is to start off by being a company that manages its cost base actively and constantly.

cutting 200 jobs in one fell swoop either. Whichever way you look at it, this is something we should all strive to avoid.

So maybe people will start listening when we talk about managing your cost base actively, constantly, from the start and even when times are good. And for the avoidance of doubt, the only way to manage the cost base is at a company-wide level.

It doesn't work otherwise.

I have deep, indelible scars from situations when I managed the cost base of my team or division, keeping an eagle eye on our footprint and margin only to be hit with a redundancy target because one of my peers didn't do it for their world. And why didn't they do it, I hear you ask? Because there were no prizes for doing what I was doing, even though it was the right thing: when the CFO didn't consider it as important as hitting a number for the end of year board pack.

So if the CFO isn't looking at the cost base, why should the business leaders? Is the rationale. People do what they are measured on. Humans default to the behaviours that are rewarded.

So not only were there no prizes for the discipline I exercised in my world. There was always a penalty. Because when the time came to cut in a blind panic because the cost base had crept up on the very people who should have been keeping an eye on it, *then* we all gotta share the pain alike.

> Cost to serve has to be managed holistically across the company. There are no prizes for managing the cost in one division if it is blown up elsewhere.
>
> Everyone will share the pain in the end.

So I had to lose people even though I had been within my envelope, because that guy across the hall hadn't. And not having done the right thing meant that the guy

---

5   https://www.efinancialcareers.co.uk/news/2023/07/fintech-layoffs
    https://www.standard.co.uk/business/layoffs-cloud-uk-fintech-prospects-revolut-railsbank-zilch-zego-truelayer-b1062962.html
    https://www.fintechfutures.com/us/category/job-cuts/

across the hall had a buffer, and making cuts didn't hurt him as much in terms of his delivery. And I didn't have a buffer, because I had been a good corporate citizen, so the cuts hurt me both coming and going.

You could argue that I am the chump here.

But the reality is you cannot build a sustainable business without control over costs. And *not* controlling the cost because nobody is making you is not adult behaviour.

Don't be that guy. Be the other guy. The guy who understands that economic models need the simple mathematics of profitability to leave you in the black. Be the guy who understands that this has to be done early and done with intent.

I once worked with a company that absolutely subscribed to magical thinking. And why not, it had worked well for them for a time? But then things changed, and pressure was felt, real or imaginary, it doesn't matter. What matters is that when the pressure was felt, the person in charge of that business called his leadership team into his office one day and asked us to put all of our team members' names into a spreadsheet in the order we would fire them if we needed to. Top of the list should be the most expendable, bottom the most critical. The chap who would turn off the lights before going home if things got really bad.

We would be done then. The last man standing.

It's an awful thing to have to do, by the way. Even if it is necessary. It's an awful thing that leaves a scar if you do it. And it is also a stupid thing to do because when we all kicked off saying this is insane and we needed a clear sense of what we were cutting *towards* in terms of either a plan or a number: so that we could determine operationally what was needed to achieve whatever we were going to try and do: are we cutting so deep that the product roadmap lengthens by three years? If so, maybe I don't need a sales team right now, no matter how good they are. Are we just slimming down? Are we pooling resources? Is there even a strategy?

We clamoured. We reasoned. We pleaded for some targets or guidance as to where this had come from and what we were trying to achieve. So that, if we are going to do the terrible thing, let's at least ensure we achieve something workable. The answer was: just do it. We called those weekly meetings the Death Squad sessions. And they didn't work. In case you were wondering. Knee jerk decisions rarely so.

So manage your cost to serve from the get-go and keep doing it. Do it intentionally, do it holistically, do it relentlessly. But do it with intent. Having a list of people in the order in which you will execute them may look like *method* (see here, I have a spreadsheet) but it is lunacy.

Managing Your Cost to Serve Is an *All the Time* Job: The Wise Story

It is impossible to talk about relentless focus on unit costs and not speak about the phenomenon that is Wise. Fun fact: I met the TransferWise (as was, originally) founders when the company was less than a year old, at a swift Innotribe showcase, and singularly failed to realise I should have bought some shares pronto. More fool me.

I have been a customer pretty much since then, though. And a fan. So when I spoke to Harsh Sinha and Steve Naudé in the Wise offices in London in the summer of 2023, that relentless focus on margin was the first thing I wanted to unpack. Because if anyone got this right from the get-go, it was them.

'Our mission is to build an FS business that helps customers and is aligned on principles' stresses Harsh. 'We talk more about how much money we have saved our customers than our revenue.

There is a lot of tension in many business models around who the customer is or what principles they are serving. We are clear on those. We want to build a profitable

> **Harsh Sinha, CTO Wise and Steve Naudé, Head of Wise Platform**
> Wise is a UK-based foreign exchange financial technology company founded by Estonian businessmen Kristo Käärmann and Taavet Hinrikus in January 2011. Wise specializes in cross-border payment transfers. As of 2023, it offers three main products: Wise Account, Wise Business and Wise Platform.

business and achieving that is a stake in the ground for sure. But we are not done solving the problem we set out to solve.'

'So we maintain and encourage a long term view of the world' adds Steve 'we say no to short term ideas and this long term view drives everything. For instance, we don't give bonuses here. Everyone gets stock. Net worth is a long-term play.' That sounds amazing.

And given the success and steady growth Wise enjoys today, it is almost hard to remember these clear-thinking commitments were made at the start of a journey that had not yet been mapped, not yet certain, not obvious, and, in the grand scheme of things, not so long ago. So the question is how does a company that is yet unproven, that is yet unfunded and doesn't have customer traction yet, a baby company, frankly, with its back against the wall because that is the reality of any company seeking funding, make these meaningful, strategic choices?

> Not compromising on your unit economics, not cutting corners, not going 'let's do it anyway' when things are tough is the only way to build a sustainable business.

When or indeed how do you have the presence of mind to make these bold moves? The answer is, to paraphrase: you don't even consider doing it differently. What's the point of doing it at all, if you don't do it like this?

'In 2015 we were talking about our unit economics, what would it take to reach profitability with a view to getting the company to a good place for a raise' says Harsh. 'Honestly, it didn't look good. So we started looking deeper. We developed a Dry Land Plan. We became more deliberate and thought long term. We have always had a high NPS score and referrals but we were spending a lot of money on marketing. We stopped. We changed some vendors. We focused on our desire to build and be around long term, especially as we knew that the next raise would be harder. So our focus was twofold: unit economics and cultural alignment.

In 2015–2016 we only invested in product and engineering. But we found that killing the marketing budget didn't kill growth and, to this day, two thirds of our growth is through word of mouth. And our addressable market is huge as people are online much more than ever. Plus the cross border space is getting bigger.'

I have nothing to add here.

I am tempted to paraphrase in order to force you to think about the implications of this. Really think about the implications of the choices made here when things didn't look good. The choice to double down on unit economics, manage the cost rather than fuel growth and hope for the best. It seems obvious when written down

> We have an insanely close and clear view on our unit economics. And we incentivise our teams to understand the cost levers of the business with a view to always lowering prices for customers.
> **Steve Naudé**

like this but very few people actually choose to do it because it is harder than the alternative and requires more discipline. It requires you to stop doing certain things, swap out vendors and suppliers, not indulge in fantasy. And the fantasy could take two shapes: the extreme looks like the founding team doubling down on what is evidently not working in the name of staying true to their vision. The less extreme and extremely common looks like the founder or founding team working themselves to the bone doing stuff that doesn't move the needle. Doing more of the same. Or things of mixed importance and significance and claiming (and actually believing) that they don't have the time, money and energy to do what is really needed to save the company because they are too busy keeping their head above water. Like the proverbial Winnie the Pooh opening salvo of Christopher Robin coming down the stairs pulling Pooh Bear by the leg. Bang goes Pooh Bear's head against each step. 'There must be a better way to come down the stairs' thinks Pooh to himself. 'If only my head could stop hurting long enough to think about it.' It's the most common reaction but it is a terrible one. What you need to do is what Wise did. Stop and think. What isn't working and what do I need to do differently to get to dry land?

What do I stop, what do I pause, what do I double down on?

And some of the changes you make may be long-term ones. Not just survival moves but long-term strategic commitments to how you will operate going forward. For instance: 'Our Dry Land Plan has one additional principle as well and that is that we *do not* cross subsidise, we do not spend with the right hand what the left hand makes. If a product can't sustain itself, we don't fund it from elsewhere' stresses Harsh. That is true discipline around unit economics right there. Steve concurs, 'this is helped by the insanely close and clear view we have on our unit economics. And we incentivise our teams to understand the cost levers of the business with a view to always lowering prices' for customers.

If you are thinking 'why of course: is there another way?' the answer is yes there absolutely is.

Speaking to Mariam Ogunbambi, Chief Client Officer of Engine (a core banking solution leveraging the technical capabilities built for Starling Bank) during London Fintech Week 2024, she explained that Starling was doing the exact opposite. The parent is intentionally using its profitability to power this product. Although the entities are separate (one is regulated, one is not) they cross-pollinate in terms of ideas and talent, learnings and accelerants and they share the bounty. The parent company is profitable so it can invest in Engine. Which frees up the team to focus on building a good product rather than chasing their tail to secure investment with everything that brings in its wake.

There is separation but fundamentally Engine is benefiting from the power of the collective and from everything the team has learned from building a digital bank from scratch – which they can apply to servicing banks. Which comes into its own when they can take a client (Salt Bank in Romania) live on the new stack in just under 12 months when industry averages are in multiples of that.

> If we offer a client a certain price and a competitor undercuts us and the client goes with them, our offer stays on the table. We won't do business at a loss. And we won't spike our prices if the client comes back after first going with a cheaper option. We are transparent at all times.
> **Steve Naudé**

> There are many ways to think about your unit economics (cross-subsidise or not) and many ways to achieve profitability (organic, venture-backed, inorganic) but you need to be intentional about which way is your chosen way and what metrics tell you how you are doing.

When you put it like that, it sounds like a winning model too, doesn't it? And that is the point with strategic choices: once you have picked a direction, it looks obvious, but when you are in the thick of it making decisions, leadership is needed. You need to choose a model for the right reasons and then implement it and protect it with focus and intent. Because challenges along the way will abound. And because, unless you are crystal clear about what you were doing, you will not have any way of knowing if it is working. Simultaneously, when you have chosen a model, you need to make sure that you keep an eye on the metrics that apply to your model. We have already said that the industry often measures things that don't matter enough to tell you whether a company will survive. It is easy to measure what is easy to measure. Or what someone asks you to measure. But, since what you measure becomes what you focus on, be mindful that you don't measure what everyone else is measuring in the industry but what is a health metric of your chosen model. Because the Wise and Engine models are different and therefore their health metrics are different and if you keep an eye on the wrong gauge then more fool you.

The intent in choosing a model, executing against it and keeping an honest eye on the numbers as the only source of truth about how you are performing is ultimately hard but essential. And in many ways, what you see when you listen to Harsh and Steve talk about the discipline of this decision-making process is leaders who haven't believed their own myth. And I ought to take a moment to remind you what the alternative looks like.

What Is the Opposite of Wise?

On the aftermath of the SVB... demise? Collapse? Wobble? I don't know what to call it as it collapsed but didn't die leaving us with a thing closer to a wobble than a death, dramatic though it looked at the time.

Tell you what. You choose your word there. Whatever you call it, you will have spent time thinking about 'what the heck happened here' if you work in our industry. For me, the sentiment in my own head was best captured by Alex Johnson who wrote, reflecting on the fintech industry more widely on the aftermath of the wobble, that ultimately magical thinking and drinking your own Kool-Aid leads to decisions that are the opposite of what I describe above. They are not intentional, they are not disciplined as to the cause and effect relationship between actions and desired outcomes.

And we have seen a lot of it: retractions like Railsbank, scandals like Wirecard or Frank. And don't get me started on the crypto world.

> Researchers have discovered that you are more likely to go bankrupt if someone in your neighborhood wins the lottery. Over the last three years, a bunch of folks in fintech won the lottery. And now we're all going bankrupt.
>
> *Alex Johnson*

What we see time and again and what we saw on the runup to the failures including SVB's is, in Alex's words 'magical thinking that is completely at odds with basic logic and the lived experiences of these institutions. And yet, I can't think of any other explanation that would cause otherwise sober and analytical bank executives to take these obviously-stupid interest rate risks.' That applies more widely frankly to all the founder teams that were faced with the stark mathematics of growth and chose not to do what Wise did.

'This is a symptom of a larger problem in the recent history of financial technology' continues Alex. Language that is toxic and charged has been pervasive over the years and it has a corrosive effect, as Alex points out, essentially suggesting that anyone who doesn't feel comfortable taking risks and shortcuts is dumb. 'And that same impulse – to believe that only fools and losers don't take shortcuts, even when those shortcuts are clearly risky and/or immoral – has permeated the entire fintech industry' continues Alex. 'I see it everywhere. I see it when founders and VCs debate what the most *believable* interest rate for customers will be, rather than what would be the best or the safest.

I see it when a stablecoin issuer opens bank accounts using falsified documents. I see it when B2C fintech companies ignore fraud in pursuit of growth. I see it when the hosts of a popular podcast casually joke about dumping inflated tokens onto retail investors. I see it when a founder says, "fuck it, we're doing it anyways," and launches a new product while lying about it being insured. I'm tired of seeing this shit.

Researchers have discovered that you're more likely to go bankrupt if someone in your neighbourhood wins the lottery. Over the last three years, a bunch of folks in fintech won the lottery. And now we're all going bankrupt. I hope, as an industry, we can learn from this and do better.'[6]

This is important. Because Alex is right.

Economic Models and Risk Models Are Not Either/Or Choices. They Are Conjoined Twins

The SVB story is in so many ways an exercise in poor risk management.

And it was the most visible case, perhaps, but it was not a unique set of failed economic and risk management decisions. Good decisions are risk management too, by the way, even though you don't think of that when you look at a successful venture. Both because we tend to think of risk management as 'bad things not happening', not 'good things happening' but also because, as Alex said above, we tend to think of success and risk-taking as coterminous or at least regularly overlapping.

Would your opinion be different if I asked you to think of the operating model Starling chose or the choices Wise made in terms of investing or not investing in a different vertical (different as these models are) as exercises in risk management within the parameters of a

> When I talk about getting the business model right, I evidently don't mean 'do the business model canvas and put it in a drawer'. It is an ongoing discipline.

---

6 https://workweek.com/2023/03/11/ngmi/

particular operating model? Which is exactly what doing the hard, disciplined work is: an exercise in risk management.

Literally, doing the maths.

Incidentally, the discipline around economics isn't an isolated thing. You are not disciplined about that and laissez-faire about everything else. So it goes hand in hand with a lot of other good habits.

The 'startup mentality' that Alex describes above often survives after the growth of a business, reflects Maha El Dimachki. And it is imperative that it does not. 'How do you develop a mindset around governance and regulatory awareness that is not about box ticking but enablement for business? How do you think about risk tolerance, capital allocation and reputation management? A scaling company won't always have the right mindset' which is understandable but a concern. A concern young companies need help to get right, perhaps. And you'd think that the investors would help with that but, so far, the indication is that they don't. So if you look around your team and go 'oops, I don't have anyone who's done this part before' use some of your runway to bring in NEDs or advisors or, if you can afford them, a couple of executive team members who know how to manage cash flow, operating costs and a risk governance model.

At the same time.

'From a regulatory perspective' continues Maha, 'consumer duty is all about outcomes. A lot of things can be foreseen. It shouldn't have to take the regulator to come in and take steps. Why can't this be industry-led? Is it habit? Is it industry inertia and box ticking? Part of this is the interpretation of regulatory frameworks as well. We want outcomes-based regulation because we want to give business the space to create and yet often you hear *our compliance department ties our hands*'. Maha is thoughtful and measured but she's right on the money.

And I would say (not putting words in her mouth: this is *me* saying) the same mindset that doesn't keep an eye on its cost base, that isn't disciplined about its own proof points is fast and loose with governance. And because this is the money business, we all pay the price. So when I talk about getting the business model right, I evidently don't mean 'do the business model canvas and put it in a drawer'. It is an ongoing discipline. And it doesn't start when your business starts being grown up. Or when money is tight. It doesn't even start when you are in an established patch of the market. It starts at the start and then it is always there.

Pismo took a year working out what kind of company they would be. Enfuse sized their ambition, their cost expectations and all eventualities that may cause shareholder tension before they even made a penny. They spent the time working through how they will work through tensions from a moment of calm. This is, by the way, the best real-life application of John Rawls' Veil of Impartiality[7] that I have ever

---

7 A concept socialised in John Rawls' 1971 seminal work *A Theory of Justice*.

seen. I am going to oversimplify here but essentially Rawls says that the only way to be fair and just when making provisions and decisions is if you didn't know how they will affect you and yours when the time comes. If a theoretical veil of impartiality descended upon you as a decision-maker and suddenly you didn't know if you are rich or poor, male, female or trans. You don't know the first thing about your race, ethnicity and religion or sexual orientation. What decisions do you make about social justice *then*? Decisions that protect everyone, right? For all eventualities. Effectively, that's what Monika and Denise did. They sat down and worked out how they will navigate crises before they knew how they would feel in the moment of the crisis. They created a risk-register with not just appetite statements but action plans from a first-principles base. This is inspired. And rare. And tells you a lot about the people involved.

> Procurement and legal can't negotiate a contract for you if they don't understand your strategy, your unit costs, your required cost to serve, your NPS levers.
> *Rolf Eichweber*

'How you are built as an entrepreneur starts very early on' reflects Monika with a smile. 'Success becomes an equaliser.'

Perhaps.

But maybe success distracts from the very deliberate steps that came before it.

As I already stated (yes, yes: repeatedly, I know) OM Bank, the insurance-backed challenger in South Africa, has the clearest view of its cost to serve requirements as a necessary condition for achieving its mission that I have ever seen. When I complimented Rolf Eichweber on this, he had this to say: 'You have to sit down with a value management strategy. Bankers, from the CEO through to management and actually, often, any other corporate, rarely understand their own business. If you ask a senior executive inside a corporate to name the levers that affect their income statement, they wouldn't be able to tell you. That applies to a lot of successful exits as well. More luck than judgement. What is a bank? How many bankers can explain it to a call centre operator? How often have you done that? Ensuring that every single part of your organisation knows how it all works.'

That is exactly what Rolf and his team have made sure that they do: make sure everyone on the team knows how things work, how they fit together and how they affect each other in terms of cost, risk and performance. And they did this with everyone and from the get-go because, like most things, this gets harder the bigger you are. Plus if you get this thinking done upfront, it can help guide decisions. 'Procurement and legal can't negotiate a contract for you if they don't understand your strategy, your unit costs, your required cost to serve, your NPS levers' points out Rolf. 'Everything needs to permeate across the organisation. Every moving part needs to fit together and work together as one engine.'

Reach for the Stars. Then Count Them

Remember Teun van den Dries who, after selling Geophy, decided to put all his money and energy into democratising access to electricity? I don't even know how you start thinking about that, so I asked him what was the hardest thing ahead. His answer was not what I expected. But then again, with Teun, nothing ever is.

'The hardest thing ahead is de-risking expectations. There is a strong public policy component as yet not fully formed when it comes to space, plus a regulatory component around the electricity grid. Asteroid mining is not an established industry but essentially you can't sell what you don't own, so do you colonise?'

> Being well capitalised does funny things to your head about how much you can spend. The size of the problem you feel empowered to take on is only secondarily about money. It is about pattern recognition.
> *Teun van Den Dries*

You are a pirate, I said. This appeals to me to no end. A privateer, he corrected with a smile. You can actually claim an asteroid. It is perfectly legal. For now. And this window of time is what makes the business.

'Some innovations are inevitable, just 20 years out' continues Teun. 'This idea felt like something I can accelerate. The science is solved for. It's a capital problem. And the opportunity is huge. The current annual electricity spend is 5.5 trillion dollars. How do you get around the incumbent vested interest problem on a bigger scale? That hasn't been worked out yet and the product market fit is yet unknown. But I was looking for a problem that is big enough.'

He sure found one.

Electricity may not be the only vector in the global warming and climate change crisis we are living through, but sustainable and free/cheap electricity means you can solve most others by replacing energy sources. So it's worth doing, is Teun's view. But if it's a capital problem (and it is) we are back to my very boring question about economics. Inevitably.

Even when the numbers are huge, you need to work through them. That's the ball game. So what's an MVP in this space? Literally: what is an MVP in space? What's an acceptable cost base for something as huge as this?

'We build a spacecraft, launch to an asteroid' (note for the uninitiated: they are not easy to locate as they are dark and fast moving) 'then rendezvous with the asteroid… touch down, grab the minerals we need… then fly back. The MVP will take 25 million dollars and 6–7 years. It's been done before by both US and Japanese scientists and we aim to be 1,000 times more cost-effective than them'.

Just because the numbers are big doesn't mean you should keep an eye on them, is the point I am making (although I totally get you that want me to shut up about unit costs and go back to talking about star pirates. Sorry: privateers).

To really do this at scale, even pumping all his exit money into the venture, won't be enough and that is no accident. Teun could have decided to do something he could do end to end with the money he had. He specifically chose not to.

'Being well capitalised does funny things to your head about how much you can spend' stresses Teun. And that applies to everyone. 'The size of the problem you feel empowered to take on is only *secondarily* about money. It is about pattern recognition. Ultimately, I wouldn't be intellectually engaged doing less.'

You are welcome to come back to this if your day ever starts feeling overwhelming, to create a sense of perspective. Both in terms of the size of problem some of our fellow travellers choose to address, but also for the universality of certain facts. Whether you are trying to mine asteroids or give me an easy, fast, secure and cheap way to send money home, you don't get to *not* keep an eagle eye on your unit costs. Or if you do, you pay the price for it. Eventually.

> It doesn't matter whether you are on a shoestring budget where every dollar matters or dealing in the hundreds of millions where thousands of dollars here and there are rounding errors. Whatever your scale of operations: do the math.

The Unappreciated Art of Saying No

Are we talking about the price of innovation here or putting your money where your mouth is? Are we talking about the inevitable successes of people making hard choices in a way that ultimately sets them and their businesses apart?

I hope that the inevitable conclusion you get to as you read both the product market fit section and the unit cost section is a realisation that you need to get good at saying no, in order to do justice to your vision and actually get anywhere. You won't get product market fit if you pursue every idea. You won't scale if you don't focus. You won't live long enough to get to profitability if you spend your money indiscriminately.

Saying no is key.

And not just for startups. The same challenges affect large institutions as we have already addressed. You may not run out of cash, if you are sitting inside the giant that is ING but you may squander good will, time, energy, talent: 'it's the same problem, just a different currency' observes Simon Boonen.

> You need to get good at saying no, in order to do justice to your vision and actually get anywhere. You won't get product market fit if you pursue every idea. You won't live long enough to get to profitability if you spend your money indiscriminately.

But what do you say no to? And when? Sadly, the answer is: it depends.

Have you had the privilege of meeting Curt Queyrouze yet? He is the man who will tell you context is everything and that, partly, is your answer. Curt is the President of Coastal Financial Corporation but 'I've been in banking over 40 years' exclaims Curt. You wouldn't think the maths adds up, if you met him. In terms of the looks or the energy he exudes. It just doesn't add up. But the stories do.

Curt Queyrouze, President, Coastal Financial Corporation
Formerly President and CEO of Tab Bank

'My dad was a banker. My first job was at his bank, running a coin counting machine. A year later I graduated to working as a teller. I didn't even have a terminal. If a customer came in that I didn't know, I had to go check last night's ledger to see if they had sufficient funds in their account for whatever transaction they wanted to go for. *Manually.*

At the end of the day someone took all the credit and debit slips in different colours and they would tally and initial every stub. *Manually.*

> The bankers are trying to avoid making the one mistake and the VC funded innovators are focused on making the one big hit.
> *Curt Queyrouze*

Back then, a financial institution in Texas couldn't be serviced by a bank more than 12 miles from their HQ. The law changed soon after I entered banking but at first banking was manual, hugely local and fragmented.' And none of this is that long ago.

For anyone entering banking now, that seems like an impossible statement. And yet inter-state banking in the US isn't that old. It just led to such a radical consolidation and reshaping of the landscape since it happened. A change so radical that it's hard to remember how recently it wasn't so. 'As late as 1984/5 I remember visiting a small bank in Oklahoma' says Curt 'and they had a paper ledger. A 14 column ledger book.' That was not so long ago either, all told.

'The speed of change is crazy' continues Curt. From paper ledgers to AI-first architecture is a huge distance to cover in not such a long period of time. And the pace of change keeps increasing.

'Now AI changes everything. Chatbots were cool but we never thought it was a game changer until ChatGPT came into the mix. And now this is a different ballgame. Star Trek territory. Everything other than transportation (you can't quite go *Beam Me Up Scotty* quite yet) is here. And yet the role we play for communities hasn't changed.'

Why am I telling you all this?

Because the context of rapid change is the context in which we do the job. The mental load of everything that goes on at once is additive to the mental load that comes with the day job anyway. The mission and the communities you serve, the product build and the sales efforts, the meetings and the continuous anxiety around getting the product market fit right, deciding whether it's too soon to call it and pivot, keeping an eye on your unit economics… it's a lot, right? And in this context you need to decide what to say no to. You don't want to be left behind. You don't want to get distracted. How do you keep that balance?

> In my former shop, we would hold up squirrel signs at meetings if we got the sense that we were about to get distracted by shiny objects.
> **Curt Queyrouze**

Context is everything. As are your team members.

'In my former shop' says Curt 'we would hold up squirrel signs at meetings if we got the sense that we were about to get distracted by shiny objects. I have tried to maintain a focus on infrastructure, for instance, because although running towards shiny objects is attractive, you need to have solid foundations. At the core of it all is data mastery.'

That focus on the fundamentals and a belief in your own strategy was key to Bianca Bates' description of how Cuscal made its bets. When I asked her whether hindsight makes her wish they had done things differently her answer was illuminating as to the value of

> The line between the messianic founder who won't take feedback and someone who lacks conviction and won't stick to their guns isn't as broad an avenue as you'd want it to be.

focus: 'With hindsight we focused on the right things but we also allowed too many things to claim our time.' And time is money in the most real sense.

'We were less discerning at the beginning about funding or time given to too many things. We may have given too many ideas oxygen' continues Bianca. 'Years ago, we spent a lot of time with small, occasionally crazy startups, while trying to work out what the next great thing is. We have learned now that we do not have endless capacity. We have become more discerning and there is nothing wrong with that. Good ideas will still survive. We will still partner and support smaller companies. We just need more demonstrable alignment and value. Good ideas will still come through.'

Saying no is a learned skill.

And you won't always get it right and you need to be ok with that.

'There are some things I said no to in my old job that my current firm didn't say no to, and I see them now as runaway successes' continues Curt. 'Some others were 100% the right call. It's a game' and we won't win each hand we play. That is a given. 'But on the day to day, making decisions is the most important thing. Accepting some level of risk is important to move forward during a disruptive period. You can't do it all. What *will* you do? When will you be ready to make mistakes, particularly the bankers who were trained to reduce risk to zero?

Everyone is chasing the same wealthy, no-risk customers and there is very little money left to be made in that arena. The allocation of capital can actually be a distraction. You have to allocate it in a way that doesn't pull you off track. What happened to good old Research & Development? There was a time when banks had R&D budgets. Now the innovation sits in the realm of VC funding and the economic motivation is inverted from where bankers are. The bankers are trying to avoid making the one mistake... and the VC funded innovators are focused on making the one big hit. As our world transforms, you have to make bets. We have to lean in, but you will struggle if your culture is not right or ready.'

> In time we have become more discerning in terms of what we spend time on.
> Nobody has endless capacity.
> **Bianca Bates**

Because Curt is clear – and right – that the most important thing is making choices. When you don't commit to a course of action and let optionality linger (invariably in the very human hope that some external factor will de-risk your choice or highlight the right path and make your life easier before long), what you do in that time is add mental and material strain on your organisation, deplete resources and potentially rob yourself of valuable time to deliver against the things you say yes to.

Effectively, indecision is a drag on your operating cost. From a multitude of directions: from the simple fact that if you need to cut costs today to the tune of 1 million, every day you don't act that number gets higher; from the productivity loss of overwhelmed people to the cost of optionality and all the decisions not made in-between.

So *No* is better than indecision. Always. Even if it is not the right answer.

But it is still risky and it takes leadership to reflect and make the call. That is the point of leadership after all. So the question you should be asking yourselves, my young padawans, is what does it take to make this kind of intentional, continuous decision-making part of your DNA as you grow?

I turn to Wise's Harsh and Steve with this same question. The answer is deliberate but not necessarily easy. It takes discipline and *intent*.

> You won't get every decision right. And you don't need to say yes to everything.
> But the most important thing is to keep making decisions.
> **Curt Queyrouze**

Steve reflects that Wise's platform business started as a startup within Wise, two to three engineers and 'all principles were applied from day one. Again relentless focus on unit economics. And constantly asking: do we have the right Dry Land Plan for the right moment in time? There is so much you *can* do.

We give our teams power to assess what our focus should be by looking at what is in the market. That is how the platform came about. It was bottom up, not an abstract strategic decision. And we continue to behave like a startup within the startup which means we don't cross-subsidise and we are writing quarterly updates pitching for money.'

And that is important. It's not just living up to the principle of not cross-subsidising. It's the discipline of the whole thing[8]. 'We have practices that keep us honest', stresses Harsh. 'We present plans to the whole company. You have to explain *to the whole company* what you are doing and why you are getting funding someone else is not getting.

> Intentional, continuous decision-making needs to be part of your DNA. It takes discipline and intent. It doesn't just happen.

Peer accountability is key.

And this is harder to scale as we grow. When we were smaller, cross company engagement every time we presented a plan or an idea was amazing. Now that we are bigger it's harder. But leaders are encouraged to lead by example and seek peer feedback. Leadership turns up for every squad day. All our slack channels are open. We used to have feedback coaches. This cuts all the way through. So deciding to accept that we will be loss-leading in the B2B for a while is a public decision. Deciding not to drop our prices under what is sustainable is a public decision. The teams are aware.'

That transparency is woven in with the discipline around unit economics and wider values in a way that is hard to untangle and separate and that is also the point. The long-term vision, relentless focus on cost to serve and transparency means that the tenor of conversation inside the business is different.

Steve reflects that pricing is top of mind for everyone. Consistency, integrity and not playing games with the pricing become a default behaviour. Wise won't undercut their competitors. They won't compromise on their cost to serve to win business, the delivery of which may break them. If you recall, Enfuce took a similar stand and were not surprised to see that their competitors who had cut their prices had also cut corners to make the thing stack up.

'Over time we believe consumers always notice when the price others discount to get the business, spikes soon after they land the business' observes Steve. 'We see our competitors pricing below what is sustainable. We play a long game in this as

---

8   In case you are worried what became of the platform… it is thriving, thank you very much… landing a huge marquis client before this book even went to print https://www.fintechfutu res.com/2024/04/nubank-partners-wise-platform-to-power-new-global-account-offering/ #:~:text=Nubank%20partners%20Wise%20Platform%20to%20power%20new%20Glo bal%20Account%20offering,-Written%20by%20Tyler&text=Brazilian%20challenger%20 Nubank%20has%20partnered,offering%20and%20international%20debit%20card

well. So, say we offer a client a certain price, a competitor undercuts us and the client goes with them. Our offer stays on the table. We won't do business at a loss. And we won't spike our prices if the client comes back after first going with a cheaper option. We are transparent at all times. At times it has felt difficult to hold the line but the economics have washed their face every time.'

> Work out your price point and your margin. You need to be able to operate your business in the envelope of what is left between the two, or you don't have a business.

Hold that thought, even if you forget everything else.

'You have to keep the focus' says PensionBee's CMO Jasper Martens. Uncertainty is the name of the game in a young company. We spent a whole chapter discussing the impact of luck, the power of timing, the exogenous factors that could accelerate your journey or make your life very, very difficult.

Realising the significance of all that from the comfort of your chair while reading this book is easy. Imagine being in the moment when the pressures are real, the answers not yet known and the responsibility of making choices to drop or not drop prices, to hire or fire, to invest and double down or not are on you. These things loom large.

The decisions are not always clear-cut and the line between the messianic founder who won't take feedback and someone who lacks conviction and won't stick to their guns isn't as broad an avenue as you'd want it to be, really. But ultimately saying No is the key. Saying No to the distracting ideas. Saying No to the things you can't afford.

And saying No to the things that take you off course: financially or existentially.

'It is possible to pivot too much' reflects Jasper. 'It is possible to do too much in the name of *growth is everything*. We [at PensionBee] stuck to our guns. We said no to things. We did the boring work around risk and compliance. We said no to other savings products, beyond pensions, because it's a different product with different regulations. We stayed focused. We are pension specialists!'

That clarity of what you are here to do, ultimately, guides what you say no to.

And there will be moments of doubt and worry. Jasper thinks back to the early days of PensionBee and recalls the team was aware that success depended on getting the customer to trust us. But there was never a moment of 'we will not make it' recalls Jasper.

How come, I ask.

The team, he says with a smile.

So it is time, my tribe, to turn to the next of our four fundamentals: your people and your culture.

But before we do that... here's your homework from this section.

Calls to Action

- Your business model is your plan to reach profitability: it is not powerpoint filler. You create a plan so you can follow it. So don't put it in a drawer. It's a tool. Not artwork.
- Do you know what it costs for you to exist, as a business?
- It is easier to work out what your cost to serve needs to be early. You need to be able to operate your business in the envelope of what is left between your operating cost and your price point, or you don't have a business.
- Your economic model is what proves your business. Early traction is just a ticket to the dance. Not a proof point.
- Managing your cost base is a *top of the house* job and an *all the time job*. If you do it in a panic, you will do it badly.
- Your most significant decisions will be committing to the things you won't do in the name of maintaining focus.

Chapter 5

People Are (Not All That) Strange

It is not a surprise (or should not be) that any account of success or failure, greatness or short-sightedness in startups or big corporates comes down to people. Even going asteroid-hunting, Teun already told us, is a people problem. People are flagged by everyone I interviewed as the single most significant factor for success, as the biggest risk and the greatest asset. Human failures, by the way, account for *all* the reasons why digital transformations fail. It could be failures of leadership, alignment, collaboration, talent retention or culture. But it is always people. Never tech.

On the startup side you could argue that failure could come due to failed product market fit or money running out but, as Nektarios pointed out in an earlier chapter, product issues usually come as a result of a misaligned team. And running out of cash comes from a team that delayed critical decisions, failed to control costs or underestimated their ability to make it rain. So it's people again. And again, it is *all the things* at once.

> When we talk about people, we mean leadership, talent, team composition, culture and the ways in which you preserve and protect those as you grow.
>
> And they are not interchangeable or sequential.
>
> They all need to be happening at the same time as each other and at the same time as everything else in this book.

DOI: 10.1201/9781003395577-5

So let's unpack this.

Because when we talk about people, we are talking about leadership, we are talking about talent and team composition, we are talking about culture *and* we are talking about the ways in which you preserve and protect those as you grow. And they are not interchangeable. And they are not sequential. They all need to be happening at the same time as each other and at the same time as everything else in this book.

Much in the spirit of everything we have seen so far, this work is hard because you have to do all of it, simultaneously. All the time. For ever. And that is hard, so it is often tempting to drop something or at least park it for later. And that 'something' is very often the people part. Although everyone pays lip service to this. Everyone will say that this is important. Most will pretend they are actually doing it and do little more than pay lip service to 'culture'. They will talk about how it is everything and it needs to be defined and protected.

Over the years it has been my favourite thing to do, asking employees what their company values are. Most don't remember. Or remember for the wrong reasons. Some, for instance, remember because there are inside jokes highlighting how far from the lived experience of the organisation the corporate narrative is. And some, very rarely, beam and shout out values that feel real, lived and true. Because that is what your culture is: a living thing.

And although you need to get it right from the start, the question is: can you?

I asked the co-founders of Enfuce what was their thinking and intent around culture when they started and they answered me with their trademark disarming honesty: 'Nothing!' said Denise with a laugh.

'That is not how you start! We started building. Then when we were about 14–15 people we started asking our team *what about us brought you here, what keeps you here?*' Start with what is real. Note to self. 'It's weird to talk about culture when it's two of you but, if you want to build a 100 person company you start with your own values and build something around it. And the core values need to be true because you will be tested. And the culture will evolve with every employee that comes in. And you will have to let that happen but also act if something isn't working.'

When you get started with a business and it's just you and your co-founder, you know the culture of the business will be important but you cannot even pretend to build towards it when it's the two of you sitting at your kitchen table.

There is a moment though when you are no longer around the

> It's artificial to try and pin down your culture when it's just you and your co-founder at the kitchen table.
>
> But it's too late if you haven't done it by the time there are 100 of you.

kitchen table where it is clear that you need to be intentional about 'what kind of place we are'. Because 'what kind of place we are' determines not just how people feel about coming to work, although happy people work harder so that should be reason enough, but also because 'what kind of place we are' determines whether people feel safe enough to put their hand up and admit a mistake or ask for help. Whether people feel trusted enough to take initiative or bring their ideas to the table. Whether people go the extra mile for you or each other when things get hard and you need to pivot and change your organisation mid-flight or when you need to grit your teeth and do more with less until the next round of investment comes in.

Culture is also what colours the feelings people – potential customers and influence-yielders in future – carry about your business years after they have moved on. I recently had breakfast in what was my old office: with a friend who has recently joined BNY and one of the senior leaders who was there when I was there, ten years

> Culture is about what it feels like to work here. It is about 'what kind of place we are': are we the sort of place where people can admit to making mistakes and are willing to bring their most creative ideas to the table?

previously and counting at the time of the breakfast. 'You should visit more often' he told me as we were parting ways 'this is always going to be your home'. It wasn't just words.

He meant it. And I feel it.

And that is what culture is, ultimately, an invisible glue that holds people together and their efforts are the fuel of your company. So it matters.

Everything we have talked about so far and everything after this section (including how you manage your culture) are leadership decisions so, although this chapter is about people, it is secondarily about heroes and lead actors. It is about people as a collective and the dynamics between them and how the context your business creates determines what that *feels* like. And what it feels like dictates what happens next when the rubber hits the road.

So I am sort of dying to call this section 'it's people, stupid'. But I know you know, so I can't justify the exasperated aggression of the line, much as it captures the fact that although we all know, we keep getting it wrong. We keep believing in false idols, we keep acting like talent is fungible. We keep assuming culture can be 'fixed'.

I get offered a job to turn around a toxic culture about once a year. The recruiters keep a straight face when they describe the job to be done. The title that comes with the poisoned chalice of a job varies. It can be an operational role, a delivery role or a revenue-generating role in a company that has become toxic and is beginning to feel it.

How?

That varies, to be honest and it depends on how perceptive they are. It could be talent retention and Glassdoor reviews, exit interviews and employee survey impacts. It could be performance metrics. It could be angry clients (it usually is). It could be lawsuits. When the leadership, talent and culture are not aligned, all the things can and invariably do go wrong. And although those turnaround jobs pay well, they pay well for a reason: it's danger money.

Culture can't be fixed. It can be mended, healed and nurtured but it can't be reinvented. So get it right from the start and protect it with your life.

Do Something Every Day That Scares You: The Capital One Story

I won't lie. I never thought I'd be quoting Eleanor Roosevelt. But when we talk about transformational leadership, there are traits involved that go well beyond showing up every day and sitting in the biggest chair at the top of the table with a fancy hat on. Leadership always matters. In all aspects of life. But when driving complicated, first-of-its kind work, leadership becomes more important than ever, both because it creates constancy, as Arthur Leung already noted, and because it sets the tone of exactly 'what kind of place we are'.

'At the end of the day, every story is about leadership', points out Michael Anyfantakis, sitting in a quiet corner of a buzzing Finnovate get-together in London in 2023. 'The Capital One story is a story of a business that has reinvented itself three times. First it was data-first when nobody else was doing it, then it focused on targeted acquisitions, then it became cloud-based before anyone else in the space even thought about it.'

> **Michael Anyfantakis, Chief Architect and Head of Product, Capital One UK**
> Previously FIBR, Capita, Lloyds, EY and IBM

Capital One announced its intention to move to the cloud ahead of anyone in the market, to be honest. That's not them bragging. That's a fact.

As early as 2015, when another big bank CTO was telling me (and I quote) 'the cloud will never catch on', Capital One announced that all new applications would be built on the cloud[1] and by 2020 they had completed the migration from all eight of its on-premise data centres to Amazon Web Services (AWS), becoming the first US bank to report that it was all in on the cloud[2].

How was that possible?

'Our CEO is one of a kind: unafraid of a pivot' admits Michael, with understandable pride. And that set the tone of what kind of place they were.

---

1 https://aws.amazon.com/solutions/case-studies/capital-one-enterprise/

2 https://www.capitalone.com/tech/cloud/

'Today we have 0 mainframes, 0 data centres. But he is not your typical bank CEO. He is a *founder* CEO. He is a different animal. And of course with scale and regulatory oversight come constraints, but the instincts remain. The clarity and richness of the message from the CEO directly to all of the employees is key. He spends four half-days talking in detail to everyone in the company. He spends time understanding and learning all the context from the people around him. He gives detailed examples and shows greater understanding of tech than even some of the tech leaders.

> The clarity and richness of the message from the CEO directly to all of the employees is key. In Capital One, people quote the CEO to their boss, when they want to explain why something should be done in a different way.
> **Michael Anyfantakis**

As a result, people quote the CEO to their boss, when they want to explain why something should be done in a different way.'

Hold onto this image of the CEO as a very active and very different state, folks. We are going to need it later. But hold it comfortably, like in a pocket or something. Because we won't need it again till the final chapter. I don't want you tiring yourselves out.

I love the Capital One story. Because it's a live example of radical, visionary and applicable leadership. Someone who sets a vision and paves a way in a way that teams feel they can apply it to their work. But a leader, as the famous John C. Maxwell quote goes, is someone who knows the way, shows the way and goes the way. And part of going the way is making a clear commitment to the path chosen, making it very clear that this is the way and saying no to everything else.

> When he declared that we will move everything to the cloud our CEO also made it very clear that we will *burn the ships*: legacy tech/platforms were finished so everyone needs to get off those or they will go down with them.
> **Michael Anyfantakis**

'When he declared that we will move everything to the cloud' continues Michael, he also made it very clear 'that we will *burn the ships*, meaning some of the legacy tech/platforms on mainframes, so everyone needs to get off those or they will go down with them. This was a very clear message to the whole of the company. Which is how we managed to move the full bank from on prem to AWS in seven years!'

Anyone who has read my first book (which should be all of you, seriously) knows that this kind of decisive decision-making is rare inside banks. And the decisiveness extending to migrating away from legacy systems *and then switching those off* is even rarer.

This decisive leadership means that, when a mistake occurs (and it will, because… humans) you have no choice but to fix forward. And this is vital. When doing something new, the first major reversal is when advocates of the status quo will start clamouring for leaving things well alone, prolonging migration timelines and 'parallel running' systems.

If you accept that mistakes *will* happen but going back is not an option because you will burn those ships, so to speak, then what choice do you have but to find a way forward within the parameters of your new strategy? You double down to find a solution. You don't just roll back at the first sign of trouble.

> Decisive leadership means that, when a mistake occurs (and it will) you have no choice but to fix forward.
> **Michael Anyfantakis**

Once you have made that decision at the leadership level and demonstrated that it is meant as intended and not just words, then that is the sort of organisation you become. That becomes the lived reality of how people face into problems when they occur. And they will occur.

'That was in response to a data breach' explains Michael. In the early days of the migration, there was an incident. Of course there was. There are incidents inside banks every day and that's not when they are attempting transformation of this kind. Of course issues will occur. But because of the 'no way back' mentality, what they did was *not* go back. Instead, they fixed forward, doubled down and now 'we probably have the safest bank running on AWS'.

Standing Alone Is a Choice Not an Inevitability

The leader that inspires, commits and delivers is not just a rarity. It is also an extremely heavy 'ask' of a single person especially when the job is to imagine, execute and scale a vision while also convincing investors or corporate decision-makers of your direction of travel.

> Given how many things need to happen all at once to successfully build or change a business, it is madness to expect that all the leadership will come from one person.

Within the context of a startup, you have to fundraise, manage shareholders, build your product and run your business. Within a corporate, you have to convince and manage the corporate and build and run your business. Whichever way you are doing your new work: it's a lot.

Rolf Eichweber reflects that 'if you try to give the job of convincing a corporate entity to do all this work… *and* do all this work… to a single person, you will fail and they will fail no matter who they are. It is too complicated. It is too much. One human doesn't exist who can do it all. The CEO needs to find their partner and that partner has to be an equal and a twin. Who is paid exactly the same. Whose bonus increase is exactly the same. Who is treated by the CEO and the organisation as a twin *and exactly the same.*'

I must admit, this degree of partnership is rare to behold.

But Rolf is not speaking of an abstraction. He has such a twin (you will meet him imminently, or as he would say 'now now'[3]). Success, to Rolf, is tied to the balance of this partnership: the division of labour and the honesty that comes with it to ensure that blind spots are avoided to the extent possible. So my first question was *how do you find this person, who balances you and challenges your blind spots and has complementary skill sets and all that jazz?* Where do you find that business twin?

I expected to hear a tale about trench buddies who came up through the same fires. Friendship, old colleagues, army buddies. Because how else do you find these people? 'In my case' says Rolf 'it was blind luck'.

'Roy is smarter than me, understands detail better than me, has expertise I don't have. The thing I am better at is navigating politics. I am lucky and I know that if I lose him, the whole project would fail.' I am only a little jealous of Roy being appreciated like this. But I do firmly believe that celebrating the value of people is good leadership. 'You need to practise being ok with being in the room, complimenting one another on the good stuff and calling out one another on the bad stuff' says Rolf. And that's not just between him and Roy but across the entire team.

You need to surface the dropped balls. Confront the reasons. 'Why did you drop that ball: Should you have asked for help? Did you just forget about something that needed doing? People will often say they have that openness but mostly they wouldn't actually because it feels like shooting yourself in both feet.

> You need a partner for the road that shares the burden and complements your skills and temperament. You may get lucky and find that person or group easily. But whether you find them easily or not, create clear rules for the road ahead.

When I first worked in a bank, I was called up on it. *What do you get for being the courageous town crier? What's your benefit?* Was what I was asked.

You can end up really isolated. And in traditional, old-school banking that was true. Thankfully things are changing. But the question is always are we putting the right people in the right place. Are we asking the right questions of them? At all levels.'

---

3 Now, now now and just now are not the same thing. I appreciate this joke is only funny to South Africans. And me. And it took me a while to get the joke but I am here now.

This sounds amazing, doesn't it?

It particularly sounds amazing when you have lived through the alternative. The boss that penalises you for not keeping your head down as we heard from Dharm in the first chapter. Or the toxic co-founder. Observe just for the benefit of comparison: Speaking to someone who is currently in court with their two co-founders (and hence asking to remain anonymous), I heard a tale that was harrowing in its specifics but familiar in shape. The founders got together and excitedly started building something. They seemed aligned. They worked through 'what' they would do and how they would do it but they didn't work out what they would do if things went wrong. Not everyone does what Enfuce did.

And what happened next? Things went wrong. Of course they did.

And one of the founders started strong-arming the others into heavier dilution, selling shares, reducing their salaries. There were justifications. There were reasons. Whether they were good ones is, of course, heavily subjective. 'Ultimately, our principles, values and work ethic were not aligned. What we all considered "fair" in terms of dividing the work or the equity, wasn't the same. We all used the same word but didn't mean the same thing and by the time we realised that... we were too far into it to "reset".'

The alternative?

The Enfuce story. Where the bad experience of one co-founder meant they sat down when they had nothing and divided how you will divide things when they have something. Where they didn't take the trust between them for granted even though they had known each other a long time. Not everyone lucks out like Rolf... So back to the idea of leadership through partnership.

So you gotta ask. If the key is putting the right people in the right places and Rolf's secret weapon is Royden: who is this man and what can we learn from this partnership?

'I have a deep desire to change the way things are done. In everything I have leaned into. What starts as a small idea becomes a *let's change an industry* imperative. I am incapable of keeping things small. I am drawn to the creative process of not just solving a problem but working out what we are solving for. So building a bank from scratch appealed to me. Plus, when I was first approached to join this work, I was drawn to the idea of banking as a societal good for the average South African.

But I was worried about the culture. I wanted to be confident about it, so I flew up (Roy lives in

Royden Volans, formerly COO of the OM Bank Build, seasoned consultant and banker
Futurist at Kearney
Formerly Chief Risk Officer at Woolworths

Cape Town, the team was assembling across the country, in Johannesburg) to meet them. And the first thing that struck me is the way the team treated Rolf. As an equal. I had a conversation with Rolf about the role of culture but I already could see it in practice. And Rolf, in his own right, was an appeal. We have now emerged as partners. He equalised our relationship. He chose to. He didn't have to.'

Only he *did* have to. *If* having a culture of equals at his top table was important to him. That's the only way it can happen: if the leader makes it happen. It sets a tone about the overall culture that is, like all other things in this chapter, next to impossible to fix along the way. So get it right at the start.

So the Leader Created the Team in Their Own Image, in the Image of the Leader They Created It

I am not one for biblical references normally but the connection is vital to bring to life. In bold, transformational work, the leader's behaviour forges the culture. Not the culture statements. Not the t-shirts. Not the fruit baskets (although yay for fruit baskets). But the way the leader shows up.

The things they do. And don't do.

The way the leader behaves defines what kind of place we are. Not what they say but what they do. That determines if a team will hide mistakes and cover up failures or own them and drive change where change is needed. Ultimately, in fearful cultures the need to pivot won't be seen on time and won't be executed decisively because fear is a terrible counsel and if you are afraid that speaking up may cost you your job, and you have a mortgage to pay, you stay shtum.

In Capital One, this bold, clear, engaged leadership by extension creates a culture when you learn to not be afraid to fail. 'We have opened and closed a number of new products, businesses, and countries' reflects Michael. 'When things are not working, we recognise that and are not afraid to cut our losses and close down. Usually this is within two- to three-year cycles, which is quite fast. Everyone looks at these cycles as learning opportunities, not as failures' and it all comes from the CEO. From the behaviours modelled and made (im)possible by the leader.

> Fearful cultures pivot too late for all the wrong reasons and often fail.

That, of course, is amplified or complicated by the dynamics between the decision-makers. Are they partners aligned in all things? Are they fighting over every choice? Are they each other's sounding board, like Enfuce? Are they a team that know, trust each other and stick together like Pismo or PensionBee?

Unlike your unit economics and sound leadership, that are non-negotiable things you need to sort out early on and keep getting right, having a solid founding team emerges as more of a superpower rather than an absolutely essential condition. Leadership is essential and ubiquitous, for the avoidance of doubt, but a rockstar and harmonious leadership team is less universal. It helps success but it is not a necessary ingredient for it. Perhaps because it is harder to come by. But those who have it cele-brate it for all it bestows. Those who had it, consider it key to their success. But it is obvious by looking at the market that success is possible without it.

Valentina Kristensen looks at the founders of OakNorth and has this to say: 'Joel and Rishi have been together longer than most marriages. They have complemen-tary skill sets. They have trust. And our team had stable, focused lead-ership throughout as a result.

> Behaviours are made possible… or impossible by the leader's own behaviour.

The founders of OakNorth were two of the most successful people you had never heard of' she jokes. They had money, they had vision, they had trust with each other and they built a business staying away from the fintech circus. And even today, they stick to a pretty low profile and are not on the circuit. They are entrepreneurs who want to help other entrepreneurs and the dynamic between them is as big a part of the business they built as the problem they are solving. That 'vibe' is largely why Valentina joined. And stayed.

Valentina finished university during the financial crisis. When she graduated, Metro in the UK was the revolutionary bank. Remember that? 'Open every day of the year and late into the evening… that was so refreshing… and now we expect to bank seamlessly all the time from home… that's how much the world has changed.'

> A rock-solid leadership team is an accelerant for those who have it but it is not essential for success and not uni-versal, in our success stories.
>
> Maybe because it is rather hard to come by.

She was drawn to working for challengers from the get-go and Metro was in fact her first client out of university. So 'the idea that the starting point [of change] should be what *not* to preserve is strong'. She was working with very interesting clients of all sizes, established as well as challengers and OakNorth was one of those clients. 'As a daughter of an entrepreneur, OakNorth's mission resonated and although I worked with a variety of clients who were in their own ways incredibly interesting, I had an epiphany that the days I enjoyed the most, were the days I worked with them.' The leadership and the way it felt to be part of this team was a big part of why she joined them full time and never looked back.

Jasper feels the same way about his journey with PensionBee. When I asked him about whether he ever feared they were not going to make it, his answer was a resounding no and his reason?

'We had the right people from the start. And it's the same team still, CEO, CTO, CFO, CMO. We are all still here. All the same people… nobody left: we feel we own this mission. The scale has changed but the work purpose is here and *everyone*, not just the founding team, owns equity in the business. You stick together. You work together. I work super closely with the CFO to drive customer growth in a way that he doesn't see [marketing] as a cost but as an opportunity to accelerate growth.'

The idea that everyone shares equity and shares in the long-term success of the business is one we came across earlier when we were speaking about Wise. In fact, Harsh and Steve, speaking of the Wise founding duo and the leadership vibe, are focused hugely on the fact that the founders are grounded. There is no ego. There is no bravado. But there is a lot of confidence. If asked, they absolutely believe that they could do this again. They could build something as momentous and successful just like Wise… again. They believe it and still are humble and grounded with it. That is a brilliant balance, if you can keep it.

> We had the right people from the start. And it's the same team, CEO, CTO, CFO, CMO.
> All the same people… nobody left: we feel we own this mission.
> **Jasper Martens**

Knowing Before the Fat Lady Sings

There's a lot of imprecision here.

A lot of 'knowing after the fact'. Saying 'it's a hard balancing act to get right' should not be the same as 'you will only know if you got it right when it's too late'. So I am compelled to ask: how do you tell apart a founder who holds the line and stays true to the vision versus an obstinate one, one that just won't listen? The sort of leader that isn't focused and committed but is giving off vibes à la Travis Kalanick in *Super Pumped*[4].

Harsh doesn't hesitate for a second: consistency is how you know.

'Is the strategy consistent? Is the vision consistent? Is their maniacal focus… consistent? if they are not doing something different every day and their desire to build a long term business is actually married with a desire to build a principles-based business' then you have your litmus test right there.

> Consistency is how you know if you are dealing with a visionary CEO or just a maniacally focused one.
> **Harsh Sinha**

---

4   *Super Pumped* is an American TV series that premiered on Showtime in 2022.
    Reasons to watch: Joseph Gordon-Levitt (card-carrying fan, here, reporting for duty) and the unexpected narration by Quentin Tarantino. Additional reasons to watch: it's sobering. That's all.

That resonates with me. As I have worked for the other kind. The one that gets a million ideas and pursues them all with the enthusiasm and focus of a chocolate labrador. The kind of leader whose team ask each other in hushed tones 'what is it today'?

So consistency in the maniacal focus is actually a good litmus test. 'And we knew, for instance' continues Harsh thinking about Wise's journey 'that if the Dry Land Plan hadn't worked, we would have needed to go back to first principles. Thankfully the numbers moved quickly.' But they were ready to do what it took, if it came to that. Which proves the consistency.

'Disagreement' adds Steve. 'The relentless focus on the outcome is there but it doesn't mean that disagreement isn't allowed. We are all open to being proven wrong and disagreement is encouraged. Servant leadership is a lived principle. And tenure is long here, for both the leadership team and the wider team. That says a lot.' Indeed it does.

In fact, as I have already said, many speak about culture and leadership but don't quite do the doing. Recently, I stood on a London stage with senior leadership from a fintech organisation notorious for its toxic climate and bad employee experience (not the

> If your organisation practices radical transparency and calls and slack channels are open… people will know both the direction of travel… and how you are travelling.

one you thought of immediately. The one you thought of next: that's the one). When asked how they balanced competing business model tensions and priority clashes inside their organisation the answer was 'our culture'. They were met with stunned silence.

They were neither challenged nor were they believed. Because Glassdoor reviews and employee churn speak for themselves. And as Steve says: it tells a story. And it matters. 'I am amazed how people make career choices and not look at that' muses Harsh.

So: consistency. Disagreement. What else?

Transparency. All decisions are public. All slack channels open. All trade-offs known: inside Wise, the teams know that we are not doing A because we are doing B.

Sardine's Soups Ranjan agrees. He believes that, ultimately, in a remote-first world radical transparency is how you connect everyone to the vision and everyone to each other. It is a way of checking the sanity of the enterprise and staying aligned. 'All our calls are recorded and available for people to listen to for background. Our repository is available to all.' But there is more.

'We never say no to a new idea. It is part of our culture. We always start from a place of *yes*. We want to be adaptable because fraud keeps changing. So we start from a positive place. When we decide we won't do something we make sure everyone is aware. We document all decisions: why, who, when.

We also go actively against the advice of not having too many people in meetings. If I go meet a team lead… and then they take my message to their team and take back their thoughts… why not speak to the teams directly? I do that. My team do that. Obviously it's a considerable time commitment but you want to hear things directly not through channels. All leaders (not just me) should hear directly from the teams. These are the most important meetings. And you need to show up for them.

> In a remote-first world, radical transparency is how you connect people to the vision and each other.
> **Soups Ranjan**

Even when I travel, I won't miss the sales update and the engineering update. Those are attended by the whole company because in a startup our size you should be either selling or building. The discipline of taking the time is key.

Obviously, customer meetings once they are in the diary they are set in stone and I don't like to move those. Then, if you have hired people who are self-starters and you don't need to manage their workload, if you have to miss a 121 in a particular week the team are ok. But we still have the discipline to be there. If I miss a call, which is rare, I will make the time to listen to it. Because being aligned on a variety of topics when you are remote first is hard.'

Radical transparency means that if all sides take the time to stay informed, you have supreme alignment. It means everyone in the company knows which direction you are going in. And why.

But it also means that they know how your driving is, so to speak. If I think back to organisations I have worked in, junior employees listening to a library of calls would soon build an image of a CEO shooting the messenger, or a CEO who kicked cans

> If you are stubborn and fail, you are just stubborn.
> If you are stubborn and succeed, you are resilient.
> **Daniela Binatti**

down the road and decisions onto the next meeting. They would see bad behaviours and good habits much more starkly than if they only navigate those relationships from their own vantage point where the context of the conversation always weighs heavily.

So transparency is definitely one way of knowing whether you are dealing with a lunatic CEO or a visionary one, from an employee standpoint.

Ultimately however, Daniela Binatti muses, the narrative changes according to the outcome. 'One investor told us: if you are stubborn and fail you are just stubborn. If you are stubborn and succeed, you are resilient. But we believed in our vision. So much.' And they also believed in each other: a founding team that had a long history and had each other's back. So 'every time something went wrong or we were discouraged we would get together and come back to the belief that this change needs to happen and if someone else does it and not us we will be so frustrated.'

This image feels right.

A group of people united by trust, friendship and a shared sense of mission. If you have a founding team like that, it becomes a leadership team who project and instil this way of being: that's something isn't it? It feels right and it is right.

What it isn't is common.

Conditions Suitable for Growth

Toxic work environments are such a commonplace occurrence, such a staple of our lives, we don't even blink when we hear of another toxic workplace any more. When a friend or family member laments their toxic workplace, most of us react with 'tell me something new'. But the reality is such work environments are neither inevitable nor naturally occurring. They happen because people's behaviour enables them to emerge and allows them to continue.

'People who don't recognise the value of other people, I just have no time for that any more' reflects Radish's Nektarios Liolios. 'VCs don't care about the inherent value of people. Corporates don't. So I have founded a company that does. I have opted for being politely polemic.'

> Everyone talks about the singular importance of culture and yet a sizeable majority of employees in the UK and the US say they have experienced a toxic work environment.

What is Nektarios referring to?

A 2023 survey from the American Psychological Association[5] revealed that 19% of workers say their workplace is very or somewhat toxic, more than one in five workers (22%) said they have experienced harm to their mental health at work, and the exact same percentage of workers said they experienced harassment at work in the past 12 months – compared with 14% in 2022.

An *MIT Sloan Management Review* article[6] found that in 2021 over 40% of people were considering quitting their jobs and between April and September of that year more than 24 million Americans *did* quit their jobs.

An unprecedented number. And the stated reason? Toxic work environments.

If the great resignation is a metric of what is going on out there, there is only one word for the state of cultures in offices and that word is: bad. A toxic work

---

5   https://www.apa.org/news/press/releases/2023/07/work-mental-health-challenges
6   https://sloanreview.mit.edu/article/toxic-culture-is-driving-the-great-resignation/

culture is to blame for resignations but also for over 60% of negative outcomes at work[7] including burnout, anxiety, depression and intent to leave. The number of UK employees that say they have at some point experienced a toxic work culture is a whopping 75%[8], a similar study in the US found 64% of respondents felt this way[9]. Better, but oh my god, still bad.

Everyone talks about culture being important and yet culture seems to be pretty awful in most workplaces.

So let's unpack it. What do we mean by culture, before we attempt to address why it matters and how it goes so wrong so often in the high-pressure change-focused environments we deal with in this book?

Although when we speak about culture, we generally mean 'the social behaviour, institutions and norms found in human societies, as well as the knowledge, beliefs, arts, laws, customs, capabilities,

> To culture (verb): to maintain (tissue cells, bacteria etc.) in conditions suitable for growth.
> ***Oxford English Dictionary***

and habits of the individuals in these groups', as a *verb* 'to culture' means 'to maintain (tissue cells, bacteria, etc.) in conditions suitable for growth' (both definitions from the *Oxford English Dictionary*, for the sticklers amongst us).

I like the verb.

Because it is exactly what we are talking about here: the intentional curation of an environment that maintains human talent in conditions suitable for growth: their own and that of the business. And arguably this is exactly what Royden was looking for when he took that plane to Johannesburg.

'When you start work like this, the hardest thing, at first, is to find people with the combination of the skills and culture you need' he explains. 'In a skills-deficient market such as South Africa, that is a challenge. Especially when you need to keep the balance of skills and culture. We expected this to be hard. In fact we expected it to be harder than it turned out to be. We have exceeded our own expectations. Around every corner there is a world of talent that you can actually attract to ventures like this. Especially now. Pre Covid you had to hire in-market, in the city your "office" was in. Even with us being across two cities (Cape Town and Johannesburg), we expected it to be hard. We expected we would need to explain [to the Board] why we are willing to pay a premium for the best people. That was corporate PTSD. We've never been challenged. There has always been trust.'

---

7 https://www.mckinsey.com/featured-insights/sustainable-inclusive-growth/chart-of-the-day/toxic-exodus

8 https://employernews.co.uk/news/toxic-work-environments-exposed-75-of-uk-employees-admit-they-have-experienced-a-toxic-workplace-culture/

9 https://employernews.co.uk/news/toxic-work-environments-exposed-75-of-uk-employees-admit-they-have-experienced-a-toxic-workplace-culture/

Which is great.

But there has also, evidently, always been intent. Building a culture and building the product were treated as jobs to be done from the get-go. Because this stuff doesn't happen by osmosis.

You Don't *Have* a Culture: You *Build* One

Somewhere between starting a business and having a business, creating conditions suitable for growth becomes possible. You can't do it at the kitchen table, as Enfuce told us already. But you can also not do it by the time it becomes imperative. It has to happen early on to be foundational but not so early as to be academic. As with most things in this book, it is more art than science. But thankfully for us, for some folks that elusiveness is the appeal.

'There are entrepreneurs who are really passionate about a specific sector. For me the sector is irrelevant. My passion is in the excitement of leading a business and building a culture' reflects Simon Merchant, CEO of Flagstone. 'And that has been my biggest learning at Flagstone: building a culture. It

> If you hire someone who turns out to be 'off' culture... and you tolerate that because of other skill sets, the team don't look at them in disappointment. They look at you, their leader.
> *Simon Merchant*

was the first time I got my company past that threshold where the business gets too big to know everyone and see everything.

We are 300 people now. The biggest learning has been the importance of a great culture because, once you have product market fit, success or failure is about scale. And your ability to scale boils down to three things: execution; funding; and finding, motivating and retaining good people. That is the only measure of success: creating a leadership team that is high performing and has trust in each other and has fun together. It sounds trivial but it is really hard to achieve and seeing a team fly is where I really get my kicks from. Everything else will follow.'

But it will not follow unassisted.

This is important. Curating the culture, protecting and ensuring it thrives is a constant occupation because a great culture is more fragile than we would like to think.

'In the past' recalls Simon 'I have recruited people in the leadership team that have the right skillset but were off the culture and I tolerated that because I wanted them to succeed or I was focussed on other skill sets and success. I realise now that when you tolerate that, the team don't look at the person who is off culture. They look at you.'

I wish I could tell you that doesn't resonate. But I have done this. I have been this person. I have hired someone who was perfect on paper. And then they arrived and they were absolutely perfect on craft. The clients loved them. Their output was impeccable. But their behaviour was terrible. And because they worked for someone who worked for me, I didn't see it immediately. I didn't see it often. It didn't jar as much as the results he brought shone. So, even after I saw it both with my own eyes and through the escalations of team members who trusted that I cared enough to intervene, I hesitated. Losing him caused me a problem. Both in terms of output and in terms of the clients. What the team said mattered and yet I hesitated. I removed him in the end. But I paid for that hesitation dearly: I lost a fantastic member of that team because of this and had a slump in morale that took a few months to right.

> You need to live and breathe your culture and it needs to start from the top otherwise it feels hollow.
> **Simon Merchant**

It was not worth it. And it was on me.

'People are scared about [the need to fire] because it means you messed up hiring which is true but what is the alternative? Not taking action? Not cleaning up?' reflects Enfuce's Monika. 'You need to be merciful to the team and yourself. We are clear about our expectations. We have a no-nonsense mentality, transparency and integrity. We have built a company we can be proud of. Which means I never want to be ashamed of the things we do: errors will happen and you need to take accountability and correct them.' And that could mean letting go of someone who can't upskill or keep up with the pace. Or letting go of someone whose behaviour doesn't align with the values.

If you tolerate either poor performance or behaviour that doesn't align with the culture, it's not the person misbehaving that is the issue: it's the leader. Because in tolerating the thing that wasn't meant to be who we are, the entire culture promise feels hollow. And there are no two ways about it: if this

> People often don't talk about the need to fire because it suggests mistakes were made. But mistakes will happen. What is the alternative? Not correcting them?
> **Monika Liikamaa**

happens you have to move fast. 'You need to trust your instinct and action a change as soon as' continues Simon. 'I have learned that now. If I think someone is not a keeper in the long run, I used to think *I will fix that but now is not the right time.* I don't think that any more. You need to move and act as soon as you realise someone is not a fit. Because *then* you need to repair the trust. And there is no workaround here and no substitute.

Trust is absolute and it takes far longer to rebuild and repair than it does to establish it in the first place. And it takes a long time to correct a mis-hire. The process of bringing someone in… realising they didn't work out… getting them out… can take two years and you can lose other good people on the way if they don't see consistency of judgement and focus from you.'

Don't I know it.

So you are what you tolerate. Everything else is window dressing.

This vigilance and swift, decisive action is key. And it is hard at all times, but it gets even harder as you grow. 'As you scale you need to be explicit about defining the culture of a business. You need to write it down and commit to it' continues Simon. 'You need to hire for it, live and breathe it. New people need to come in already sharing values. When we are hiring, we eliminate about half the candidates on culture fit. We have culture ambassadors and every first interview is with them. Which means that a C suite candidate could have a first interview with a junior product manager. Those cultural ambassador roles are formalised and we choose people who share the values and show consistent evidence of behaviour that aligns with those values. Ultimately you have to involve everyone in this process and still it has to come from the top. The behaviour of the leadership is key. Otherwise, the culture feels hollow and artificial and it is demotivating.'

> Culture isn't about 'loosely defined positive stuff'. It needs to be real. It needs to be about what it feels like for a particular group of people to get together and do good work and enjoy themselves.
> **Gareth Richardson**

Thought Machine hires with an aggressive focus on culture fit as well. And they are clear and unapologetic that it's all about the 'fit'.

Gareth Richardson reflects on the fact that, in our industry, 'culture' is usually the term we use to denote some loosely defined positive stuff. But the thing about culture is that it needs to be real. A group of people getting together and having a lot of fun solving some really hard problems. The specifics of what that looks like differ from team to team and may not work for everyone. Gareth worked in places before Thought Machine that had a strong culture and the specifics of that culture wouldn't work at Thought Machine and vice versa. What is universal is 'that we need to work together every day and all work on the same problem so we need culture *fit*'.

> You should stop thinking about your culture in terms of what is 'good' but rather in terms of what is 'real': it is not an abstraction. It is the lived reality of your teams.

What that culture is, is specific to the organisation. The need for the fit is universal.

Similar to Flagstone, Thought Machine do culture fit tests first, when hiring. 'For engineering in particular' explains Gareth. 'We bring people in for beers and a chat before we find out if they can do the job. Sometimes you see a totally different person in an interview vs in a group. You see who engages, who seeks to dominate a conversation, you see who you want to speak with and work with. Do you want to be next to this person every day?

We don't always get it right of course but what we find is that when we get it wrong there is "organ rejection". Within six months either the people the person is working with will raise a red flag, or that person will go "I don't like this place" and leave. Of course, we will have discussions and warnings if behaviour is seen that isn't aligned with our values but if organ rejection happens, we have to listen to it.'

The culture of a company has to be a consciously maintained artefact but it is, clearly, also visceral.

Arthur Leung, CPO at Shawbrook, reflects that one of the reasons for the business' success inside his organisation 'is the paradox that the people who have been here longest are the most adaptive to change.' This sounds counter-intuitive and we are used to hearing that the old hands will be the first to resist change, but not at Shawbrook. This *is* their culture.

'There is this antifragility concept' explains Arthur 'they have survived change and shaken out those who are not true to the core of the company. You know they can navigate change and lean forward, they will have the curiosity to see what would happen if we made any change. They understand that change is like fitness. It's a way of being. It is not a phase. You stop running… it gets harder to get going again. So we have to keep up our fitness.' And part of the way to do that is by hiring people who get it, and firing people who get in the way.

Values over Value

Culture is not an abstraction. It needs to be a lived reality that your teams both believe in and thrive in. By definition, not every *place* is for every*one* and that is not often spoken about, but it is as significant as everything else we have discussed here.

Your culture needs to be true and a positive ecosystem to thrive in for those that are suited to it and for those it suits. That means that some people you just shouldn't hire no matter how good their CV, some people you should fire fast and some folks, as Gareth points out above, will fall by the wayside naturally.

> You need to be intentional about your culture and invest in it. Actively and materially. It won't just happen.

A strong culture is key. What makes up that culture is, frankly, up to you and your business. In that sense, a toxic workplace for me could be Loki's dream playground. And that is, or should be, ok. What is needed for success is a strong, self-sustaining culture. Not an objectively good one.

That said, the specifics of your culture need to be aligned to your business in a way that isn't jarring for your people. The culture itself needs to be a lived reality but it also needs to jive with the work itself.

If you are an animal welfare charity, you don't kick puppies in the face. If you are the Green Party, you recycle (yes, yes there is a story there but it is *resolutely* for another time) and if you are building an empathy engine (such as Bond AI), your team needs to carry a culture that puts empathy at the heart of everything. It is not a thing apart, says founder and CEO Uday Akkaraju, because how can you build the product if you don't share its fundamental purpose. 'And of course if you have an empathy based culture, everything else becomes easier. The question is what happens when in certain behaviours or situations those values don't come through? You need to be always on alert for that. You need to have the conversation. You need to course-correct. We are lucky to have the right people that make this easier but we remain vigilant at all times.'

This author doesn't think it's luck, dear readers, it's judgement and active curation. And I mean very *active* curation. Remember Uday takes every potential hire to dinner with their spouse to get to know them in a relaxed environ-

> Building and maintaining a company culture isn't 'light' work. The leader needs to take time over it. And be seen taking time over it.

ment. And it doesn't stop there. 'We have six locations globally and every month two people from one office will visit another. We make the cooperation component of our work key. Visiting is part of how we do things. And, of course, none of those things are cheap. You need to spend time and money on them. We care about the balance sheet. But we care about the mission more. So we will invest in the mission and our people. This model won't fly in any corporate. We know that.

We also give people six months to get themselves into the groove. We don't expect people to be operationally effective in a shorter time frame. They need to learn and acclimate. That also costs money. Our investors make this possible.'

How you retain this at scale is a question Uday is losing sleep over every day. He knows he will have to adapt. He knows he won't want to give it up.

Soups agrees. 'We used to have all new starters travel so that people could meet each other' he recalls. 'As we now curtail travel, we have to overshare on slack. Every win. Every investor conversation.' Ensuring people feel connected and informed isn't just about going through the motions. It takes time and effort and money. Even if you don't travel: maintaining the culture you want is resource-intensive because if it's not dollars you are spending, it is time.

You need to be intentional about your culture and invest in it. Actively and materially. Time, money, attention and interventions when needed.

It won't just happen.

'This is my third enterprise software and SaaS startup. Yes, of course we want to sell to banks but our long term success is in helping our customers' customers (end users) to make better financial decisions' reflects Kasisto's Zor Gorelov. 'The focus is always on the end customer user: We believe every conversation in banking matters. We *all* believe this. *Believing* this is key to the ethos of the company.' Which means that part of what Zor looks for in people when hiring and part of what he seeks to instil in people when onboarding and managing them is this belief as lived experience. Because that is key to doing the job. Everyone in the company needs to believe that every conversation in banking matters. That's the culture.

'As CEO – and maybe this is not scalable – but since we started, I always sit down and explain the Kasisto vision, culture and values and what kind of company we want to build *to every new employee*' the emphasis is mine but since I can't do a dramatic pause in written text, I use what my elementary school teacher used to dismiss as orthographic posturing. Yes, I know. So in an act of sheer pre-teen rebellion, Italics it is. But back to Zor.

> There will be principles and values that are key to the business you are. The product you are building. Actively recruiting for those and managing for those is key to both your culture and any commercial success.

'I still personally onboard *every employee* and focus on our values. The relentless focus on the end user matters. Every conversation matters.' And who do the employees learn these values from? The boss. And how does he make it clear that these values matter? By taking time over them. By committing *his* time to them. By making company decisions and company metrics about them. This works but as Zor asks does it scale? Uday worries about the same thing as we mentioned above.

'We are 75 people now' he reflects. 'Honestly? I don't know what will happen next.' But he expects it to remain time-consuming and frankly expensive. The trips and the dinners may not be the way anymore. But they will be replaced by something that works well at scale. They won't just stop.

What Will You Be When You Grow Up?

Pismo set out to democratise financial services. Not a small feat but the four co-founders were ready for it. They had worked together before, solving difficult problems, as you recall, and they knew what they were taking on. They were prepared for fundraising to be hard. They were prepared to have to evangelise and build demand as well as building a product. They were prepared to bootstrap. And they were determined, as we already covered, to do things differently and learn from everything they had seen and learned before, good and bad.

And then they landed their first deal. And it was a big'un.

Itaú: a giant controlling 50% of money movement in Brazil. Which sounds amazing. And it is. But it comes with its own problems. 'When we signed them, we were a 19 person company, we were smaller than their squads!' recalls Pismo CTO Daniela Binatti.

The company had to deal with huge volumes overnight.

They had to convince the client that they had the tools and know-how to support their giant partner on the journey they needed to go on while showing them how a different way of working was better, faster and cheaper than what they were historically doing. The team had to scale while holding onto the differentiating posture they had when there were 19 of them. They had to help the client with the new tech and the psychological transition that comes with big change. And they needed to scale their own team to cope with all the extra work, without losing all the key traits that they had spent so long building. The easy thing to do would be to cut some corners and become more like the client than your former self. But that was literally the opposite of what they were trying to do.

> There is a big sense of the underdog in our culture: a Brazilian team, selling tech to the world! This matters to people and they need to remember this is all about them!
> *Daniela Binatti*

'Retaining our culture is not easy.'

Every time growth comes is a cause for jubilation of course. But adding a lot of people in short periods of time can cause dilution, confusion and on top of that, the relationship with clients 'when you are a company our size selling to enterprise clients… the relationship is hugely asymmetric' which itself puts pressure on the culture.

And then further strain as the world goes into lockdown and 'we became remote-first when the pandemic started' recalls Daniela.

'We were 40 people then and we added 250 during the pandemic.' The orders of magnitude matter when you are trying to retain an elusive culture from afar and the new folks outnumber the carriers of the culture by some margin.

'We are over 300 people now in Brazil but less than half in Sao Paolo. So we have had to learn how to manage the culture when not everyone is in the same office.

We have needed a very strong HR team with a clear mission to be closer to the team. We talk to the team a lot. We take concerns head on.'

Every major change, even the most positive ones, have to be treated as a potential threat

> Every major change, even the most positive ones, have to be treated as a potential threat to the culture.
> *Daniela Binatti*

to the culture. Even positive events such as growth. When the deal with Visa was announced, for instance, everyone should be jubilant (and the rest of the market, I can confirm, green with envy). And they were. But the joy was tinted with concern.

'We were worried about losing people when the deal was announced' admits Daniela. 'We know that when the conversations with Visa started, there was a real concern among the team about the founders leaving the company. We addressed it. We reassured people. But we were still worried. Thankfully nobody left. People are motivated and excited about the next challenge. There is a strong sense of the underdog here: a Brazilian company exporting tech to the world. This is such a big story for our people. Big global players using our tech: so it is important that the team remember it is all about them. Because *look what we built!*'

Soups Ranjan is losing sleep over the exact same thing as he is scaling.

'One of the hardest things is running a remote-first startup. How do you ensure everyone is on the same page? How do you do that? And how do you detect issues in a remote model?' because of course the radical transparency and over-sharing that Sardine practices helps with staying connected but it doesn't solve for finding things that are about to go wrong in a timely manner.

'If something is wrong with a deal or with a person, I will get on a call immediately, reacting to something going south. Sometimes you are too late of course but hopefully you learn even from those and the company or the product gets better for next time. But it is an interesting conundrum.

The people team have a very aggressive goal for themselves to meet everyone at least once a month and "debug" things before they go south.'

Proactive is the watch-word from both Pismo and Sardine. Constant is the unspoken concomitant. Constant, proactive, intentional curation. Especially as you deal with the positive but undeniable stresses of growth.

There is no way around this need for commitment. Curating and maintaining a culture is not done by osmosis and it is not 'light work'. It takes time. It takes resources. And its ties to leadership and vision need to be real, lived and continuous. And it needs to deal with the challenges – exogenous such as growth or a global pandemic – and endogenous, head on.

I have worked with a company that had gotten the inclusive, friendly, playful culture it wanted to project down to a T. We had t-shirts and fluffy unicorns (we genuinely did). There were beach balls flying overhead for no reason other than to communicate what kind of place we were. There was an incredible vibe in the office. On a good day, it was the best place to work by a country mile.

> You will have culture wobbles. Some of them will be down to bad hires. Some will be down to bad behaviours you didn't eradicate quickly enough. And some will be down to phasing: because as your company changes and matures its culture also shifts. And some people will resist that.

But on a bad day, there existed no language, constructs or intentionality to deal with the behaviours that really don't go with the projected narrative. When things went great, it was great. When things were not great, 'under the carpet' was the preferred solution. Which is the surest and fastest way to kill a culture. Which is exactly what happened there. How do you deal with that?

'Of course we have had some culture wobbles' reflects Mettle's Ken Johnstone. 'They came down to the phasing actually. As important as it was to our evolution and focus, it took effort and leadership to help people go on this journey. Businesses do evolve and when things are ok and the culture is strong, people will resist change away from something that is happy and good.'

You need to help them. But you also need to keep moving forward. People will resist change for reasons that are not at all destructive in intent but are problematic anyway.

Zor reflects that, when Kasisto decided to double down on Gen AI, although it was not a big departure from what they were doing anyway, some folks resisted. Not because they didn't like change but because they felt their work was important.

They weren't being petulant. They were committed. And you can't turn a blind eye to that, dismiss or just ignore it. And you don't want to lose these people either. People will not always resist out of ignorance, laziness or malice. They may resist because they believe in what they were doing or because they love what you are changing away from and want to protect it. But evolution is inevitable and the process and structures by which you manage those transitions without forcing them but also without wasting time is key.

Everything is a dialogue, after all.

When the Going Gets Tough: The PensionBee Way

Jasper Martens reflects that PensionBee's values: *love, innovation, honesty, simplicity and quality* form the basis for everything. And he doesn't mean the decorations on the walls and HR material for new recruits. He means actual business decisions. 'Everything we do is structured around [these values].' Although it is hard to keep the focus on values singular, especially as you grow, it is vital to do so as the values become a filter for decision-making and prioritisation. The values 'help streamline as you go'.

> This is a partnership. And culture is an ingredient for success. It is a driver of it.
> You can't add culture later. Like a hat.
> **Jasper Martens**

And if things go wrong? What happens to the values then?

'Of course things will go wrong' reflects Jasper. 'I have made some interesting mistakes myself. I have made a 30k mistake when 30k was a lot to us and I had so much angst to fess up to my boss. But what she said was "did you learn from it"? And I had. And we moved on.

Next time make the mistake as small as possible. And that was it. This is a partnership. And culture is an ingredient for success. It is a driver of it. It is not just protected because of the success we have now had. A culture of support, no blame and trust enables you to make sacrifices and move forward even though you won't always get what you want. You need to have this from the get go. You can't add culture later. Like a hat.'

I cannot tell you how much I love this phrase.

And the implications of what it means.

Because for PensionBee the culture is not a statement of intent on a wall and some community events here and there. It is reality or it is nothing. And you know that by looking at what happens when things don't go right. Not when they do. For employees and customers alike. As a customer, I once had a quick email exchange with my beekeeper about something I was trying to do.

It couldn't be done because of the way the company had set their KYC up. If you must know, I interchangeably use my preferred spelling (Leda) of my middle name (Lida) and my *actual* first name (Agapi) in formal paperwork which, in the pre-digital era, was fine, but nowadays it is getting more and more complicated. The problem is I've been doing it for years so my footprint is messy. My life is lived as Leda Glyptis (not just my public persona but also my mortgage, degrees, salary contracts, pre-digital bank accounts) my passport is Agapi Lida Glypti. This meant that my pre-existing pensions were in a variety of versions of my name depending on whether pension providers followed the employer's record (where you may get to be a Dan and not a Daniel) or the passport (where you are definitely a Daniel). I wanted to register 'alternative' spellings for my name which some providers have no issue with and they let you do it in the same field as people register maiden names, names changed by deed poll etc.

It wasn't possible yet. Maybe at some later stage but not right now.

I should be annoyed.

But I wasn't. Because my beekeeper was responsive, gentle and polite and fully transparent about what was happening and why. She also gave me three options on how to move forward. I didn't take any of them, by the way. But I was given them and I couldn't fault the interaction. In every way, it lived up to their values fully.

> Toxic people are like Teflon, nothing sticks to them so they stick around.
>
> You have to be intentional about not allowing that to happen. You can't add values suddenly and go *from now on we will love and respect each othe*r, it doesn't work that way.
>
> **Jasper Martens**

As a customer, I saw it. But as an employee? What happens when someone doesn't live up to those values? Because when you have an ever-growing number of people working together all day, every day, the encounters are numerous and the chances for not living up to values sadly proliferate. Do people fall short? Of course they do.

'Toxic people are like Teflon, nothing sticks to them so they stick around' reflects Jasper, delivering another perfect one-liner. 'You have to be intentional about not allowing that to happen.' So live and die by the sword: promote and fire according to your values. And if your values are love and respect that means you *only* keep people who demonstrate those values around. It doesn't mean you love, respect and tolerate everyone. You need to fire, respectfully, and swiftly or your values die and you can't just restore them later.

'You can't add values suddenly and go *from now on we will love and respect each other*, it doesn't work that way' reflects Jasper. And I agree. And yet that is how most organisations try to do things. Values are seen as 'positive things' ergo, seems to be the implication, they are deployed in a *positive* way. They are present in celebration but usually absent in firing decisions, when justifying a downsizing or explaining why a strategy will no longer be pursued. That shouldn't be the case but it often is.

I once worked with a company that listed 'integrity' as a core value. The same company during the course of one year reassured the workforce that 'there would be no further cuts' six times and each time the next round was already planned and approved. They approved RnD budgets knowing it would be cut the following month. There were reasons for the secrecy but there were ways to not mess with what needed to be cautiously handled and not compromise yourself by saying things you know are not true.

> Protecting your culture will entail firing people who jeopardise your values. But it will also entail allowing your culture to evolve as you grow.
> Knowing what to protect and what to let go is one of the biggest decisions you will have to make. Again and again.

The values looked good in print and that is as far as their reach would go. Because the behaviours that contradict the values are perpetrated by people and while those people are around and your workforce sees them saying one thing and doing another, your values are forfeit.

So Jasper's point is valid albeit hard to implement. If you allow toxic people to stick around and do not protect your values from them, then your values are just window dressing. Living by the company values means letting go of people, ideas or practices that jeopardise those values.

'And of course we feared the values may be compromised when we went public' reflects Jasper echoing the concerns Daniela Binatti faced as Pismo went from strength to strength and growth put a strain on the culture. The same concerns Uday, Soups and Zor are losing sleep over right now.

'We had to make sure the transition to scale didn't hurt us as the pressure can absolutely hurt the culture. But that doesn't mean no change. We changed a lot during lockdown for instance. Lockdown made us remote first and, again, we had to protect our culture, move it online. We started doing things, activities, rituals... and then settled into a new way of working. It's harder to get this right but you get used to it.' And it is important to get this balance right: protecting the values, embracing change that comes with scale or just life and knowing what to keep and protect and what to let go.

Changing Cultures for Changing Times

Everything we look at in this book is centred around change. And change work is scary, as Simon Boonen reflects. Whether it's a big organisation or a small one 'change is always about people'. And the more people you have, the hardest it gets. So how do you mobilise ING's 57,000 people? Because, to affect change in a large organisation, you need to change systems and learn new ways of working but you also need to shift and move away from old habits and espouse new ways of working and being. The culture of a big organisation needs to shift, or change won't stick.

And that goes against the grain. Both of how people feel and act inside big organisations where habit drives most actions and interactions but also of the main tenet of my argument thus far: that you can evolve your culture but you can't change it. You can't fix it.

Evolution is inevitable of course and you can influence its direction but it will always be a continuation of where you were when you started the journey. The culture will always reflect the realities of working inside your organisation and whatever you do to influence it needs to work with and align to the purpose of the business.

> Change is not quick or easy to affect across an organisation such as ours.
> And it's not meant to be. You have to work one step at a time, one department at a time. Year after year. With consistency. Until it becomes the default way of working. You make small changes that compound to something bigger.
> **Simon Boonen**

All that is hard work made doubly hard by the fact that, instinctively, a bank's culture is anti-change, stability being the name of the game. A culture that resists new things is actually the right culture for a stable, scaled, regulated organisation. But it is the wrong culture for what those organisations want to become.

'The reality is, nobody joins a bank because they want change' observes Nektarios. 'The organisations are not meant to do that. People are incentivised not to. People operate in a very specific way.' And that is widespread across the traditional institutions of our industry. It is the way.

'One of our ecosystem friends' recalls Nektarios 'was forced by organisational expediency to work with a big consulting firm on a project. Traditional behaviour meets traditional practice. *I don't want powerpoint from you* he said to them' implying he wanted actual work. Not vapourware. *'No problem* they replied *we can do keynote and Prezi.'*

Funny cos it's true. But also telling.

So if culture is defined as conditions suitable for growth, then *traditionally* culture inside a big corporate would fight change because that is what protects the body corporate. But that fight is never all-out war. It is usually passive, time-wasting resistance. A painful slow-down rather than an all-out fight or a resounding 'no' to whatever you are trying to do. Which, we have already stated, is worse for morale and resource management than a No. So, given the changes in the world around us, given the relentless need to engage with new

> In a big company, the culture is already geared towards survival. That is why it resists change. But the world around us has changed so the culture needs to evolve so that it can ensure continued survival in a changing world.

technologies and business models in a timely manner, all big organisations would need to evolve in line with the needs of the changing world to retain their dominance medium to long term. The needs of the company today and the needs it will have tomorrow are currently at odds. The way individuals instinctively react to change is at odds with their and the organisation's self-interests.

Arguably, it is not a fix or massive departure but an evolution of the existing culture that focuses on survival adapting it to reflect what continued survival entails in changing circumstances. In other words, focusing on survival is good, but the very thing that would have killed you back in the day is the thing that will save you now so the focus is right but the understanding of what you see needs to change.

In short, it isn't the culture that needs to change as much as the way it manifests itself as the conditions around us have changed. Which is just as well, since culture can't radically change. Plus any evolution is gradual and it needs to start from where you are today and carry a lot of who you are into the future with you, otherwise it is a departure and those things don't work when it comes to culture.

'Change is not quick or easy to affect across an organisation such as ours' continues Simon. 'And it's not meant to be. You have to work one step at a time, one department at a time. Year after year. With consistency. Until it becomes the default way of working. You make small changes that compound to something bigger. Small accomplishments that show each individual they can contribute.

And you need to learn about people: the problems they encounter and the opportunities they want to pursue. You need to open a conversation and then create a coalition of the willing. You need to find who is willing to take the step and put in the work. You need to find the particular opportunity that you can get commitment around, in order to get started. Then you need management to have conviction to help.'

This is the main difference when it comes to culture, by the way, between a startup and an established entity: the tie between the leader and the culture can be looser. There is enough stability around, that inspiration and support can come from a few more quarters than in a startup.

If the leader is a caretaker, steady-state CEO, it is possible for an innovative, change-focused culture to develop inside the organisation and apart from the way the main body of the organisation feels and acts. Not at odds. That will never survive. Just different. Like siblings often have very different personalities but coexist under the rules of the same household and share more commonalities than they often wish to admit.

> The cultural dynamics you need in order to make change stick inside a big organisation are weirdly even more important in that context than they are in a smaller entity as banks are not structured in order to keep you on a path of transformation.
> **Mike Cunningham**

This creates options but that change still needs to be nurtured, stresses Simon.

'You need to make room in the organisation to make it happen: you need to secure access, headspace, people and eventually budget' none of which is easy to come by (and we will speak about it all very soon because it would be naive to suggest that if you get the leadership and culture right you are off the races: you are not).

The cultural dynamics you need in order to make change stick inside a big organisation are, weirdly, even more important in that context than they are in a smaller entity and that is because, as Mike Cunningham observes, 'banks are not structured in order to keep you on a path of transformation. I have been a lone voice at times' he reflects. 'People agreed [with the path I was advocating for] but never voiced that agreement publicly. They didn't want to stand up to be counted or be quoted in support of change initiatives. Many people, especially in smaller markets, don't want to rock the boat. They are either comfortable and can't be bothered with change or they want to support change but they are aware that they are playing in a small market and cannot burn bridges. Not everyone can pick up and go work somewhere else if things don't go well and often that limits people's willingness to voice dissent.'

> The culture you end up with may be accidental: forged by silence and the absence of dissent rather than active choice.

And make no mistake, when transformation efforts inside big organisations fail heads do occasionally roll. Not always. And not everyone. But for every failed or delayed transformation, someone loses their job in a very public way, impacting what their next move can look like. It is human nature to *not* want that to be you. But that means that what you believe in and what you do, on an individual level, is at odds. What you say and what you are willing to back. Which means that the culture you end up with inside a corporate entity may be entirely accidental. One forged by silence rather than active choice.

> After every failed transformation effort inside a big company, some heads roll: it is human nature to *not* want that to be you. Which may result in your beliefs and actions being at odds with each other. But only the actions matter.

'Maybe that's why I want to be the CEO of a big thing' reflects Mike. 'Because as long as I have a supportive board, I have no excuses. The power to execute will be in my hands.

If I have strategy, people and money, the impact can be multiplied. The feel-good factor of seeing the joy in people's faces when you are doing good work: that's better than any bonus. That feeling is the biggest motivator.'

And he is right. About all of it.

About the fact that if you have strategy, people and money, the sky should be the limit and that getting culture right is key always, especially in big organisations where the prevailing culture means that the natural antibodies of the shop aren't geared to help you achieve what you are setting out to do.

So you need to watch out for the body corporate antibodies. But that is not all. You need to also watch yourself.

> The job is the culture and you need to watch yourself, as a leader, because when pressure mounts everyone reverts to learned behaviour.
> *Rolf Eichweber*

'We can all buy the tech' reflects Rolf Eichweber. 'The job is the culture. Yes... managing a culture feels elusive but that is the point. It is the most important thing and you can't buy it. You need to actively work on it. As a leader', reflects Rolf, 'you must spend half your day on it. When pressure mounts, everyone always reverts to learned behaviour. So you will forget to pause and ask and check if things are ok.' And you could become your own culture's enemy by letting yourself default to type, indulge in old habits or not trust your gut. Which isn't the same as allowing yourself to fall into your old habits.

Observe: Bianca Bates led a big, established entity in Cuscal. Her view on the balancing act required between the people who run the shop and the people who change the shop and the cultural tensions this creates is illuminating.

'Of course it all comes down to people. In every big implementation you invariably find yourself with your back against the wall at some point and you need to rally. It is in moments like that where you see who is helping and who is not.

What I have learned is: if your gut tells you someone isn't helping the team, but you hesitate from removing them because you don't want to disrupt the effort and lose momentum in that critical moment… don't.

Follow your gut and move bad people away fast. Make the change, fast. You always think *I can't do this now, too risky.* Yes you can.'

This is the exact same sentiment we got from Enfuce, Flagstone and PensionBee: different verticals, different sizes, different markets. And yet the imperative is 100% aligned: there are people aligned to your purpose and people detrimental to it. Get rid of the people who are detrimental to your purpose. You want to talk about culture? And values? And protecting those? Fire the people who damage it all. Fire them and do it fast. It's not very fluffy advice but it's the only truth there is.

> If your gut tells you someone isn't helping the team, but you hesitate from removing them because you don't want to disrupt the effort and lose momentum in that critical moment… don't.
> **Bianca Bates**

What Got You Here Won't Get You There

It is true in a startup.

And it is weirdly even more urgently true in a big organisation, as your change-makers who need to sustain the work are effectively a lonely cultural outpost, so it is imperative that they not be overrun by the culture of the main shop or get exhausted by the isolation, before the work is done. And protecting yourself against those two dangers is in itself a cumulative effort. That always complicates matters.

'Inside a bank' reflects Curt Queyrouze, 'you can hire people from different backgrounds.' In fact… you need to, in order to keep the talent pool fresh. And you can bring in people from startups and mix them in with your existing talent pools to enrich both but 'the question is always the same: how do you create a culture of execution inside an organisation that is focused on minimising risk?

In a startup mentality, you are prepared to take huge risks to find the one hit.

> Inside a bank you need to bring in talent from startups and mix the talent pool but the hardest thing is to reconcile the way these different types of talent perceive risk.
> **Curt Queyrouze**

In banking, you try to minimise risk to zero with an eye to not making the career-ending mistake. The mentality of how you approach risk is the hardest part to reconcile.'

If you are trying to build a new culture by mixing startup elements and banking elements and hoping that 'the best of both' will prevail, you need to be vigilant 'and you need to always look at people's motivations to be able to understand how to make the talent you bring in, fit in and not work at cross purposes so they can have an impact. As the industry is shifting, how do you bring those people who can imagine what is possible and find focus for customer success? In a context of constant regulatory scrutiny?

Everything is about people, fundamentally.

> In banking, you try to minimise risk to zero with an eye to not making the career-ending mistake.
> **Curt Queyrouze**

Every hiring decision you make is seeking to bring knowledge together. Just as Google fast-tracked our productivity by getting knowledge out faster, AI via tools like ChatGPT will do the same. The ability to minimise the work needed to get to the decision point will increase productivity in tremendous ways. This acceleration will once again disrupt whole industries. In finance, it will accelerate a disruption that emerged over the past ten years.'

As I said before, Curt is the man who has 'context is everything' literally sown in the lining of his suits. And he is absolutely right. The context defines the backdrop against which we do our thinking. So when we think about the culture we need to preserve in order to enable the work we need doing, the shifting context is, in so many ways, what makes the work of building and protecting a culture so hard. Because what it is and what it needs to become and how it needs to change is an ever-shifting ball game.

As true as it was to say that if you get your culture wrong, it's next to impossible to change it, it is sadly equally true to say that no matter how true and good your culture is today, it will need to flex and evolve as you grow, as you encounter opportunities and challenges. And although protecting the culture and retaining the people is always

> As you grow, you need a different kind of skill set. A different kind of person. Your culture will shift correspondingly.
> How do you change and evolve… and still retain what makes you… you?
> **Valentina Kristensen**

a primary motivation, as we have already seen. It is also inevitable that some will fall by the wayside as you grow and change. It is sad and hard on occasion, but it is necessary and inevitable.

'Our first office had mouse traps in it' remembers Valentina, back when OakNorth was a scrappy startup. 'The second office had no air-conditioning and some seriously sweltering credit committee meetings were hosted in great discomfort and good cheer. The current office has a barista and sushi Thursdays. And that is amazing but it also sets a different kind of expectation. You get a different kind of person *now* than you did in the early days' and it is important to notice that and be aware of it. As a necessary reality.

Some of the people who enjoyed the scrappy days may not want to be around the days of plenty. Some folks who are doing great work today couldn't fathom working in an office with mice in it (although I had a very fun afternoon chasing a mouse with half my engineering team around the floor of one of the best capitalised banks in the world a few years back...

> As a company you need different skills and attitudes at different stages of growth. And different people are attracted to the scrappy early days who many not like the days of plenty. That shift is inevitable. And your culture needs to change to reflect this without losing your core values.

so... you know... mice are not discerning. They may come find you anywhere). Some folks could not take the financial risk of joining a startup.

It is ok.

In fact it may be necessary. What it takes to build something and what it takes to run it is very different and it is important to acknowledge that. What you need to do changes as you grow, so the type of person you need to do the doing also shifts as you grow: both in terms of aptitudes and attitudes. And the culture that these different people will do their best work *in* may also need to evolve. As long as the fundamentals remain.

'OakNorth never believed in the hustle culture we hear so much about. But passion and drive matter... I think of it as the hunger culture' continues Valentina. 'The team needs to hold onto that while also growing into new structures and a new size. The shape of the organisation, the stage of the organisation attracts a different kind of person. That is inevitable. So how do you make room for them and retain what makes you... you?'

What Goes in The Box Is Up To You. *Almost* Entirely

As we already said, protecting the culture is a universal imperative. What that culture is, is for you to determine. What values your company is built around is up to you. How you protect them is universal, what they are should not and cannot be. The specifics are deeply personal to your business. The need to have them and uphold them consistently and robustly is universal. As is the need to do the hard work to defend your values when they are side stepped or violated. Yes: that means firing and disciplining people. It's uncomfortable but it is what it is. And you don't have a culture, really, unless you do that.

I worked for a startup many years ago who had a 'no (insert expletive here) policy' actually written in the HR manual. I laughed uncomfortably when I saw it because you can't get 20 years of banking propriety out of your system easily. I wanted to like it but it also made me a little uneasy. Anyway, a few weeks in, I had someone working on my team who was being exactly what the policy suggested we don't tolerate to a couple of other people.

So I spoke to him.

His behaviour, sadly, didn't change and it got to the point rapidly where we needed to remove him from the team. I expected the CEO to push back as the dude had been his hire. Instead, the CEO read the file, spoke to me and HR and then walked into the room with me and very calmly said 'we have a clear no you-know-what policy and you are being a you-know-what so this is not the place for you'. Can't say he wasn't warned. Can't say I didn't love it. I absolutely loved it.

> The challenges to your culture may not be what you expect especially as your values are intentional, your curation of the culture also… but the culture itself is a living thing. Not 100% predictable or in your control. And your context matters as much as your intent.

My point is: it is vital to actually act on the cultural intentions and statements. It is existential to uphold them and defend them and yes that looks like stopping behaviours that don't chime *on their tracks*. It does look like firing people occasionally. And it also looks like keeping an eye on protecting the culture as you scale or as the work evolves. Because the challenges may not be what you expect especially as your values are intentional, your curation of the culture also, but the culture itself is a living thing you can't always script.

It is neither 100% predictable nor fully in your control. The culture will evolve and it will be the things people do and the way people react and anticipate those behaviours. If a couple of folks are backstabbed and thrown under the bus and nothing happens: your culture becomes one of people watching their backs. No matter what your culture statement says.

So your context matters as much as your intent. The lived reality of 'what working here feels like' matters more than your vision. And that means that the things you are afraid to tackle or the things you miss may define your culture

> Your culture is not fully in your control: it reflects the lived reality of working here. So if people throw colleagues under the bus and nothing happens… your culture is one of people watching their back. No matter what your culture statement says.

ahead of the things you curate. 'The things you worry about are the things you focus on and solve for' reflects Royden. So the biggest danger comes from the things you haven't spent time worrying about.

'The things that concern me consume intellectual and emotional energy. For instance, I didn't underestimate that building a bank inside a big corporate would come with challenges. But I vastly underestimated the cultural difference between us.' First there is the relative size difference.

Then there is the 'going concern' difference. As a startup venture inside a big entity, you have a blank sheet of paper and, for a while, all you do is build. The pressures of running a scaled business operate to different timelines and risk considerations.

And then, as if the above wasn't hard enough, you are building a bank inside an insurance company and although they are both in FS and understand regulation and understand scale and complexity, they fundamentally relate to money differently.

'We have had fantastic coverage from the CEO' reflects Royden. Without which most of these endeavours don't even start. And the tensions between new and existing, build-mode and scaled business are not failures to be overcome. They are facts to be navigated. At senior levels, differences can be appreciated and solved for intellectually. But as you move through an organisation, culture is the scaling factor.

If you are thinking David vs Goliath, scrappy startup vs big corporate, you are proving early Royden right. And you would both be wrong as it turned out. This is the challenge everyone had anticipated, both inside the challenger and inside the parent organisation. That is the challenge they prepared themselves for. But it wasn't what they got.

'We knew building a bank was going to be hard. Some things I would do differently now' reflects Royden. 'When we started scaling, we didn't have the foundations for scaling our culture, we didn't have that robustness buttoned down and building independence in the teams can lead to deviation from the culture that you want. Great ideas and perspectives are key but not enough.'

You have a vibrant team. The culture is great. You add a person. Does that tip it? No. Do five? Do 20? What you need to do to scale your culture and when you need to do it is, as I am sure you have noticed, not an exact science. But there was more and that is the point, there is always unforeseen tension and the cultural challenge Royden hadn't anticipated is not about size, but about existential purpose. They are building a bank (which is hard), inside a corporate (which is hard) and that corporate is in a different business. They are not a bank. They are an insurance company. And it turns out they are a lot more different than you expect.

Explaining it with much more nuance than me, Royden clarifies: 'customers demand instant access to cash from their bank. In many cases they are using the bank as a funding line (which sometimes won't get repaid). The bank is part of an industry moving and settling money to keep an economy's cash flow alive. Expectations on cash repatriation from claims or investment payouts do not seem to carry the same degree of urgency while for an insurer they carry a high risk and a material obligation [on the insurer] to get this step right, and they are therefore not instant'.

When put that way, it is so obvious that what the organisations get good at, what they value and what mindsets they cultivate would be radically different. *When* put that way.

'Insurance companies approach risk management differently from the way banks do. The nature of the risks they face and how they mature over time differ.

Whilst financial services reflect this all as Risk Management, and there are indeed similarities, they are different. Differences in business models re-enforce differences in cultures. It's not unique to insurance, it's a different comparison but a similar outcome when comparing how retailers with interests in financial services learn to appreciate that profit doesn't accrue to a new account that is opened in the same way it does when merchandise is processed at the Point of Sale. The tension is hard to reconcile, but it is important. Both because it is, after all, the mothership and because the tension between the two models is up to the challenger to manage.

Because they have more to lose.

Retailers trade by the hour (or minute), banks profitability emerges over years (and is lost in an instant), life insurers measure time in decades. Responsiveness, energy, rigour. They are all present in all these types of business, but they are different. And although we are a strategic initiative inside Old Mutual, the mothership is a huge ongoing concern with thousands of people operating at scale with this difference in culture. Our hundreds, still building and figuring ourselves out are easily overwhelmed if we aren't careful. This is hard to reconcile. But it is important.' Both because it is, after all, the mothership and because the tension between the two models is up to the challenger to manage. Because they have more to lose. That is my view, not Royden's. He tells me he agrees though!

But also, and this is important, because the cultural tension isn't because one is intractable or 'stuck in their ways'. It is because different missions are being served in ways appropriate to their circumstances. So that means the tension has to be navigated, not resolved. That's both a moment for relief but also a moment to realise that yes, yes you don't need to take on the Herculean task of solving this tension, you just have to navigate it... but... It will always be with you. Navigating this tension will forever be part of the job.

Royden's view, once he put words to the cultural challenge and identified what he needs to navigate, is that the way to achieve that is through 'retaining constant information asymmetry. The team and I are always extremely well prepared. Partly because that is the environment we are familiar with, and the paradigm of how we do

> In a situation where there is huge asymmetry between a parent organisation and a new venture, you need to retain constant information asymmetry on your side as the new venture, to bridge the gap.
> **Royden Volans**

things. And partly because the organisational asymmetry easily goes the other way. The greater the gap the harder the task'.

Any parent organisation will have the size, cash and corresponding power, so their paradigm of how they see the world will always be dominant. That is the deal with every incubation effort of this type as we also saw with Wise Platform: the new thing needs to keep the existing thing informed of how the experiment is going until it is an experiment no more.

Royden deploys information to bridge the gap. And so should you.

'It was extremely important for us to let the other side of the equation feel part of the process. So we worked hard to be prepared for any question, but we also tried hard to wait for the question to be asked. I still don't always get this right by the way. We recognised early that we needed to be both a teacher and a student. So we have provided a lot of information and training to bridge the gap on banking, and we continued to seek insight into insurance. What we didn't realise at the beginning is that this was never going to be enough. It has to be a constant dialogue. Distracting? Very. But necessary.

This cultural tension is familiar to all companies being built inside corporate 'parents'. The tension of knowledge and business models may be there but the cultural divides are undeniable.

Ken Johnstone, reflecting on Mettle's relationship with NatWest, highlights that it has all been a journey. 'Ultimately, our work was seen as an experiment. As all experiments, it could have failed. Now it has grown into a credible business but that wasn't always a foregone conclusion. We started with a 'fail fast' mentality and it is possible that there were folks inside the bank that thought we would do exactly that: fail and fail fast. Failure is always an option with an experiment, of course. We focused on getting product in the hands of customers as quickly as possible.

We didn't fail.

And now we are no longer an experiment. We are no longer insignificant. But you need to earn that place.' And then the dynamic changes. The context changes. And how you navigate them changes. And that has a massive impact on what you need to do and how. And with whom.

> When you are building a new venture inside a corporate there is power asymmetry plus you are a cultural outpost It is up to you to manage that.
>
> You earn your right to continue existing.

'For us, getting a mix of bank people who speak that language and tech people who get how to go fast was important and getting the organisational congruence was key. The mix of talent inside a cohesive culture was key. Getting this right *is* key. It's not what you write on a slide. It's what is lived reality. Values have to be lived and real. And it has to be top down. It's so influential and can't be faked. The flow of information, for instance. Transparency.'

That's a hard one to fake for sure but it's also a hard one to scale. 'Transparency is easy in a small company. It gets harder as you grow. You need to focus on it. You have to be intentional. You have to *choose* to focus on it. To keep the right dialogues going. To make sure people stay connected. It gets harder so you have to actively focus on it.'

It's All Fun and Games Until Someone *Causes* Hurt

Fun fact for you. The original quote is by James Hetfield and it goes 'it's all fun and games till someone loses an eye, then it's just fun you can't see'. I can't help but think ole James would be fun in a party and useful in a scrap.

There is little left to say about culture. It is important. It is fragile. It is hard to get right and it takes intent and effort and resources to maintain and it can't be an after-thought. You can't behave abys-mally and then throw a party quarterly and feel it's all taken care of. Although, I have worked in many places that did exactly that. Excellent parties, mind. As they had a lot to make up for.

> If you want to build long term value, you need to find and retain long term thinkers.

And why does culture matter? That one is easy.

'The thing to lose sleep over is human capital' reflects my former boss, Antony Jenkins. 'You have to have the right people in the team. One highly talented engineer is worth three mediocre ones.'

So finding and keeping the good people is existential. As Simon Merchant also explained earlier in the chapter, talent retention is a major reason why culture matters. Happy people stay. Happy people work harder. Both excellent things if they are the right people. But the right people aren't just a function of talent. It is also a values thing as we already explained. But above all it is an *alignment* thing.

Wise's CTO, Harsh Sinha, reflects: 'for the wider company the challenge is how do we continue building a team that is here long term, when others are not? How do we find and keep the best long-term thinkers? How do we build the DNA that will outlast those people? How do we retain the culture and ambition?

Allowing for the culture to evolve but also knowing that we will make new choices, different choices and we want the next gen-eration of leaders to make those choices based on the same values and principles as we hold today?' Part of the answer is you need to know what you are looking for when you are recruiting, promoting and rewarding.

> The talent you need and the culture that will be right for them to thrive in depends on your mission and circumstances.

Look for the right traits and incentivise those with the right traits and behaviours to stay. Those traits and behaviours are specific to you, needless to say. What you need depends on your mission and circumstances.

Kelvin Tan, for instance, while building audax 'curated a team with a profound understanding of the banking sector, possessing knowledge and proficiency in navigating the intricacies of an established bank.' That felt like a critical skill set and, given what we heard from Royden and Ken above, rightly so.

'To complement this, we strategically incorporated external talent in the fields of technology and data. This inclusion not only introduced contemporary and competitive skillsets but also contributed to the diversity of our team, blending the expertise of seasoned bankers with the innovation brought by technologists. This dynamic mix ultimately enhances our ability to address the multifaceted challenges of our industry.' In short: bring people in who can navigate the bank (they know who to call, they know the history of people, systems and divisions, they know the landscape and culture and language and dynamics) and people who can navigate the newest technologies and ways of working. That sounds brilliant. But it does not a culture make and tensions are inevitable.

Your culture is forged in the *way* you navigate those tensions. By anticipating that they will happen and offering guardrails for them to play themselves out in a civilised and above all predictable manner.

> You need to create structures and ways to address dissent, conflict and tension.
>
> Nobody wants it to happen. But to assume that it won't is naive.

Kelvin's answer is to 'leverage best practices across the entire industry, transparent and open communication culture, reminiscent of Netflix's radical candour. Disagreements are encouraged and a commitment to decisions, even in disagreement, follows the Amazon model.' And if that's not enough?

'We've established a clear escalation process for unresolved matters, allowing any steerco member to challenge decisions deemed detrimental to the company. This accountability extends to the organisation's structure and team dynamics. We emphasise working with each other, not *for* each other. The structure encourages collaboration, and there's a defined process to challenge decisions. In instances where adjudication is necessary, I play a role, often supported by candid feedback from the team, ensuring accountability and constructive critique are integral to our growth.' Accountability is the magic word here.

You have the option to escalate and essentially challenge another SteerCo member to a duel (my words, not his, but you catch my drift). You can challenge someone suggesting they are wrong. There is

> Culture is always associated with positivity but the stark reality is that the way to protect it is through firing and disciplining the people who don't live up to it.
>
> Culture, it turns out, is not fluffy.

a way for you to do it. There is a path available. Not so easy that it can be flippantly over-used. But, also, not a sacred cow: you can challenge. You can critique. This is a partnership. We are in this together.

Building things is hard.

Getting the right people working together is hard in the first place and continuously getting it right is not an accident. It is an intentional engagement. A leadership commitment. How you spend time and money, how you make decisions (Wise's and Sardine's full transparency, for instance), how you discipline and, when needed, fire, are all key. And as we already saw with the OM Bank and Mettle cases, how you manage relationships with investors or your corporate parent is also key. And the power dynamic cannot be ignored.

Culture is key because it becomes the way you achieve success. It is the way you negotiate trade-offs and make decisions. And the context in which you are building and nourishing your culture is a huge influence on how you work. So we will turn to that next. But first… your homework.

Your Calls to Action

- Be mindful of your founding or foundational team. It won't kill you if you have to make changes but it will supercharge your efforts if you don't.
- Do the thing, don't just talk about it.
- If you want a team of equals, as a CEO or senior leader, it is up to you to equalise relationships. It won't work any other way.
- Be the sort of leader people brag to their friends about by understanding that your work begins when you get the top job. It isn't an accomplishment; it is a beginning. How you show up is how you earn it.
- Consistency and willingness to listen to dissenting voices is how you can tell apart a committed leader from a tunnel-vision one.
- You need to get the culture of your team right early. You can't add it on later. Like a hat (thank you Jasper).
- You need to do the hard work of protecting your culture: let it drive decisions of prioritisation and hiring/firing. Spend time, energy and money on it.
- Do not hesitate when you need to fire people on grounds of toxicity, bad behaviour or misalignment to values. Do it fast.
- Habit may be the enemy of the culture you are trying to build. Be vigilant and intentional. Take feedback. Apply all the lessons of *Bankers Like Us* (what do you mean you haven't read it yet? Go get a copy immediately!)

Chapter 6

Negotiating Trade-Offs and Other Superpowers

In case you are desperate to skip this section because you leafed through and realised the next section is talking about money and sponsorship and board dynamics and you are itching to go, the summary of this section is people – process – governance. That's it. I really think you should read on, though, you know. The devil, as ever, is in the details.

If you have had the joy, privilege (and, admittedly, absolute pain) of working with me in the past, you will know through painful, personal experience that I am the Queen of catchphrases and one of my most oft-used ones is *all the things need to be true at the same time.*

Not everything, everywhere. But all the things we are working on, assuming we have time and budget for; all the timelines we commit to; all the client deliverables and their associated dependencies: all of those need to be true at the same time. If three initiatives are eyeing the same budget pot, three feature teams are assuming the other feature teams can lend them resources to meet their deadlines

> All the things we are working on, all the things we are assuming we have time and budget for... all the timelines we commit to... all the client deliverables and their associated dependencies... need to be true *at the same time.*

DOI: 10.1201/9781003395577-6

and client deliverable timelines are not aligned to the feature team work schedules then you have dropped balls all over the place. You have misunderstandings. You have chaos. You have stress. And you have waste. You also have realities inside teams that cannot be true at the same time as each other. You have magical thinking at its most destructive.

You also have one of the most common problems in the industry.

It seems so obvious to state that all your commitments, as a business, all your dependencies and resource allocation need to be true at the same time. But it doesn't happen. Do you know why? Because organisations do planning all together but in an abstract way. People are in the room, they have the conversation, but nobody ever puts their commitments in a full sentence that includes the magic word 'therefore'.

Observe.

I have sat in meetings that put the same person (me) in four different succession plans celebrating how much better female representation was going to be in our next generation of leaders. Assuming I would do all four of those jobs, at once. The sentence that was missing was 'Leda is in four succession plans but can only do one of those jobs *therefore* our succession planning work is not complete and the future is not quite yet female'.

> Negotiating trade-offs become the single biggest discipline of leadership teams because there will never be enough time and money to do everything, so what you do, what you don't do and how you decide that is vital.

More recently, I have sat in two successive meetings. Literally back to back. The first one allocated budget to a project. The second one discussed an *equivalent* cost cut affecting the same team. The overlap of humans in the room was about 80%. So it wasn't an information flow problem. It was an ostrich problem.

When I asked whether the budget allocated was additive to the cost target, was actually what was behind the cost target or a different pot altogether, I was told this was not the topic of this meeting. That is corporate speak for 'the emperor is naked and we all know, but nobody else seems to feel the need to point it out, so whose side are you on?'.

I have sat in meetings agreeing to client commitments with all relevant teams and the client in the room: look me in the eye, shake my hand, we are doing this type territory… only to walk from that meeting, across the hall, to an internal meeting of all the same people minus the client, only to hear about how none of those commitments will be met because other commitments were made in a different meeting by the same people. The same people who knew, when they were saying yes, that what they were promising was *theoretically* possible. But not if the other promise they made (also theoretically possible) needed to be kept.

In other rooms, other wonders[1], you may say.

But that is the point. The same wonders have to apply in every room. The reality of your resource allocation needs to hold true in every room. And you need to find a way of keeping that reality constant and aligned. In every room and across every room and across every day and week of your working life.

Negotiating trade-offs becomes the single biggest discipline of leadership teams because there will never be enough time and money to do everything, so what you do, what you don't do and how you decide that is vital. Having a process for deciding is vital.

We have already heard that Wise and Sardine practice full transparency. Team members always know what initiatives time and money is being spent on instead of whatever else they may have wanted. You may not like the outcome but you know the commitment. But even more importantly, you know that money is spoken for and it can't be double and triple allocated. Audax has a process for escalation and resolution in case team members feel really strongly against decisions. Again, the idea is you discuss, you surface, you resolve and then you commit. You don't get to go rogue. To get that negotiation right you need several things to be done right. And the first one is: you need the right people around the table.

Who's There Is as Important as Who's Not

Having the right people around the table when making a decision doesn't sound like rocket science because it isn't. But its logical extension is sadly a rarity so it needs to be talked about. When we say you should have the right people in the room, we also mean not having anyone but the right people in the room.

We briefly mentioned the significance of firing toxic people who are bad for your culture but the reality is, important though culture is, firing toxic people or people who are not helping the boat go in the right direction, to paraphrase Bianca Bates, is actually critical to your business focus.

> The obvious concomitant of having the right people in the room also means not having anyone but the right people in the room.

If 90% of leadership is negotiating trade-offs and deciding where your time, money and talent should focus, having the right knowledge and attitude in the

---

1 You little rascal. You recognised the title of the short story collection by Daniyal Mueenuddin, didn't you? I like you.

room when you are having this discussion is key. Having no empire-building is key. Having people who will make the decisions and trade-offs required with an eye firmly on the company's mission and values is key.

So having the right folks around the table (both from an attitude and an aptitude perspective) is how you remain focused and negotiate trade-offs.

That means several things: people with the wrong attitude are actively damaging but also, less insidious but as dangerous: anyone who is not actually needed is superfluous. Not just a cost centre but also a distraction, because in their attempt to make themselves appear useful they will create noise. You know these guys.

I worked with a colleague once who created 32 hours of internal

> You need to have the right people in the room:
>
> Do not hire or fire people who distract your business.
>
> Do not invite people who distract the meeting.
>
> Have the right talent in the room for the work. And nobody else.

recurring monthly meetings in an attempt to show everyone how 'on top of things' he was. He didn't contribute anything material to those meetings, by the way. He just called them, ran them, created action logs and publicly humiliated anyone who didn't show up with all green RAG reports or was late in a deliverable. He created discipline and transparency, was the message. He made sure the meetings happened so we could stay connected and informed across silos. He sent a flurry of emails and messages before and after each meeting, cc-ing people with Cs in their titles to ensure everyone knew the meetings were important and, by extension, so was he.

There is a special place in hell for this man *especially* because I don't think he cared how much of a productivity drain he was to the entire organisation. But if you asked him, he would probably tell you that this was a version of Sardine's transparency, a version of Wise's openness. What it actually was lip service and a profound drain on people's time.

Does that sound familiar? I bet it does. Especially if you have worked in a bank where this type of behaviour is very common Middle Management Heaven. We have all been there. It is awful but we often accept it as inevitable. It is not.

There *is* another way you know.

ABN AMRO's Klaas Ariaans, on stage with me, in May 2023, gave the most rebelliously straightforward alternative to just living with the pain of having superfluous bodies adding activity for no reason and derailing the process of doing your work.

We were discussing 'leadership and people management in a constantly changing world' at the Banking Scene conference in Brussels and he shared with us the following story about how stark the mathematics of 'only having the right people around' may look.

On the first of July 2018, he reminisced, there were 278 managers across the teams he was responsible for. On July second there were 25. For 300,000 (three hundred thousand) plus people.

What did he do to the other 253 managers? He did exactly what you are thinking: he fired them. Why? Because he didn't feel that that traditional, over-hierarchical, layered structure of the bank (and that is *every* bank and almost every scale-up I know) was conducive to executing against the transformation goals they had set themselves.

> If you want to affect change, you have to do it wholeheartedly. And not everyone will like it. And that's ok.

'You obviously need to prepare people to ensure you understand how the change will affect them and ensure that, in the change, you make people want to stay on… working with you… Some will leave but the ones who stay, will drive the journey. And you drive the change in behaviour: if you always turn to your manager… and your manager isn't there… what do you do instead?'

And what people did was they stepped up. They took initiative. They were empowered and it worked.

That change happened in the largest division in the bank while other divisions carried on with the old ways of working, alongside it. Not everyone liked it, of course, stresses Klaas 'and some even compared me to the leader of North Korea' he recalls with a laugh 'but the reality is if you truly want to affect change, you must do it wholeheartedly.'

Frankly, that's what having the right people around the table looks like: *only* having *them*. Anything surplus to that is overhead, distraction and a complication. Anything less than the best is a felony after all. Vanilla Ice has been saying it since 1990.

Kissing Frogs: In Pursuit of the Right Talent

Remember Antony Jenkins said one talented engineer is worth three mediocre ones? And instinctively that feels absolutely right. But finding the right one is not an exact science. Every frog in the swamp believes themselves an enchanted prince and interview techniques are imperfect.

> If people are *everything* then getting and retaining the right people is actually whatever comes above 'everything'. But the process for doing that is imprecise and prone to error.

The market swings and shifts regularly and there are times when the battle for tech talent or the niche combination of skills FS transformation needs (deep banking knowledge, process design knowledge and tech knowledge) create scarcity and real struggles here. Finding and retaining the right talent is top of mind for everyone in tech.

You need to have a method, an approach and rigour.

The productivity loss of getting it wrong and having to let go of someone and recruit for the role afresh is huge and for companies managing cash burn or striving for growth, every month and every penny counts. In fact, I have worked with many a founder who realise they have hired the wrong people for the job or whose team's skillset isn't growing at the pace the work requires but they don't have the time or money (in terms of runway left) to replace them. So this can get existential and companies focus heavily on hiring and developing methodologies that can minimise that risk for error. With mixed results but absolute dedication.

Revolut, for instance, has a very rigid and specific recruitment policy and process developed by its leadership. Although the approach has come under criticism not least by some of the recruiters who worked within it[2], it has been known to work. Or at least it is believed to be working by the people running the business especially in geographies where the brand is strong.

For my friend Juan who we met earlier in this book, this equation didn't quite stack up. He is the CEO of Revolut in Mexico. In other words, he is CEO of a brand very well-known *elsewhere*. For him, applying this process while hiring was expected, but it has been a challenge.

'The thing I expected to be easy and is a challenge is recruitment' he reflects. 'The brand is not known here yet… the style of interview that is common to the company's process doesn't fit culturally in Latin America. Added to this, is the difficulty in getting a seasoned executive to leave a job and join a startup in the current climate.'

If anyone can find a solution to any problem, that is Juan and having successfully obtained his banking licence in the time since we recorded this interview must, inevitably, help, but the conundrum raises an interesting challenge. Because you do need a process to ensure you have the right folks around the table. And you need to keep sanity-checking that the process is working in all the places and all the ways you need it to be working. That the provisions you have put in place continue to work at all times and in all the places where you need them to work.

You then need to be actively mindful of the fact that your processes may not apply across geographies, as Juan found, or across talent verticals. As we already saw, audax, Mettle and many others need to attract a mix of banking talent, tech talent and startup talent. How you speak to each before they become part of a whole needs to reflect your understanding of the world they come from and assess their ability to come into the world you are building.

---

2 See Sophie Theen's *The Soul of Startups*, Wiley, 2022.

Because a lot of the trade-offs you will need to negotiate as you go, will not be around scarcity of resources necessarily but rather around balance and focus. The trade-offs will be about what is relatively more important than all the other important things. Negotiating with yourself about what will give the best outcome, what deserves more attention and effort and what doesn't is a big part of building.

Dancing with Myself[3]

We usually think of negotiations as something happening between two distinct parties sitting at opposite sides of a table. But actually most negotiations in business are internal: you are negotiating inside your own team about what will get priority and how you will deploy scarce resources. Furthermore, trade-offs are not normally negotiated by people passionately advocating for one side over another. Rather people, who are not necessarily invested in one idea over another, have to become so, in order to keep the business focused and moving and resources allocated meaningfully.

'We constantly keep ourselves on our toes about not doubling down on things that won't work' says Mettle's Ken Johnstone. That applies to the product, of course: features and capabilities. But it also applies to structures.

> If you know what is important in this phase of our journey, you can tell if your work is moving the needle against what is important. And what is important can't be a long list either.
>
> **Ken Johnstone**

'How do you ensure you have alignment of objectives and the right metrics? We find that phasing is key. If you know what is important in this phase of our journey, you can tell if your work is moving the needle against what's important.

And what's important can't be a long list either. What are we here to do? Are we doing it? Acknowledge what's not working. Celebrate the wins. Create psychological safety for saying *I tried this for three months and it's not working, let's stop*. We are not perfect at this, by the way. But saying *I know this is my job but I don't think it's a job that should be done* is key to having an empowered team. You need the trust.'

Essentially: the person saying *the thing I spend my days doing isn't worth doing* should know they are not talking themselves out of a job in the process of being honest and mission-aligned. You need to make sure people don't become entrenched or defensive. What Ken is describing here, is the opposite of empire-building, for the record.

---

3 Billy Idol, 1980. If you knew that already, you are my people. If you didn't, go have a listen. You are welcome by the way.

'You need to coach and support and occasionally you need to step in and set a firmer direction or if the team gets distracted' continues Ken, 'Re-establish focus.' The things we are doing now are not set in stone. If they are not working, we stop. That effectively means that the idea of internal negotiation, trade-off balancing and assessment is consistently constant. That dialogue is part of BAU. It requires discipline to ensure you do not indulge in pointless navel gazing but it is important so that you can allocate resources properly, stop things that aren't working or start things that may need to be revisited when the time is right.

'The parking lot is not a graveyard' continues Ken: things that were not the right thing to do last month may be the right thing to do now. Having the process for these discussions is key. The process itself brings discipline. And is never done.

That is for many reasons. Firstly, not everyone thinks holistically and some people will double down on what they are working on because it's interesting or because it's theirs despite what is good for the wider business with the best intentions in the world, as Zor flagged. But also because sometimes people, like my former colleague of the 32 meetings, sneak into your organisation and it takes a while to work out who they are and how what they are doing hurts you.

That said, sometimes, you need process to drive focus for the exact opposite reason. Uday Akkaraju agrees that developing a process that allows your talented, passionate people to focus is key. 'We are so passionate about [what we are here to build] that it is possible to get carried away. We now have a process in place to validate ideas. Our own passion sometimes needs to be checked. Not the intentions. But the practicality.

> We have a process in place to validate ideas. Our own passion sometimes needs to be checked. Not the intentions. But the practicality.
> **Uday Akkaraju**

You need to say no. You need to say stop. Sometimes the sacrifice is small: you choose this piece of tech over that. Sometimes the sacrifice is bigger because you need to stop working on something you feel strongly about because it isn't working or it is distracting right now.' As Ken says, the list of what is important needs to reign supreme and it cannot be a long list.

No Business Is an Island: Keeping the Peace with Key Stakeholders

Nowhere is the need to balance competing priorities and negotiate alignment more pronounced than in new ventures backed by existing concerns. 'The tension between *being here to be different* and respecting the way the main bank does things needs to be balanced' reflects Ken.

'There is immense value and advantage to the knowledge inside the main bank.' Only a fool would ignore that. So your job is not to keep them out or at arms' length but learn and cross-pollinate without being drawn into the orbit of the main shop. But even that resistance and push-back is a negotiation. 'As a *renegade*' continues Ken 'you don't have the right to push the boundaries from day one: you earn that right. When the main bank learns that you won't do anything stupid. That you understand what is at stake. You negotiate your way to negotiating leverage: even if you are given a seat at the table, you earn your voice.'

> You need to balance 'being here to be different' with the way the main bank does things.
> **Ken Johnstone**

If you are sitting there thinking 'that sounds like a lot of work' that is because it is.

It is ongoing work that happens at the same time as your internal negotiations and all your market-facing work. And all that happens while you are negotiating the negotiating, for good measure.

'There is a lot of advice' reflects Ken with a smile. 'And knowing which to take and which to politely ignore is important. You need real clarity on what you are trying to achieve in each phase of the work. The advice you get may be helpful overall but a hindrance right now. It may be advice for six months down the road.

Actively managing the phases of the work is key for success.' And that is also a negotiation and trade-off. As is knowing when a gear-change is needed.

'Transition between the phases is also key. You need to say ok now we have solved this, what is next. What buys me the next survival period? What does good look like in the eyes of all my stakeholders (customers, investors, budget holders?) for the next step.'

> You need clarity on what you are trying to achieve in each phase of work. The advice you get may be helpful overall but a hindrance right now. It may be advice for six months down the road. Actively managing the phases of the work is key for success.
> **Ken Johnstone**

It is vital to accept that you will always be in the midst of negotiations like this. It is important to know what you are working towards (what does your 'next survival period' look like) and you also need to be mindful of who needs to be negotiated with. Which is the point Royden made above: this is the job. It's not a side show.

Louder for the people at the back: negotiating with your stakeholders whoever they may be for each phase of your work is not a distraction. It is not a necessary evil. It is literally the job of the leader: ensuring survival so the amazing team amassed can do the doing. Who you are negotiating will vary depending on your setup. It may be your investors. It may be your parent company or companies. For Mox, for instance, the negotiations involved the parent bank, the JV partner *and* of course regulators.

'This ongoing dialogue' reflects founding CEO Deniz Güven 'extended beyond the organisation to include regulatory authorities. In a rapidly changing world, we worked closely with the Hong Kong Monetary Authority (HKMA) to establish parameters for electronic Know Your Customer (e-KYC) processes, risk modelling and regulatory compliance. The regulator's input also benefited internal discussions.' Throughout this process, the team had to remain focused on making technology choices and assembling the right stack to achieve their mission. They had to stay focused on building. But there was never the illusion that building an incredible modern stack and user-aligned interface would have been enough without full stakeholder alignment.

The Time, the Place and the Art of Finding It: The Mettle Way

Having fewer and better-chosen people around the table helps with negotiating trade-offs. I know you have noticed that Soups Ranjan earlier fundamentally disagreed with this view. He believes that having more people in the room, so they can hear things from the horse's mouth is important. And I don't disagree that you can make that work and, if you do, it is valuable but the danger of being distracted is high. Soups' point is: don't get distracted. And you can't argue with that. My point is if you can't achieve discipline with numbers, then being focused on who needs to be where for decisions to be made is the next best thing.

Having agreed filters to enhance focus is also key. Knowing who you need to make sure you are aligned with, internally and externally, is key.

There is a lot that needs to happen at the same time so part of the art of getting this right is finding a way to remain aligned on what is discussed, decided and conceded in each room, without needing the same people in every room. How do you ensure the left hand knows what the right hand is doing, without talking all the time, or being in all the same rooms?

You do what Wise do. You do what Sardine do. You create repositories of information that are accessible to all. You document, as Soups stressed, when and how decisions are made. Who decided what and why. You create discipline about record-keeping and a culture of actually going back to look things up. This takes work. From everyone involved. The easy alternative, the less tiresome way to ensure alignment is to float all decisions to the top. I worked somewhere once that had a weekly four-hour alignment meeting (it wasn't called that, but that is what it was). Yes weekly, that is not a typo. The CEO and her entire top table sat

> Management provide guardrails. Those closest to the data and the customer make the decisions.
> **Ken Johnstone**

at this meeting. Plus all the function leads and some of their leadership. It was a lot of people spending a lot of time on a lot of detail. I mean project-level detail. JIRA ticket level of detail.

Why?

Because the company had been making one too many isolated decisions that weren't true at the same time as all its other decisions it was making and ended up in hot water with clients.

See, if you spend the same budget twice you end up with a deficit. If you commit the same engineers to two pieces of work, only one piece of work gets done. Or none as, in a desperate attempt to do too much, you may complete nothing. If you don't make sure all things are true at the same time, you get caught out before long.

So, the idea here was, bring everyone in one room in the presence of the headmistress, have the discussions, stay aligned. Inefficient, but it should work. Right? Wrong.

Hundreds of decisions are made daily in every company. Whether to extend a supplier contract or not. Whether to increase storage capacity before going on holiday or not. Whether to hire a candidate or not. Whether to move an internal meeting to accommodate a client pitch, whether to give preferential pricing, whether to prioritise this piece of work over that. Whether to go to lunch before responding to an email. And that's before you calculate how many hundreds of decisions each engineer makes daily.

So even if you wanted to, you cannot float all decisions to the top. And even if you wanted to float the important ones, you don't always know which ones will turn out to be important. But the real issue here is that you shouldn't want to bring decisions to the top. The top is rarely the right place to make decisions. The right place to make each of those decisions is where most of the information and knowledge is. So the question is not how do you bring each of those decisions to the boss but rather how do you ensure each of the people making decisions (i.e. *everyone* in your company) knows what the bigger picture trade-off decisions already made are so they have the right context for their decision-making.

For Mettle one of the ways they have devised for negotiating trade-offs is vesting the people with the information with the power to make relevant decisions at the right operational level. For the record: inside a bank, that setup is one click below all-out rebellion and I love it.

> Ultimately, you need genuine conviction that you are doing the right thing, solving the right problem in a meaningful and differentiated way. But you also need evidence that you are doing the right thing.
>
> **Ken Johnstone**

'The power inside Mettle' stresses Ken 'is at the squad level. Those closest to the data and the customer make the decisions. Of course within guardrails. But getting that right is key.' It is key to efficiency and to an aligned organisation.

It is rebellious, though, inside a bank. *And* key. Because, without this, you end up either with leadership becoming a bottleneck or with disjointed decision-making that double-counts resources and double-commits time and money. The challenge is that when agreeing to nurture a different venture, the parent organisation doesn't necessarily anticipate changes in such visceral things. And you need to negotiate your way to this change for all the reasons explained above.

Curt Queyrouze agrees although he puts it a little differently (and it may fit your organisation better to think of it in these terms): 'What you see looking back, the lesson to be learned, is that the things you bring focus to change according to the environment [you operate in]. The only constant is focusing on where the work actually gets done': that is where you need to negotiate your trade-offs. That's where you need to embed the changes. 'So when you do the digital thing' reflects Curt 'focus on the back office.'

Where is the work getting done in your organisation? Where the work is getting done and the information is being held, focusing there is good advice and a common theme.

In fact, looking at the Mettle approach, a lot of it is about breaking decisions down, making them in the right place and moving on quickly.

'I am proud of the methodical approach we took' says Ken. 'The fact that we chose to not worry about the tech stack, for instance,

> The journey we are on is staged: making the decisions appropriate to each stage at the right time and then moving on is key.
> **Ken Johnstone**

and focus on proving value gave us focus and clarity. Now we have built our own tech and we can start thinking about how others in the bank can benefit. It has been a staged journey and remains so. That doesn't change.' The decisions you need to make at each stage do change, of course, but the process does not. And you will need to work out the language and cadence and fora for this dialogue to be ongoing because trade-offs will be needed (nobody ever has enough time and money to do everything) but also – and equally significantly – because mistakes will be made.

'There is always something keeping me up at night' reflects Ken.

'For instance, we dropped the ball on focusing on quantitative data. We had such a relentless focus on qualitative data that we realised at some point that we needed to go back and re-work certain things. Unlock and re-do. But that's part of the journey. Ultimately you need genuine conviction that you are doing the right thing, solving the right problem in a meaningful and differentiated way. But you also need *evidence* that you are doing the right thing.'

And that is also a muscle you need to build as part of your trade-off engine. How do you get better at framing the dialogue of what you should do and what you should stop? You create an evidence-based culture. Such as, I hear you ask. What evidence is compelling enough? Cash flow, obviously, is a powerful one. But not the only one.

For Ken the data that matters the most depends on the phase of the work but, ultimately, it boils down to 'customers using a feature. Giving feedback. You need the mental strength to push on, because this work is hard, but you also need evidence: to convince yourself, before you convince others. You need to highlight the positive green shoots even before they grow but you also you need to not be afraid to admit it when you get things wrong. Killing things is hard. But you have to *not* double down on things that don't work. We have done a lot of work on some hypotheses that were just wrong.'

What did they do when they realised they were wrong? They stopped (are you taking notes?). *How* did they know they were wrong? Data.

Not gut, not preference. Data. Just as Kelvin did with his pricing strategy. That data-first approach is key not only for informing trade-offs but also for creating the right culture in approaching trade-offs.

Ultimately, you are not guaranteed that your decisions will be the right ones but if you have the data, allow the decisions to be made by the people who have and understand the data in the service of a set of agreed priorities, you are on the way to having the right mindset and the right language for successfully navigating whatever the world throws your way. That, and the transparency of what decision is made, why and what is not being done as a result.

> You will make assumptions and you will be wrong about some things.
> What do you do when you realise you are wrong? You stop.
> How did you know you are wrong? Data.
> Not your gut. Evidence.

The process that Harsh and Steve described as Wise's transparency culture is key in developing a workforce that understands that, with finite hours in the day and finite resources, decisions cannot and should not be made in isolation. Everything is a trade-off and needs to be spoken of in that language. In a startup, it is key as wasting time could mean death as cash runways are always tighter than you want them to be. In big organisations, the problem of navigating choices and negotiating trade-offs is as urgent, but for slightly different reasons.

Roadblocks and Fairy Godmothers

Michael Anyfantakis has driven material transformation work across several banks both as a consultant and as a product and architecture leader inside the shop. In his experience (and mine, since you asked) transformation and innovation inside a bank is always hard and almost never a creativity challenge but almost always about the negotiation of what sits where, who owns what and what doesn't get done instead.

'When we look back at the beginning of the journey of innovation inside big organisations' Michael notes 'the ability to innovate was actually there. Inside all the large banks I have worked in or with, you could see teams arriving at some very good ideas very quickly.

And then we would get stuck.

We would have proven an idea, shaped it… and then we would move to leverage what the bank had in order to bring the idea to life.

We would need to shift owner-ship [from the innovation teams] to people who had the closest possible business inside the bank and, although the idea was good and passed all its stage gates, they wouldn't necessarily take it on because *it wasn't invented her*e. They wouldn't kill it exactly. They would agree it's a good idea, but

> Inside a big organisation, the biggest challenges to innovation are not cre-ativity but ownership: where will something sit, who will own it and how can you incentivise people with separate P&Ls to collaborate.

they would want to start again. Maybe introduce new vendors. Maybe recast the hypothesis. They wanted to do it. But not as something someone else started.'

And that is not all.

Finding an owner inside a bank is key and wanting to really own the idea isn't the only challenge. Innovative ideas often result in a 'product or service that did not fit within the existing divisions and product lines of the bank. When looking at a new product from a customer perspective, often we came with a proposition that would bring together multiple services that the Big Bank offered, but these were owned by different departments and different executives, so finding a single owner to bring this to market was very tricky. Sometimes those departments even competed with one another, but even if not in competition, they definitely did not see benefits of collaboration, as they have had different P&Ls.'

This is a challenge of a different order of magnitude and complexity. Because you may budget for the time it takes for people to come to feel ownership of an idea, even if that means covering the same ground twice. But how do you negotiate trade-offs when it comes to the holy grail of revenue sharing?

Plus, the challenge Michael highlights here, occurs when the trade-offs that need to be negotiated for budget, prioritisation, timings and decisions that impact other parts of the organisation are made by people with different definitions of what is important, different incentive structures and different pri-orities. How do you negotiate trade-offs when 'good' isn't the same for everyone around the table?

With difficulty, is the answer. But it is not impossible.

None of these were terminal challenges. 'We made it to the finish line' recalls Michael but given all of this, 'the speed was crawl rather than run. And yet we made it. We saw a number of big propositions come to life.

Some of those ideas were impressive and capital intensive. Ideas that needed collaboration across divisions (e.g. investing in buildings that allowed people to rent and then buy their own flats as a mortgage path). This was not one P&L. And yet we did it.'

It took perseverance. Patience. Negotiation. Also… A Fairy Godmother helps.

'How did we make such an idea work?' asks Michael. 'The idea had sponsorship from the get go, that's how. The business owner was involved from day 0. That creates an emotional connection. They were involved. They were interested. That matters. You want that senior, engaged sponsorship.'

> How do you negotiate trade-offs when 'good' isn't the same for everyone around the table?
> With difficulty, is the answer.

A senior sponsor helps you navigate and short-circuit internal tensions. A senior sponsor can under-write bold solutions and spear-head trade-off negotiations and tit-for-tat arrangements that could enable you to get the green light for things such as creating a separate entity (a new department, a new business line, a new brand) aside from the same shop. And once you get going, a senior sponsor will give air cover when negotiating trade-offs. A senior sponsor is key. But it helps if they are not your only weapon.

You need a process for negotiating trade-offs that doesn't involve a 'my dad is bigger than your dad' moment. A process for this is key in companies of all sizes. And particularly significant in big organisations changing themselves while carrying on with the main business.

The Dirty Secret of Innovation Is Process

When I was running innovation functions inside banks, the face of stakeholders would often fall when they realised that we were not the department of lego, crayons and crazy creatives. And as if that was not enough, we were also *not* the department of the magic money tree, where budgets that are hard to find anywhere else in the organisation flow freely.

It was always a little disappointing that what we did was create a repeatable process of approvals, budget and resource negotiations and accountability for ideas that didn't have a natural home or that needed space and speed that didn't naturally occur in

> Everything is a learning opportunity. We learned how to learn in this process. And we learned how to negotiate with each other: 12,000 colleagues learned how to negotiate with each other.
> **Simon Boonen**

the organisation. I was a little disappointed myself, truth be told when I realised that was the job. I expected more bean bags, fewer gantt charts.

Simon Boonen agrees. You need a process. Tried, tested, developed and agreed. ING has developed a structured innovation methodology called PACE. This combines a focus on skills, expertise and mindset. It comes with small empowered teams that move quickly, it comes with clear rules for getting the support functions involved when needed and allows ideas to flow through without getting stuck in all the usual places of neglect, lack of access to shared resources or management mind-share when decisions are made.

The commitment to the process is intense: over 12,000 colleagues have been trained on applying PACE, in innovation and/or in their own work environment. Which means that over 12,000 colleagues *know how to negotiate* with a colleague from a different department about access to the testing team or the risk team. The process also drives awareness. In a context where we can't do everything and neither should we, focus emerges because an organisation has the language to negotiate holistically and, by doing it often, it starts developing self-awareness about the sorts of things that work best within the body corporate.

'The reality is we all love working on opportunity-based innovation ideas' chuckles Simon 'but a challenge-driven piece of work will get focus faster. That is a lesson we learned: challenge-driven innovation vs opportunity-driven innovation is 90/10. And

> Innovation is less about creativity and more about a repeatable process for creating space (read: time and money and talent) for ideas that don't have a natural home inside the existing organisation.

that is ok. It creates space for collaboration and then changes come across the board. Everything is a learning opportunity. We learned how to learn in this process. We learn how to tell what works and what doesn't. We learn from the knowledge brought to us by the third parties we collaborate with. If the specific experiment we are working on works, great. If it doesn't, we still learn.' And whatever happens, you have to go again. So you need a repeatable process.

And you need to spend the time feeding the process. A total of 12,000 colleagues going through the training with the expectation of applying the knowledge is no small feat. And it isn't even the full story as you need to keep getting smarter, through the process. And

> The whole thing is a funnel: you get practical real quick as time is always constrained.
>
> **Simon Boonen**

reviewing the process in the process of the process being applied.

'We have evaluation meetings' continues Simon. 'What works, what doesn't and why. We feed that knowledge back constantly. What to keep, what to improve, what to stop. Post mortems are key. Why do things fail? Did we make the wrong assumptions? Did we not get the right sponsorship? Was there a change in external circumstances? The whole process of getting a new idea or partnership through the commercial process is like a pregnancy. The agreement is a starting point. It feels like a finish line but it's only the start. Sometimes miracles are expected but the reality is things take time and although getting to the start line is never easy, that's when the work actually starts. The only way around that is constant open communication including the "innovation disclaimer" that *things may not work*. Everyone knows it but in the specifics it is often forgotten so if you say it often enough people may remember in the moment when something doesn't work.'

So what have you learned in this process is my obvious question.

'Size matters' says Simon with a laugh. 'Instead of working with super small startups, we de-risk the process by working with scaling companies. We can control for that and we have learned what works.' That is the exact same realisation Cuscal came to, as Bianca Bates told us in Chapter 5.

> We realised that banks don't have the luxury of setting expectations any more. The bar you are compared against is higher than ever before. You need to rise to that.
> **Simon Boonen**

'We have also learned to work in a collaborative way with business stakeholders. It's their show after all. We help them navigate the market and our own organisation but at the end of the day it's their signature on the agreement. So we need the people with the right mindset and you find them through the conversations we have talked about before. You find people with an appetite for collaboration. And the whole thing is a funnel: you get practical real quick. You can tell who is ready to work in a different way.

This is key as time is constrained. There is only so much you *can* do. You learn to prioritise against the organisation governance, the things you know you can control for, the overall priorities of the organisation. You find the accelerants. You also trust your instinct. That comes with experience.

The world has changed in the years banks have been learning how to innovate in tandem with the market. Platforms have emerged as a new business model. We realised that banks don't have the luxury of setting expectations any more. The bar you are compared against is higher than ever before. You need to rise to that. You are fighting for attention. We need to prepare the organisation to be more flexible and nimble and to be able to respond to these major external changes as they come. And they will keep coming. The number of successes helps also. It helps the organisation feel joy when we get traction. That energises people.'

The Most Important Work Isn't Glamorous

We speak about change management and innovation, we speak about founding new businesses and pushing the boundaries with new products and services, new business models and more empowered ways of working. It sounds cool. And it is. But if you are doing it right, the work itself isn't all that sexy.

'One of the first things I did at my current job was centralise the PMO office. Not a glamorous task but we found hundreds of initiatives that needed focus and management attention' notes Coastal Financial Corporation's President Curt Queyrouze. 'The staff did not have the correct structure to support the rapid execution of so many initiatives. Where there may have been a handful of "important" initiatives in years past, now there were more than 160. The constant readjustment of focus is inevitable but *not* distracting yourself is an active choice. Resource allocation becomes your first priority.'

> One of the first things I did was centralise the PMO office.
>
> Where there may have been a handful of "important" initiatives in years past, now there were more than 160. The constant readjustment of focus is inevitable but not distracting yourself is an active choice. Resource allocation becomes your first priority.
> *Curt Queyrouze*

Getting the process to negotiate what you will do and what you won't do is not the creative part of the process and many organisations (of all sizes) chafe and say inane stuff like 'that's not how you do innovation'. Only: it is.

'The market will be constantly transitioning' continues Curt. 'The pressure will always be picking up. And of course there are always things I wish I had that I don't... and things I wish I didn't have to contend with, that I do... but even with a clean sheet, the next big decision is not any easier. Because humans are humans.'

So a process for determining what gets done and what doesn't in a repeatable fashion is key no matter the size of your organisation and the stage of your evolution. As is the process of learning from the successes and failures and improving your tooling, methodology and support structures. So the process will help you even if you don't necessarily think you need it right now because when big decisions need to be made, humans won't always think in a linear fashion.

'If you remember that people will always revert back to *what's in it for me* you will lay a better vision for the future for your people. You speak about grand ambitions and someone is sitting there thinking *yes but that person over there has an EVP title and I deserve one too.* There is no getting around that. You need to tie the two.' Your strategic vision and people's very personal needs and ambitions need to work together. 'Employee engagement is key to success always' reflects Curt. And that doesn't just mean the odd holiday party, cupcakes and surveys. It means actively reflecting on what is important to people: big, small, lofty or petty.

Amen to that.

If you are constantly alert to the fact that people buy into the mission but also want to feel personally looked after as well, and that doesn't make them bad people; if you remember that people may resist change because they like the work you are asking them to stop, or they believe in it, or they are comfortable with it, you see the significance of all this coming together.

'You have to be alive to the fact that people will want to protect their world as they know it' stresses Curt. So all your processes for negotiating trade-offs need a level of selfishness-proofing as people 'will want to feel they have some personal incentive to be part of something bigger. You have to show them a path forward. You need to help them feel protected. You will need to provide an answer to the often unspoken question "what about me, will I be ok?". Whatever you do from a tech

> Your strategic vision needs to coexist with people's own concerns from 'why does that person have an EVP title and I don't' to 'will I be ok through this change'.
> **Curt Queyrouze**

standpoint, you need to get people feeling safe and engaged.' If you are in a big organisation, there is no getting around the significance of Curt's point. Because, ultimately, in a startup you could argue that people signed up for rapid and constant change. And even then, it's hard and folks react and resist. In a big organisation people aren't necessarily equipped for the change you are foisting upon them.

'Your mechanisms for enabling trade-offs then' continues Curt 'need to be mindful of the fact that humans bring to the table a variety of motivations depending on who they are, where they sit and what they are measured against. And they need to be mindful of what you are trying to achieve. In a startup it is about surviving to the next cycle. In a scale-up it is about getting to stand on your own two feet as a business fulfilling its mission.'

And in a bank?

Curt is adamant that in all your trade-offs you need to retain 'a constant awareness that our job is to protect consumers' so 'as you move into the new tech world, how do you test for these fundamental protections? How do you know that they are in place?'

Innovation's Greatest Friend Is Governance

'There is value in my grey hair' jokes the unfairly handsome and debonair Curt (I am not even being nice… and yes I know it sounds like a cheap line in a romantic novel but it happens to be the truth. I dare you to meet Curt and not think exactly the same). 'I know the pitfalls of the past as we head into a fully digital future. I know governance is key' stressed Curt.

'I have been through seven recessions. I have seen banks fail in droves. It's the best education you can get. And although I was too early in my career to be responsible for what happened, I was in the middle of the mess starting my career in an industry beset with fraud and litigation.

It was an education. I have seen what can go wrong and how wrong it can go and how important governance is. We are currently seeing shocks like SVB or the even more dramatically FTX[4], etc. Each wave of spectacular failures (Enron, Worldcom, FTX) look different, but there is always a common denominator: Lack of governance is always present.

I had a mentor years ago who had two senior leaders working for him. One was an evangelical vision guy. The other was a governance freak. He taught me he needed them both. They created balance and they were each as important as each other. You need vision. But you need to protect your consumers as you move forward. It can never be an afterthought. Fintechs often only *concede* the governance part. It is 'forced' upon them as they grow. That attitude needs to shift and governance needs to be seen as a key part of maturing. Especially as the industry matures itself. When I started in banking, we didn't have KYC as we understand it now. Everything is evolving, it's not just fintech. And as new speedy ways of working are available, we need to keep a balance between doing the right work, servicing clients and not bending rules.'

> I have been through seven recessions. I have seen banks fail in droves. I have seen what can go wrong and how wrong it can go. I know how important governance is.
> **Curt Queyrouze**

This is, of course, the trade-off that never speaks its name. Because cutting corners and bending rules is sadly an ever-present danger when decisions are being made and trade-offs assessed. And for the avoidance of doubt: trade-offs are inevitable. Cutting corners is not.

'I remember I was in the process of boarding a flight to go see a client' recalls the Client Service Director of a scaling fintech that asked to remain unnamed. 'It was an overnight flight and I was looking forward to a glass of wine, a movie, some sleep before a

> When I started, we didn't have KYC as we understand it now. Everything is evolving, it's not just fintech.
> And as new speedy ways of working are available, we need to keep a balance between doing the right work, servicing clients and not bending rules.
> **Curt Queyrouze**

---

4 Just in case you have been living under a rock or you pick this book up decades into a future where the FTX fiasco is forgotten, FTX, short for Futures Exchange, is a now bankrupt company that operated a cryptocurrency exchange and a crypto hedge fund both of which were found to be riddled in fraud and resulted in a 25-year prison sentence for Founder Sam Bankman-Fried (under appeal at the time when we went to print).

   https://www.nbcnews.com/business/business-news/sam-bankman-fried-sentenced-25-years-prison-orchestrating-ftx-fraud-rcna145286 pretty busy day ahead on the ground. My cell phone rang as I was taking my seat. It was one of the product team leaders. That never happened... He never called. It was not a good sign. He was calling to say timidly that I was going to land into a rather tense atmosphere because the client had found a plethora of defects in the latest release of the service I was negotiating an extension for on this very trip.

How come?

Things were running late and the decision was made to release without testing thoroughly because they were too scared to ask for an extension as they were always late and the client was getting annoyed.'

So they opted for cutting a corner and hoping for the best. Needless to say, the best did not materialise. Hope being, by and large, a terrible strategy. Was there a process that said 'we don't release without testing' in this company? Of course there was. Was there oversight? No. In the interest of speed and in the name of a respectful culture, they operated on the basis of an honour system: in other words, do the right thing because we agreed this is how *we* do things, not because someone is policing you.

It turns out, in their particular case, policing was necessary. More governance was needed. And yes it would slow them down but it would also stop them from doing things like releasing untested code to avoid difficult conversations. And before you ask: no, nobody was fired as a result of violating the honour system of their company. I had the same question too. And this was the answer: 'the incident was treated as a case of *worse things happen at sea* which is the real summary of the company's culture' reflects the Client Service Director. 'The honour system was just words.'

But words that created real problems and, frankly, real risks for the business.

We Are in the Risk Management Business

'You can't be so locked down with governance you can't service the customers' observes Curt 'but equally you can't have no regulatory concerns.' You need to ensure you have the right mechanisms for ensuring your trade-offs take into account all the things that need to be true at the same time and that, in our industry, includes regulation and governance.

'We know what it takes to run a bank. Where you sit on the risk spectrum is up to you. What you need to do to service your clients varies depending on the communities you serve. But the need for people to be able to trust us is constant. Sound infrastructure plus governance is key in delivering against that trust. Mistakes will happen. Infrastructure and governance is how you keep trust when things go wrong.'

> Mistakes will happen. Infrastructure and governance is how you keep trust when things go wrong.
> **Curt Queyrouze**

It is how we prove to customers and regulators that we have things under control and minimise mistakes.

'This is a mindset question' confirms Maha El Dimachki. And it is a mindset we need to see in all companies in financial services, no matter what their size. Especially from a regulatory perspective. 'A lot of younger companies don't engage in active risk management' reflects Maha 'and the risk that hits you is always the risk you cannot see. Did you not see because you weren't looking?'

Governance is how you make sure you keep looking. Regulators encourage younger companies to start actively managing their risks and putting governance in place so they develop the habit of being 'on the lookout for those signs' continues Maha.

> The risk that hits you is always the risk you cannot see.
> Did you not see because you weren't looking?
> Governance is how you make sure you keep looking.
> **Maha El Dimachki**

'If the risk is in your line of sight, you will do something about it. That is why you should do scenario planning. That is why you should always spend time on mitigation, pivot and wind-down plans. We are human and we like to believe we are rational, but the reality is emotion is key and entrepreneurs believe they *will* be successful. You need that optimism. But how do you retain that optimism without leaving the big decisions behind? Scenario planning is how.

Plan for the most devastating scenario as an exercise. Do it even if your investors don't ask for it (and they often don't, as they focus on the more optimistic stuff like total addressable market and growth projections).

> Entrepreneurs believe they *will* be successful. You need that optimism. But how do you retain that without leaving the big decisions behind? Scenario planning is how.
> **Maha El Dimachki**

Also: We tend to be predisposed towards a particular set of skills but a founder has to be *all the things*, both visionary and operational. And if they don't have those skills, they have to bring them in: investors want vision but both are needed. And in fact the expectations of investors and regulators and the needs of businesses (although they often produce competing priorities) need to coexist in harmony. Competing priorities are ok but if you are dealing with too many tensions it becomes difficult and they need to be solved. It's complex. And in a digital world where does one thing stop and another begin?'

Governance becomes the mechanism through which you stay alert to the needs and challenges of an ever-changing world.

The Medium Is the Message

It is very rare that your trade-off mechanisms, your ways for keeping yourself honest about the decisions you make and the way you make them are directly bound to your purpose and business model proof point. But for OM Bank it is. For them, that trade-off question is existential. They set out to have an impact on society and their belief is they will achieve that not just through a good product, nice UX and great marketing, but by controlling their unit economics. Why?

They have seen what happens to businesses that don't.

'The problem our competition have' flags Royden 'is that executing change is expensive and hard. So they make few bets, understandably, and those few bets still come with huge political capital expenditure.

These bets are made around the board table and, strangely, there is more focus on getting ideas funded rather than getting them executed. In an organisation where change is cheap and easy, all good ideas have merit you can test.

And even then, you can't do everything as your operational complexity will go through the roof if you do that. So you still have to be selective.

To get that right, you have to build a business where change is a lived reality with constant experimentation and learning. We are digital so we define that ability as a baseline for everything we do. So, success as an organisation would be being extremely flexible so that when the world changes or we find out we are wrong in our hypotheses or assumptions, we can change.

> In big organisations executing change is expensive and hard. So they make few bets, understandably, and those few bets still come with huge political capital expenditure.
>
> In an organisation where change is cheap, all good ideas have merit you can test.
>
> You have to build a business where change is a lived reality with constant experimentation and learning.
>
> **Royden Volans**

The culture you need for that to succeed entails a much higher degree of accountability across the board. Plus you need to get the fundamentals right. Customer focus is key. Getting your economics right is key: if that is your vision, what are your trade-offs. You need to produce an economic manifesto. And then you need to follow it.' And by 'you' he means everyone in the business. Everyone in the business needs to make trade-offs that are in line with the economic manifesto since that manifesto is, as we have already seen, the proof point and strategic lynchpin of the entire business.

See how all the bits are coming together? You'd think I'd planned the chapter sections that way…

Inside a big organisation and for all the reasons Roy describes, agrees DNB's Trygve Aasheim, it is rare that you would be able to completely reinvent yourself. Apple is an outlier.

Most organisations, once they achieve size, double down to protecting their business model. That is even more complex for a regulated entity such as a bank whose 'auditors want to see your software development lifecycle from business requirements to development work and back to business outcome. So we are not only "rigged" as an organisation to our business model, but also regulated to do just that.'

Within this context you can still iterate and innovate but need some very clear guidelines on how to follow new concepts that are mature enough to be verified. 'Digital is not biology. It is not something that needs researchers and theories and consensus to be proven. Digital is made out of tools and processes created by humans. So if you want to, you can easily understand it and apply it to your business with great benefits but always within the constraints of your process and governance.' And if it is too disruptive to fit, you will have to run it in parallel to your wider organisation. But that's Chapter 7's consideration, where we turn to money and governance models.

I know… that's what you've been waiting for! But first… your homework.

Your Calls to Action

- Having the right people around the table is about who you have there (both in terms of attitude and aptitude) and who you make sure is not there: so fire toxic people and ensure you don't carry passengers.
- Who is not there is as important as who is.
- Get processes in place early on for hiring, firing and accountability and keep checking they work.
- Bring decisions as close as possible to the people who have the information needed to make the decision. Decision-making should be about data, not hierarchy.
- Never debate trade-offs or decisions without facts. Information should always trump gut feel and preference. So make sure you gather data as a matter of course and review it regularly.
- Be clear about what is important. Make sure it's not a long list.
- Make it ok for someone to say 'I know this is my job but I don't think it is a job that we should be doing' (thanks Ken).
- In a big organisation, make sure your new venture has a big sponsor early on.

■ No matter how big your organisation, establish a process for negotiating trade-offs. Create the language and forum where this is meant to happen. Don't leave it to individuals to work things out in the context of specific situations.
■ You can have the grandest plan and the greatest strategy. People will still worry about themselves. You need to bring them on the journey.
■ Governance is how you check your blind spots and how you keep trust when things go wrong (thanks Curt).

Chapter 7

Gods *and* Masters

Money, Money, Money

Yes.

This is a reference to the anti-hierarchy anarchist slogan 'No Gods, No Masters'. And, yes, it is followed by an ABBA song reference. And, yes, I am well pleased with myself thank you very much. And, yes, of course the insinuation is the exact opposite of what the slogan was going for. That's why it's funny.

Because *of course* power dynamics abound in the world. From the kindergarten playground to the world stage, everything is (for better or worse) about power and influence vectors. And business is no exception.

So in this section, I want to talk about the dynamics of power introduced by money in the context of new ventures: namely who

> Whether you are backed by a VC, a group of investors or a corporate 'parent', there is asymmetry in a relationship where money flows one way. You need to actively manage that and be clear about what you are giving up in exchange for cash each time.

holds it, who gives it, what they get in exchange and what are the things you should be thinking about when considering the money you are taking: how much, from whom, when and how.

DOI: 10.1201/9781003395577-7

As you would expect, the specifics of where money comes from, how you pitch for it and what you are 'giving up' for it, so to speak, are different between startups and corporate-backed ventures but the significance of the power dynamic is equally present.

There is an asymmetry in every relationship where money flows one way so, even though the specifics are different between a startup and an enterprise-backed venture, the mechanics and trade-offs that come with securing investment are very similar. Ultimately, you are being funded on a promise and the way you manage the process and the proof points of said promise will determine to a large extent whether you will get more money next time you ask for it. And you will be asking for more money without a doubt. So: managing the expectations of the folks who gave you money to get started, so that they can carry on giving you money, so you can finish what you started, is equally significant whether you are a venture-backed startup or a corporate-backed entity and have many parallels.

You need money to build a business, after all. And there is no such thing as free money even if it does seem like it at times. Ultimately, you will always give something up in exchange for money. That is inevitable. You give up some equity, some freedom,

> I don't mind giving away equity, but it's like blood: there needs to be a bloody good reason for doing it!
> **Dharm Mistry**

some decision-making power. 'My first rodeo was during the .com boom and crash' recalls Enfuce's Monika Liikamaa. 'I first built with other people's money and to their ambition level. We were building something similar [to Enfuce] as early as 2011/ 2012. And the ceiling to our growth was other people's ambition level.' And now?

They didn't take the money that came with loss of control. They didn't decide to build to the tune of someone else's ambition level. 'Now', continues Monika 'our ambition level was so massive that we went global faster and cheaper. It is not typical to be born female in the Nordics and want to change the world and at the start we were called insane. Then… we were called lucky. Whatever. Find someone who wants it as much and as big as you. Your business partner is a marriage of ambition.'

As is your investor. Because if you are not aligned, you are not giving up just equity. You are giving up part of the reason why you are on this journey in the first place. And even if your investors are as ambitious as you, equity is only part of what you are giving up

> When you are building with someone else's money, you are also building to their level of ambition.
> **Monika Liikamaa**

so whatever it is, make sure you are clear what the exchange you are entering into is. What you are *actually* giving up and whether it's worth it. Because giving up equity comes at a price beyond the equity itself.

'I don't mind giving away equity, but it's like blood. There needs to be a bloody good reason for doing it' says Dharm Mistry with a laugh. He's been through the founder journey three times now and is very pragmatic about it.

You have to take money and give equity away, much as you may not like it. And you will need to take the market hints and change, hold back or sell when the opportunity arises. Even if you don't like the idea. And exactly because decisions will need to be made under pressure, it matters who is in a position to weigh in on those decisions. During those moments when you have to make decisions under pressure is when who your investors are will make the most difference. Who you take money from will have a big bearing on decisions around pivots, market expansion or, indeed, sales.

'Recently I had my third exit, not the ideal market conditions, but a real £5 is better than a picture of £50' reflects Dharm. Selling a business may not be an easy decision, but it often is the pragmatic one. Thinking back to an earlier exit that saw his business sold to Temenos (and Dharm joining the Temenos top table as its CDO for a while) he reflects 'I didn't want to sell at the time. I felt we were two years away from true glory. But the investors had been there with us for seven years, we were the last company in their portfolio so they applied pressure.

> A real £5 is better than a picture of £50.
> **Dharm Mistry**

I also remember my previous CEO turning down 100m [expecting much more] and exiting with next to nothing. So [when the offer came] we took it.'

So when you take money on day 1, expect this kind of conversation at some point in your future. Ultimately, investors wanting to be made whole is only to be expected. The question 'is this the best offer I am going to get' is a valid one. Especially as, Dharm recalls, 'urgency and pressure is always there in a small company, and it's a constant rollercoaster. On the downs you ask yourself should I quit and get a job, the ups are glorious, you feel you can conquer the world. A big company will spend years questioning something rather than investing in it. So as an employee you have a choice to either get paid and put up with that pace or leave and do something you believe in.' But even when you believe in what you are doing, you need to be pragmatic when negotiating with investors, when accepting or rejecting money.

The Early Bird May Get More Than It Bargained for

We can all agree that change is expensive and it takes money. No matter what you are doing, you will need investment to get going and keep going. There will be times when you are desperate for money and that is when it is important to remember that not all money is good for you. That's both because the provenance of the money matters (who is behind this money). But also because where you are *at* on your journey also matters. The same money may be bad for you at different times of your journey and great at others. But also, depending on where you are in your journey, you are more (or less) likely to make bad decisions around money. We have already talked about pressures put on the product decisions Lizzie Chapman and the Zest team made by the investors they had around the table.

That is a really common challenge because for most entrepreneurs getting the money to get started is the biggest concern when they get started. Joel Blake thinks back to the start of his journey 'If I go back to when I first had the ambition to start a business, I thought I needed to get money as soon as possible. I thought *I know my idea is going to work so I just need to get the money to make it work.*

> Money, early on, when you are not proven tends to 'cost' more in equity given up and concessions made. But it is also usually less valuable for the business: because you rarely know how to make it extract maximum value, really early on.

That was naive and it almost killed me.

It wasn't about the money. It was about the value money had for me at the time: what it was worth to me at the time. I genuinely thought that if I can get money then I am in the game. I came from a context of struggle, so my attitude was that *I want all the money I can get, if I can get it. Give me all of it.* But the strategic value of money is not just about your strategic plan. It is relative to your own psychology vis a vis money… your overall context, technology advancements, maturity of thought.'

Of course that makes sense. Money is never just about the sum. It is all about the context and the relative impact. But nobody who has ever fundraised can tell me that they didn't feel the same urge as Joel. If you tell me that you started fundraising for an idea you believed in and didn't think at least briefly 'I will take the most money I am given', I won't believe you.

But of course, 'give me all the money' may well not be the best decision for you. Let's unpack this.

First of all, money, early on, when you are not proven tends to 'cost' more in equity given up and concessions made. You give up

> When your back is against the wall… that is the worst time to make decisions.

something that isn't worth anything specific yet, of course, and your investors will always joke at some point in the process that '10% of 0 is 0' which is true but also it's the game they chose to play so what you should be thinking about, while they think about their potential upside, is your dilution at scale. Will you still control the direction of your business after one or two more rounds? Will you still have the ability to give equity to employee? All of that stuff may be stuff you give up for early cash and few have the discipline of the Enfuce founders to sit down and work out what they are and aren't prepared to do, when they have nothing to divide.

Incidentally, when I asked Monika and Denise about the board dynamics around their top table on the back of having turned down the investment early on in the journey they had one word for me: control. Monika didn't pull her punches: 'We are in control. People around the table know that this is the deal: the investors have invested in us and they have invested because we know our shit. So we are in control of our business. In the next round the most challenging thing will be understanding what we need to give up so that the company can keep growing.

And, as always when the time comes we will need to sit down and think what is best for the company and us as individuals.'

So the time comes when you will give up control even for the most seasoned entrepreneurs. And most entrepreneurs don't start the journey knowing what the build journey will look like.

So in fact the second most serious issue with fundraising is that, early on, you have no idea how much you need. You may severely underestimate the challenge as Lizzie described or raise more than you need. Remember Soups said if

> Money early on in your journey 'costs' more in terms of equity and loss of control and future optionality. And it comes with the danger of not actually knowing how much you will need to raise: are you raising too much? Are you raising too little and diluting too much too soon?

he had his time again he would try to do what he did with even less capital.

Why is that? Because companies that raise too much bloat or lose their edge. Staying lean and focused is very often a function of needing to keep an eye on burn. That is a common and, frankly, not very sinister scenario.

But the moment-in-time your company is in when raising money also determines heavily how much of a poisoned chalice that money may turn out to be. It is a well-known industry truism that you should raise when you don't need the money and the reason may look like this: As part of my research, I spoke to a founder who asked for his firm to not be named for reasons that will become apparent very soon.

> Money is never free. What you give up to get it may make it a poisoned chalice.

The company was early stage and, although it had some early traction both in terms of user numbers and some seed investors coming into play in the first few months of operation, everything that could have gone wrong, did. Timing is always a factor, as we have already discussed, and not always a kindly one. Exogenous factors (including the pandemic) created delays when the team could least afford them and simultaneously the founding team imploded in a rather public, spectacular and expensive way.

Public spats between the founders on social media made it hard to hire, unpleasant to work there and (predictably) annoyed the early investors. Private empire-building by the two co-founders meant that they found themselves with two competing product-build priority sets being pursued simultaneously inside a team of 14. That shouldn't be possible. And yet.

This feud diluted scarce resources and created toxic divisions in a very small team under a lot of pressure already. As if this wasn't bad enough, the process of discovering what was going on took a little longer than it should have done because of the pandemic forcing a change in ways of working that took a few weeks to bed in. Isolating who was instigating what and who thought they were doing the best they could in the circumstances and exiting one half of the founding team (which is the solution they arrived at eventually) was fraught with legal interventions and compensation battles.

> Anything that distracts you (from a falling out with your co-founder to a product feature that isn't the right one) will cost you a lot down the road, when you need to raise again to make up for the time you lost.

It distracted the team; it wasted valuable time. And it depleted scarce resources.

At the time of this interview, things were almost fully sorted but the surviving founder and CEO didn't look like a winner. He looked like a shell of a man who had been through a war he barely survived. He had aged ten years in the space of two. He was hollowed out. And he was not done.

Because although the drama with his co-founder was over, what was left of the company was in disarray. But he couldn't just call it quits. He had employees and most importantly he had investors.

Remember those early-stage investors that had come into the mix and were greeted as great news and a fantastic sign of early traction? Well. In a happy world, they would pump some more money in roundabout *now*, make sure lessons were learned and move on. It can happen. It does happen. But it didn't happen here.

> Your investors, even the best ones, have to manage their own exposure and their own returns.
>
> Even the friendliest ones are never fully aligned to your business.
>
> Do not forget that.

The early investors, instead, put considerable pressure on the remaining founder to take some emergency capital from a third party that they identified. New to the cap table. Willing and able, so to speak.

So what is the problem, I hear you ask? The investors are being helpful.

Well.

This chap had the money alright, but he had also failed every AML screen you could think of. I hardly need to say that this is terrible in any context but in financial services this decision is potentially catastrophic and criminal proceedings are not out of the question. Which is why the founder asked to remain unnamed.

Given the company in question was in FS, not regulated itself but dealing with regulated activity and people's money, the first failed AML check should have been where *all* the investors around the table shouted ABORT. Only they didn't. They put immense pressure on the remaining founder to take the cash, so they would manage their own exposure. Their interests and his interests weren't exactly aligned here.

This, of course, proves that they were the wrong investors and the early traction proof point they offered came with a cripplingly high price down the road. The founder, since you are wondering, felt he had no other options. So he took the money. True or not, it is how he felt at the time. It was that or shutting down and, as he felt he was responsible for the situation at least partly since he picked the now departed co-founder, he felt responsible for the 11 remaining employees who had put their faith in him and the company and who would lose their jobs if he didn't do something.

'When your back is up against the wall' he recalls 'that is a terrible time to make decisions'.

So. When thinking about fundraising, timing is important. Try to not leave raising money so late that you are desperate and have no option but to take what you are

> Even if nothing goes wrong, an early strategic investor may discourage other investors down the line if their strategies and time horizons don't align.
> Every choice comes with a trade-off.

given. 'Because' he continues 'even knowing what I know now, if the circumstances were the same… I would do it again, for the same reasons' even though that doesn't make it a good choice for anyone involved. It was a bad choice then. It is a bad choice now. And yet.

That bitter realisation of 'even knowing what I know now, I am not sure I would have been able to turn down the money' was the conclusion of another founder, in a different geography, who also asked not to be named as he is mid-litigation with an early investor. Full-on ugly court battle that isn't set to end any time soon as the investor has deep pockets and a message to send to the market.

The story starts well for this founder too.

Early traction in their chosen market but a mammoth task ahead and an early investor comes in and says 'I see you. I like what you are trying to do and here is some money to help support this mission'. In their case this was a strategic investor who could also support with product distribution as well as give cash. What's not to like?

How do you say no to that, and why would you?

Well, the vanilla cautionary note is that a highly committed, early strategic investor may put off more valuable long-term investors down the path. They may not want to share the board room with someone whose horizon and methods don't align with those of a different kind of investor. So that is a vanilla consideration for everyone to weigh before saying yes to an early investor of any kind.

The less vanilla story is that there may be other incentives at work. In this case, the investor started using data shared in this startup's board packs to fuel their sales efforts and product development elsewhere in their portfolio. This is rare, before you ask. It is breaching confidentiality and fiduciary responsibility agreements – hence the lawsuit. It is unethical, of course it is. It is demoralising. It becomes a massive drain on time, resources and energy.

Drastic steps had to be taken and some are still being played out (hence the anonymity) but the losses were considerable, both in terms of material expenditure of time and money and the morale loss, the energy loss. 'We had early product market fit' he recalls. 'And this was crazy bubble time. There was money to be had, there were new companies coming up every day and we were so desperate not to f'up and miss our moment. We knew we could do what we set out to do but, because it was Fintech Fever times, our fear was someone would beat us to our market because they had the money to do it faster. We felt we had everything worked out, other than the money to make it happen fast. With hindsight, we took money from the wrong people on the wrong terms. But I am not sure there was an alternative. I am not sure I would do things differently if I had my time again: I am not sure it would have been possible.'

Nobody Sets Out to Fail

'Look at the WeWork example' reflects Funderbeam's Kaidi Ruusalepp. 'They were pushed towards growth at all cost and that meant that they were pushed towards crazy funding rounds and stupid mistakes. Companies fail as a result.' And nobody sets out to fail. Nobody knowingly takes those risks. Maybe people fly too close to the sun, high on the optimism we have agreed founders and change makers need in order to do this work. Or, soberingly, at

> How you make decisions while scared may be your greatest test as a leader.

the time poor decisions are being made they seem objectively better than the alternative and that is important to remember.

It is scary, building new things. How you make decisions while scared may be your greatest test as a leader.

Looking back at the last decade and a half, where money was plentiful and investment into fintech reached dizzying heights, a lot of mistakes were made by companies who were trying to do their best. 'Nobody teaches you about how to assess how much money to take, whose money to take, as you dilute your business, and who is around the table' reflects Lizzie Chapman thinking back to those days.

Investors are often seen by entrepreneurs as the people who've done this before, seen it before and can actually help navigate. But that isn't always the case: they come with their own agendas as we saw above and their experience, while benign, may not always be useful. Remember the Client Services Director we met earlier who got the bad news of the untested code as they were boarding their flight?

'I don't sit on our board' he recalls 'but I occasionally present to them. Usually when something has gone wrong. So, on my return from the trip, I had to give an update on what happened and remediation. During the briefing, I was bombarded with questions. Some valid. But most left me wondering whether they even understand what we do.'

And they may very well not. Investors don't always have specialist knowledge in the things they invest in. And even if they do, it is rare that they have built businesses before. So the knowledge they have won't be operational and the insight you hope they bring, may not be there. Besides, continues Lizzie, you could 'easily and unintentionally invite the fox into the henhouse, so to speak'.

> Startups often see investors as people who have done it before and can help navigate.
>
> But they haven't always done it before. They may have invested before but that is different.
>
> Their experience may not be useful and they always have their own agenda. That is not sinister. But it is a fact.

And it doesn't even need to be a sinister situation like the ones we discussed before, to be problematic. It could be a question of whether you give investors a board seat, how you manage their expectations, how much of your time you give them. Do you need to speak to them every week? Probably not. And yet most early startups do. And they don't do that because they are stupid. They do it because disrupting an industry is expensive and keeping your investors sighted and on-side is important. Building platforms is expensive. It is rare for anyone to only need the one round of funding and fairly common for investors to 'follow their money' so the bad habits of giving too much time, headspace and attention to the investors are actually sensible habits. Speaking to your investors every day distracts you from the job of building a product and spending that time with your team

> Money that allows you to spend it in order to achieve what you set out to achieve, rather than spending it chasing after more money, is more unusual than should be the case.

or customers. But without the money of those investors you have no business, you have no product and the team are out there looking for another job. So what choice do you *really* have as a founder?

'That is another thing you don't think about at the start' recalls Lizzie 'you need to bring the money in of course. But do you need to speak to your investors every day? How you divide your time is important.' Money that allows you to spend it in order to achieve what you set out to achieve, rather than spend it chasing after money, is more unusual than should be the case.

Some VCs are mindful of that and help protect you. 'One of our investors' Lizzie recalls 'left us alone to work but would reach out and challenge us if they thought we were about to do something stupid'. And that, arguably, is the difference between money that is good for you, and money that isn't. Because money that isn't good for you exacts its price at the worst possible moments: when you have your back to the wall.

'You get your *oh shit* moments. Especially in the first couple of years' recalls Christian Nentwich. Those moments when your resilience is tested and giving up is a very real option. 'Resilience and determination vs obstinance is a hard one to call. How do you know when to give up? It's so hard. And

> You should DD your investors. Take reference calls... because you want investors that are 'do no harm, do no evil'.
> **Soups Ranjan**

you are dependent on so much external stuff. Du.Co had, at one moment in 2015, two weeks of cash flow left. A bad investor could torch you at that moment. Hold you to ransom. Take out immense amounts of equity. Mine didn't.'

This is the sort of investor you want. And it's not always easy to tell which is which before working with them. 'As a first-time founder' reflects Sardine's CEO Soups Ranjan, 'I luckily made no mistakes on the investor side... yet... but I have learned a few things I would do differently if I went again. For instance, I would do reference calls. Not just the ones that the investors themselves recommend but also back channel. You can and should DD your investors as much as they DD you. Because you want to find an investor that is *do no harm, do no evil* and willing to back you in good times and bad.'

It's Not All Doom and Gloom

How do you determine whether the investors who just gave you a term sheet are the good kind, like Christian had, or the other kind? You have to be careful. You have to do your homework. And you have to be lucky. The cautionary tales shared above are well known in the industry, so when I asked about how they approached funding, everyone echoed the single word used by Pismo's Daniela Binatti: 'cautiously'.

Of course, it is important to flag that there are happy investor stories out there. Although, reflects Gareth Richardson 'As with all things, time will tell if we have shielded ourselves to be honest'. So far, their story is a good one. They have been cautious about what money to accept but they have been consistently successful in raising capital.

'We have been, as an industry, on a remarkable run of, if not free money, then easier money' reflects Gareth. 'We [at Thought Machine] got investment fairly easily and, so far, it has been good. But we don't expect that much from our investors. Maybe it's a bit of "we have done this before", maybe it is the nature of the problem we are looking to solve and maybe it is a bit of arrogance, but there have always been good options for us on the table. [As an industry] we have just gone through a miraculous period when money was sort of free and investors were trying to sell themselves to you. It was less about what they wanted *from* you. And we never put a huge onus on them, never expected too much.

> Expect that different investors will have different needs. Manage those. Then, make realistic commitments. And deliver those.

Our Seed and Series A came from a lot of pre-existing relationships that Paul [Taylor, Thought Machine CEO] already had, alongside two of our first bank customers. In general, they were people who were used to deep tech and they understood that it is harder to build and the investment cycles will be longer. These investors have stayed all the way through. They are used to seeing complicated tech businesses. Later investors came in with a portfolio/industry view and now, as we move towards IPO, we are looking for wider financial markets credibility, we do not look to them to help with the business tactics per se. But they are a very useful sounding board.

So far so good. But we need to see it all play out, through the next few years.

It is natural that investors will always have different priorities around the table and people who came in during series A or series D

> There are always trade-offs: a foundational customer-investor will impact your roadmap but will also deepen your relationship and accelerate market credibility.

have different needs and requirements to institutional investors or patient capital. So far we have made generally realistic commitments and deeds followed promises but the balancing act is never over and in tough times it obviously gets harder. Of our bank investors, Paul was originally reluctant to take the initial investment from Lloyds as he didn't want that relationship to define our product build or market perception. His initial concerns were partly right: we did have to go back and revisit and redo some of the early work, but that turned out to be a positive learning experience for the company. There was a slow-down after the original go-lives before we sped up again. But overall this has been an unqualified success. It has aligned our goals with our largest customers in a much deeper way, they have helped us in many, many, ways over the years.'

There Is Always a Catch

Ultimately, investors give you money because they expect to see a return. That is a clearly understood exchange. They accept they are taking a risk but believe that there will be return and they will seek to guide you in a way that maximises and speeds up said return. The pressure applied by Dharm's investors at the start of this chapter sounds reasonable enough, in this context, doesn't it? They are investors not charity donors. They will want to see returns at some point. That was the *point* of them investing in the first place: believing that there was a chance for a profit. But how they encourage you towards that liquidity event, what pressures they exert and when isn't universal. Different types of investors behave very differently and we know that some Venture Capital firms have, in the past decade, set the tone for a 'growth at all cost' mentality. In fact, growth at all cost has been the name of the game for a while and although we accepted it as a given or at least as 'the way of the world', it is a counter-intuitive way to work.

First of all and as we have already seen, growth at all costs becomes addictive for your team and distracting for your product roadmap, as you keep needing to bring fresh stuff to fuel the investment and valuation machine. Soon

> Aggressive growth needs capital. Before you know it and if you are not careful, fundraising may be all your leadership team have time to do.

it becomes all the leadership have time for. 'For five years' recalls Lizzie 'it was grow, raise, grow, raise. You're either closing a round or getting ready for one. You stop talking to customers or thinking strategically. It is not what you came in for and you didn't know to expect it at first. If you are a second or third time founder you know that VCs operate in this way.' Maybe if you are a third time founder you know

how to manage them better, or you know to opt for patient capital. Or (like the cases above) you are not naive in believing that you will always have an option.

It's the proverbial rock and a hard place. Because you can't do any of this without serious deployment of capital and yet 'sometimes the money is the reason you fail' reflects Rolf Eichweber.

'VC money is *sell your soul and get it done* money sometimes.

> Sometimes the money is the reason you fail. VC money is 'sell your soul and get it done' money. Banks are not the right money either when it comes to changing themselves. The antibodies will kill you every time. Tech money is often dismissive to the regulators.
>
> **Rolf Eichweber**

Banks are not the right money either, when it comes to changing themselves.

The antibodies will kill you every time because you are standing against the product owner and the P&L holder. Tech money is often dismissive to the regulators which is naive because you can't do this without your regulator – plus the regulators know what they are doing. So for me… working with an insurance company was deliberate.'

There *are* choices, evidently. There are alternative constructs and different sources of capital. But they are not as plentiful as the aggressive VC money has been for the past decade and a half. And, arguably, we couldn't have gotten to this set of realisations without going through what we have collectively gone through, as a market.

'Some of the components that were top of mind for early fintech are fading away' notes Kaidi. 'Will they come back? It's hard to tell. There is global change in banking', it is not just fintech that is feeling the shockwaves.

> It's not just startups that have been burnt by investors, it works the other way round too. The successive, highly visible scandals and constrained funding environment makes investors very cautious now.

Who would have expected the Credit Suisse and SVB failures? Who would have expected the audacity of the Theranos and Binance scandals? Or Frank[1]? Who would have expected that level of shamelessness? Arguably, we all should have. But we didn't. So it's not just startups that have been burned.

The combined shocks to the system coinciding with the radical shift in the global financing climate will make investors cautious. 'If they could avoid investing altogether right now, they would' observes Kaidi. And banks are going back to basics when it comes to risk management. 'And let's face it' continues Kaidi 'the issues we have seen come down to inadequate risk management. Across the board. So the question is *what will emerge as the solution to gain back the trust of the customers.* Because it's not Credit Suisse or any other bank that has the money, it's their customers' money so we owe the end consumer to get this right: to find a way to renew and transform this industry without introducing instability, volatility and worshipping false gods. Such as growth at all cost.'

Kaidi is right. But how do we build new ventures *while* getting this right?

---

1 Let's see: Theranos became a huge success over tech that didn't actually exist (https://www.busi nessinsider.com/theranos-founder-ceo-elizabeth-holmes-life-story-bio-2018-4) Binance has been found deep in a money laundering scandal
(https://www.theguardian.com/business/2023/nov/21/binance-settlement-crypto-excha nge) And Frank, acquired by JP Morgan, seems to have inflated their user numbers by 10x to boost their valuation
https://www.cnbc.com/2023/06/15/jpmorgan-frank-case-startup-employees-questioned-customer-stats-before-acquisition.html

Seeking Alternatives: The Bond AI Story

By now everyone has heard a horror story or ten about the possible pernicious impact of bad investor advice or the pursuit of hypergrowth. Short-termism. Expansion over sustainability. Paper valuations over steady, repeatable sales and the rest. But we have also acknowledged that VC capital is not always a bad influence, despite their bad rep. Besides VC capital is not the only way. OM Bank is being nurtured by an insurance company, Mox by a joint venture. And we will look at banks fully owned by other banks in a moment. But if you don't want to go down the corporate route or the VC route, what are the options?

There are two, as it turns out. You can seek non-equity funding (more on that later) or you can choose to work with patient capital. The kind of investors who by design, temperament and investment horizon will not agitate and push. But more than 'patient' capital, you want *aligned* capital. Investors whose mission is aligned to yours.

Uday was adamant in our conversation that he wouldn't even accept money from investors unless they 'buy into the mission'. The people who seek impact, not a quick exit. 'They are the right audience for me'.

> The way you choose to spend time inside your company, takes money.
>
> Your investors need to see eye to eye with you on what matters or they will derail you.

Getting the right investment mindset around the table, he reflects, is how he manages to invest time and money into his team the way he does.

Remember Bond AI and the time investment they make in recruiting, onboarding and keeping employees connected?

The way Uday Akkaraju spends time takes money. And intent.

The focus of the business itself *also* takes away from easy profit. Their mission is not to maximise profit but to be sustainable as a business to fulfil a mission.

'We have one single KPI: a financial health score. Are we moving the needle on that? Everyone in the company knows how what they do impacts this single KPI.' In itself, this is what dreams are made of: an entire business geared towards one single metric that each individual affects differently, *this* is the stuff of business books, mission statements and dreams. And it is actually very hard to achieve and maintain. And Uday's team manage to achieve and maintain it and yet that single-minded focus is on neither growth nor profit.

'Our business is about impact. We try to have a direct impact on people's lives.' Imagine being the investor who sees this single-minded determination and ability to move that single KPI forward. What are the chances of you not demanding that the focus is shifted to profit? Or profit... *as well*? Arguably because a profitable business can 'afford' to think about impact.

Uday's view is that an impactful business can be profitable without seeking profit first and then turning to impact. And now, having been running long enough for his numbers to tell their own story, he can demonstrate that to be true. But it wasn't always easy.

'When we started, nobody was buying into the idea [that this was possible] but we showed that if you do this with focus and consistency you achieve both the desired impact *and* generate revenue. We believed it but we had to show that. We had to demonstrate the art of the possible.'

That moment, by the way, when the vision is not yet proven and the founder is under pressure is the moment when it is easy to take

> Your impact requires integrity and focus from day 0. And it requires resources from day 0 too. You need to ensure you have enough resources to do this work, *in this way* when you start. Otherwise, you will get distracted, it won't be possible.
>
> And even after you've done all that, you need to keep doing all that.
>
> **Uday Akkaraju**

the wrong money, water down the metrics or shift the focus in the name of survival and the belief or hope that you can come back to it. That moment is when the 'let's compromise so we live to fight another day' decisions are made.

Doubling down to find the right investors to allow you to demonstrate that impact-first businesses are viable is a choice. And a hard one to make when you are under pressure. A hard one to maintain and stick to, when you are under pressure. And you will be under pressure, that's inevitably a part of building a business. The easier path, when your back is against the wall, is to give investors something they *can* believe in, in exchange for the cash to get started in the naive and erroneous (but understandable) belief that we can get back to what we were originally doing once we have some gas in the tank. It doesn't work that way.

But it often happens this way.

Businesses very often veer off their original direction in order to attract investors and then veer off even more (for instance, adding features they don't need as Lizzie already mentioned) to placate investors.

I once worked with a product business that had changed its pricing strategy three times (from consulting, bespoke time and materials revenue, to pure licence fees, and back to rate cards) in 18 months to placate their investors and avoid having a rather uncomfortable conversation about what the investors thought the target addressable market was for the business and what the reality was. It is often much easier to give the investors what they are asking for in the quarterly review meeting and tell yourself you have no choice.

So it is worth acknowledging just how hard and just how important getting the right investors is, or standing up to them to do right by the original deal: the numbers as well as the principles.

'If what we are is an impact business' continues Uday, 'that impact focus has to be understood and shared in the company. Otherwise the work ahead is going to be very hard. The relentless focus on impact requires a lot of integrity and focus from day 0. And it requires resources from day 0 too. You need to ensure you have enough resources to do this work, *in this way* when you start. Otherwise you will get distracted, it won't be possible. And even after you've done all that, you need to keep doing all that. You need to keep investing in the right things: you need to keep yourself on the hook.'

That doesn't mean you will always get the balance right, continues Uday. Especially when you are trying to avoid being lured into a particular direction, you may find yourself over-correcting.

> Don't raise money from VCs if you are an impact business. Even impact-driven VCs will push you towards an exit.
>
> **Uday Akkaraju**

'At the beginning, my focus was developing the product and focusing on the bigger picture. Looking back, I didn't focus on revenue enough. And we want to have a sustainable business. We want this to be a successful business. So that we can solve the problem we set out to solve. And to do that you need funds.'

The business needs funds for growth. So revenue is important. But growth towards an exit isn't. Not for Uday.

On a personal level Uday is clear: 'money is not a motivator for me.'

So he knows he has to make a profit and wants to make a profit. But not at the expense of his impact. The only way to reconcile those competing priorities, he says, is 'don't raise money from VCs. Even social impact VCs will push you to an exit. The investors I did select care about impact. And in a recession, like we are now, this all becomes even more important. The people we do this *for* are suffering, banks are richer than ever and VCs become stingier.'

Uday is right.

In the two-year window of researching, writing and publishing this book, the economy has been in a very weird limbo: very high interest rates and massive cost of living increases. That meant that if you had money in the bank, it worked for you for the first time in decades.

> You need to go for investors that will allow you to operate in the way you have chosen.
>
> And that takes a lot of time.
>
> **Uday Akkaraju**

If you were the bank, you were effectively printing money, but lending became extremely hard. If you had cash, you were in heaven. For everyone else it was a dire, difficult time, and not a short one either.

People raising capital in this environment struggled. People who had already raised found themselves under immense pressure for down-rounds, exits and mergers as investors wanted to protect and manage their exposure. If you had the wrong investors around the table, the pressure to move away from your mission would be immense.

'Meanwhile out there people are suffering' continues Uday. 'So what we should be asking is what can we each do to help out?' What Bond AI did was give back: 'We have started monetising our customers' data for them: so we can give them money back. You need to always try and identify your own way of being helpful.' And you need your investors (and your board, a topic we will explore in Chapter 8) to support that course of action when things get hard. When a lucrative option would also be an easier option.

Again, there is only one way to ensure that you will be 'allowed' to operate this way. 'The investor community I go after is very specific' reflects Uday. 'But that means I have to be patient too.' You won't be surprised to hear that finding the right investors and ensuring alignment is not a quick process. Plus timings may not align even if values do.

'Some want to join the journey but for whatever reason can't. Those who love the mission and who have made enough money to seek impact are the right audience for me. And then it's a conversation about the kind of impact they want to have. People still say to us that we are too philosophical, too mission-oriented. We have rejected advice that could potentially have made us a unicorn. Because for me, for us, it's not about the exit. If you really are addressing someone's need' continues Uday 'I believe that will go a long way. We are now cash-flow positive and make good money. Not big corporate money but good money. Money that will allow us to keep doing what we are here to do. And because of what it feels like to work here, our people scout for more people. If we can find a formula for that, it will be amazing as it will help retain our culture as we grow.'

So I couldn't help myself. You don't want an exit, I said, so what are you growing towards? 'I just want to start the engine,' Uday said. 'This business has to be bigger than me and it still needs to be going after I am gone. My job is to make sure this focus isn't lost as we grow.' And a big part of achieving that is finding the right money that won't distract it.

Horses for Courses

Now this is a good place to say that, if you are a founder and you are *all about the exit*, then the right money for you will be the exact money Uday is saying no to. No judgement from us. You do you. But do it intentionally is the point.

If you want a fast and aggressive exit, there are investors out there who are perfect for you. Equally, if you want a different path to growth, you need to ensure that the people whose money you take have expectations aligned to your intentions because, when the chips are down and decisions need to be made, whoever holds the trump cards makes the calls. That means shareholders, board members and investors. And let us not forget that an unhappy board *can* fire a CEO, in case you were wondering about who really holds power in those situations. But the point being made here is not about keeping your job. It isn't even about getting your way.

Which, incidentally, is also something you need to reflect on when you are considering whose money you take because some investors (corporate venture arms and pension funds, for instance) will be more demure, less pushy. It's part of their ethos, not a personality trait. So you need to be thinking about what kind of board you want when you say yes to the term sheets. If, like Enfuce, you want to retain control of your business so you build to your own level of ambition, then saying no to a certain type of investment is necessary. Hard but necessary. Ultimately, the money you take affects the kind of business you are, not least because of who gains access to your boardroom and what they do once they get there. And, arguably, no matter whose money you take, there will be challenges in the boardroom. That is as it should be. That is what it is there for.

> Do the right thing for you.
> If you are all about the exit, take money from a growth-oriented VC.

In fact 'it is always the same challenge in the boardroom and you need to hold the line of what you are trying to build' stresses Wise's Harsh Sinha. 'One investor wanted to give us 4,5x the money we were looking to raise. We said we don't need it. We didn't want to be capital-heavy. We didn't want the bad behaviour that may encourage.'

> The kind of money you take... determines what kind of boardroom you will have.

Steve Naudé concurs: 'We have a strong sense of mission, so investors needed to buy into what we are trying to do. They needed to buy into the long-term vision, they needed to believe in a 100-year business.'

Saying no to capital is so hard when you are cash-starved and all businesses are cash-starved at the start. Wise, Enfuce, Bond AI and so many others said no to money when money was what they needed. Digest this for a second because that is the lesson. You will need to look a gift horse in the mouth. You will need to go against the belief that beggars can't be choosers. You will need to reflect on turning down the thing you need the most and that is hard.

Where did the wisdom to say no come from, I wonder (*and* ask. I didn't just wonder. Obviously, I asked). Because it is so easy to know this is the right thing to do with the benefit of hindsight and so hard to actually do it when you need to raise capital and there is money right there in front of you and (at the time) there is no visible alternative necessarily. It's easy to know you need to say no to money that will pressurise you and take you off course. It's another story altogether to actually do it. So where did the wisdom and strength to say no come from?

'The founders are level-headed' replies Harsh. 'They were raised in Estonia, with a different worldview. Plus there was a realisation across the leadership team that we want to ensure this company behaves in a certain way long term. You raise too much and your valuation goes up, and then you have a very different type of conversation. Our aim was for sustainable long-term growth, we

> When people offer you money, you absolutely need to look a gift horse in the mouth and perhaps turn down the thing you need the most at the time you need it the most.

wanted a sustainable business. We never gave any free transactions [as competitors did]. We priced from the get go. Equally, we were as deliberate with how we spent and continue to do that. In 2017, for instance, we were under [investor] pressure to hire engineers faster. But the pace of hiring was dictated by how quickly we could onboard them, not how quickly we could find them. And the investors accepted that.' How? I asked. By now you have worked out the answer: 'the founders had been deliberate in whose money they took.'

Sometimes Less Is More

Admittedly, there are very few ventures in general and particularly in FS that start without investment. The heady romantic notions of entrepreneurs starting with a battery, a screwdriver and some sand paper in their parents' garage and emerging with a multi-million-dollar prototype, A Team style, are unusual in businesses that are capital-intensive. Most FS businesses need capital and few can bootstrap for long. And if you are in the majority and need to raise, you need to give something up, as we discussed. But there are ways to side-step the dangers of giving up too much too soon.

> Look at all your options: may your business qualify for a grant?
> Investment is not the only way to get started.

Joel Blake reflects on the three things that enabled him to be cautious and patient with GFA so that it could grow into the space that it is now. The first was the lessons learned the hard way with previous ventures. 'The good thing about my own teething problems before was that it made me really alert' he reflects.

The second is that, this time, when an angel investor came in, he knew to channel the money towards product build with the clear realisation that the product is still being refined and not ready to sell. 'That was a key distinction for me and all of that helped GFA get into the space it is now as it forced me to validate and demonstrate the potential of what I could do. And because the prime sweet spot of what we are doing is to help manage risk *while* being inclusive, the business qualified for a government grant.'

And that was the third thing. Because a grant gives you a different kind of breathing space. 'Because we qualified for a grant, the quality of that funding gave me a choice and I was fortunate, I could build a product *with* the market. The beauty of our original MVP failing, having to take time to build version two and talking to the market, is that during that time we built a demo, MVPs with clients who were not yet commercial agreements but they were getting us what we needed: data, delivery credentials without having to worry about revenues because of the government grant. Revenue came. 18 months later.'

Not everyone qualifies for a government grant, I hear you say. Perhaps.

And besides, these businesses need a lot of money, I hear you say. There is no way the government grant would cover your needs Actually: you may be wrong there.

GFA wasn't Joel's first experience with government funding.

'In February 2012, I sat in a pub sketching an idea out with my co-founder. By April we had a business. By June we had a £2 Million per-year pot for the next five years to lend to SME businesses. We used the HSBC credit ethos and lending model. We followed the system. We got paid £1,200 for every loan that we did and we were away. Of course we realised that we needed money to cover our costs so we could scale in a way that is commensurate with our business model. So we negotiated with the government: they would cover all our costs for our early days. We went national immediately. We were profitable. We were the darling of the government as we provided a solution in a much-needed space. And we made progress.

We realised we had to be more refined about the business model, so we devised our own questionnaire, reducing default rates considerably: getting them down to 17% down from the government average of 48% for startup loans. So we had a scalable profitable business.

Profitability will come if you can find the money to take care of all the things that are in your way. "Scaling" is not exactly in your way though! Scaling is a choice, not an inevitability. And scaling fast can diminish the quality of the money you take.

Having our core costs covered allowed us to reach profitability fairly easily… and we started pursuing scale.

But when we [started having] to cover our own costs, those [costs] started going through the roof: staffing, marketing and wider competition outside the region (when we no longer enjoyed exclusivity). You could argue that we found ourselves operating at the level we may have had at the beginning, if we hadn't enjoyed that period of "protection". So we had to change our business model. In order to help our business survive, we made changes. And we found ourselves in a place where we were helping our business by saying no to three times the loan applications that we were saying yes to.'

Nobody asked Joel and his co-founder to move away from their mission, the reason they were doing this anyway. The pressures of profitability led to a set of cumulative, 'erosive' decisions that looked after growth ahead of the mission.

As Uday said already, unless you give it relentless focus, this happens.

As Joel also highlighted, growth may be a false god. It is a choice. It is not an obstacle you need to remove. You don't need to grow at all costs. Let that sink in.

So throwing money at the growth dream can and will distract

> Profitability will come if you can find the money to take care of all the things that are in your way.
> 'Scaling' is not exactly in your way though!
> And scaling fast can diminish the quality of the money you take.
> *Joel Blake*

you from your mission. Joel learned that the hard way and is doing things differently with GFA to protect its mission. But the danger of growth eating your purpose is common. And the way it happens isn't intentional, direct and obvious. It is usually gradual and looks like gluttony.

Augustus Gloop

'Success often relies on getting funding at the right time' reflects Maha El Dimachki (who, as you recall, spent time with the FCA and is now with the BIS) 'and that usually means *not too soon*. Money itself isn't actually a factor. It is having it at the right time.'

Why?

Because, as we have already heard, investors will rightly push you to spend the money they just gave you, to achieve whatever it is you promised them to achieve with it. They will push you to accelerate product development. They will push you to realise that geographic expansion you spoke about. And on occasion they will ask for things that make little sense, but they will

> If investors gave you money for something… they will put pressure on you to spend it towards achieving that something. Product build acceleration or geographic expansion,: growth can all come too soon if you are not careful.

ask anyway: like the time an investor asked a treasury management startup to 'do BNPL' because it was all the rage at the time.

How do I know?

They called me in a panic asking for advice on how to 'do BNPL' given what their product does. Because their CEO had said 'let me take this away' to their investor and now they had to do something. The same is happening right now in a boardroom near you, by the way, only the ask is for AI not BNPL.

The investors will ask for you to open the office in the new geography you mentioned even though you haven't really done any go-to-market work about how you should really approach that brand-new market. They will pressure you to hire the people you said you'd spend the money on, as we heard from Harsh, and the hiring process becomes a metric in itself. And what you end up with is bloating. You hire more people than you need. More people than you can meaningfully onboard or manage. You dilute your culture (a danger we already discussed). You expand into geographies you don't understand. And then when things get tough, you withdraw. You close offices and pull teams out of geographies in droves. You fire people and it makes the news as we have already seen.

'We did so well until 18 months ago when we raised a series C with the explicit strategy of geographic expansion' says someone who asked for this part of the conversation to not be attributed. 'And then our investors pushed us to accelerate the growth we raised the money for.' The result? Hires. New locations. More hires. And of course you have to give them time to settle in. You can't judge whether the experiment worked or not immediately. You need to give it a few months. If you are operating in enterprise sales, you need to give them longer because you want to see your teams working at different stages of the work cycle and the cycle is long. The outcome? 'We are undoing now what we did 18 months ago, having wasted a heap of money and 18 months'.

If you are thinking 'you told us this story twice before' you are right. Only it is three different firms. If this sounds bad then, let me tell you, it could be worse.

One of the companies I spoke with was very well capitalised very early on. Which meant that they built a team *with* frills. Bells. Whistles. They had the luxury to

> Once you take money, you will be pressured to spend it to achieve the thing you said you wanted the money for. If you bloat in the process, getting back to the right size will burn twice the amount of money... and time. Which amounts to more money.

staff the procurement team and employee engagement initiatives from day dot. They opened RnD centres and swanky offices in five cities before they even had the first customer signed. They had t-shirts and stickers and a barista in the office. Everyone had an EA. The CEO had three. There was a corporate travel team before they had an MVP. And they didn't have the urgency to hire with prudence. They didn't have the existential angst of managing burn.

The outcome? An army of people 'tilling a field with tea spoons when a tractor was needed' to paraphrase an old manager of mine, who wasn't speaking about this particular company but he might as well have been. And, for the avoidance of doubt: the tractor existed, the tooling existed, but the spoon people didn't know how to operate it.

Why am I telling you this?

Because in the situations above, where a company suddenly bloats, right-sizing is difficult and wasteful but possible. But if you start off bloated, right-sizing isn't available to you. You can either keep doing 'crash diets' boom and bust, cutting people then hiring them back again when you land a client and carrying inefficiency and terrible Glassdoor reviews with you like a bad odour or you scrap and start from scratch knowing that the market set-back reputationally and operationally will be huge.

What investor in their right mind would let you do that? A crazy one, you may say. And yet that is the most common story in the market. And to stand a chance of having an investor that doesn't behave like that, you need to be cautious right at the start when optimism and hope make everything seem possible. You need to be intentional from the get-go. And very present. As Kaidi rightly notes, 'putting the customer first rather than the shareholder is a leadership choice and a leadership problem' but if you have taken the kind of money that piles on pressure and you have spent it badly leading to more pressure, plus you don't have the kind of leadership that can hold the line then you have very few options at that point. And they all look like compromise.

Living Happily Ever After

Some of these stories have happy endings by the way. Some of these businesses set out to change the world, to disrupt the industry and did exactly that. They knew they needed backing and got it. And although they made mistakes along the way, that is kind of the deal. That is an inevitable part of the process.

> Few entrepreneurs talk about the significance of exits. Even those who had them.
> The journey and the people in it seems to be the most important thing to everyone.

Some of the businesses I spoke to for this work, such as Bond AI, OakNorth and PensionBee among others, are planning to still be here 100 years from now.

Others focus on the outcome rather than the business itself.

When I asked Zor Gorelov what the plan was for Kasisto: growth, IPO, exit, he was neither particularly invested in one outcome over another nor did he see his success in terms of whether he ended up with the right size of prize at the end[2].

2 And, as if to underline that point, he left his position as CEO soon after this conversation, appointing a successor who can take the work to the next level of its growth while Zor continues to pursue impact in a new way and I wish him luck and can't wait to see what he does next.

'Banks are our customers but we are a B2B2C company and the C is key to success[3]. Part of our product is that end customer experience so we measure it throughout the platform. I love what I do. I love working with customers. I love solving problems. For me it's all about people: employees and customers. I have met so many nice and super intelligent people, that's what it's all about.'

For so many folks, the journey is the point. The problems they solve, the people they meet and the people they help. Success is doing that *well* and leaving the world and the tech space and the FS world a little bit better than you found it before solving the next problem.

> Whose money you take and the motivations they bring to the table will determine what kind of boardroom you have.
> Think ahead.

Impact, as I said from the start of this book, is the connecting thread of all I spoke to.

Few talked about exits. Even those who had them.

The exits were seen as events, not destinations. And their timings had a lot to do with exactly what we are talking about in this chapter. Depending on whose money you took, whenever you may have taken it, there will be motivations and considerations around when is a good time to see returns that you will need to be mindful of.

One of the boards I observed (you won't find it on my LinkedIn profile, so don't go looking) ended up being one step away from toxic even though every individual around the table was lovely. People were nice. They were decent. But as investors around the same table, they just didn't work, not least because they were *so* radically misaligned in their expectations for what the money should be used for, how soon and with what parameters as to be irreconcilable. They were so far apart in their expectations that there was no squaring the circle. And when pressures mounted, it got ugly.

Arguably, those considerations would and should have been obvious before the company took the money, of course.

> An exit isn't always a happy story. It may be forced by investors, poor product market fit or circumstances.
> To get a good exit you need to go looking for it, on your own terms. Or get very very lucky. And jump when the opportunity comes.

---

3 In the unlikely event that this volume somehow makes it into the hands of someone who isn't of the industry… welcome… B2B2C is a business to business to consumer service. So Kasisto's customer is another business, not an individual… but that business uses the service to offer a better service to an end customer, a human. And Kasisto cares about that end customer, their customer's customer.

But sometimes you don't know enough to realise how important this factor is (remember we said most successful leaders in this space aren't succeeding in their first rodeo partly because the first rodeo is where they learn these lessons) and sometimes you've left it so late that you have no choice. Sometimes you also overestimate your own ability to manage those tensions or your investors' willingness to play nice once they have committed. Sometimes you also just don't care, admittedly, but I didn't speak to any of those guys so I wouldn't know what they would say about this.

This is the message, by the way, there is no other message from this section. You need to be deliberate in whose money you take and say no to cash (when you most need it) if it will demand, as part of the price, a change in your mission, time horizon or values.

What happened in the case above, by the way, was a forced exit. The board decided that their options were to fire the CEO and start from scratch or force a firesale exit. Not all exits are unqualified success stories if you look closely. Some are. Some aren't. But the vast majority are somewhere in the middle.

I asked Christian Nentwich about his own hugely successful exit: it was a proper fairytale wedding ending from the outside, in that Du.Co still exists and is thriving, he is still involved with his business on a much bigger stage until he chose to step back from the CEO role but remain on the board. Of course, no story is uncomplicated but as happy endings go, this is pretty great. How did it come about?

'We went looking for it' he replies. 'We needed, at the time, to balance shareholders with different time horizons and needs and our own aspiration for growth.' Pause to digest that, because frankly it is all you need to remember from this section. It is in some ways the exact same problem that I described above albeit not toxic. The difference is Christian decided to lead his company to the next stage rather than allow the tension to play out. He acted when he had options. He didn't wait for his back to be against the wall in the hope that a miracle would occur in the meantime that would make the work easier. 'We needed an inorganic event to sustain growth. You have to run at it with scale and speed that you can't do organically. Any PE-backed firm will outrun you if you try to do that. And I never wanted a lifestyle business. So now we have the backing, we can take it to the next level: we can get the solution horizontally outside its FS concentration; and we can solve a wider data automation problem.'

The mission continues. But Du.Co is now a very different animal.

Your Calls to Action

- Money isn't free and you give away more than equity when you accept investment.

- Be clear you won't compromise what you are trying to achieve by accepting the wrong kind of money.
- Saying no to the thing you need the most when you need it the most may be counter-intuitive but at times it is exactly what you need to do.
- Try to not make decisions with your back against the wall, leave yourself time and options which means start working on things before you need them.

Chapter 8

Shapes, Sizes and Colours

A Thing Apart

We finished the last section talking about how Du.Co went about actively looking for an exit, an inorganic event to fuel its growth. Even though Du.Co as a business very much still exists after the Big PE firm entered its life, and although its mission still holds, it is undeniable that this change of ownership changes things dramatically. It fuels growth as funding of a different kind is forthcoming, but it also introduces layers of accountability, governance and bureaucracy that a scrappy startup simply doesn't have. The new relationship is nuanced and complex and it entails tensions and balancing acts you didn't have to contend with before.

What of the entities that start life with this level of account-ability requirement? Businesses that are set up as corporate-backed ventures? Entities that start with some of that complexity baked in? Like Mox, Mettle, :86400, OM Bank or audax who we have met before in these pages. What is the reality for them? What are the tensions and balancing acts of their daily existence?

> For a corporate-backed venture, the *money equation* may be simpler than for a venture-backed startup. But it comes with complexity around governance and demands around account-ability from day 0.

DOI: 10.1201/9781003395577-8

Although big FS players have, historically, and still do undergo large, ambitious change projects internally, the consensus of recent years in the market is that transformation is one thing, running a fully digital business is quite another. To do it right, it needs different tech, different rules and different economic models to apply. So you *must* build it outside the main bank. How far outside is up for debate but the separation is not.

And this 'arms length' separation doesn't apply just because the big bank with its habits and inertia may strangle the new initiative (although, also that) but because a traditional FS organisation and a digital-native FS organisation have different business models. Remember those? The cost to serve conversation, TAM and profit margin? They are different and therefore it helps to not try and serve them at the same time and in the same way, prove them in the same way and submit them to the same timeline.

And that applies to any organisation, of any size and digital readiness, that launches a product or service that has a different set of economic assumptions to their primary business. Do you want me to spell this out?

If you are a product business that is five years old (and born digital) and decide to launch a new

> The main reason why a new venture should be separate from the main shop is not the fact that it may fail... it is the fact that it invariably comes with a different business model.
>
> It is set up as a separate business because it is a different business.

product or service, you need to separate that out. A new product or service has different risk profiles, different liquidity realities and different revenue multiples then 'arms' length' is the advice for you too. You are probably sitting there going: that is not what Starling Bank is doing, you told us they are leveraging the power of the collective and servicing three – soon maybe more – distinctly separate businesses: a bank, a SaaS product and a service business. My answer to that is twofold: if they have managed to keep the creative energy unified but separate the governance and talent allocation, if they have managed to separate the sales cycles and margin expectations and retain the unified funding mindset of 'we win together and lose together' then more power to them. And I am a customer and a fan of their team so, honestly, I hope they have. The second part of the answer is: their way is harder. There is more to go wrong. I am a big advocate for control as you have seen in this book. And if you want to control your variables, then you allow your wheels to spin at the pace that is appropriate to them.

So, if you are trying to balance two different business models inside a challenger, you should remember what Steve Naudé of Wise had to say about not cross-subsidising different parts of the business. You should also be mindful that if you change what you do, the dynamics inside your own business will change whether you meant for them to change or not. Hence another reason for a separation.

'For the platform' explains Steve, 'we see the internal dynamic changing away from B2C or SME going to servicing bigger businesses. It's a shift in our understanding as the expectations of a big bank are very different.

How do we align to that and build the best cross-border infrastructure to achieve our mission, so that we are not just the service people use, but we are the *infrastructure* people use. It is not about downloading the app anymore.' This is a totally different business: a different set of customers, with different needs, different time horizons and different success metrics. And a different business model to serve them. Any time you create a separate business, you need to create a separate business model. Even if it feels similar. But especially if it does not.

And, to state the obvious, you need a clear and clearly articulated business model. Both to guide your new venture's growth and – and this is equally important – to manage the accountability towards the corporate owners and manage the rules for the road. And because people revert to type and old habits when they relax, when they forget, when they are under pressure (aka all the time and at every opportunity) it is good to be explicit about these things.

Getting Agreement on the Differences

Being deliberate about the business model and governance structure, being explicit and prescriptive about how the governance ties to the business model and what the guardrails and expectations for all involved need to be saves you a lot of headaches down the road.

Mox, if you recall, the Hong Kong challenger bank that sought to capture market share through a joint venture (JV), had several layers of balancing acts to think about in order to make its business and operating model work. In fact, the balancing acts *were* the operating model, to make the business case work.

First of all, it was backed by a bank, but a separate legal entity. And then it was a JV on top, further complicating the structures,

> Mox was separate because it needed to move in a different way and at a different pace and because it was a JV, not just a SCB business. But also because we had a clear strategy of re-use, we developed every component of the new model with the intention of global applicability rather than solely focusing on being the "Monzo of HK."
>
> ***Deniz Güven***

relationships and stakeholder conversations as the two venture partners were not from the same business background and they had different expectations, assumptions and requirements when it came to... well... everything. But this complexity was central to the plan, recalls founding CEO Deniz Güven as the idea was not just to launch a successful challenger but use the construct of a JV as a commercial accelerant. The idea was that by marrying two parents from different markets you could accelerate market penetration. Yes you needed to manage how you set it up carefully but if the construct worked then the idea was to 'explore the possibility of expanding into other markets [after Mox was launched], replicating the operating model. This strategy was especially cru- cial in the face of emerging giants, particularly within the Chinese context. The goal was to build a challenger bank *and* create a future operating system for Standard Chartered Bank (SCB).'

> Banks are controlling things, usually.
> Getting them comfortable with building something new, in a new way... a priori giving up control... is hard.
> But it is not impossible.

But being separate, a JV *and* having a clear strategy of re-use, meant that Mox had to balance several sets of pri- orities, requirements and proof points while developing every component of the new model from scratch with the intention of global applicability rather than solely focusing on being the 'Monzo of HK'. Building the Monzo of HK would have been new enough for a traditional bank. But Mox took it a few clicks further.

And it is worth saying that, at the time that Mox was launching, being the Monzo of anything was cool enough. In fact, the focus on UX was such that the uniqueness of Mox's business model wasn't what captured the imagination at the time, even though it is what has differentiated it down the road. Mox itself, however, captured the imagination in a way I have never seen before. Everyone, and I mean *everyone*, claims to have worked on the early stages of the project. It is the 'I am Spartacus' of the fintech world with people who had the loosest association or had a coffee with someone from the team once claiming an intimate connection in the hope that some of the magic will rub off. That's flattering, I guess. Though for the people on the coalface it was hardly relevant, as they had a big task ahead of them, balancing all the components of their model to make it work.

And let's be frank here: Banks are controlling things, generally speaking.

This whole 'arms length' thing sounds good but it doesn't come naturally to banks. Most of the 'arms length' ventures have had policies imposed upon them, officers appointed from the top without due process, governance changes that come from above like a new bedtime your mum just announced without conversation or recourse. The intention is usually there but actually getting a bank comfortable with the realities of building something new and not fully controlling every aspect is hard.

Getting the bank to share its toys (in a JV construct) is harder.

Getting the bank to give up a priori control by accepting the viability of re-use for infrastructure as a principle feels like an impossible set of conversations.

And yet.

'We expected resistance internally, within the bank' recalls Deniz 'but actually what was harder was demonstrating value to the partner side because they don't necessarily understand the intricacies of banking, so they have a different approach to profitability and speed. It worked in the end, but it took time to build trust and get the partner to see the value that this JV holds for them. You need to put in the time to get them to see the value of doing this *together*. And you need to get the right combination of partners in order for the synergies to work, for expectations to align at board level across all partners.

We had a bank, a telco and a travel company around the table.

They have different priorities and pressures, and their expectations are different in each

> By getting the operating model right from the get-go and sticking to its core principles, Mox created a capability that is 60% portable. That, in case you were wondering, is very good.

of their verticals. You need to understand and manage that. Especially as the whole idea was that the model should be portable and repeatable.

This is now the story of Trust Bank in Singapore.'

How portable is it, I hear you ask? 'The tech about 60%' answers Deniz. 'The regulatory and risk parts need to be localised and, of course, you need different local JV partners. This is the game. If you can find the right combination of these elements you can make it work.' Rinse and repeat.

'You enter a new geography and have to find partners for the JV, align for local regulations and the rest you copy and port across. Day zero to day 1 for Trust Bank was 12 months and one-third of the cost of Mox.

The next one we do will be cheaper and faster. It is a good model. It is a weapon for the bank, if they choose to use it because it allows you to adjust the value proposition as needed. Maybe it's not fancy. But it works!'

I would say it's pretty damn fancy *and* it works.

If It Ain't Broke, Repeat It

The repeatability of a thing well done is an important lesson to learn here and not an obvious one because we do have a tendency to reinvent the wheel, in the financial services industry. We seem to be forever enslaved to what is commonly known as 'not invented here' syndrome whereby banks build

> You need a mechanism for benefitting from the collective knowledge inside your organisation, maintaining headspace vis a vis other programmes and retaining some independence.

things from scratch that could be bought off the shelf for less money, immediately. We seem to fail to learn from the mistakes and successes of others and, often, compete so fiercely internally that we fail to learn from our own successes and failures.

This is where the Starling folks would point and go 'we literally do the opposite of that' because we learn from our own learnings. If it sounds obvious, it is not. In fact, banks are more likely to compete with themselves than share learnings. And this was a question I posed to Kelvin: Is Mox an internal competitor to audax? Both playing largely in the same space. Both part of the Standard Chartered Bank (SCB) venture family. Both sharing some components including their Thought Machine core. Both playing loosely in the same space.

'Mox is not our competition' says Kelvin. 'We maintain a philosophically different approach to how we have constructed our technology stack, we are not targeting the same clients or regions nor are we addressing the same questions in our respective strategies.' Ok so no. Not a competitor in terms of the market. Although, the fact of the matter is that in any organisation the size of SCB, there will be many initiatives vying for headspace, resources and airtime. That's the other challenge you have when setting yourself up inside a parent entity. You are never alone, never the only thing. You are never the main thing. And part of the way you set up your governance needs to be geared towards protecting the headspace you need from the organisation (and no more than that). That is another lesson learned the hard way by those who went before and either went too far off the reservation that they were forgotten and starved of resources or flew too close to the sun and were stifled in governance and oversight.

Let's face it, we've been at this long enough as an industry, that actually if you care to look, there are several dos and don'ts from those who went before you (hence this book). We know now, for instance, that setting up your new venture as a thing apart but connected and governed is safer in terms of its chances of success. But this hadn't always been the industry-established wisdom. Some had to be among the first.

:86400, in Australia, was among the first digital challengers to be set up like that. In case you are not familiar with :86400's credentials, then it's worth looking them up. It is one of the early digital banking success stories in Australia and Cuscal (their corporate parent) was excited about the proposition early on.

> The things you are mindful of are the things you will control for.
> How do you set your venture up to ensure you get out of your own way in the things you don't know to anticipate?

'We were convinced that there was a need for a digital bank and, at the time there wasn't one in the market', recalls Bianca Bates. 'There were digital capabilities around, but :86400 was the first bank that had no branches. Where there was no option for a workaround. You had to do everything digitally every time.' That sounds obvious now. It was not obvious then. Neither was what they did next.

'From day 1 we knew we had to let them be their own creature. We were mindful of not killing them. But as it turned out that wasn't the hardest thing. Because we were mindful of it, perhaps. So we checked ourselves. We had seen it go wrong elsewhere.

Where compromises were made and corners cut.' There are always 'processes, ways of working and habits that are endemic inside a bank. You need to work around those while respecting the checks and balances, governance and approval processes etc. startups don't have all that of course.'

That awareness is key. And because many banks didn't have it at the time that they needed it (hindsight being 20/20), it is fair to say that a lot of the initiatives that were not arms' length, choked on these very processes and bureaucratic expectations. And failed.

The failure may look like a proposition gap (I know you are thinking about Finn[1], so there: I said it), or it may look like something that never managed to get enough sunlight to grow, forever competing for resources with the division inside the bank that does something too similar for comfort. So we have seen the alternative *not* work.

> The temptation for banks to go at their own pace is always there but the impetus to change is always there too: it is external, driven by consumer demands or big tech raising the bar.
> ***Bianca Bates***

And we have seen the arms length approach work. And yet I, for one, am not 100% convinced that the industry is getting the memo. Particularly in a high-interest rate environment.

I put the question to Bianca and this is her take: 'The shift in the global context right now may be creating an opportunity for banks to do things at their own pace. There is a possibility that banks may continue going about what feels more comfortable to them, but the reality is that the impetus to do better for consumers often comes from consumers themselves and then the major banks compete among themselves to meet the demand.

The reality is that, so far, the push has not come from digital challengers or startups. The expectations in-market are driven by big tech right now. There is always an external impetus raising the bar.'

For those whose eyes are open, in short, the imperative is there. Even if it is looking a little different than it did five years ago. And now, thankfully for the fast followers amongst us, there are tried and tested shapes out there.

Bianca reflects: 'Big organisations can be clear on purpose and have clear alignment on what drives success. It takes sensible, balanced messaging for that to be sustainable but it's not impossible to be big *and* focused: look at Square.' All it takes is intent. And once you have established a winning formula, it takes discipline to stick to it.

---

1 In case you have managed to forget all about Finn by Chase... here is a reminder: https://www.forbes.com/sites/ronshevlin/2019/06/06/why-did-chase-shut-down-finn/?sh=1d2e469b702b

'With the acquisition of Basiq², we will apply the same shape. We now know how to leave them alone. We know it worked before. We need to be clear on what we have to learn from them and what they have to learn from us (security etc.).

We are not afraid of the big bets. For instance: we have transformed our operating model. We saw the value of agile delivery. We saw how it changes the pace of an organisation. We learned the value of weekly releases. To get to that took us 18 months of really hard work. But we are here now.'

Not being afraid of hard work is key here. And obvious. None of this is easy. But some of it you can plan for.

> If you decide to set up a new venture as an 'arms length' subsidiary then it is incumbent upon you as the parent entity to actually leave them alone to do the thing you set them up to do.

A Startup Inside a Bank Isn't Same-Same but Different

When you set up a new venture and decide to allow it to be 'arms length' so it can pursue a different business model, move at a separate pace and do all the things you can't or won't do in your main shop, it is important for the new venture to not expect that their life is going to be like any other startup because,

> The 'arms length' relationship between a traditional FS and its digital subsidiary has to be honoured by the parent. The power imbalance can only fall apart one way.

I hate to break it to you, but no other startup shares an office with JPMorgan like Chase UK does (the fully digital challenger consumer bank Chase launched in the UK taking the market by storm and growing at a pace that outstripped all its competitors combined at the time of writing). But equally, the parent company has to be prepared that the new venture will, for a time at least, operate a lot like a startup.

'As a bank, it is very hard to deprioritise profitability, even for a time, and focus on doing things differently' reflects Mettle's Ken Johnstone who is operating within UK banking giant RBS/NatWest.

But that is exactly what they are called upon to do when they embark on a journey like this. 'For us, the 'arms length' approach that NatWest gave us was a massive success factor. Because you are not a corporate but you are not quite a startup and having that 'arms length' relationship is key' and for the relationship to

---

2   https://www.startupdaily.net/topic/business/open-banking-fintech-basiq-sells-to-payments-giant-cuscal/

work the larger party has to respect the boundaries. And for that to work, the Big Bosses inside the larger party have to be supportive.

'In our case' continues Ken 'the parent bank honoured that relationship. Sponsorship has to come from the top otherwise things get smothered. And we had that.' And that sponsorship is key because you are setting up a new thing that doesn't live by the rules of the main shop or the market outside its doors. A startup inside a bank isn't like a startup and it isn't like a bank. It is a different thing altogether. It is a shape that works. Which is why it is included in here in the first place. But you need to approach it the right way to yield results and part of that is realising it's not like one thing *or* the other.

> In a corporate-backed startup you don't need to pitch VCs for funding but you have to respect a budget cycle and demonstrate, at the right time, both your potential as a new venture and your alignment to the group strategy.

For instance, knowing where your money comes from and not having to fundraise doesn't mean that you don't have to go through a rigorous process around funding that dominates your calendar in a qualitatively different but quantitatively similar way as fundraising does. In short, it's a different process to an external fundraise, but there is a lot of it just as there is a lot of time commitment going into a fundraise.

'For us as a startup inside a bank' explains Mettle's Ken Johnstone 'budget cycles were part of our "calendar". With a VC, you have a different set of pressures: you have a finite pot of cash and when it's gone it's gone and you need to demonstrate enough potential to raise the next round. Inside a big business you have an annual budget cycle, you have a date by which you need to show your potential as a new venture *and* your alignment with wider group strategy and get your growth funded.

To do that you need to speak the right language. In both cases you need to do that. In both cases you need to be mindful of the timeframes. They are different but you still need to work to them.'

And that is not just for the budget cycles. It is for everything: from getting the idea socialised to getting your governance in place so it can approve your next step, if you are operating inside a big corporate you need to work with the grain of the mothership even if what you are building is intentionally different.

> From getting an idea socialised to getting your governance in place so that it can approve your next step, if you are operating inside a big corporate, you need to work with the grain of the mothership.

Kelvin Tan recalls that 'the original concept behind audax was encapsulated in just five slides' and a lot of daring. 'During the years spent building Standard

Chartered nexus, I encountered much scepticism, often hearing the refrain *this is a fantastic idea, but it may not materialise within Standard Chartered.'*

Kelvin was undeterred.

Nexus was built and on the success of the platform he created a brand new business to go after a huge market opportunity outside SCB. And SCB wasn't a newbie at this. They had already cut their teeth with many other ventures including Mox so they knew what they needed to be mindful of.

That relationship of course comes with expectations around governance, security and robustness. 'As part of Standard Chartered, audax adheres to significant governance measures, particularly in terms of information security and enterprise requirements, aligning with the standards prevalent among our clients. While this governance may occasionally result in a slower pace than anticipated, it contributes positively to our credibility with banks and ensures the creation of a more robust and secure solution.'

But as ever, the thing you worry about is rarely the thing that becomes the biggest challenge. Weirdly, the challenge for audax hasn't been SCB getting in their way but other banks perceiving Standard Chartered as a competitor. Do I want the competition owning the infrastructure on which I build my vision?

'Standard Chartered has clearly articulated its ambition for audax, aiming for complete independence, including external funding. Importantly, while audax is backed by Standard Chartered Ventures, we function as a stand-alone business entity with full ownership of its intellectual property. Notably, Standard Chartered does not impose restrictions on our choice of partner banks, and our pipeline includes collaborations with entities that might be considered competitors.'

That is an uncomfortable new space for banks to occupy. And they are learning fast. Whether it's an acceptance of delaying profitability to build something new, competing with your own main business (RBS, Mettle's parent, has a strong legacy of serving SME communities in the UK, for instance) or creating a brand new vertical, like audax, respecting the rules of the new game is key. So agreeing what those rules are and having the right people around to navigate what that looks like effectively becomes the lynchpin of success or failure.

New Ship, New Captain, Old Rope

In order to do the kind of work we are talking about here, you need the right folks at the helm of the new venture. Michael Anyfantakis reflects that 'at the end of the day success always looks like a decision at the board level to build some-

> You need a special kind of leader to lead a corporate-backed new venture: someone who can navigate the new world and the old simultaneously.

thing new... from scratch... *differently*. All these three things matter. And then you are faced with the challenge of finding the right CEO to build this new thing, from scratch, independently... and to build it *as such*.'

This is a multi-layered challenge. Because you need them to be able to build something from scratch in the first place. Not a skill everyone has. But you also need them to speak the right language to manage the corporate context, to Ken's point above.

'That person needs to be outward-looking and open-minded' continues Michael. 'They are not your traditional bank MD. Hiring for attitude towards change is key. And then the main body of the bank needs to not reject this new implant.'

> It is always tempting for the main organisation to appoint one of its golden boys to run the new venture. It is a common temptation.
> And a dangerous one.

This cautionary note isn't *just* for the leader and it isn't *just* for the start of the journey, cautions Michael. It concerns the team and its culture overall. And it also affects every step of the journey. The start is critical. Most things falter soon after inception. But equally critical is the question of whether/when to bring the new venture into the fold of the main bank. In fact, the tension on whether/when to make the decision never fully goes away. Unless you make it. The decision, that is.

Keeping the new venture to the side has advantages, so does consolidation. Each option could earn or lose you budget, talent and sponsorship.

As could the timing.

Michael thinks back to an example he lived through in a previous role, of what happens when you try to bring a new venture in too soon. He is referring to New10

> If you are building a new venture inside the corporate, having the ability to navigate the mothership is as important as having the ability to build the new thing.
> If you fail at one, you have failed at both.

at ABN AMRO. The intentions were good. They decided, on the whole, the benefits of consolidation (economies of scale and closer alignment) won out. So they brought the venture into the fold. But they did it too soon, they did it clumsily and they didn't focus necessarily on protecting the culture and ways of working that would retain the talent necessary for the continuation of the journey. The result? 'Their whole leadership team (and most of the core team) left very quickly, when the bank decided to bring it in.'

Michael contrasts this with what is happening with Mettle (yes Ken Johnstone's shop: isn't it nice when it all comes together?). 'Here, NatWest is keeping the new venture separate enough ('arms length' rather than complete separation) and growing it through a combination of external partnerships and the rapid organisational shift of NatWest's own transformation in the form of a set of capabilities expected to run differently.'

For the avoidance of doubt: the realisation that you need to incubate the different thing differently and simultaneously change your organisation (not treating your new venture as digital inoculation but as part of a developing story) is sensible and affords the organisation protection from errors we have seen committed before. But it doesn't eliminate all risks. The decisions that need to be made are nuanced, the timings imprecise. And although it is a comfort that there are precedents to learn from, in the specifics, these are hard lessons to learn.

> Your new venture is not 'digital inoculation': it is not enough to protect your main organisation from the changing world. It needs to be part of a bigger story.

'The board needs to ensure this change is sustained top down. That is where the board is key' concluded Michael.

We will come back to how board dynamics can make or break those initiatives at the end of this chapter but that dual theme of leadership inside the venture and sponsorship outside pervades, as you have already noticed. It is a balance of respecting the newness of the new thing and navigating the old shop that makes it possible: with respect in the right places and unconditional push back in the right places. The challenge is knowing which are the right places.

The recipe for success, stresses Michael, is 'the combination of CEO and Exco member overall sponsorship, the right MD/CEO to lead the new business that is trusted by the old business *and* is the right type of person to get the work done.' And that person doesn't need to be external, observes Michael. It depends on your organisation. 'If you have lots of entrepreneurial people in your

> There was a time when finding someone who can build new things inside a bank was next to impossible... and then you would bring Silicon Valley types in and they would either baulk at the bureaucracy or be frozen out by their colleagues. That is thankfully not the trope anymore.

company, like Capital One who is always hiring grads from top Universities, then you can find lots of good candidates internally.'

There was a time when finding someone who can build new things inside a bank was next to impossible and then you would bring Silicon Valley types in and they would either baulk at the bureaucracy or be frozen out by their colleagues. That is thankfully not the trope anymore. Banks are realising that and have been hiring differently for a decade now: they have been building new ventures with varying degrees of success and building innovation muscles with varying degrees of speed. But the point remains: ten years ago, you wouldn't know where to turn to find someone who can face both in and out. Now these people are still fairly rare (it is a niche skill-set we are looking for, after all) but they do exist and, as you see more and more of those hybrid models, you have people in-market who have both the right skills and, increasingly, experience.

Standard Chartered is an excellent example of this: Mox was led by Deniz who had created an entrepreneurial outpost inside a different bank before. He had proven credentials in this outside/in balance. Audax is led by Kelvin who demonstrated the fact that he was willing and able to build Nexus inside the organisation, and although he hasn't done something like audax before, he has built a successful 'new' thing inside the 'old' shop.

Plus his general approach to life is 'when faced with the assertion that something is not achievable, my inclination is to find a way to make it happen. They told me it cannot be done, I said, hold my drink'. Both of these people were *already* working for SCB when the time came to look for leadership for the new ventures. If you are reading this book sitting inside a corporate giant, take a moment and ask yourself if you know who those people are in your shop. If you don't, maybe it's time to get you know your team and find them. Or, if you are convinced you don't already have them: hire them. And soon. My guess is you are going to need them before long, even if you don't set out to build something hugely ambitious.

'If you don't have lots of those folks (like most big banks who grow executives from the grassroots), then you struggle' observes Michael. And you will struggle because, in the absence of the hybrid skill set, you may be tempted to bring one of the golden boys of the main bank in to run things. A common temptation because it feels like a smaller risk than bringing someone in from the outside. And a dangerous one, cautions Michael: 'Bringing someone of the old school into the new ways of working could break [the new venture].'

> Sponsorship is key but it can also be damaging.
> You don't just want sponsorship of the idea... you want sponsorship of the leadership. So that good intentions don't pave the road to hell for your venture.

We see it often. With new ventures and innovation programmes inside incumbent organisations. The thing starts as a separate entity, department or venture. Everyone agrees it should be so. Everyone agrees on the reasons why it should be so. But then the work progresses.

Decisions need to be made that get uncomfortable either in their complexity or because of the sheer fact that you keep needing to make new decisions on things you have no established wisdom on and it gets exhausting. Or, an even simpler scenario: the venture or experiment succeeds and grows. It becomes attractive to the main bank so a 'grown-up' steps in. Be it fear or excitement, whatever the motivation for getting closer to the new venture, the danger is the same.

'People who don't know how to do sustained change work, regularly take a project away from the innovation team or the venture team... take away its "separateness" and give it to someone who *also* doesn't know how to do sustained change work' deplores Michael. It is a 'comfort' thing, as the person chosen to run the new venture at such a juncture is one of their own. Someone who operates in a more familiar fashion and aligned to their motivations and ways of working and, potentially, politics. 'Their reasons for doing so make sense' reflects Michael. 'The result doesn't always.'

So although sponsorship matters, even a well-meaning sponsor can hurt you by appointing the wrong leader. Or backing the wrong board dynamic. Hence when we say sponsorship matters the nuance is: sponsorship of the right leadership matter. Especially if you find yourself with a well meaning and enthusiastic board who may want to be too close, go too fast or participate too much.

A myriad of daily balancing acts determine the survival (or not) of new things. Because having made the decision to do the new thing 'apart', there are still a million decisions that need to be made and there be dragons.

Do you go big? Do you start small? What is the right size for the mechanics of the work itself. And how small is acceptable to your investors or corporate backers? Is their size and the size they want you to start at in any way aligned?

Questions of Scale

The biggest challenge for a startup is getting enough money to prove your point, to disrupt the industry and to achieve your mission. And yet we already discussed the dangers of getting too much money too soon. Or the wrong money at the wrong time. That danger is ever present with any corporate-backed effort as well even though, from the outside, it may not feel as existential.

It usually looks like a board that decides they want to do something new (fundamentally a good thing) and realises that this 'something' will take a lot of money (also a good thing, because it is not uncommon that people want the moon on a stick immediately and for the price of a popsicle). And then this hypothetical board give you that sack of money and expect you to just *go do*. Seemingly also a good thing. But a challenging one.

> Too much money early on leads to bloating and inefficiency: that is common whether you are a venture-backed startup or corporate-owned venture.

'If you are given a lot of money by an enthusiastic board' reflects Michael 'you start big... and then you bake in inefficiency.' You grow too fast. You bloat.

Plus, as the CTO of a venture that meets all these criteria and asked not to be named reflected: 'you all agree you want a baby... but the board is so enthusiastic that they want you to hire nine women to be pregnant for a month each and have the baby ready in a few weeks... it doesn't work that way. But if the board have convinced themselves that it can and should work that way... if you go in too hard telling them they are wrong all you end up with is your marching orders and they just hire someone more willing to spend their money for them.'

There is such a thing as support of the wrong kind, it turns out.

Because there is no cash-strapped entrepreneur who wouldn't love the idea of a blank cheque, an enthusiastic board throwing money at you. But, actually, you would be better served with a little less money and a little more time. Actually being left alone long enough to establish the basics would be great, thanks.

The best kind of support within a corporate, actually, is not a blank cheque. Having to come back to explain your spending and demonstrate your progress is not a bad thing. It creates discipline, focus and alignment in the ongoing conversation. Way more valuable than money is the political aircover to start small 'when you can hide something in a corner long enough for it to be properly incubated, grow to something that is effective and efficient and that can prove its value' continues Michael.

> In a bigger organisation it's not the regulatory burden that gets in the way. It's the size of the organisation itself. It's the people in the middle of things who may over-interpret. Who do their own little functional thing and make a job of it around their own interpretation or job definition.
> *Michael Anyfantakis*

The ability to build something early on 'without being noticed... until you want it to be noticed' is actually key and it is 'not as easy as it sounds, because in most large banks, even small things require governance approvals that need to go very high' so flying completely under the radar is a technical impossibility, continues Michael. Plus if you have active and enthusiastic sponsorship, then the chance of not being noticed until you have something worth noticing has sailed even before you started.

What if your sponsor could help you stay quiet for a bit? You won't be hidden as such. Just shielded. But that is invaluable. This is important because Michael stresses (and I fully agree) that 'in a bigger organisation it's not the regulatory burden that makes the difference. It's the size of the organisation itself. It's the people in the middle of things who always make a job for themselves. Who may over-interpret. Who do their own little functional thing and make a job of it around their own interpretation or job definition. The biggest challenge with the large organisation and the "people in the middle" especially when it comes

> The parent company can kill its venture but trying to make it get too big too fast... or drowning it in governance that is too big for the risk you are currently trying to mitigate.

to risk and regulation is the over-interpretation and ultra conservatism, even when this is not necessary/appropriate for the level of risk you are trying to mitigate.'

I cannot put this better myself and it is absolutely key to understand the challenges new ventures face inside a big organisation.

The issue is not governance and regulation itself. It is the way that is interpreted and managed by a small army of people not always trained beyond the checklist of their own job definition inside the big organisation. This means that, if a big corporate were to revamp their compliance team, this challenge would go away. Until that happens, however, what you are protecting your 'thing apart' venture from is not risk and compliance, it is your risk and compliance *teams*. It is the ways of working and default behaviours of the people inside your organisation. Not the governance.

This is not a big reveal by the way.

'People at the top seem to be able to see that, as they have a much wider view of tradeoffs and can make better risk calls' continues Michael 'but once this is split into functionally-aligned organisations and you go a bit further down in the hierarchy and also introduce the second line/third line concept, then you lose the link across areas, and everyone just fights for their own corner'. *That* is what you are protecting against, when you set a venture to the side.

So if you set your new venture to the side and *still* unleash your mid-level risk managers upon it, you have squandered all the value of the separateness and may as well not put the effort into building a separate venture at all. You need to embed thoughtful professionals inside the new organisation and ensure they interface with thoughtful professionals when it comes to the main shop.

'Truly small, cross functional teams that are autonomous is the theoretical answer, but difficult to achieve when you have the governance structures that Big Banks put in place' concludes Michael.

An Ever-Shifting Balancing Act

When you lead a venture such as the one I am describing above, you are essentially signing up to an ever-renewing balancing act: managing the sponsors inside the main shop *while* creating space for the teams to build a brand new thing, *differently*. Creating a fledgling business that will make money differently, eventually, *while* satisfying the folks paying the bills today.

> The biggest reason why banks find themselves repeating mistakes they have seen others make in the past, mistakes they know to watch out for is the sheer mental load the CEO and top table carry. You need a plan in place for when they get side-tracked.

And although there is no denying that sponsorship for such a venture can become its own undoing, it is also absolutely key in getting started, reflects Mike Cunningham who has been through this journey more than once. And by that he means you have no way of starting without that sponsorship. Getting started is binary, inside a big organisation. How you manage the process once you have received the green light is much more nuanced.

'The leadership says *ok let's do it together*, and it feels entrepreneurial at first' reflects Mike. And you want to do everything in your power to retain that feeling.

'I always treated my board of directors like I would a VC' says Mike reflecting Ken's experience. 'I gave them investment memos, not KPI updates. I treated them as investors, not senior managers in a hierarchy because it is key to maintain the entrepreneurial dynamic.' But it is hard to achieve that. Both because of all the reasons we discussed above and for the blatant one we haven't yet, so here it is: 'Leadership changes may come'. Sponsorship is necessary to get started and great to have as you go, despite all the challenges in maintaining its focus and the necessary distance all at once.

But what happens if your sponsor retires, resigns, is fired or promoted to a swanky new job that takes them away from you and your venture? What happens when you are left in a roomful of people who were just going along, not invested, don't feel that this new venture is 'their baby' and they are thinking 'we make x billion per year, do we really need to change?'

How do you protect against that? Asks Mike. And he answers: You don't.

It is impossible to protect yourself against that.

All you can do is be mindful it might happen and mitigate. You ensure you make more than one friend at the top table. You actively manage your board. You show progress and alignment in equal measure. You manage both imperatives to build the new thing, build it fast and build it to be different, while ensuring it is not scarily different. Just the right amount of different.

This active management exercise is the job of the leadership of the new venture. And it is key. And it is a lot. But it is still not enough, reflects Mike: 'there is no getting around the need for someone other than you saying that what you are doing is right.' You need friends at the top table, vocally acknowledging your direction of travel exactly because it is new and by definition uncomfortable.

> When doing new things differently, you need someone other than you to say 'this is right'.
>
> And it has to be more than one person: because if you have only one friend at the top table if they get promoted or fired, you are all alone. No matter how good a friend or how big a deal they used to be.

'Any chief digital or transformation officer has to be the teller of difficult truths' continues Mike. 'They need to hold the mirror up and say look at things from a different angle. But to be able to do this you need sponsorship: consistent and extremely senior sponsorship' and remember: you need this sponsorship to be given to you by more than one person. 'If that goes, you are isolated and become ineffective.'

I built three banks before Bank Clearly, in big regulated environments across different jurisdictions, for big "sponsor" banks' continues Mike. 'The context matters but mostly what determines how fast you move is the Bank itself. Leadership changes at the top table will affect you whether you like it or not.

But also, if you don't do what you need to do to keep it at 'arms length', it will get in its own way. If you don't help it balance competing priorities, it will get in its own way. Using old decision-making processes is just as bad as using old tech. It is effectively relying on turkeys to vote for Christmas, you will lose out *and* it will be your own doing. If you ask what went wrong when someone else tried to do what you are doing somewhere else and then repeat the same mistakes you saw them make: the question is why? Why are you doing this? Why are you not learning?'

It is not a rhetorical question.

It is in so many ways, the one we are here to answer. Why this book exists. A lot of what we are highlighting here is not shocking. It may be more compelling when it comes with the testimonials of multiple people who have done it before but none of the pointers in these pages should be a surprise, really.

So if we already sort of know already, why aren't we learning?

This is Mike's answer, and I can't argue with it: 'The CEO of a bank has so many things on their plate. *Digital*, however important, is not the only thing. Building the next thing, no matter how important, is never the only thing. They will get side-tracked. It is inevitable. And you need to plan for that. You need to be ready. Wider politics, second-guessing decisions, low risk appetite, global events.'

Be prepared to lose mindshare. That doesn't mean 'expect it and it will suck', although you should expect it and it will suck. At times and for a time. But what it actually means is prepare your defences, shore up your team, make multiple friends and have your wits about you. Because it will happen and it will suck but it doesn't have to kill you.

> The CEO of a bank has so many things on their plate.
>
> *Digital*, however important, is never the only thing. They will get side-tracked.
>
> You need to plan for that.
> **Mike Cunningham**

We have seen how this plays out more than once, so be prepared, is the message. Be prepared always. Even after the battle is seemingly won. Be prepared, for instance, that people won't be done sniping about the budget you got, or the risk your venture represents, ages after the decision to start has been made. Even months or years into the work, counter-intuitive as that seems.

Remember the CTO of the nine-women-pregnant-for-a-month-each story? Of course you do. It is a hard image to shake. He had the purpose of the venture he was running challenged at the board level three years into their operation. By that point, they had hit all their milestones and proof points, had set themselves more ambitious targets. They were growing and developing along what felt like pre-agreed lines. And doing it well. There was reason for optimism and celebration.

But the Chair of the Board came to the end of their tenure, a new Chair came in and decided to put their mark on the place. And rather than changing the curtains they go for 'should we be doing this in the first place.'

That penchant for second-guessing a steady new venture is sadly common. Sometimes it is triggered by fatigue or the pressure of deploying resources elsewhere. Sometimes it's politics. I spoke to a founder recently who had a collaboration with a big bank killed as Covid started even though it was steady and profitable. 'It was making money' he cried out, his hands in his hair, the incomprehension palpable even years after the event. 'We were making money. There was no problem to solve. They just needed to let it be. But Covid started and the bank decided to simplify its estate so they killed it. It was making money and they killed it.'

A common story sadly. So stay alert. Getting the green light doesn't mean you are out of the woods. 'The urge to say *yes we made the decision but should we get McKinsey in to have a view anyway?* is always there' agrees Mike Cunningham. Even months or years into a build. You are never fully in the clear because senior decision-makers in banks have default behaviours to shore up the 'who has egg on their face if this goes belly up' question.

> Just because a decision was made inside a big corporate it doesn't mean that someone won't decide to second-guess it. Often months or years into the work.
>
> Be vigilant. You can't avoid it. But you can be ready for it.

'The lack of accountability resulting from this type of behaviour is endemic in banks and, weirdly, it means you can create space for great change and, frankly, get away with things provided they don't go against the grain. Provided it's all nice and comfortable for those who need it nice and comfortable. This attitude means that if you are happy to live and die by the sword' continues Mike, 'you welcome the accountability and say *if I fail, fire me.*'

In organisations where personal accountability is in short supply, Mike reflects, that can short-circuit the decisions you need to get the organisation to back you to get started. But you are not done.

If you are willing to live and die by the sword, they are most likely willing to let you but not join you. And that is fine. You don't need them to take the same amount of risk, just to give you enough scope to actually manoeuvre. 'Don't send me to fight Mike Tyson with an arm tied behind my back' chuckles Mike.

'That's the trade-off. I don't want to break rules but we need the rules to not get in the way of the work. [Big organisations] spend more money and time in the discussion than the work itself. If we agree that we need to change, then let's change the way we work towards the change.'

The idea of doing different things differently is back. How do you do that, I hear you ask?

'You create two sets of rules' is Mike's answer. 'Make the new venture go through the bureaucracy *once* but when you give the green light, let it move differently. Within rules and boundaries that are fit for purpose. Governance is key. But it has to be different.' Which means that a certain degree of accountability needs to come back to the board. It is inevitable. Hence the need for more than one friend around that table. You will do most of the work but you need them to back you not to do the same work again and again and again.

Wasn't that the point, after all: to do a new thing differently? And to do the different thing, *differently*, you need to change a lot of the established tropes. You need governance but it will look different. You don't copy/paste is the message from everyone quoted here. You create a separate, *different* thing. You give it money, time, space. You let it grow and you let it be different. And you supervise.

You are on the Board. That's what they are for. And you have probably learned by now, the hard way if at all, that your own organisation may not be very good at doing the thing you are trying to do here. And it will be up to you to square that impossible circle of wanting to do the thing you are really not very good at.

When the Thing You Need the Most Is the Thing You Are Terribly, Terribly Bad at

It is a universally accepted truth that big companies struggle with innovation. We talked about the levels and reasons behind failed transformations earlier in this book and I wrote a whole other book about it, so I won't double down on the reasons here. I will only say that those reasons are well known in the industry and inside the corporate itself. There are *millions* of reports saying the same thing again and again. Ok, perhaps slight exaggeration. Perhaps it's not millions, but trust me when I say it feels like millions.

Weirdly, the fact that we know where things go wrong is why there is so much focus on process and governance: to supervise the danger zone, albeit not always to ensure things don't get stuck inside the organisation's own habits and inertia. But as we have demonstrated above, there are increasingly agreed-upon ways for big FS players to get out of their own way.

Jordan Schlipf, Co-Founder, Rainmaking venture studio
Previously Jordan worked in M&A, has been a startup founder, investor and entrepreneurship teacher

'Why do corporates struggle to innovate' reflects Jordan Schlipf who has worked on both ends of the size spectrum and has seen the high failure rate in both startups and corporate ventures. The problem is intriguing, he admits, but in some ways 'to implement a solution to this problem is thankless. There is too much resistance.' That is why he moved into the corporate venture builder model: building startups from scratch in partnership with big corporates but outside them. The arms' length model, yet again. 'We are creating a new asset class in a way. Traditional M&A is essentially buying smaller versions of yourself' continues Jordan. 'The type of M&A we do here is looking at a different business model that traditional corporate finance teams would struggle to find synergies with. It is a brand-new capability designed to bring innovation and it requires a new and different skillset to work with.'

Right. That's what I am talking about. That's what we have been talking about all along. So. Doing this stuff again and again and again is your business, I asked Jordan: What works?

The answer won't surprise you.

A meaningful strategy from the start of the funnel, explains Jordan. And a strategy that is aligned to P&L (because each business is different). These are not tick box exercises, stresses Jordan. You have to do your strategy well at the start. You need to 'determine

> Be honest with yourself: are the new things you are building *genuinely* new business models, new ideas, new products or stuff that is BAU, just new to you because you are falling behind the market?

what innovation vehicles you should deploy. Determine which non-programmatic partnerships will work for you.' And you need to be honest with yourself about what is innovation and what is work you should be doing anyway. What is new because it is breaking new ground and what is new to you because you have fallen behind what is expected by the market. 'A bunch of stuff is now under the umbrella of innovation that shouldn't be. Growing your P&L, lowering your cost base: that's just doing your job. It's BAU. Digital adoption is not innovation. It's getting on with the day job' stresses Jordan. 'Innovation is a word that seems to cover everything. It is still a buzzword. That's a legacy from the innovation theatre days[3]. Innovation KPIs for managers have started appearing but it's still all part of the act. Strategy means having a north star that helps define what is in and what is out of scope. What direction you move towards. An innovation strategy cannot miss the fundamentals of strategy: we will achieve x, in y timeframe with z resources. Most of that is missing from innovation strategies. Why is that?'

Jordan is right. I would argue, however, that most of that is missing from most strategies. It goes back to the business model conversation earlier in the book. You need to have it. And you need to use it. It needs to guide decisions or what's the point of it? And yet focus is often in short supply despite the pressures (runway

---

3   What Jordan is referring to is the not-so-distant past of folks spending time and energy and money doing POCs and going to events and announcing partnerships and marginal investments that were never meaningful in size or intent for how the main organisation functioned or thought about its business.

for startups, SteerCo grillings for corporates). Arguably *because* of the pressures of runway, investors breathing down their necks and product market fit challenges, startups usually face the strategic and focus questions sooner and more easily. It helps that there are doing less too, obviously.

The Elephant in the Room

But there is also an elephant in this here room and I am proud of myself for making it this far without using the 'i' word. I hope you noticed I had steered clear from the word 'innovation' even though I have inched dangerously close to speaking about those theatre days when I discussed which founders I was *not* interested in speaking to. And in selecting which corporates I wasn't going to ask to weigh in on the debate.

But we got to the place where I can't avoid it any longer because, having repeatedly stated that innovation is neither the measure nor the endgame, it is a reasonable question to say well what of all the time, money and headspace spent on exactly that inside big

> For a long time, what we have been talking about in this book flew under the banner of innovation. But that banner hasn't served us well.

organisations: doing stuff that falls under the banner of innovation? Because when talking about all the ways in which bringing change about inside big organisations is hard, it becomes important to speak about the early, heady days of innovation theatre. If only just to say: that's not what we thought we were doing. For a long time, everything we talk about in this book would have flown under the banner of innovation and with good reason. It's just that the banner hasn't served us well.

Nektarios Liolios (who was for a time a peer and colleague of Jordan's and how I got to meet Jordan in the first place) recalls: 'If I look back in 2011/2012, what was needed [across the industry] was knowledge.' Incidentally, I agree fully. I remember those days. When fintech was evolving before our very eyes and it was richer and more nuanced with every day that passed and the established FS players were still grappling with *what is what* and *what to do with it*. I remember, at the time, feeling that if we understand, we will move forward. We need to learn. Then we will *do*.

I believed that fully. I was wrong.

But at the time, I believed it. We all did. At the time, we were aligned and honest in the pursuit of this knowledge. 'What to do with that knowledge came next' continues Nektarios. 'We didn't think that far ahead at the beginning. At first, we felt that inefficiency was mostly complacency and, if we could get our organisations to get on the journey, then we would be ok as the need to change is clear and the tech allows us to affect that change.

And yet the battle has been constant. By the time I was at Rainmaking, around 2015, the conundrum was different. On the one side you have the bank and they want to innovate but haven't worked out how and on the other the startups. The hackathons we held were meant to bring those together but actually what was invaluable were the peer conversations. That's where the greatest value was. Like AA meetings for innovators. For the startups the upside was access and not wasting time talking to the wrong people. And frankly we didn't know at the time that the innovation people were not the right people.'

> In the early days of fintech there was a fundamental belief that what was lacking was knowledge. We were wrong. What was missing was a clear sense of 'what is in this for me'.
> **Nektarios Liolios**

And again. We all believed at the time that they were the right people. They understood, they were willing, they had knowledge of the new stuff and access inside their organisations. Besides they were hired by their organisations to be catalysts of change. Allegedly. They thought they were the right people and so did everyone else.

'We all believed at the time that they were' continues Nektarios. 'But the space got very noisy. A lot of opinion leaders who got excited about stuff that was interesting but not useful' and as they were not accountable for a single deliverable, and theatre was of the essence, letting them play with the cool stuff was ok. But 'focusing on the cool stuff is dangerous and, at the time, people in innovation didn't always realise they had to solve *real* problems. Not just be creative but solve for things as they are today. Banks often still don't realise that they are part of their own problem (the way their procurement operates, for instance).' And that is not all.

There was another fundamental disconnect at the time, recalls Nektarios: 'we then realised that banks are not prepared to move forward without a clear understanding of *what's in it for them*. And that is understandable but, at the time, it came as a shock.'

> Innovation is not a meaningful end-game. Business value is. Is your new venture a business driver, or a shiny thing?

I am surprising myself as I type this but I know it to be true. And it was universal.

Remember Deniz describing how, in the early days of iGaranti, they focused on playing an innovation game rather than standing up a profitable digital business? At the time, the expectation was that banks would go on the journey to learn with no clear upside. That would come later. That would sort of organically follow, was the belief. We should have known that nothing about this work is effortless or naturally occurring. We should have known that banks don't know a lot of things but they know money. So, Nekrarios recalls, banks would deploy '200 million in a fund but not 200k on an exploratory pilot. And that caused frustration but shouldn't have caused surprise'.

Understandable but, again with hindsight, it should have been obvious that the decision vector was not whether the bank can afford the 200k or the 200M but whether it was money deployed or spent, money invested or burnt. Whether the money went towards an identifiable shape with a known risk profile or not. It was never about the amount. It was always about nomenclature and risk matrixes.

Is it fair to say that some of the many startup failures boil down to people working at cross purposes in the early days of fintech? I can't put a number on it but it is absolutely true that some early investment either directly or from bank-backed funds into startups the banks never intended to be a customer to, created noise and false hopes. And that hasn't stopped entirely. While writing this book, I was approached to join the board of an interesting early-stage startup. Hugely disruptive space, if they get traction. Not entirely clear how they will go about getting traction, if you read their business plan or speak to the CEO, but you would be tempted to disregard that issue as an operational issue that will easily be overcome since eight of the world's largest banks and potential cornerstone customers for their vertical are sitting around its board table and on its cap table. The right people are there and 'invested' in the company's success.

And yet.

Not one of them is a customer.

How come? I asked during the exploratory conversations. Oh well you know how it is, was the answer. Yes. I do. That is why I am asking.

It turns out... Not one of them is willing to commit to a timeline for becoming a customer. They

> We have been trying to build new things for a while under the guise of corporate innovation and digital ventures but mostly we were measuring the wrong things and hoping they would substitute for leadership intent.
>
> They do not.

have bought optionality. That is all. This was a risk-hedged investment portfolio play. Some empty innovation metrics were met inside their own banks as a bonus side effect and a very misleading market engagement set of metrics were generated inside the startup.

And now what?

The bank representatives spend board meetings beating their startup up on why it's not gaining commercial traction.

'Fintech was going to eat the world' reflects *The Banker*'s Liz Lumley, thinking back to those early days. 'But the reality was... This was never going to happen. Banks are not that easy to destroy. They even tried to destroy themselves in 2008 and they couldn't do it. Finance is everywhere. It's naive to think they won't be around overnight. [Banks] will just look different.' But even that was a worry for the banks. That narrative. No bank ever believed they would disappear. That existential fear never dawned. But they feared disintermediation. They genuinely believed it was a danger, so it felt real. At the beginning of the digitisation journey and the dawn of fintech, disintermediation was all banks were seriously worried about and startup founders in the FS world were feeding this fear. But they were also themselves feeding off it. Founders really started believing they would eat the world and disintermediate the banks. Wedge themselves between the Bank and its clients in the fattiest parts of the value chain. And founders believed that specifically. Not just that the sector would make it but *them* specifically. Each founder was the new Steve Jobs.

Understandable in the circumstances, perhaps. And we already spoke of how unbridled optimism goes with the territory and is a necessary evil but an error nonetheless.

> Banks worried fintech would disintermediate them and founders believed it for themselves as well as the industry. That may account for many of the early failures: the naive to the slaughter.

Starting a business is harder than many assumed. That may account for some of the failure rates we have seen in fintech. The naive to the slaughter.

Plus it takes more to modernise and digitise a bank than a couple of fintech partnerships and the collaboration between the two needed work on both sides. We are finally realising all that and making some progress.

'We are now better at the lean startup methodology approach' reflects Liz 'but banks are on cloud now. That's progress. The context in which we do this work has changed too. There is no beer in the fridge any more and the old version of the innovation lab is over.' Does that mean playtime is over? Not quite: 'hey everyone is doing CBDCs and quantum now' reflects Liz, which is as abstract and far away as APIs seemed ten years ago. And the intent to use the experiments in anger is as elusive. So ok not everything has changed. But banks *are* on the cloud now. API-first infrastructures are basic hygiene. And the ventures we are discussing in this book are not everywhere but there are enough of them to be more than outliers. 'You could argue that we no longer need the labs' reflects Liz. 'We have learned how to learn, they have fulfilled their purpose.' The era of innovation playgroup is over. We have graduated to the next thing, at last.

The Party Raged on. And Then It Ended

'A handful of individuals in corporate development or M&A or strategy seemed to have managed to convince their boards to give them money to play with while

> All the success stories we have seen to-date are not repeatable.
> **Jordan Schlipf**

keeping their day job perks' reflects Jordan. 'And yes they don't have the carry of professional investors but they don't have the risks either. They essentially create a fun, different job for themselves for a time.' Isn't that a hoot?

'That said' continues Jordan, 'some entities and teams have done *some* of the things well. Not everyone engaged in theatre. Some were thoughtful about what they were trying to achieve. But even if you do the strategy part well, then execution becomes an issue. And more often than not that is when organisations start cherry-picking. They look at all the things that need to be done to get to the next phase of the strategy they just devised and think 'surely I don't have to do all those things, I can just do *some*'.

Regardless of the industry, this cherry-picking is common and it is rarely about the money. Most of this work is really not that expensive actually. The issue is not budget considerations, when the chips are down, but lack of courage. Deployments of new ideas or new systems inside big organisations are done either with a consultancy leading, which causes issues of its own, or with an internal executive leading and retaining too much control. Internal people running initiatives like this will get railroaded by a silly request from their boss and everything will start unravelling.

Plus, banks will try to make all decisions upfront, from the point of most ignorance in order to get ahead of managing internal governance requirements. That instinct and behaviour combined mean that, before long, people default to old behaviours and issue

> This work is not expensive, all told. Hesitation is never down to budget considerations. It is always lack of courage.

KPIs that folks can work to, even if those KPIs don't move the needle, don't measure actual progress against strategy or do anything other than giving the team something to show bonus-guaranteed progress against for year-end and their boss something pretty and… green… to report to their bosses on a quarterly basis. Plus ça change.

'So the question really is' continues Jordan 'who can sit there, at the right level of decision-making and help those decisions *get* made. No wonder successful ventures are outside this quagmire, you may think. But even then, as we saw, you are not clear of its challenges. Plus your chances out on your own aren't necessarily that much better. 75% of startups fail "in the wild" and you start a protected initiative to avoid that happening to you, but then you start getting in your own way doing things that *are known* to cause failure in the market… why do you do this to yourself?'

> As a bank, you need to provide the time, money and space for a non-linear process of innovation to take place. It is frustrating as it runs and rubs against the organisation's normal ways of working.

Fair question, Jordan.

And it doesn't help to know the answer: humans can't help themselves. They will become, as Curt already flagged, short-termist. They will hold onto contextual habits or personal preferences. Even if they are motivated by a belief that they are doing the right thing, as Zor reflected earlier, humans will get in their own way.

When organisational inertia, misaligned incentives and multiple priorities are *also* thrown into the mix, it is no wonder that the majority of initiatives fail. It is a wonder that any have succeeded.

'The thing about the success stories we have seen to date' stresses Jordan 'is that they are not repeatable. Either the CEO forced something through the business or someone leading an initiative put in *hero* effort, using a lot of their own political capital. But then… all those behaviours are there in the [ventures and initiatives] that failed as well.' Which is the recurring theme of this book. There are a million things you need to do to avoid disaster. *Not* doing them is tempting fate. Doing them does not guarantee success. That is the game you chose to play.

It is important to be honest with ourselves about these factors of success and failure because although we started this journey believing, as Nektarios rightly pointed out, that we were solving a *knowledge* problem, 'our issue as an industry is no longer a knowledge one' stresses Jordan. 'The knowledge exists and is accessible. It is just not implemented.'

As Mike asked a few pages back, these things are not big reveals: why are we not learning? Is it the relative significance of all the things warring for mindshare? Or is it a mindset thing? In which case it is a generational thing and there's hope yet as the demographic make-up of decision-makers are changing slowly but inexorably.

'We have had a generational shift and a leadership shift occurring as we speak' reflects Jordan. 'The main thing that will prevent regression is the pace of change outside the industry. Everything is accelerating and doesn't allow for complacency.' A new generation is at the helm: this stuff is more familiar to them and it becomes their responsibility to keep the focus and pace needed, concludes Jordan.

A big job but, arguably the generation now responsible for it, has been chomping at the bit to take the reins for a while. So the question becomes more nuanced: if we are putting more appropriate people in positions of decision-making accountability inside the

> Big organisations have looked at the digital economy and tried to cherry-pick: surely I don't need to do all that stuff? But yes… yes you do.

industry, are we learning from our mistakes and the successes *outside* our industry? The question no longer is, are we learning about the new stuff. But rather are we learning about all the things we are not good at and seeking to find ways of getting out of our own way?

Because the reality is that the arms length approach, challenging as it is, is great for some stuff but it can't solve all of the digitisation needs a corporate has. Whether you want to call it innovation or not, to Jordan's point (and I personally couldn't care less what you call it), big corporates can't just create digital parachutes for everything.

They have to work out what to do with their own business in a changing economy. For that, they need an honest view of their strengths and weaknesses when it comes to changing. I am not for a moment suggesting that an era of open, self-awareness has dawned. But I am suggesting that, in this one thing, corporates show signs of learning. And the leadership tenor is changing.

Two problems remain. One really granular and in the weeds the other abstract and pervasive. The first is: how do you stop the main organisation's pace, cadence and habits from getting in the way?

I have written before (yes, yes in *Bankers Like Us*, you know you want to read it, you just know it) about ambitious and successful innovative solutions built inside banks in a matter of weeks that then had to wait for six months for a release window (that one

> Your strategy is great. But it will fail in the detail of your testing policies or procurement process... And it will fall before what you actually pay people to do. Not what you tell them to do.

happened to me). And I recently lived through a very ambitious go-live with a bank that had the visionary desire to build a complicated and market-leading embedded finance platform but wouldn't give the project team their own testing resource and we had to play around with the weird voodoo of how do you book testing resources as per the bank's policy, six to eight months in advance, when you are running three-week sprints and daily releases.

Is this even a problem you should be solving? No. Only unless you solve it, it will get in the way. And why didn't the sponsors solve it for you? Well. Because they didn't realise they needed to.

The intent, as ever, was that once the strategy is set, the kinks will be combed out on their own, so to speak. Things will shake themselves loose. Because the strategy will cascade. And whatnot.

Only the *whatnot* becomes a sticking point. Always.

Because people will always do what they are incentivised to do and strategy be damned. They will do what you pay them to do, not what you tell them to do. They will do what is measured ahead of what is right. And incentivisation inside a big bank isn't conducive to innovative or change work. Maintaining the status quo is rewarded and promoted as a matter of course. 'A bank may hold back a bonus or payout until they ensure you have done nothing wrong' reflects Mike Cunningham 'whereas growth equity will create golden handcuffs for a longer game. Working to a 12/18 month horizon and actively managing the share price doesn't allow for proper strategic thinking. Unless you have the vision on the board and executive sponsor-ship to tell a story of where we are going and why we will be going under for a few months to get there.'

So what is the answer the industry has alighted on? An 'arms length', separate venture as we saw. Which absolutely gets us out of innovation theatre and out of our own way. It doesn't solve all problems, you still need to modernise your shop. But it solves some problems and that is not nothing. But even then, there are negotiations galore that still need to happen.

Even the Most Powerful CEO Answers to Someone

The minute I wrote that, I knew it wasn't true by the way.

In startup land it is very common for a CEO to be majority shareholder and Chair. I have worked in a bank where the CEO was also Chair but at least they had the good grace to flag this as temporary. Because the CEO reports into the Chair of the Board so it's a bit cosy if it's the same person. It takes being your own boss to a whole new level. But yes. It happens when the governance is loose and even though the CEO feels unfettered, the reality is they are not free as much as they are alone and un-advised. But more on that in the next section. For now, let's talk about boards that work like they should do: providing guidance and accountability structures in equal measure.

The beautiful thing about boards is that the responsibility of those around the table and the main imperatives that need to be met are clear and personal. Or at least they should be. Weirdly, when talking about digital transformation efforts, success, failure and strategic integrity, we don't talk about boards anywhere near enough. And yet aligned boards are very often behind successful ventures, disjointed boards who refuse to learn are often behind stop/start efforts and the responsibility to consistently move in the right direction needs to be more clearly apportioned. Behind the heroic CEO there is a board that did its job, or not and a very important story as to what happened and what didn't. And what happened (or didn't) in the board room is a hugely significant part of the success stories and the failures.

> Board tenure is about three years. So a board will need something noticeable (which means big enough to make an impact to their P&L) and need it relatively quickly. They can afford the money, but not the time.
> *Michael Anyfantakis*

It is not too bold a generalisation to say that, when building new things and for all the reasons discussed in the book so far, the instinct across all ventures (corporate backed or venture backed) is to *manage* the board, not to lean on it. Corporate-backed ventures often see their boards as a very stern SteerCo, an oversight committee. Something like a PTA on steroids. Startups often see their boards as a necessary evil requested by investors either because they want to sit on them or because they want the comfort of governance and oversight. It is extremely rare for the leaders of such ventures to see their boards as an asset to be leveraged on the journey. And yet the reality is, an informed, engaged and supportive board is so much more than a tick in the box. Or at least can be.

'Each phase of build you finish, you graduate into a new league' reflects OM Bank's Royden Volans. 'You never quite reach a finish line. It's a journey. And a supportive board is key on this journey.' By supportive, however, Roy doesn't mean you need cheerleaders. Your board doesn't need to be unanimously behind you. They need to be universally engaged. Which is not the same thing.

'Practically, you need a majority to keep moving forward but it is not a board's job to give you full commitment. Their job is not to pat you on the back. It is to challenge you. They should be

> Your Board can be a huge asset if you set up and use it correctly: it should be neither a nuisance nor a PTA meeting on steroids.

asking you *why should I believe you*. The main thing is not that they support you at every juncture, it is that they are learning at every turn. If they challenge you and you show progress against the strategy, do they progress too? To the next set of questions? Or do they ask the same questions or sway in their direction and falter?

Because a startup cannot cope with uncertainty at that level. It would be a cause for failure because the team needs to know there is commitment. If the team feel that the direction of travel is not committed, *their* commitment will waver, their velocity will drop. Quality will drop.

If that happens, the CEO will need to face into the board in an uncomfortable way. They will need to take this challenge on. And they may need to fall on their sword at some point. Especially if you don't have a strong chair person.' So get one. Because you need one.

Again, they don't need to be an unwavering advocate but they need to hold the board to account

> The main thing is not that your board support you, it is that they are learning.
> If they challenge you and you show progress against the strategy, do they progress too? To the next set of questions?
> **Royden Volans**

against the vision just as they hold the executive team: the board isn't there just to hold the executives accountable. 'They are part of the journey' continues Royden 'and the way they hold the executive team accountable needs to remember their commitment to progress over perfection. There is work you can do around board induction to reduce this risk and around balancing the skillsets and perspectives around the table, because you will need to teach different board members what they don't know and you need to balance the fresh and different perspectives with a sustainable range of things to teach.'

That learning mindset and strong chairperson is key, especially as an enthusiastic but clumsy board can cause more trouble than it causes. Remember Michael Anyfantakis saying that the best thing your sponsor can give you is aircover to stay small?

'On another occasion, we had an idea that went straight to the board. It got buy-in. It had sponsorship.' We are trained to consider these conditions ideal for success. 'And yet that had the opposite effect' continues Michael. 'The dream was big' continues Michael 'but so were the expectations. We attempted to start small and we got shot down because we were too small. We were given more money than we needed and higher expectations that we could meet. How do you avoid that? A board thinks big: *if I throw money at it, will it go faster?* You can extrapolate on the business case but you can't accelerate everything.'

> You need to manage your board's expectations but you can and should hold them accountable to stay on a learning curve with you.

Who manages the board's expectations? Who makes sure they are learning and holding you to account but not pushing you to the wrong decisions?

The answer of course lies in a healthy tension between an engaged and inquisitive board and a strong and communicative CEO. But that is not always there and it is always a challenge. And if the challenge becomes too great then it becomes a distraction. And if the tension becomes unhelpful, the board conversations become heavily curated. The possibility for a genuinely value-additive dialogue goes out the window and we get a tick box rather than an asset to the business.

To be a material help and accelerant, the relationship between the Board and the team needs to be actively managed on both sides.

If the Board decides on a strategic direction, then they need to hold their proverbial horses and sit on their hands. They can expect quarterly progress updates but not material progress between sessions.

> You can extrapolate on a business case but you can't accelerate everything: a Board thinking big and throwing money at you isn't always a good thing.
> **Michael Anyfantakis**

Especially if the aspiration is sizeable: building a platform or building a bank. That takes years and it will suffer reversals. Progress will feel slow and at times it won't feel like progress at all. And the board has to expect and manage their own impatience. And that is difficult. Not least because the lifespan of a board (usually three years for a big bank), and the time horizons of ExCos, the targets they need to meet, the cycles they are measured in and the bonuses at stake don't always align.

So a board, especially a bank board, stresses Michael, will 'need something noticeable (which means big enough to make an impact to their P&L) and need it relatively quickly. They can afford the money, but not the time, and this is very different to fintechs, Investors, VCs: they have more time and not much money, so they can start small.' And although startups may not like the fact that they are forced to start small one little bit, Michael is adamant that they should count their blessings.

'Starting Big is a Big challenge!

We were saying that all we needed was a team of 35–50 people to set up this new venture and we were being laughed at. *You got to add a zero to that in order to be credible* was what we were being told.
The board didn't want an experiment on the side, they wanted to migrate the existing business. But the business owners were nervous by the magnitude of this. They were finding a million problems. They stalled.'

The venture had intense attention and that was what killed it.

> There is no way around the tensions, governance and competing time horizons of your stakeholders.
> You need to face into them. You need to manage them. And you need to accept that you can't solve for them: only balance them.

Which is the opposite of what we have been saying all along in some ways. Engaged sponsorship at the top and all that.

The issue in everything we have said in this book is a balancing act. If you are building inside a corporate, your board being engaged is a necessary but not sufficient condition. Because if they are pushing you, they may draw the wrong kind of attention from the wider business which means you can't start small, you can't stay to the side of the main shop. All the advantages we have been discussing in this section evaporate.

The obvious release valve here and the right move from a governance perspective is, of course, that your new venture gets its own board. A board that reflects its needs and ethos. That reflects its business model (Mox for instance had its JV partners around the table, alongside the parent bank). That reflects its regulatory standing (OM Bank needs its own board, as a regulated entity, where representatives of the parent company are present of course but whose mission here is slightly different). Getting your own board is important. From a governance and an alignment perspective. But it doesn't solve all of these challenges. It just brings a subset of them into a different room.

All the Way Up. All the Way Across

Juan Guerra, CEO of Revolut Mexico, reflects on his experience, 'sitting on the board of the oldest financial institution in the Americas: a 250 year old pawn shop which must transform or die. They serve some of the poorest people in Mexico and folks who have a bad or a thin credit history. They need to radically change their relationship with their union and build digital capabilities.

I am glad I can learn about the former and, especially, bring my skills to bear on the latter. But as the "innovation guy" on the board, there's only so much I can do. In reality, the Chief Innovation Officer of any business has to be the CEO with full support from the entire board. Anything else is just a waste of time.

I saw that done well at Santander, where Ana Botín puts a thoughtful bet on the future. You can't expect a manager further down the hierarchy to drive that. A manager lives and dies by the quarter. You can't think about material change in that timeframe.

> The only way for transformational mandates to stick is from the top... and aligned to the mission of the whole business.

Furthermore, managers are always punished for any failures and seldom rewarded for the success of a bet. They are just not transformational leaders, they can't be. And the environment reinforces that.'

The only way for true transformational mandates to stick is from the top. Right from the board and CEO and all the way down. But also all the way across a business rather than in an isolated department or division.

You need a clear mandate from the board to transform a business or build a business. You cannot be a lone voice. You need a holistic view. Translated into strategy by the leadership. Then the teams further down will execute. But by then, this imperative will be part of the DNA of the company, not a side show. Even if the venture is separate, the behaviour will not be.

That is, to Juan's mind, how you keep your company on a path of constant renewal. 'Revolut is technically not a startup any more' he says reflecting on his day job. But they are still a young company. Still scaling. 'And yet the CEO drives a clear resource split between core business and innovation. That

> Transforming a business has to have board-level support and be cascaded down across the entire organisation: it cannot be the domain of one person or division.

could mean new markets, new products. Think about it. We are new. Our history goes back eight years. Not even a public company yet and yet we have a good chunk of money placed on new bets. Why don't you see that split in cash-rich companies?'

It's a fair question but a rhetorical one. We know why.

They are not set up this way and every structure, habit and metric makes it hard to change so fundamentally. But exactly because change is always so hard, Juan reflects 'be it a start up struggling to make it or a big company trying to transform... unless the top people (the CEO and the board) are determined and fully aligned, things won't happen. In a big company it's the board and CEO who need to drive transformation. Bottom up doesn't work.'

But it doesn't have to be done by someone 'edgy' and you don't have to reinvent the wheel 'Look around you' encourages Juan. 'Mimic success where you see it.

It's not mysterious: observe and copy. Learn and do. Minimise the instances in which you need to come up with something entirely new – only truly innovate when absolutely necessary. That's a safer way to minimise risk and move at pace.'

Jasper from PensionBee agrees.

Although a listed company, PensionBee still sees itself as a challenger brand.

> You don't need to innovate to transform: you can mimic successful strategies you see around you and risk-manage the process.
> **Juan Guerra**

'We are not one of the old boys and we certainly do not intend to become one! Being a public company can come with a bit of a slowdown as you add regulatory layers and oversight but the company is fundamentally the same. You want those layers as we're managing billions of pounds of our customer's pension money.'

That means culture, people and the commitment to innovation stays top of mind, no matter how big they get.

Which is a *big* commitment even before they get properly big. Because size matters. As we have seen, size creates challenges despite the best intentions. So to stay ahead of it is a conscious commitment by the executive leadership and their oversight bodies (boards included). And this is a commitment that is hard to get and even harder to retain as you achieve scale and people's habits kick in.

Thinking back on why he left 'the corporate innovation game' Nektarios is adamant: 'I couldn't stand to hear another CEO, a few brandies into the evening saying *I get it but I can't get my leadership to do it*. At the end of the day, I have met more than 100 bank and insurance C suite and the things they won't do because they are too hard always boil down to managing board and shareholder expectations

> The things [Bank and Insurance C-suites] won't do because they are too hard always boil down to managing board and shareholder expectations and incentivising their senior leaders the right way to sustain change. And it's all solvable.
> **Nektarios Liolios**

and incentivising their senior leaders the right way to sustain change. And it's all solvable.'

And Nektarios is right. It is solvable. Through all the ways we have discussed at length in this book. All the things you need to get right upfront, all the factors and variables you need to control. But above all it is solvable through people who will push through no matter how hard it gets.

Which is why, for the last chapter, we go back to the people leading the successful transformative ventures. I know that's where we started. But it evidently all boils down to them staying the course and managing to do all the (admittedly numerous) important things, all at once. And since it is all about the leadership that stays the course and manages to do all the things, there is one more thing about these people that is key to remember, and given all we have talked about so far, it is fair to talk afresh about the leaders that break through the inertia. And how they do that.

But first, your homework.

Your Calls to Action

- As a leader you need to keep yourself on the hook and do the work in the right way. All the time.
- Doing the right things doesn't guarantee success. But not doing them guarantees failure.
- If you are building a different business inside your company you need to be clear about what will need to be done differently to succeed and you need to create clear lines of separation and accountability.
- Whatever you decide to do, you need to be able to sustain the effort within your organisation and repeat the model. None of this work is one and done.
- A startup inside a established entity is neither a startup nor a established entity. The model works but you need to understand it and respect it. It is not a smaller version or a bigger version or a slightly altered version. It is a different model altogether.
- In a big organisation, be prepared to lose mindshare. Be prepared for habits and structures to 'leak'. And by 'be prepared' I mean anticipate and resist.
- Whatever shape you opt for, your Board needs to get it.
- They need to want it, support it, not lose interest and not rush it. That's why the right money matters for startups. That's why top of the house sponsorship matters for corporates.

Chapter 9

Between Steadfastness and Adaptability

Who Tells You That You Are Being an Idiot?

Many moons ago, I was approached for a job. It was shiny, this job. There was nothing about the job I didn't like. It's not just that I was a good fit for it; it was more like, it was so perfect, it felt like it was designed for me. Which, with hindsight, it probably was. The job was perfect. The team would have been mine to build. The package was pretty close to perfect for what I would have wanted at the time, truth be told. And the company was a mixed bag, to be fair. As is usually the case. They had some amazing things going for them. Some more questionable ingredients in the mix. And a charismatic CEO who didn't just drink his own Kool-Aid but he did so publicly, unashamedly and repeatedly.

This is gonna end in tears, I thought. Question is: whose?

But I still had the chat.

It's hard to do the things you know you need to do, like eat your vegetables and avoid the things you know you should avoid sometimes. I can resist everything but temptation and whatnot. So I had the chat.

And when we got to the 'do you have any questions for me' part of the conversation, and he looked at me all expectantly, *all* I wanted to know from him was, 'who, in your leadership team, tells you when you are being an idiot?'

The stunned silence that met my question was my first answer. And this wasn't in reaction to my use of the word 'idiot' in a work context, by the way. Those days

 DOI: 10.1201/9781003395577-9

are over and the fintech world in the UK (where this took place) is a very sweary industry. The silence was not because my vocabulary shocked him.

The silence was followed by an awkward laugh. That was also answer enough, I guess. But there was more. The third and only intentionally spoken words also spoke volumes: 'well, I guess if you join us... you will'.

Very funny. But no thanks.

So, fast forward to many years later, and I am chatting with the wonderful Kelvin Tan about his experience building and running audax. We speak about the vision and challenges, the opportunity ahead and the operational decisions he needs to make to set this up, calibrate it and grow it. So in the context of a lot of decisions needing to be made with speed and conviction, I ask him: who will tell you when you are being an idiot?

> In order to have a company where genuine feedback is offered, you need a culture that allows it and a structure that enables it: neither is enough on its own.

And I get a trademark Kelvin chuckle and he says: everyone.

Somehow, I doubt that, not least because Kelvin is not an idiot. But I like the sentiment that everyone is allowed and everyone is welcome to shout foul. Because the challenge of *how you keep yourself true is* real for every leader.

How do you keep looking for your own blind spots?

And how do you empower the team to do the same for themselves and actively do it for each other, including you? The answer to that is multi-layered and intentional. When Kelvin says everyone *can* tell him he's an idiot, he means they have created a culture that allows it and a structure that enables it. Both important and not interchangeable.

So the first step to building a company where this is possible is mechanical. You need to put in mechanisms that intentionally gather feedback from every member of the team, fostering a culture that values and solicits input across all levels. 'Utilising methods like 360-degree feedback and skip-level meetings, we ensure a comprehensive understanding of perspectives within our 180-strong team. As we grow, scaling this approach is a challenge, but our commitment to ensuring aligned values within the team remains unwavering.'

> Soliciting and actively listening to feedback from both your team and clients is how you spare yourself unpleasant surprises down the road.

The thing to remember here is that you put the structure in as a default. You don't do 360-degree reviews or skip-level meetings when something has gone wrong and you need inputs. You do them (or whatever your version of them is) by design. All the time. As part of 'how we do things around here'. So when you need them, they are part of how things work. They are trusted. They are used. They don't feel artificial and don't arouse suspicion.

Secondly, in order to really have a clear sense of how things *really* are inside your shop, you need feedback from clients. If you recall, Kelvin road-tested his pricing with the market (and not in a fit of confirmation bias but actually taking a few hypotheses out into the open world and seeing what works). Active dialogue with clients is a key part of how he is taking audax to market. He even meets with every prospect, even before they become a client. And before you say it: they have a pretty sizeable pipeline (I checked, just in case he was doing this for something to do while there wasn't enough work to go around, but no).

So why does he do it?

Because, ultimately, if they don't buy, you don't have a business, so their ongoing feedback matters more than anything. Their feedback is how you avoid unpleasant surprises in a timely manner. They will tell you the truth around your product readiness, size of your product market fit and pricing. Theirs is the opinion that matters the most regarding your delivery discipline, coverage model and how your team shows up. The way they present themselves. The way they make the client feel about the prospect of working with you.

In an industry where sales cycles are long, integration phases fiddly and contracts span decades, looking forward to spending time with the people on the other side of the table is an often unspoken but key part of any vendor selection. So get the feedback.

Soliciting and actively listening to feedback from your team *and* clients as an ongoing activity is a fairly rare exercise by the way even though it should be an obvious one. Because it is time-consuming and very public, you need to follow it up with action depending on the feedback. Most companies go

> A good way to find out what is really going on inside your organisation is talking to clients. Your product, your pricing, your service, your culture: they are the truest witnesses of it all.

through the motions of doing it. Usually with surveys and perfunctory gestures that tick a box but rarely seek to engage.

How *Not* to Do It

Soliciting feedback with honesty and integrity and with the intent of acting upon it runs counter to the fundamental habits of the industry. Surveys exist. Every organisation I have ever worked in, big and small, did client surveys. Sometimes the input was used to determine individuals' bonuses and performance reviews. In short, if your clients liked you, you got a gold star. But that was largely it.

The opportunity to find out how you are *really* doing is often squandered. And the clients know it, so they rarely fill the blasted thing in. So how do you get around that? Well. The CEO actually picking up the phone or going over to speak to the clients regularly helps. Client Advisory Boards (CABs) help too. I have never witnessed a CAB that didn't deliver value. You can keep them small and vertical-specific, closed-door and structured like most banks do. Or you can be more open (if you dare) and invite prospects to their sessions like many tech companies do.

> If you solicit feedback (from employees or clients) you need to be seen to do something about it in a timely manner. You need to action it. And you need to action it visibly.

If you are willing to listen, they are a powerful way of keeping you on your toes. But you need to be seen to be listening, and you need to action the feedback in a timely manner. You need to hold yourself visibly accountable or it will be worse than doing nothing.

'A bit like employee engagement surveys' commented one of the interviewees who chose to remain anonymous for reasons that will become apparent very soon. 'We knew we had morale and retention issues in our company and the new HR director made a big production of launching an employee engagement survey as part of the remediation plan.' Tell us what you really think, was the message, give us a chance to do better.

'They said all the right things: this is not a fix but an opportunity to get everything out in the open: tell us, we are listening. So the first year we had something like 100% response rate. And it all came out. Accusations of bullying and racism in the verbatims. Accusations of favouritism. Descriptions that would make you ashamed of the company but above all descriptions that made us all go oh yeah I know when this happened. Plus the culprits were named.'

And then what? And then what happened?

'Nothing. The people whose teams had filled out the most surveys got an engagement award and then the next year we did the survey again and people got penalised for their teams not being as engaged, because nothing happened in year one so people didn't come back to fill out the thing next year... and that became a management issue. Why are your teams not engaged?'

Why indeed.

So. Don't do that.

It is hard enough to find out what your teams are thinking without squandering the opportunities. Largely, people don't communicate up unless it's good news or the world is on fire.

I remember shadowing our regional CEO as part of my professional development when I was at a very large bank myself. It was an education in the amount of self-control and context-switching the day of the top brass entails. The experience made me realise that I did not want his job. But the most uncomfortable and most unforgettable thing he told me during the course of the two days I spent following him around like his literal shadow was that the most important thing to *retain* as you rise through the ranks is *people who will still bring you bad news when something can still be done about it.*

> Be the kind of leader people are unafraid to bring bad news to.

It stands to reason that when the news gets really bad, the top floor will hear about it. Or at least they will hear the bang of things spectacularly imploding. They get to hear about the bad news because there is no way to hide it once it gets really bad. That means that they hear about it at a time when it can no longer be hidden, usually at the same time as the clients, regulators or the Street hear about it. Whatever it is.

Not great, in short.

You have no time to fix, prevent or foreshore. You just react. Usually with egg on your face. Why were you not told before?

Such dramatic situations are always brewing inside big entities, by the way. Things don't always explode, but at any one moment there is always something that could go really badly south. And there is always someone who knows what that is and where it is developing.

In theory, your SteerCos and risk committees are there so that the people who know inform each other and the organisation in its totality is informed because forewarned is forearmed and all that. So assuming that for every thing that has ever gone wrong, at least someone, somewhere in the organisation knew it was going wrong before it went all the way wrong, why didn't they tell the big boss until it was too late?

Well.

Part of the problem may be the boss themselves. Is he prone to shooting the messenger? Shooting from the hip with incomplete information? Looking for someone to blame or fire in a pursuit of swift conclusions? Because if he is, who wants to have *that* conversation?

But that is not all.

Even with the most equanimity you could possibly muster, junior folks in big bureaucracies often assume that any good idea or valid observation they may have can't be original. There is the pervasive assumption that for *any* idea 'someone above my paygrade will have thought of this before me. There will be a reason why this is not already done'.

Only there isn't always. So it is very often the case that people see something wasteful or counter-productive and stay silent because they assume there is a good reason for it. Or they see something bad brewing and assume that people above their paygrade have noticed, have it in hand and have informed the relevant authorities. And if they have not, well. It is a matter of time before someone else notices, so keep your head down, Timmy.

Timmy is not a real person, by the way. But Timmy's desire to not be the messenger in an industry where the messenger is very often shot or belittled is as real as real things get. Besides, why bring the Big Bosses bad news when there is still a sliver of hope that whatever is going wrong can be fixed and there's still a chance that there will be nothing to see here?

Understandable instinct. Terrible practice.

So, make sure you are a leader that people are not afraid to bring bad news to, the CEO I was shadowing told me. He said *be a leader that people are not afraid to say things to*. Bad things, uncertain things, still-developing things. Things that don't make the person who brings the news seem smart or heroic. Just… things. Including when the thing they need to say is that not just that something was missed but that *you* missed something.

> Be the kind of leader who is ok to be presented with 'unfinished' thoughts. So that people will not wait till things are fully developed before they seek your help or guidance.

He was right.

Being the sort of leader who can be told things you don't want to hear (without shooting the messenger, if you shoot the messenger, it really doesn't count). Mastering this art means that you are a teachable leader. A leader who can reflect and adapt if that is needed. Because (spoiler alert: it will be needed.)

Changing an Industry Isn't a Light Workout

I was leafing through an industry book recently. I will confess I didn't choose it for myself. Someone 'traded me' at a book signing for a copy of my own book. I explained that it is not how it works, that barter was not necessary: our kind hosts had bought copies for their guests. But I did so most feebly because I like books and I wasn't going to turn one down. Plus, this one had a foreword by Garry Kasparov, so I will have it *thankyouverymuch*.

Inside the volume there is fairly standard digitisation-there-be-dragons fare. Nothing you haven't seen before in a Big Four report. But in one of the articles[1] it said this, and it made me laugh out loud: 'After all, leaders in large organisations don't actually *do* anything. Their job is

> In large organisations, leaders don't need to actually *do* anything. The ship, largely, runs itself.

---

1 George Westerman, 'How to turn your company into a master of digital transformation' in *Hyperautomation*, published by and for Appian in 2020.

to get others to do things. If they do it well, the company succeeds. If not, then the company finds a new leader. That's why vision is so important. If it's compelling for you and your employees, they'll help you make progress'.

I mean. It is an accurate description of what actually happens in large organisations. In large steady-state organisations, the leaders don't need to do things. They just need to make sure things keep happening. And by *make sure*, I mean don't get in the way of them happening; I don't mean that they need to cause said things to happen in a specific way. Which isn't the same as leadership. It is more a case of loosely letting 'things' carry on happening in that voodoo way of theirs. And it is voodoo.

Because, the reality in a big organisation is that the CEO doesn't *really* know what the bond issuance team *actually* does 9 to 5. Whether they are understaffed and overworked or cruising inefficiently along. He may be told, but he won't *know* how to confirm the truth of such a statement. Across every team and every function and every geography. It's not an indictment, by the way. It's a statement of inevitability. Any CEO doesn't and can't really know which bit of activity is achieving which outcome inside their huge global organisation.

Which is why, of course, when we look at change work there are no known scripts and guardrails. That is true both when starting a brand new thing when nobody is doing anything yet so you need to be pretty clear what you want them to do, show them or explain it and somehow measure impact or otherwise satisfy yourself of progress made; and when changing an existing thing where people carrying on as they were is the opposite of what you are here to achieve.

It is all *literally* the opposite of the job at hand.

So actually, the way leadership works in large organisations is not designed for what we are talking about here. The people, the practices, the habits, the language. The training. It's just a different animal.

So yes. George Westerman is right. That is how leadership behaves. It is a fact but it shouldn't be an endorsement. You are *meant* to lead. You just get away with not doing it in a big organisation if steady-state is the name of the game. But if you want to change what is going on, then, I hate to

> Vision is necessary but not enough: to change an industry you need leadership that is visionary and yet practical as teams have no default to fall back on.

say this to you, George, but vision alone ain't going to cut it. Vision is good but it is not enough. To change the organisation you run, in order for it to be fighting fit for a changing industry, you need to know what to stop and what to keep and what to do with the bits in between.

If you read that article and thought, 'ah vision, I have that from a McKinsey report I commissioned last year, we are good to boldly enter the digital era at last'; get your money back. From both George and the vision deck people. For this kind of work, leaders need to behave differently in *all* things. They need to engage differently. They need vision, but they also need to know how to lay out the specifics of what they are asking their teams to build. They need to know how to guide the work: *actually* guide the execution, not just visualise a desired end-state. They need conviction, but they also need the humility to solicit and listen to real-time feedback. They need to think, act and react differently in all things.

Which is why they tend to also be an altogether different kind of leader as their instincts help them point away from the 'as you were' attitudes of traditional leadership in large corporates.

Interestingly, the narrative we have been seeing in the fintech world during the Years of Plenty, when money was cheap and the court cases that have, since, sobered everyone up were unthinkable outcomes, *that* narrative created an image of an unflappable, visionary CEO that was in every way modelled on the outward characteristics

> The narrative of 'me vs the world' that we have seen in start-up culture: the unflappable captain of the ship, is outwardly modelled on the corporate CEO at the helm of their huge vessel. Only it is a false analogy. Neither the ship nor the journey is comparable.

of a big company CEO (even if they were only running a team of four engineers and a pet gerbil).

The image of the visionary, *me vs the world, my way or the highway, I tell you to jump and you ask me 'how high'* (actual conversation I had with a founder CEO[2]) is actually copying the vibes of the Corporate CEO tropes. The Big Bosses who don't do things. *Any* things. But instead set direction and then lean against the prow of their ship scanning the horizon, vaguely unsure as to what all the skivvies are doing below deck but convinced it doesn't matter as much as their vision.

I say *outwardly modelling themselves* on that because, of course, the mechanics of building a new venture need to be put in place. The ship won't sail itself until someone builds it and sets the direction and calibrates the navigation. You can't just stay out of the way and hope for the best, with a new venture. That is literally the opposite of your job.

---

2 If you must know, it went like this: I explained that engineers should be allowed self-determination when it comes to non-operational meetings. Effectively each engineer should be allowed to decide which optional, internal update meetings they should attend in order to minimise context-switching and interruptions. So they shouldn't have to go to sales meetings or Town Halls or all-hands or Show and Tell or Lunch and Learn sessions unless they wanted to and it fit in with their work schedule that day. They should have to go to operational meetings, but everything else should be left to their discretion.
His response?
Everything I ask for is compulsory. I say jump. You don't ask why. You say how high?
A case study in 'how to make friends and influence people' that guy.

And yet the Years of Plenty saw many a venture (now failed) where the CEO was neither an engineer nor a product person, neither a banker nor a compliance expert. Not a sales person. Not a people manager. But a visionary. Like a cult leader only for investors. Or, if you have seen the Barbie movie: Like Beach Ken. He does Beach. And that is all he does. We should have known then this wouldn't work, by the way. But whatever. We know now.

We have seen the failed ventures after the sky-high valuations. We have seen the Glassdoor reviews and the court cases, the tell-all accounts and the failures. And we have also seen the dawning realisation across the market that, acting like the ship will sail itself, doesn't make it so. Unless you have a ship

> During the years of plenty we saw founder CEOs who had no expertise in engineering, product, compliance or anything, actually. They were visionaries: like cult leaders for investors.

and a crew that know what they need to do, which, in a new venture, you don't.

Or you have a ship and a crew that know what they are doing (which, in an established, going concern, you do), and you just want them to carry on doing it. And in a change mandate, you don't.

In fact, across the board of what we are looking at here, doing what they have always been doing is the opposite of what you want from your people. As you would expect, in a start-up, this gap is starker. The company is new. Nothing exists unless you create it, and those gaps loom large as you go, the things you may have neglected, left for later or didn't realise you needed to do in the first place. With transformation, you have the added pressure of every gap being filled by habitual behaviours oozing back to fill any reluctance or gap: people reverting to type, going back to the very thing you are pulling them away from. Either way, it is hard work. And the leader needs to be involved in both setting the direction and the sailing of the ship. You need a destination, of course. But you need so much more.

Vision-First. Just Not Vision-Only

Antony Jenkins used to run a big ship like the one I described above. One of the biggest, actually. Barclays Bank. You may have heard of it.

And what he learnt captaining that ship became the vision he used when building his own venture.

> Knowing a problem inside out isn't the same as knowing how to solve it. Where do you look for ideas, inspiration and guidance?

Because the 'default to what we have always done' attitude of leadership and practice in large organisations means that bold decisions are hard to make and therefore are made rarely. In practice, what that means is that ways of working, habits and the technology estate of large banks suffer as a result because it is ageing rapidly. 'As you were' may work well in certain contexts. Technology isn't one of them. And yet it is exactly the prevailing attitude. So, having run one of these ships, he set off to build a company that played right into that space: the very thing that Big Ships are very bad at doing for themselves. Speaking when he was seven years into his entrepreneurial journey with 10x, Antony reflected: 'the tech banks have today is seven years older than when 10x started and it was 30 years old then. It will fall over. That's the belief and the vision behind 10x.'

It is also the truth. And there are very understandable reasons why this happens. The leadership styles we already discussed. Things happening that always feel more urgent in the day, week or quarter than replacing your technology estate, making change that isn't mandated and may not feel inevitable. 'Ultimately short-term drivers always have an impact and cause upheaval.

> The irony is that for a whole generation of entrepreneurs and intrapreneurs the vision is to clean up the mess accumulated by decades of the 'you don't actually need to do anything' style of leadership. The years and decades of doing exactly that when it came to building digital competences: nothing.

The interaction between the tactical and strategic will always be in play. Demand and supply conversations are constant' reflects Antony. And context is always key. Having lived through this, he set out to create the thing he wished he had when the shoe, so to speak, was on the other foot.

'I had lived with the limitations of existing tech and I was expecting regulators to be understanding. I had invested time to see how tech worked and believed the direction of travel was inevitable. But fundamentally understanding how technology is driving change is key to ensure you don't miss an opportunity… and yet it is equally key to not become too enthralled by a tech idea and miss the problem you set out to solve.'

Of course, as we have been saying throughout this book, you need to find a problem big enough to be real and stay focused on the problem rather than your preferred solution. And even then, you have no guarantee that what you are building will be the right solution, the solution that will capture the imagination of the customer you are doing this for.

But at the start of the journey, the vision is what drives most of our heroic figures here. The irony, of course, is that for a whole generation of entrepreneurs and intrapreneurs, the vision is to clean up the mess accumulated by decades of the kind of leadership described above. The 'you don't actually need to do anything' type. The years and decades of doing exactly that when it came to building digital competences: nothing. So there is a cumulative, *huge* problem to solve in FS and a whole host of businesses and ventures coming in to solve it.

We know what problem we are trying to solve and why. But that doesn't mean we know *how* to solve it. If nothing else because, by definition, this new problem will require new solutions, delivered in a new way. So the people institutionalised enough to see the problem and know how big it is don't necessarily know how to solve it, as 20 years of fintech mostly failing prove.

And that shouldn't be surprising, as, the more we know, the harder it is to get back to first principles. So although the greatest inspiration and driver for change comes from knowing what is broken, that doesn't become a self-

> When managing change work you need to balance the tension between your people seeking familiarity and predictability and you needing to push yourself to challenge your perspectives and maintain perspective to avoid complacency and stagnation.

sustaining force. So how do you find the energy and ideas to drive constant renewal?

Especially as humans are supremely ill-suited to constant change. We crave familiarity so, often, we go out of our way to create it. Even when the very thing we set out to do is change, we still try to create familiarity in the process of change. The paradox of humanity in its full glory.

If we need to constantly keep our perspective fresh, and humans default to the comfort of the familiar, consciously or unconsciously, where do we get the impetus to do that?

Don't say vision. Yes, yes, you need the vision for change, but underneath that? Where do we do the learning and get inspiration and energy to keep going towards the vision? From each other may be a good answer. But it is rarely enough as inertia sets in.

'If I look back', reflects Curt Queyrouze, 'I can attribute some of the success we had at TAB Bank to Twitter of all things. That's where I saw a knowledge-share I had never seen before in my career. People thinking outside the box and sharing freely and in real time. Now it is less about instigating new thoughts and more a question of how you sift through what's real and what's not.' This spark of creativity cannot be replicated, reflects Curt, not least because Twitter is no more and what has replaced it is an altogether different beast. But also because 'that moment in time has passed.' We are now on the journey. The catalysing influence is gone but arguably no longer needed. Now we need to find ways to keep going, avoid distractions and work out what to do and what not to do.

Seriously.

How do you decide what *not* to do? How do you bring focus and governance to ensure durability to your change efforts? And how do you make sure that the decisions of what not to do are not driven more by fatigue, fear and giving in to the urge for familiarity? How do you, as a leader, ensure that what you do and don't do is constantly realigned to what you are trying to achieve and not dictated by the very human urge to just leave well alone for once? The tension between the organisation craving predictability and you needing to constantly maintain perspective is ultimately up to the leader to manage.

As I asked folks that question, the answers all pointed in the same direction as Curt. Not Twitter necessarily, but the need to put yourself in a position where your perspectives are constantly challenged and refreshed. The leaders that navigate the bad times

> Every leader needs to find a space where they can learn new things, find new perspectives and check for blind spots. What is yours?

as well as the good times tend to be those who go out of their way to make sure someone challenges their blind spots. They don't ask for everyone's advice on all things. That is a case of paralysing insecurity. Don't do that. But ensure you have advice when you need it, and people who will call out blunders before you make them… when you most need it.

Avoiding Two Unforced Errors A Year

'Imagine the impact you can have if you surround yourself with people who will give you the sort of advice that will help you avoid two unforced errors a year and move all actions six months earlier than you would otherwise do them' reflects Christian Nentwich. These are the people you need around you as a leader: the people who will help you see and prevent two unforced errors a year. They may never need to tell you that you are being an idiot because they will help you not get there.

Because the reality of our industry, for all its bluster, long hours and sense of desperate urgency, is that the things that matter usually play out in slow motion. The things you probably need advice on play out over weeks and months, not hours. It is

> You need to surround yourself with people who will help you avoid two unforced errors per year.
> *Christian Nentwich*

rarely dramatic and therefore timely interventions should be possible. Things usually evolve and build up, and there are several moments in which you can change the course of a set of events. It is possible. Is what I am saying. We are not talking about the stars aligning here. Timelines permit those kinds of interventions. You just need to have the right people around you, and when the advice is given: face into it.

'To achieve [avoiding two unforced errors a year] you need to have the hard conversations when they are needed', continues Christian. 'You have to fix things that need fixing and you need to have a few people around you who call the things that need fixing out, in case you miss them.' And the timing. Because in my experience I have often bitten back 'I told you so' when a leader parked my advice because they felt they had time, and when it was existential, they looked at me accusingly and told me they didn't have the luxury of implementing my solution any more. So the advice is no good unless you take it in a timely manner, and to take it, you need self-awareness of a particular type.

There are three parts to this awareness. The first is knowing you need these people around you. The second is creating conditions conducive to being told it is happening as it is happening (the right team culture, the right leadership structure, the right advisors and the right flow of information and this is key because if you only share beauty pageant-grade information with your advisors, you will never get the advice Christian is talking about here. And most people sanitise the information their advisors see to such an extent as to render them incapable of seeing the forest for the trees or vice versa).

And the third is your willingness to act upon the feedback *in the moment.*

We are all good at being humble and open to advice in the abstract, but the feedback won't be abstract when it reaches you. And it won't be delivered in a zen-like

> You need to solicit advice. You need to provide the information for the advice to be informed. And then you need to act on the advice. In the moment when it matters.

manner, in a moment when you are most open to it or can reflect and react in your own time. That is not how the universe packages life lessons.

The process of engaging in this dialogue has to be intentional and constant. As a leader, your ability to take the advice when it comes is key: take it when you need it, even when you don't want it, even if it is not when you are most ready for it.

Oh. And one more thing. It cannot be an echo chamber.

I was speaking to a CEO recently who recounted how he had a 'Come to Jesus' conversation with his executive team. He had a difficult but necessary meeting with them during which he effectively told them they were falling short. They were operating below the level of accountability he needed. The conversation was hard but, unexpectedly, it landed well. They reacted in an adult fashion. They acknowledged his point of view was valid. They were operating weirdly simultaneously above and below their functional responsibility. They could see it.

They had fallen into a pattern whereby they held their CEO to account like a Board would but with the benefit of unfettered access to real-time information, as they were executive leaders, but, simultaneously, they didn't feel accountable for the performance of their functions beyond executing tasks set by said beleaguered CEO. He was right to call it out. They could and would do better and start taking accountability for their areas.

Sounds amazing, right?

Literally as they were walking out of that very meeting, news came through that a big payment from a client was delayed and it may affect payroll unless some actions were taken immediately. The head of client success, finance director and HR director all turned to the CEO and said, 'what are you going to do about this?'.

And what did the CEO do?

He actually went off and dealt with it, realising he had wasted his breath in the thing that had until a moment previously felt like a good meeting. But he also didn't do anything further. Reverting to type is sadly a danger for us all, and, on this occasion, the failure was on both sides of the table but, ultimately, the responsibility to stop the charade only on one. The leadership team was happy to play the feedback game and ignore it the minute they left the room.

If their CEO let them, then why not?

So: you know. Having feedback sessions and frank conversations is not, in itself, valuable. Being able to take feedback, understand it, internalise it and act on it, that is the ballgame, and it is not a single thing but an ongoing mindset. You need to be willingly looking for it. It needs to be an ongoing discipline.

> As a first-time founder, I created an advisory board and was intentional about mentoring relationships. Which felt like a good idea. But it created a bubble and the advice became very specific. Consistently specific. Now I seek different sources of advice when I need it. I go out of my way to find fresh perspectives.
> ***Uday Akkaraju***

When I asked Rolf Eichweber, who challenges his thinking, he pointed at Roy.

What about you, I asked Roy, half expecting him to point back at Rolf in full bromance mode. And I was ready, dear reader, to challenge the cosiness of it all. Because when do cosiness and effectiveness go together, really? Never, that is when.

But Roy didn't give the answer I expected.

If *he* is expected to hold the leader to account, he needs to hold himself to account too in a non-cyclical way. 'So I ask a lot of questions all the time from a lot of people', says Roy. 'I remain curious. I value getting perspectives particularly regarding conduct. I value seeing how things from other contexts apply to mine. And I play the *the more we talk about it, the clearer it get*s game. The team tease me, they call me the pendulum because I revisit ideas all the time.'

'It is vital to find people you can have these conversations with', confirms Bond AI's Uday Akkaraju. 'The first time I was on this journey, I created an advisory board and was intentional about mentoring relationships. Which felt like a good idea. But it created a bubble and the advice became very specific. *Consistently* specific. It became a well-meaning echo-chamber. Now I seek different sources of advice when I need it. I go out of my way to find fresh perspectives.'

That sounds amazing. But the whole point of a blind spot is that you may not know it's there to go looking for help around it. It's a hard balance, getting advice, getting challenged, growing as a person and still getting the job done without second guessing every breath you take. How do you ensure you don't paralyse yourself with constant navel gazing but still know someone is watching out for your blind spots?

Who do you get advice from, I asked Antony Jenkins? Who does the man who used to run one of the biggest banks in the world get advice from? Friends, who have been on similar journeys, he says.

And Amanda.

Amanda is Antony's wife and life partner. She is 10x's Chief Impact Officer and one of the sweetest people you will ever meet. She has also been there every step of the way as she and Antony got together when they were very young. 'She is the co-founder of my life', says Antony. Wipe that tear, I won't tell anyone. I had exactly the same reaction.

> There are no right and wrong answers, who you are determines your choices.
> *Antony Jenkins*

'Ultimately there are no right or wrong answers, who you are determines your choices', continues Antony. Which is why who the leader is emerges as such a big part of these narratives from the beginning. Who the leader is as they come into the fray and what 'who they are' does to them once they face challenges. Because the experience won't make you the person you need to be to face it. That, you bring with you. But make no mistake, the journey will change you.

Whether You Think You Can or You Think You Can't, You Are Right[3]

During the interviews conducted for this book, I asked every single person I spoke to whether there was a moment when they thought 'this ain't gonna work'. To my surprise, the answers were divided right down the middle between those who calmly said 'no', the mission was strong and so was the team, the journey has been hard but we knew we were going to make it, and those who laughed and said 'oh my god, every day'. So it turns out that whether you are quietly confident or feel the fear and do it anyway, Henry Ford and a whole generation of entrepreneurial self-belief drivel on Instagram may have been wrong: the mindset does *not* determine the outcome. Teachability does. Tenacity does. Hard work does. Doing the hard things consistently and simultaneously does.

Because what followed both sets of answers was an account of what came after the moment of crisis, whether people feared it would be terminal or not: how the

---

3   The quote is attributed to Henry Ford.

teams ensured they were on a learning journey, no matter how confident they were in the outcome at the start of each day.

Antony (who was in the camp of having many moments when he thought this was not going to work) reflects: 'I had extensive business experience but hadn't run a tech company before. You need to constantly augment your knowledge. You constantly challenge yourself: can you build it? Can you make it work? Can you make it better? All in the context of long cycles for development and sales, multiple stakeholders and multiple exogenous factors. Ultimately, every business is one day away from disaster. You never *don't* lose sleep. If you stop losing sleep your business starts to die. You always need to keep moving forward, keep working out the next frontier, the next challenge. Given the context of the technologies that dominate our lives, when you run a tech business you have to be part of the next thing, or you become a Harvard Business School case study on why Blockbuster failed.'

> Ultimately every business is one day away from disaster. You never *don't* lose sleep.
>
> Given the context of the technologies that dominate our lives, when you run a tech business you have to be part of the next thing, or you become a Harvard Business School case study on why Blockbuster failed.
>
> **Antony Jenkins**

So staying on a learning journey is key. Write that down.

But that is often easier said than done. Nobody sets out to *not* learn from the journey they are on. Even when that is often the outcome. Does hindsight help? Yes and no is the answer.

'If I did this again', reflects Antony, 'all with the benefit of hindsight.... Migrating databases: I wouldn't do that again if I had the choice! But there is one thing I would not do differently

> The thing about success is that it is always just outside your grasp.
>
> **Antony Jenkins**

and that is identify a real problem and seek a solution that is 10x better, not fractionally better. *That* I would do again. I would also work with clients from the start again. 100%. You get insight and also get paid! What I would also do differently is that I would have a better sense of what good looks like when it comes to engineering. I would have focused on that more, if I did this again. And it isn't just about the type of talent but also timing. Businesses grow and change and knowing when to bring in the right talent is key. The thing about success is that it is always just outside your grasp. Especially in a young business where everything changes very quickly. For 10x, seven years ago, success would have been winning a client. Four years ago it would have been going live. Today it is about achieving repeatability. And as you achieve each milestone, success redefines itself. If you ever think *I am successful now,* that's the kiss of death.'

That state of restlessness, of not feeling quite done, may itself be a necessary ingredient for success. It is, after all, ever-present. As is the realisation that the journey of building a business from nothing or transforming an existing venture into a different animal is a staged journey. And the only way to succeed is to be mindful of the realities and needs of each stage. The work needed and the people needed to do it.

Maha El Dimachki reflects on all she has seen at her time at the FCA and beyond and agrees: 'talent is key and not a simple question. This is not about technical expertise alone. Needs are different depending on the stage of the company. What the company *needs* changes. What the company *needs from you* as the founder or CEO changes. How do you learn to be flexible? How do you adapt to the needs of your company in its various stages?'

To Thine Own Self Be True

When you were invited to build Revolut in Mexico from scratch, I asked Juan Guerra, did you go, 'here we go again'?

Juan, after the heart-breaking experience of Student Funder, had not been idle and, although he took on big corporate roles, the pull of building things from scratch never left him. 'After some time at Citi, I met Rappi – the leading delivery platform in LatAm, aiming to become a super-app that did a thousand other things on top of food delivery, like financial services. They were looking for a bank partner to launch their financial services platform. I tried to make Citi their partner, but we lost the RFP and a partnership was struck with Banorte instead. But a few weeks later I got a call to lead the JV. I landed a $700 million fundraise, designed the product, built the team, and, 15 months later, we had broken into the credit card market in Mexico and were active in Brazil, Colombia, Peru and Chile as well.

> Are you the kind of leader that prefers planting to harvesting? Are you better at creation than management? Can you evolve from one to the other? Do you even know?

At that point I was invited to build Revolut in Mexico from scratch and I could not say no. I like planting, more than harvesting, it seems', Juan reflects with a laugh.

That is a very important piece of the puzzle: are you a planter or a harvester? Are you the person who starts things or the person who scales things? Are you a pioneer? Are you a *forever* leader? An all-weather practitioner? Are you good at all the things that will be needed? And do you even want that for yourself?

There is no right or wrong answer, by the way. There is no answer that is better than any other. There isn't an answer you should aspire to. The only thing you need is self-awareness. Which one are you? Where are your skills and preferences, and how do you support yourself with the leadership team and mentoring team that enhances your skill sets? And how do you time when you are no longer the right guy for the job? If you are a builder, do you want to run the steady-state business? Yes or no, there is no right or wrong answer. But there is a right and wrong answer *for you*. As a person.

And as you probably have noticed in the stories told on these pages, most people work out their answer in the process of going through the first rodeo and maybe the second. Most people don't have a fully formed and accurate image of their own strengths and preferences at the start of the journey, but they do after a few

> A grown-up business needs grown-up things.
> If you prefer the chaos of the early days then you are not right, you are not wrong, you are just not fit for the whole journey.
> And it pays to know this.

rounds. People's self-awareness evolves and changes. Everyone changes. Interestingly, in many of the stories told in this book (and without any statistical significance) that journey of change seems to be a little different for men and women. Most of the men I spoke to, suggest they learnt humility in the process. Interestingly, and in what is probably a banal indictment of how we are all socialised: women going through the tumbler and with every knock acquire greater confidence. They all, without exception, learn the hard way not just what they are good at but also what they enjoy. What they want for themselves.

'Do I want to still be doing this when I am 80, like the Rolling Stones?' reflects Antony Jenkins with a smile. 'Maybe. Maybe not. I need to be open to what the universe presents. This is the life I chose. But I need to ask myself periodically: do I still want to be doing this or do I do it out of habit?'

'Personally', reflects Jasper Martens, 'I joined a startup for a reason: I want to build a brand and see it through. I liked the uncertainty of the early days. And I like this stage. Now I have a completely different job albeit the same title in the same company[4]. If you want to build a company, you need to go on the complete journey' that means you need to grow and shift. You need to learn what the company needs from you at each stage. And not hold on for dear life on the things you like the most.

Speaking to a friend not so long ago whose start-up is about to click into the next phase of its growth, I asked him why he's not leaning into a bigger leadership role for himself. He has the experience. He has the clout. But he doesn't want it. His answer was joyous as it was self-aware: 'because I am not done playing yet'.

---

4   That is technically no longer true as, by the time we are going to print, PensionBee has expanded
     to the US and Jasper now has a global role and a new title to go with it, changing yet again and
     growing with the company.

And the company will need you to stop playing as it grows. And he doesn't want it for himself, so he will let someone else do it. Someone like Jasper (though not him because it's a totally different company) but someone who knows what it entails, and above all, someone who wants it. Because going on this journey, continues Jasper, 'means you are also doing less exciting things so the company can stand on its own for the long term.' A grown-up business needs grown-up things. Many of which are less exciting than the chaos of early days. But no less necessary.

But to be able to evolve like this, you need to be willing to notice the need for that change, you need to be willing to accept the change, and you need to be able to actually make the change happen and adapt.

All three are key; all three are challenging in different ways and they are also true of the entire team to a certain extent, not just the leadership. The type of talent you need and will attract at different stages of the business will be radically different. We already talked about this and Valentina's reflection that the type of person that joined OakNorth in the early, uncertain days when there were mouse traps in the office and the type of person that joined when there was a barista on the premises and a sushi lunch provided on Thursdays (I am pretty sure she said Thursdays) is radically different, and that is part of the deal and par for the course. In fact, it is as it should be.

The team evolves. People will leave and other people will join as needs change. The transition at a team level is understood, inevitable and often celebrated as a proof point or growth. That transition is harder when it comes to the leader, though. And of course the start-up chronicles are filled with stories of CEOs ousted by investors so that a 'grown up' can come in. The language we use in those situations varies depending on how popular the outgoing CEO was with the industry press. It is either fond, understanding and a celebration of all that was achieved or confrontational and brusque. But whichever language we use, the reality is that, as a business or venture grows, what it needs from everyone changes. Its leader included.

Pivot Yourself!

Every leader must change. That change doesn't need to be dramatic. It can just be an evolution. Sardine's Soups Ranjan reflects on his own evolution. 'I am not shy of expressing my opinions anymore! I have learned the hard way how to sell and I am confident in this now.

> Knowing your strengths and weaknesses and working towards them make you a better leader. Confidence is good. Self-awareness is better.

I have also learned how to balance work and life. I exercise more. I take my health more seriously. I will go on a bike ride listening to a call and when I reach what I call my outdoor office, a space in the woods, I will make some calls before cycling back.

I realise I need to brood so doing physical exercise helps me ruminate. And it is important to enjoy the journey and not forget to look after yourself and family. For the first few years I took a pounding and realised it wasn't worth it.'

If you are reading this thinking *I like it, this is what maturity feels like* you would be right. But also, you would not have the full story. Because you need to have self-awareness in the mix. Soups needs to ruminate to do his job better. So he creates conditions that allow him to do just that. What do *you* need?

Do you have that awareness? Do you ensure you create the conditions suitable for your growth, mental well-being and good performance? We operate in an industry where 'heroics' are seen as tantamount to performance, and treating your health poorly is seen as a proof point of commitment and success. Are you even trying if you don't have a stomach ulcer and have missed at least three school plays and every other gym class you ever committed to?

It takes courage, self-awareness and strength to not follow the industry trope and work out what you need to do your best work. And then actually do it. Protect your own health and productivity and not treat it as an optional indulgence.

> Conversations about success are hard because everything's made to look like an overnight thing.
> We underplay how hard this is.
> ***Daniela Binatti***

It also takes work: maintaining the equilibrium you have found works for you. Just as in an earlier chapter we talked about the need to take the time to do the things that matter, time that occasionally feels indulgent. Well. The same applies.

Maturity doesn't come free. You work your way to it.

'I came from a humble family', reflects Pismo's Daniela Binatti. 'My parents left school when they were nine and they always encouraged me to get a good job. Not start a company. I had impostor syndrome and anxiety around this at the start. But everyone has challenges. Everyone is intimidated by other people.'

Enfuse's Denise concurs. 'I never doubted myself', she says, 'but I looked up to people with big titles and big names'. And now? I ask. 'I am becoming more like Monika!' she says with a laugh. Monika, as I am sure you recall, is the zero hoots given powerhouse that is her co-founder. That is a learning. And it comes the hard way. Because, I hope you appreciate, I have not held back at any juncture from stressing just how hard this work is.

Daniela reflects: 'It is hard actually talking about how hard it is. Now I know I am as good as anybody else. When I travelled to San Francisco to meet the Visa execs, I was so nervous. But it was great. They were great. Ultimately we break new ground from both a tech perspective and a life experience perspective. We do something from scratch and it is amazing but the pressure is huge. That is the deal we signed up for'.

As someone who has far outgrown the lived experiences of the home I grew up in (that's me; I am talking about me), speaking to Daniela was like a balm. When going on this journey, we do break new ground from a business, tech and life perspective. And they are all equally significant and hard in their own ways *at the same time.*

> I don't overthink the decisions I take: I will look at all the information I have when I need to make a decision and make it. If things don't turn out as expected, I do the best I can with what I have and move on.
> ***Daniela Binatti***

And for the avoidance of doubt, what that deal looks like to individuals differs. Even inside Pismo, the four founders are very different personalities and have different motivations. Even their reasons for doing this work differ. The way it feels while doing the work is different. Even the realities of the sacrifices made feel different. The things that are at stake depending on each person's life and personality are different.

Bootstrapping, for instance, for Daniela and her co-founder husband Marcelo meant that 'we spent every cent we saved, we sold the car to ensure we could still pay the school for our daughters. The worst moments in this journey have been worrying about whether we can keep our girls in the same school. Now with hindsight we can say we were lucky enough to be in the right place, right time and we were experienced enough to keep going and every time I would be thinking about giving up the others had my back and vice versa. Thankfully we didn't all four have doubts at the same time. But conversations of success are challenging because everything is made to look like an overnight success. People underplay how hard it is. I am actually uncomfortable by how people talk to me after the Visa deal: I am still the same person.

> We take the resilience of founders as a given but we don't speak anywhere near as much about teachability. However, if you survive the knocks and learn nothing, you are nowhere.

Would I have done something differently? I don't think so. But I don't think about success and failure in those terms. My daughter was writing an essay for school: she had to write about a time she failed. This is psychological: I never think about failing. I don't fail: I win or I learn. I don't overthink the decisions I take: I will look at all the information I have when I need to make a decision. If things don't turn out as I expected, I do the best I can with what I have and then move on.'

How did you feel reading that?

Did you go straight for the montage? From humble origins to a determined but struggling founder to a lucrative exit? Or did you actually listen to the pattern in her words? I look at the information I have, I act and if it works great. If it doesn't work, I learn and go again. The resilience we expect in founders is a given. But the teachability is not. And yet it is the single most important thing to take away from this. You need to learn. From your mistakes, from a changing environment and in line with the changing needs of the things you are building.

Thought Machine's Gareth Richardson echoes the sentiments of both Jasper and Dani, above. He started his career as an engineer, so his evolution hasn't just been a personal journey but a fundamental skills overhaul. 'As an engineer your day is structured. You are under pressure but all you need to do is solve problems. There is a beautiful simplicity to it. Yes you have challenges and deadlines may slip which brings on big pressure, but in management the pressures and outcomes are very different and much more personal. And in learning that… you also learn that there are some things you are just bad at.'

And learning what you are bad at is key so you can manage it. Key but not easy because, as you go through your career and especially 'if you are competent, you will get platitudes about how great you are, as you go through your career', reflects Gareth, 'but the reality is… in management sometimes you fail and you don't even know [you are failing] because the feedback from people isn't there and the impact won't be felt immediately. My solution used to be to keep working hard and hope it all works out eventually.

The reality is you need to reset at some point. You also need to recognise your gaps and have people around you that help to round you out. For me, the optimist, I realise that I need people to point out the problems – but not too much. I need some of that culture around to balance me. You learn that with experience.'

The Version of You That Started This, Can't Finish It

'The version of me that started this, can't finish it', notes Christian Nentwich, reflecting on his journey with Du.Co. 'You reinvent yourself every couple of years. You have to. I had a moment in 2015 when I realised I had overlooked the fact that *I* needed to do different work. The company now needed different things from me.'

If you are doing something and it works, everything in your being screams, 'do more of it'. So for a CEO and a business that is on the journey and doing well, doubling down on the things that are working seems like a sensible approach. But it is not necessarily the right one. How do you tell the things you are good at and therefore should keep doing more of and the things that you are good at and doing well but you need to do just enough of them to

> How do you tell apart the things you are good at and doing well that you should keep doing… and the things you need to do well enough to get to the next stage?
>
> To double down on the latter would hurt your business.

get to the next stage? And then stop or hand them over to someone even better than you at what is needed next?

Christian, for instance, is strong in sales and good at communicating with clarity in a way that allows clients and prospects to come on a journey with Du.Co. That was something that the business needed from him at the start and needed from him up until the moment he stepped down as CEO. But as a founding CEO, product was something that was so close to his heart and so *alive* in his own mind that, as he evolved into the role the company needed him to be performing, he needed to give it up. And that was the hardest thing to give up and delegate.

Partly because 'so much of it lives in your head, particularly around brand value and the ethos of the product' and partly because it's *yours*. It's personal. It's your baby and it is hard to let go. And frankly, that is partly why you need to let it go. And why the only way to do so is evolve and pivot. Yourself, not just your business. Because you need to acquire the skills and maturity to do what is needed next, and part of that is realising that changing needs and dynamics of growing organisations.

How do you do that?

Well.

It helps if you anticipate it. Yes. I am back to the rodeos.

'For most of our leadership team', reflects Gareth when I asked him about how they keep each other accountable and focused inside Thought Machine, 'this is not our first rodeo. We wanted to build a 'proper' scale business from the start. We did not want to build something small, sell it and be done with it. We had all done that in different ways before. We came here to build grown-up things from the start. We came here to do something market-leading. We wanted to build an organisation

> You need to build the right culture for the problem you are trying to solve. You need to be intentional in building it and intentional in maintaining it, if it will be part of how you keep on track.

that can scale safely and maintain its culture. Because both the organisational culture and its maintenance have to be intentional. A lot of people talk about culture and actually espouse a particular type of mono/Silicon Valley culture and any other permutation is bad. You need the right culture for the problem you are trying to solve and be intentional about it.'

If you recall, Dani and her Pismo co-founders spent a year whiteboarding the kind of company they want to be and the kind of company they don't want to be. And part of that is the relationship between the leadership team; and the leaders and the wider team. That intentionality helps. So do the people around you who can identify your blind spots as we said before. Because we all have them. The question is not how do you eliminate them but how do you find them before you make an unforced error.

'A good mentor would have caught me six months earlier', adds Christian. 'A good mentor is key. These are unsafe conversations that need trust and need to be had with someone not involved with the business.' So. Intent. Structure. And outside help.

But mostly intent. Because these are hard, emotional conversations. They are necessary. But they are extremely hard because they feel deeply personal to the leader as they revisit choices, motivations and competence level. And on top of being uncomfortable, these discussions may often feel indulgent, like a luxury you can't afford while the world is on fire. So although they are existential, they become easy to avoid when you are drowning in work and what you are doing seems to be working, in the moment. And nobody gives you the feedback, as Gareth and Christian pointed out. Or they give it, but you are not ready to listen. So you let time pass. And as Christian said repeatedly: it only gets harder the longer you leave it, especially as you get bigger.

Situational Leadership on Steroids

'We are 230 people at Du.Co today', continues Christian. 'You'd think that we can run multiple verticals and do everything we want in the way we want to... but business itself is distracting. It keeps you busy in the day-to-day. There are always operational

> People either grow with the business or need to exit. And you as a leader need to make that call. It is necessary. But it is brutal.

challenges. Always a need to focus on the right people doing the right things, *right.*'

Getting bigger isn't just more hands on deck. Growing creates its own business. And any intentional retention of cultural behaviours or rituals you want to add on top is exactly that: additive.

So to ensure you have the right people and they are focused on the right things, and everything is done right, you need to do a lot of things you'd rather not do. You will need to create structures you never needed before. You will need to spend a lot of time on a lot of

> Business itself is distracting and its needs constantly change. You need to fire and promote fast. It is a terrible skillset to develop, firing people fast. But a necessary one.

things that may have happened naturally before.

You will need to exit a lot of folks who are no longer right.

You will need to make changes to keep getting things right. 'And that is brutal.

People who are good for one phase of the business' growth need to change themselves or exit as the business grows. People need to reinvent themselves or leave at the next stage. And you as the leader need to make that decision and make it fast. You need to exit and promote. Fast.' It is hard. But it is necessary.

Soups agrees but is philosophical about the fact that, as a leader, you need to always be parting ways with people. 'Everyone is growing and the company is growing. If it is time to part ways it's not an indictment. Just not growing in tandem. If you made a bad hire of course – and it happens – you have to fire immediately. But if someone has been with you for a year and a half, say, and need to part ways then it wasn't a bad decision, you just stopped growing at the same pace. It happens.' He is right. But that doesn't make it easy.

That was the biggest challenge for Teun van den Dries as well, as he thinks back. Building an organisation and a team is usually thought of in the creative, flowery language of finding and developing talent. But that is only one part of it; it also looks like holding talent accountable and letting go of people who are not a good fit or are no longer right for the business. 'The first time I fired someone I couldn't sleep for three days. You need to be able to do it but it is a shitty skillset to develop', recalls Teun.

And it's not just about firing folks, hard as that is. You need to keep managing the expectations and desires of the team you keep. They may have joined your start-up full of energy and creativity and, as the company grows, you need to box them in, you need to be more prescriptive about roles and remits. You

> If you don't have the resilience gene you are nowhere as a founder.
> *Christian Nentwich*

need them to do what you need them to do, which may not be what they want to do. Which is a hard conversation. Even harder if they have been doing what they wanted to do and now you need them to stop. You need them to focus differently. You need them to address a different problem in a different construct because, it turns out, your seven-person start-up didn't need five C-level folks, and as you grow, the remit of 'the person who used to do the thing' doesn't grow proportionately to being the head of said thing in a scaled organisation.

Maybe you called your mate Bill the CTO because he was the most senior engineer when it was the two of you. Heck. He was the only engineer. But maybe he is not the CTO who will run the 250-person distributed engineering team that you now have. Telling him this may cause conflict. It may hurt his feelings. But you need to resolve this and do it fast. Your pre-seed start-up doesn't

> Job title inflation is common in start-ups. You need to fix it as soon as you realise it's happening.

need a Chief Innovation Officer; your mate Dave, who joined you on day one to help design the product, leaving his second ever job before his 27th birthday, is not a Chief Product Officer who can scale an enterprise solution without solid new skills, and the question is: can he grow into the function and the skills and the title, or do you need to start calling the work he actually does something else?

I had just had a run-in with a very arrogant and very mediocre over-promoted specimen of exactly this variety about two hours earlier, as serendipity would have it, when I had the conversation with Christian, so it resonated more than I can tell you. It is common. It happens a lot. But you don't have to live with it forever.

'You need to avoid title inflation or at least at some point swallow the pill and fix the title inflation that will have happened in the early days. You need to unravel that. People dodge it because it is difficult', adds Christian. Of course it is hard. It is a difficult conversation to have. Imagine: 'hey Marie, I know we have been calling you a CTO for the first few years of the business but the reality is you are a very talented senior engineer and we need a different type of skillset in the CTO chair that you can learn from as well'.

Marie may not like it. It will feel personal. She will have no choice but to accept it – leave or live with it. But the conversation itself will be unpleasant for both you and her. 'I was so bad at this

> Situational leadership requires a sense of urgency.
> **Christian Nentwich**

when I started', recalls Christian. 'I was worried about what people would think, which meant I slowed down. You have to learn how to do this fast. Mentors, experience and an executive coach all help. It helps with self-awareness. Because you need to work out how to balance taking care of people and making the necessary changes. Situational leadership needs a sense of urgency. An ability to say *we have talked about this three times, we will not think about it again.*' How I love this man. He speaks my language. If what he says sounds self-evident, let me give you a little taste of what doing the opposite of what Christian describes looks like.

Three times in my career I have lived through huge cost cuts. That means firing people to balance the books. Every single one of those times, each function leader was given a target. Cut this much FTE (full time equivalent, 'humans' in normal speak). And each time,

> Making difficult decisions fast is hard for the CEO as a person. But not making difficult decisions fast is hard for the organisation in the long run.

someone (usually someone with a disproportionately large team) would just not comply. They wouldn't choose violence as such. They just wouldn't have the conversation. They just wouldn't do the doing. And months would pass. Because they were counting on the CEO *not* wanting to have the 'whatever the hell do you think you are doing, Mark?' conversation.

Mark is not real. Only he is. Every company has a Mark or ten who do exactly this. And 6, 9, 12 months down the road, the CEO wouldn't have the conversation with this imaginary Mark. Instead, magically (and inevitably) all of our cost-cutting targets would get bigger to accommodate the operational drag of Mark's willingness to play the CEO's reluctance to have it out for all it was worth.

I am guessing you have met a Mark or ten in your travels?

So Christian is right. Doing these things fast is sadly vital. You need that sense of urgency at the top. You also need resilience. Because this stuff is hard. All of it is hard. Dealing with a diminishing runway, fighting for your life and right to exist every day, firing people you actually like because the books won't balance or they are no longer a perfect fit. Changing your own work focus. Second-guessing your sense of comfort. Becoming the sort of person who knows they have to do these things and doesn't hesitate when the time comes.

All of this is hard. It is hard to do, and it is hard on you, on a personal level.

And that's before you have started trying to sell the product and get commercial traction.

> In enterprise sales success rate is always low. So you are mostly losing. If you don't have resilience, you are nowhere.
> **Christian Nentwich**

Which, in this industry, is another hard slog of long sales cycles and brutally low conversion rates. 'If you don't have the resilience gene you are nowhere as a founder. We have a 25% win rate in enterprise sales. You are *mostly* losing. If you are affected by that, you are nowhere', reflects Christian. He doesn't mean you need to become an unfeeling machine. But you do need to not let the reversals deter you. Because they will affect you, that is inevitable.

'The biggest sales losses we've had… I don't think I will ever get over them. That drives you though. And there's plenty of adrenaline left, despite being scaled. We can never lose data for instance. That is always top of mind. And sales are always the same no matter what size you are: you depend on one or two big deals and you can go from zero to hero. And I love it. I like the complexity. I like how many people we need to convince, turning the detractors. I love B2B enterprise sales.'

I know it seems obvious… but it needs to be said: it helps if you love the work. Not the allure of being a founder. Not the money or power that may (or may not) come. But the work. It helps if you love it. Because this is hard work. On the person and their family. 'I missed father's day', reflects Antony Jenkins. 'Flew to see a client on my birthday. Cut a vacation short. All in the past few months. There are constantly things that you give up when you do this work. And there is no choice.' Please digest that.

There is no balance to be had, there is no choice. If you choose to do this work, there is no option to fully protect yourself. It takes its toll. You can get better at protecting your health and your family, as Soups mentioned already. You can get better at protecting your organisation. And you can get better at protecting yourself. But there is no way to shield yourself fully. It *will* take its toll. 'But equally you can't let the work define you. You have to be deliberate. Time is our most precious resource. We need to spend it intentionally. I work hard, but I am not a workaholic. I make sacrifices knowingly', says Antony. They are still sacrifices, but at least they come with intent.

And it's fair to say that the people on their second rodeo knew what they were about to do to themselves. And did it anyway.

You Get Knocked Around, When You Go on This Journey

'It is a volatile journey. You get knocked around and beaten up', reflects Lizzie Chapman. 'Founder PTSD is a real thing. I had been genuinely fearless most of my life, hence my move to India, hence starting a credit company', but after a few years of working at full tilt on a grow-raise-grow-raise treadmill, Lizzie found herself at a low. Not a permanent low. 'But it was a shock to even experience that. Another thing nobody tells you about.' The personal toll this takes on you.

'Now I am back to myself and the experience gives you an even stronger sense of who you are. And you know you will survive. It can

> Founder PTSD is real.
> *Lizzie Chapman*

sound trite and cliche but it is true: what doesn't kill you makes you stronger. Nothing deters me now especially as I know that because of all I have been through... *now* I will make better decisions.

And I have stopped using the "failure" word because, originally I thought if I use it to describe my journey nobody else could say it to me. But the reality is, looking at *Zest*, most of it worked. And for a time it worked really well. And I left nothing on the table. I did it. Most people never do. So success or failure is a "point of time" thing. Now I am not panicking about each decision. Whatever happens, we will figure it out because the worst happened and we figured it out. So we will be ok. Even the dramatic parts, with hindsight I am grateful for because I know it didn't knock who I am.

> Success or failure is not an absolute: it is a 'point in time' thing.
> *Lizzie Chapman*

Knowing that, in different situations, I made choices that I am ok with. That, having made them, I can sleep at night is important. Because I have lost sleep over the things we had to do. The people we had to let go. Anyone with a normal human moral compass would lose sleep over that. It is hard but it is inevitable. But when there was pressure on us to make choices that would be wrong and we resisted. Knowing that I didn't make those choices is what I don't lose sleep over.

So I am tougher. More idealistic and more realistic at the same time. I will be more practical and balanced next time. Life isn't black and white. There is so much luck and randomness. You have to get a little more zen. You need to not sweat the small stuff.'

Would you do it again? I asked Lizzie. Remember? I mentioned this at the start of the book. Before we had looked at all the things doing it again entails. Of course you remember. And you remember what she said: 'I would. In fact I am!' Stronger, wiser, more determined than ever.

She is not alone. That's how you get the second rodeo. The people who know how to avoid some unforced errors and focus on the right things. It's those majestic lunatics going again. Joel Blake has a similarly philosophical attitude,

> One of the many things that will change for you on this journey is your relationship with both time and money.

reflecting on his own journey and his decision to go again and again. The ventures that didn't work out and the reasons why. The challenges around money. Having to take a full-time job in between attempts at pursuing the dream. He is not alone in that: having a family to look after can be a sobering factor.

'During that time – when I had taken a full-time job for the stability that money offered me and my family – the value of that money was very obvious to me. Security for my family. Stability. And I was very aware of how different money felt and looked when your position vis-a-vis it changes: I went from access to funds, profitability within my own business… and then a straight run to a position of securing stability for myself *while* having responsibility for money I didn't manage, in a policy role inside local government, running strategy for the local SME ecosystem from a bureaucratic point of view. That was a huge change for me. I had influence on how money was deployed and had responsibility over money I did not actually manage. All the while building GFA in the background.' The journey to appreciating the distance between the sum of money and its value was complete.

> When I am at my most vulnerable is when I am at my most positively dangerous.
> **Joel Blake**

GFA is now a full-time reality and a revenue-generating business.

'And now we have an opportunity to grow. Lending is our primary market but the technology we have built for GFA is sector-agnostic and we have made a conscious choice to sacrifice profitability short term to invest in partnerships. Again the value of this money right now is the profit margin but it will fuel growth through greater access and bring scale. I basically built GFA off 85k and that money brought growth and initial revenue. And now we have a commercially viable, market-validated product that was built in the leanest possible way.'

The journey to date explains the wisdom. We saw in earlier chapters what taking the wrong money early on does to many entrepreneurs, including Joel. So *knowing better* protects your business. Having done it wrong once before helps your business.

But how much do you as a person change in the process?

'You find yourself learning to embrace your own vulnerability more than ever before. Ego is a wonderful thing when used correctly. Ego is that fire in the belly, that wish to be the one who makes a difference. And I have learned that it can be a great positive catalyst when matched with vulnerability, because when you are faced with your own vulnerability everything else goes out the window. When you go through this journey you experience fear and anxiety. And you try to mask it as a husband and father but, if you are honest with yourself, it can be liberating. Because you get to a point where you have to make a decision: do I go ten steps back into my comfort zone, regroup and start over or do I take half a step into the unknown? That half step is more terrifying than ten steps in your comfort zone or ten steps of learning and you probably need to do all that anyway before taking that half step. You have to embrace the fear and do it. And then do it again next time. And again. And maybe after you've done it a few times the half step becomes a full step. But you need that honesty with yourself.

> This journey will almost kill you at times. But if you survive you become fire-resistant.
> *Joel Blake*

When I have been at my most vulnerable is when I am at my most positively dangerous and that has forced me to realise that being aligned to my values has nothing to do with being in business. Business is just a vehicle. And then, once that clicks, you can focus on the best, cheapest, fastest way to do the thing you were trying to do in order to have the impact you were trying to have. But you have to be willing to pare down to who you are. Honestly, I didn't think I was built for this... but those pivotal moments have stopped my ego taking over, have helped me remember why I do this in the first place. They have made me fire-resistant.'

So there you have it. The whole truth about building new things[5]: This work is hard. It has to be done consistently, all at once, with intent. It will almost break you at times.

Almost. But not quite.

Your Calls to Action

- Surround yourself with some people who will call out your blind spots and help you avoid unforced errors;
- Keep yourself on an active learning journey: learn from others, learn from your mistakes and dissect your successes so you can learn from them, not just bask in their warm reassurance;

---

5 Thank you Jen Smith for this tagline.

- Be honest with yourself about what parts of the journey you are good at, where your heart is and where you need to change yourself, or your team. Both hard in different ways and both need you as a leader to develop new skills, some of which you wish you didn't have to learn;
- There is no easy way to do this work, you will need to make sacrifices while doing this work. It helps to do so knowingly.

Index

Printed in the United States
by Baker & Taylor Publisher Services